FASCISM AND THEATRE

Comparative Studies on the Aesthetics and Politics of Performance in Europe, 1925-1945

Edited by
Günter Berghaus

Berghahn Books
Providence • Oxford

First published in 1996 by

Berghahn Books
Editorial offices:
165 Taber Avenue, Providence, RI 02906, USA
Bush House, Merewood Avenue, Oxford, OX3 8EF, UK

Library of Congress Cataloging-in-Publication Data
Fascism and theatre : comparative studies on the aesthetics and
politics of performance in Europe, 1925-1945 / edited by Günter
Berghaus.
    p.   cm.
Includes bibliographical references and index.
ISBN 1-57181-877-4 (cloth : alk. paper). -- ISBN 1-57181-901-0 (pb
: alk. paper)
    1. Fascism and theater--Italy--History--20th century. 2. National
socialism and theater--Germany--History--20th cventry. 3. Fascism
and theater--Spain--History--20th century. I. Berghaus, Günter,
1953- .
PN2684.F27 1995   95-20516
792' 094'09041--dc20   CIP

British Library Cataloguing in Publication Data
A CIP catalogue record for this book is available from
the British Library.
ISBN 1-57181-877-4 hardback
ISBN 1-57181-901-0 paperback

Printed in the United States on acid-free paper

CONTENTS

Introduction

Günter Berghaus

> Do we seriously believe that *we* would have been immune?
> (...) It has filled us with horror to realize all that man is capa-
> ble of, and of which, therefore, we too are capable.(C .G. Jung,
> *Aufsätze zur Zeitgeschichte*, Zurich 1946, p. 86)

Since the 1920s, an endless flow of studies has analysed the political systems of fascism,[1] the preconditions for the rise of fascist parties, the marketing of their ideologies, the methods employed in the seizure of power, the forms of executing authority once the régimes had been established, and finally the atrocities committed against the internal opposition and the wars waged against enemy countries.

Our image of fascism has been much influenced by the terror systems imposed onto several European countries. Much less attention has been given to the attraction fascism offered to millions of people and to the subtle strategies of persuasion employed by the régimes to win over the masses to their cause. Political scientists and historians have traditionally viewed fascist propaganda as the key means of influencing public opinion. Only more recently has the 'fascination of fascism' become a topic of enquiry. This is where the function of this volume is located: to provide a wide-ranging analysis of the rôles and functions played by theatre and other performative means of expression in fascist States.

The fifteen essays presented in this volume are the outcome of a collaborative and inter-disciplinary research project undertaken by the universities of Bristol, Granada and Berlin. Our starting point was a conference and a subsequent volume dealing with the activities of theatre and film artists exiled from Nazi Germany.[2] As a follow on to this, I had planned to publish a collection of documents illustrating theatrical life in the Third Reich. However, at the same time I was also undertaking research in Italy on the theatre of the Mussolini régime and, struck by the similarities between Fascist and Nazi theatre, I began to investigate the history of Spanish theatre during the Franco period.

Through a lucky coincidence at the time I had a visitor from Granada, Blanca López Román, who introduced me to Antonio Sánchez Trigueros, director of a Grupo de investigación de teoría de la literatura y sus aplicaciones. In 1990, they invited me to Spain to talk about my research on fascism and theatre, and from then on a plan began to take shape: our intention was to gather an international group of experts, who would produce a truly comparative and inter-disciplinary study on the politics and aesthetics of performance in a number of countries governed by fascist or para-fascist régimes.

My publisher, Marion Berghahn, was fully supportive of this idea, and so began my long search for a dozen or so specialists, who would possess more competence in these fields than I could ever muster.

The general objective of our undertaking was outlined in my first call for papers:

> The aim of the project is to investigate a wide spectrum of theatrical activities carried out in countries ruled by fascist régimes. The main emphasis will be on those theatrical manifestations that were organized by the State as part of their propaganda efforts. But attention will also be paid to other forms of theatre which were supported, condoned or simply tolerated by the State authorities, but which did not necessarily express open support for the ideology or politics of the government. The project is not in the first instance concerned with fascist drama. This does not mean that literary aspects will be ignored, but contributors should focus primarily on the performative aspects and processes of fascist theatre.
>
> The essays will examine all forms of theatre the contributors see as being relevant for their enquiry: literary theatre, opera, dance, mass spectacles, marches, rallies etc. Analysing the use of theatrical performances for political purposes, detailed reference will be made to:
>   - performative aspects such as acting, directing, choreography, stage and costume design;
>   - the physical characteristics of performance spaces - from play and opera houses to sports stadia and open-air festival grounds;
>   - the internal organisation and management of theatrical institutions;
>   - the political strategies employed by the régimes and their transformation into aesthetic language;

- audience structures and the relationship between audiences and theatrical institutions.

In June 1991, after a visit to Berlin, where Henning Rischbieter had set up a research centre investigating 'The Structural History of German Theatre, 1933-1945', and following consultations with many other scholars in Europe and the United States, the research group was formally set up. Contributors were invited to summarise their past research and write a résumé of their current lines of enquiry, which was then circulated to all members of the group. In order to integrate the different aspects of the topic into a unified whole, and to arrive at a proper *comparative* study, a forum for discussing the research carried out by individual scholars in their respective areas of expertise was required. A symposium seemed to be the best solution for such an exchange of ideas and for discussing the notion of a generic fascist theatre aesthetics. By examining the whole spectrum of theatrical manifestations in a number of States with a varying degree of fascistisation we hoped to arrive at a truly comparative analysis of performative phenomena and establish which similarities and differences existed in the theatrical cultures of several countries during the fascist era. Divergence of opinion amongst historians and political scientists on fascist systems and doctrines had to be reflected, as well as the major political and cultural differences between the countries under investigation.

No attempt has been undertaken to impose a monolithic view on contributors as to what qualifies to be designated 'fascist'. The problematic nature of the term is highlighted in the first contribution to this volume, written by Roger Griffin. An entirely different, and much wider, concept of fascism is employed in Reinhard Kühnl's essay. Both authors represent major schools of thinking with regard to fascist systems, but this, of course, is not to imply that other approaches to the study of fascism and the rôle of culture in fascist countries were disregarded or undervalued in our discussions. Different approaches are reflected in other contributions to this volume, which not only address fascist theatre in its 'classic' form, but also fascist performances in non-fascist countries and non-fascist performances in fascist countries. Although the key focus of this book is Fascist Italy and Nazi Germany, the hybrid cases of Spain and France are also included, partly because such borderline cases can sharpen our instrumentation of analysis, partly because they help to clarify the criteria of what qualifies to be designated 'fascist' (see, especially, Sultana Wahnón's contribution).

For reasons described below, our investigations concentrated on the period from 1925 to 1945, when fascist movements had a major impact on European history and developed a performative aesthetics to propagate their political aims and to influence public opinion. The roots of these symbolic forms of representation in preceding cultures, and their impact on post-war society could only be given cursory treatment. Again, different approaches to the study of these wider-ranging phenomena have been taken by scholars from a variety of disciplines. The essay I have contributed to this collection focuses on one aspect, the ritual core of fascist theatre, and how the relatively new discipline of theatre anthropology may offer possible explanations for the pervasive use of ritualistic modes of performance in fascist States. I have incorporated some references to the older, psychoanalytic, understanding of ritualism as far as it seemed relevant to our study of fascist reactions to situations of crisis. However, any in-depth discussion or critical assessment of the psychological literature dealing with the 'fascist mind' falls outside the scope of this contribution. Here, as well as in the other fourteen contributions, the emphasis is on performative processes. Related phenomena in the other arts, in the various branches of popular culture, and in political propaganda via the printed media have found treatment in other studies, a selection of which can be found listed in the bibliography at the end of this volume.

The 'theatricality' of the public displays in fascist States has always startled observers. Therefore it hardly needs justification to devote a volume of studies to this phenomenon. Rather, it is astonishing that more historians have not devoted their attention to it, or at least not in an interdisciplinary, comparative fashion. Critical opinion may vary as to whether theatre and ritual performances were central to the functioning of fascist systems, or must be regarded as an epi-phenomenon secondary to the military execution of power. There can, however, be no doubt that even within a dominant framework of economic, social and political coercion some effective means of persuasion and soliciting consent had to be found and that these aesthetic and political forms of propaganda played a significant rôle in the fascist State.

It appears to be a typical trait of fascist régimes that they sought to translate their political creeds into a theatrical language that drew heavily on the traditions of ritual and mysticism. Theatre as a symbolic expression of fascist ideology made use of performative conventions derived from religious and secular sources. Like all ritual theatre, it had the function of offering a healing power, or *katharsis*, in a moment of crisis - in this instance, a perceived national crisis - and to communicate a binding belief system to the participants. Theatre, because of its immediacy, touches a deeply irrational core that no other form of propaganda can reach. It conveys political messages in an overtly non-political form. In addition, it provides the participant with an experience of the self in communion with others, all of whom are potential subscribers to the presented belief system. Therefore, fascist theatre could fulfil the function of leading the spectator out of the everyday sphere and away from the realities of an alienated existence in societies undergoing major structural crises in the aftermath of the First World War, in order to bind the community in an emotionally elating experience that transcended class divisions, political divergencies, individualism, uprooted existence in a modern metropolis, and so on.

Mobilising mass audiences and manipulating the emotional impact generated by the event for political purposes seems to be a common trait of fascist theatre in all countries.

However, what requires detailed study are the aesthetic forms employed in these spectacles and the performative traditions on which they draw. Since they differed from country to country, extensive investigation of the full range of theatrical modes of expression and performative circumstances is required before they can be compared country by country and related to the political systems that generated them.

This was exactly the task the eighteen participants in this project had set themselves when, in February 1993, they gathered in the splendid surroundings of the Universidad Euroárabe in Granada.

The resurgence of neo-fascist movements in many European countries gave the conference a contemporary relevance, which was repeatedly referred to in the papers. The topic of the symposium was, moreover, of special significance in Spain. The country has only fairly recently emerged from the Francoist ashes, and there still prevails a pronounced reluctance to conduct a full investigation of the past. Too many turncoats are still in positions of power and influence and, understandably, offer resistance to having their 'dirty linen' displayed in public.

Research on the rôle of theatre in Franco-Spain and the influence of the fascist Falange on the performing arts of the country is still in its nascent phase. The very existence of a fascist cultural policy and theatrical practice has been repeatedly negated; documents have been destroyed, and access to archival material is often restricted. Antonio Sánchez Trigueros, who was the Spanish secretary of this symposium, reported on many incidences of how the work of his research group had been impeded for clearly political motives. Therefore, it is not astonishing that the symposium provoked considerable interest, not just within the confines of the academic community.[3]

Although the papers given at the conference addressed historical phenomena, the resurgence of a New Right in Europe, with the accompanying acts of violence and murder, again revealed that fascism is not a closed chapter. Moreover, the permutations of fascist theatre are far from exhausted. I have been able to witness, for example, productions of the national-socialist avant-garde co-operative 'Neue Slowenische Kunst' and was shocked to see how young audiences - utterly unaware of the political convictions of the group - enthusiastically submitted to the emotional power of the performances. A year later, I produced an up-dated version of Brecht's anti-fascist drama *Turandot* and chose the music of the neo-fascist group 'Laibach' to characterise the enormous attraction exercised by the Hitler-figure in the play, the political gangster Gogher Gogh. The younger members of the audience in particular were sucked into the emotional drive of the performance, until the production made them realise what, unintentionally, they were identifying with.

Fascist theatre of the 1990s, it seems to me, no longer takes the concrete forms that were discussed at our symposium and are now presented in the essays of this volume. However, by comparing a variety of historical forms and distilling their performative substance, we can arrive at an analytical perspective on historical *and contemporary* developments. Modern youth culture is offering a whole range of expressive forms that can be used and exploited for political purposes. One only has to visit the heavy-metal stage performances of Neo-fascist rock groups such as 'Böhse Onkelz', 'Radikahl' or 'Endsieg', or the open-air celebrations in Italian *Hobbit* camps run by the 'alternative' Right linked to Pino Rauti and the neo-fascist MSI, and one can observe the metamorphoses of fascist theatre in response to changing audiences and their sociopolitical concerns.

Moreover, the most recent political developments in Germany and Italy, and to some extent also in the post-Communist countries of Eastern Europe, indicate that neo-fascism is a well-and-truly living force even at the end of the twentieth century. The international community has been shocked by the spectacular murders of 'guest-workers' in Rostock, Mölln and Solingen. The statistics of the increase in racist attacks in Germany (3,300 alone in the first half of the year 1993, compared to 1,300 in 1992) offer clear evidence that these widely reported occurrences are not isolated incidents. Similarly, attacks on refugees and migrant workers in Italy can be linked to the phenomenal success of the MSI in the communal elections of November 1993. The Duce's granddaughter, Alessandra Mussolini, won 31.1 per cent of the votes in Naples, which was no exceptional result, but compared well with the Party's support in Rome (30.8 per cent) and other cities. It is still too early to predict if Shirinovskij's ultra-nationalist programme, which led him to gain 23.5 per cent of the votes for the Russian Parliament in December 1993, was a transitory phenomenon or is going to escalate into a neo-fascist danger coming from the East. There can be no doubt that the economic crisis of the early 1990s has led to a resurgence of phenomena that bear a close resemblance to the fascist mass movements resulting from the acute hardships endured during the early and the late 1920s.

A volume such as this is therefore a timely reminder that the study of history is of topical relevance to contemporary developments in the political and social fields. Art is not detached from the society that produces it, but rather it reflects and shapes public consciousness. Theatre has proved to be an important instrument for fascist movements of the past. Just as their political ideologies have re-occurred in a developed industrial world, so have the performing arts supporting them, albeit under new guises. I hope that this volume sharpens our understanding of what constitutes the performance aesthetics of fascist movements and how, under different historical circumstances, they can re-appear in modified form.

Some readers may reproach me for not having included any papers on these more recent phenomena in this volume. Unfortunately, these, as well as several other relevant topics, were excluded not by design, but coincidence. I partly take the blame for not having approached the right people to cover the contemporary developments in fascist or proto/para-fascist theatre. But what was offered to me - in draft form - was not promising in terms of scholarly acumen or simply did not fit into the framework (methodological or thematic) of our project. I regret not having pursued other routes to find better contributors knowledgable in theatre and performance studies *as well as* contemporary right-wing politics. But time was pressing, and in the end an imperfect, but hopefully inspiring volume on the politics and aesthetics of fascism and theatre in their classic form has resulted. May it encourage other scholars to bring it up to date by analysing the corresponding phenomena in the late twentieth century!

I have, however, no guilty conscience when faced with the question: where are the promised analyses of theatre performances in fascist States? In order to compile this volume of essays, I had to approach scholars in many disciplines. Those who are knowledgable in fascist theatre are not necessary professors of theatre studies. And even within this discipline, the methodology of performance analysis is still underdeveloped. This certainly is one reason why my exhortations for more detailed analyses of performative processes did not find the response I had hoped for. Another explanation for this shortcoming is that we are dealing here with transitory phenomena that were badly documented in the first place. Theatre critics at the time did not provide analytical write-ups of the shows they saw; directors and designers did not keep sketch or prompt-books of productions they regarded as politically compromising; photographic records are not easily available and are often scarce for the 'fascist years' in a given theatre's history. Finally, professional theatre scholars of the post-war period did not extract enough verbal information from the actors involved in fascist theatre. As Bettina Schültke points out in her essay for this volume, they often had their own reasons for keeping quiet about the preceding decade and preventing younger scholars from turning over stones of the past.

For all these reasons, this volume is – I regret to say – incomplete in its coverage of the subject matter indicated on the title page. Critical judgement should take into account that this is the first book of its kind that attempts a comparative and inter-disciplinary analysis of fascist theatre. Our undertaking is only a first step in the direction of a comprehensive examination of theatrical and performative phenomena in support of fascist movements. The field is still open to further research!

Attempt has been made to render this collection of essays equally interesting to political historians and theatre historians. Specialists in the one or the other field may find certain paragraphs going over familiar ground. However, the context of adjacent chapters may bring a different perspective to these phenomena, and the overall balance of contributions with their many inter-connections and cross-references will produce, we hope, new insights also into some well-known matter.

I wish, at this point, to express my warm thanks to the many scholars who responded to my initial call for papers. I received valuable advice and help in finding the authors presented in this volume. Unfortunately, the areas of dance and theatre architecture could not be covered, despite my long search for qualified specialists to write on them. Other papers that had been promised never materialised, and some collaborators - due to pressure of other projects - had to withdraw at a relatively late stage. I am extremely grateful to colleagues who, in some cases at very short notice, agreed to produce an essay for this book or to incorporate new aspects, discovered during our discussions in Granada, into their contributions.

All collaborators showed exemplary patience when confronted with my endless flow of queries, emendations and suggestions at the final editorial stage. Needless to say, all essays went through various draft stages and were often considerably re-written in the light of comments received from me and other collaborators, sometimes changing in scope and focus. I am most grateful to the authors' constructive response to these criticisms and suggestions.

Finally, acknowledgement must be given to the translators, who extended their services far beyond their call of duty (and remuneration). Carmen Vadivia Campos and her colleagues provided an excellent simultaneous interpretation service in six languages during our conference in Granada. Ian MacCandless operated as *secretario adjunto* throughout this project, translating essays, letters, documents, organising meetings, providing hospitality, building communication bridges between three universities that - even in the age of fax and e-mail - sometimes seemed to exist on two different planets.

Where though, would idealism and scholarship lead, if they were not supported by appropriate funding? Therefore, we are much obliged for the financial assistance received from the University of Granada, the Regional Government of Andalusia, the Spanish Ministry of Education and Science, the Asociación Andaluza de Semiótica, the Goethe Institut, the Alliance Française, the British Council, the British Academy, and the University of Bristol.

NOTES

1. Throughout this volume distinction will be made between generic fascism (spelled with a lower case) and Italian Fascism (with a capital F).
2. See Günter Berghaus (ed.), *Theatre and Film in Exile: German Artists in Great Britain, 1933-45*, Oxford, 1989.
3. See the report published in *The Drama Review*, vol. 37, no. 3 (T139), Fall 1993, pp. 13-15.

1

Staging the Nation's Rebirth

The Politics and Aesthetics of Performance in the Context of Fascist Studies

Roger Griffin

Generic fascism

Those who are reading this volume with the trained eye of the historian, and in particular the reader with an interest in the history of the theatre, may be disconcerted to encounter a chapter such as this, which unashamedly applies theoretical perspectives drawn from the social sciences in treating fascism as a generic phenomenon. However, the need for such a chapter is made pressing by the fact that, with the possible exception of 'ideology', there can be no term in the political lexicon which has generated more conflicting theories about its basic definition than 'fascism'. Thus, a work such as this which attempts to throw light on an aspect of it in a comparative perspective, must offer at least a working definition so as to provide a rationale for inclusions and omissions. This chapter sets out to offer such a working definition, but also to go beyond this by elaborating an approach which, hopefully, illuminates the central subject under discussion, namely the theatricality intrinsic to fascism as a political ideology.

My main contributions to the tangled debate over how best to approach fascism as a generic phenomenon have been a new model ('ideal type') of fascism constructed and applied to a number of its aspects in *The Nature of Fascism*,[1] and the primary source reader *Fascism*[2] which provides extensive empirical

underpinning to that model. The definition of the 'fascist minimum' which the latter offers while corroborating widely shared
'common sense' perceptions of the subject, has two distinctive
features: extreme concision (fascism is defined in a single sentence, albeit one which requires considerable 'unpacking' before
it is intelligible), and a central emphasis on the mythic dimension of fascism as a key to its underlying ideological coherence
and causal dynamics. Moreover, its premise is the obvious, but
still relatively unusual one of treating fascism on a par with
other political ideologies such as liberalism, socialism, imperialism or ecologism (all of which pose intrinsic definitional problems of their own), namely by defining it in terms of the vision
(utopia) of the ideal society which determines its critique of the
status quo.

To be more precise, the genus 'fascism' is assumed to be defin-
able in terms of the *core myth* which is common to its different
permutations, and which underlies its diagnosis of, and remedy
for, the social and political 'crisis' of the present order of society.
There is an almost total consensus among experts over the crucial
rôle played by 'illiberal' or 'integral' nationalism in fascism. There
is also agreement among a number of them that, rather than
being a reactionary or conservative force, fascism aspired to create a revolutionary new order. Artificially forged into a single
concept by the faculty of 'idealising abstraction', these two elements produce a new ideal type of the fascist minimum. When
applied to Fascism the conceptual framework thus created reveals
the structural link between the different, and in many respects
conflicting, currents of political activism (Futurism, revolutionary
syndicalism, the nationalism of the National Italian Association
etc.) and the political careers of individual ideologues and activists
(e.g. Gentile, Bottai) which formed an uneasy alliance within
Mussolini's régime. The same core myth of revolutionary nationalism (though inevitably articulated through historical and symbolic discourses peculiar to the national culture in question) can
also be shown to lie at the heart of the propaganda, policies, and
social dynamics of other movements and one régime widely associated with fascism (e.g. the Falange, British Union of Fascists, the
Iron Guard, the Third Reich), but not all (e.g. Peronism, Fran-
quism, Vichy France).

How are we to characterise the core myth of generic fascism
which results from the fusion of a revolutionary project with anti-
liberal but populist nationalism? It can be expressed in a single

binomial term, albeit an initially cryptic one: 'palingenetic ultra-nationalism'. 'Palingenetic' refers to the myth of 'rebirth' or 'regeneration' (the literal meaning of 'palingenesis' in Greek). Clearly, the triumph of a new life over decadence and decay, the imminent rebirth from literal or figurative death, is a theme so universal within manifestations of the human religious, artistic, emotional and social imagination throughout history, that it is in itself inadequate to define a political ideology. For example, the faith in the possibility of regeneration from a present condition perceived as played out or no longer tolerable, is arguably the affective driving force behind *all* revolutionary ideologies, be they communist, anarchist, or 'dark green' (or even liberal, as a study of the speeches of the leading French Revolutionaries such as Saint-Just or Robespierre shows[3]). The adjective 'palingenetic' first acquires a definitional function when it is combined with the historically quite recent and culture-specific phenomenon of 'nationalism', and only when this takes a radically anti-liberal stance to become *ultra-nationalism.*[4]

Fascism thus emerges when populist ultra-nationalism combines with the myth of a radical crusade *against* decadence and *for* renewal in every sphere of national life. The result is an ideology which operates as a mythic force celebrating the unity and sovereignty of the whole people (except, of course, for those considered its internal enemies) in a specifically *anti-liberal*, and *anti-Marxist* sense. It is also *anti-conservative*, for, even when the mythic values of the nation's history or prehistory are celebrated, as in German *völkisch* thought, the stress is on living out 'eternal' values in a *new* society. The hallmark of the fascist mentality is the sense of living at the watershed between two ages and of being engaged in the frontline of the battle to overcome degeneration through the creation of a rejuvenated national community, an event presaged by the appearance of a new 'man' embodying the qualities of the redeemed nation.[5]

The ideal type of fascism presented here boils down to the following thesis: what all permutations of fascism have in common (i.e. the 'fascist minimum') is that their ideology, policies, and any organisations formed to implement them, are informed by a distinctive permutation of the myth that the nation needs to be, or is about to be, resurrected Phoenix-like from the forces of decadence, which, without drastic intervention by the forces of healthy nationalism, threaten to extinguish it for ever. Thus, when in an overtly anti-liberal and anti-socialist spirit the Fascists celebrated

the creation of a Third Rome, the Nazis believed they were founding a New (national and European) Order, Mosley promoted the
idea of the Greater Britain, or Codreanu looked forward to the
appearance of the Romanian New Man, all were being true to the
core mobilising myth of fascism. In their idiosyncratic way they all
invoked elements of 'traditional' values, but did so not to create a
modern form of *ancien régime* based on the traditional ruling élites
and institutions, but to inaugurate a new era for the nation in
which even the common man (though rarely the common woman)
could form part of the élite charged with the mission to combat
national decay.

The implications of this definition for the dynamics of fascism

To conceive fascism as a 'palingenetic form of ultra-nationalism'
has a number of consequences for the way its dynamics are
approached which have been spelt out elsewhere.[6] The aspects
most relevant to the study of fascist theatre are as follows.

Fascism as a modernising ideology

Far from being a form of anti-modernism, cultural pessimism,
nihilism, or 'resistance to transcendence',[7] fascism is born precisely of a human need for a sense of transcendence, cultural
optimism, and higher truths compatible with the forces of modernisation.[8] It offers to its followers *not* the prospect of returning
to the idyll of a pre-modern society with its dynastic hierarchy
and religious world-view intact, but rather of advancing towards
a new order, one consonant with the dynamism of the modern
world, yet able to purge it of the social, political, economic and
spiritual malaise which liberal and socialist versions of modernisation have purportedly brought about. In particular, the
regenerated national community promises to overcome the root-
lessness and chaos, the anomie, attributed to the breakdown of
traditional community, cosmology and hierarchy under the
impact of secularisation, materialism, pluralism, massification
and industrialisation. It claims to do so by offering a *new*
dynamic source of rootedness, community and hierarchy based
on the organic nation, and many forms of it actively embrace
modern technology and industrial civilisation, though only if

integrated into a cohesive socio-economic order consistent with the needs of the nation.

Fascism as a tendentially charismatic form of politics

In the inter-war period at least, fascism specifically repudiates the rationalist and political tradition of the Enlightenment, and in particular the principles of universal human rights, egalitarianism, methodological scepticism, pluralism, tolerance and individual responsibility. Indeed, it encourages the individual to subsume his or her personality unquestioningly *but willingly* within the greater whole of the national community caught in the throes of its transition to a new order, and so participate in the special historical destiny allotted to it. By a similar token it rejects all forms of socialism, whether as a revolutionary or reformist force, which promote the concepts of materialism, internationalism, or equality, because they are held to undermine a 'healthy' national identity and the new hierarchy which is to accompany it. Some forms of fascism do, however, claim to represent a 'national' form of socialism whose task is to destroy capitalist values (though not all its institutions) and abolish class distinctions (though not hierarchy as such). In both cases, fascism thus rejects what Max Weber called the 'legal-rational' concepts of authority.

Being both anti-traditionalist and anti-rational fascism, with few exceptions, manifests itself as a *charismatic* form of political ideology. This aspect expresses itself in inter-war fascism's drive to replace all genuine freedom of opinion and all democratic processes based on individual consciousness by a 'permanent revolution' founded on ritualised authority and an elaborate civic liturgy sometimes referred to as a 'civic' or 'political' religion,[9] the most well-known manifestation of which is the leader cult. Fascism therefore operates as an *identificatory* ideology, encouraging total symbiosis with the ideological community (as opposed to an *integrative* ideology, which liberalism and socialism are in theory, encouraging individual conscience, a spirit of inquiry and the tolerance of difference).[10]

Fascism as an élitist form of populist nationalism

In principle fascism offers solutions to three central problems of modern society: 1) the socio-political integration of the masses into society; 2) the need for a pervasive, all-embracing sense of personal identity and values; 3) the need for political institutions which create order and authority. It does so by creating a new type of nationalism which is neither the anti-democratic kind promoted by traditional (aristocratic or restorationist) conservatives, or modernising ones (e.g. post-monarchist royalists, anti-liberal political Catholics, militarists), nor the populist variety associated with the liberal revolutions of the eighteenth and nineteenth centuries. It is a nationalism with a populist, revolutionary, hierarchic, and charismatic thrust, bent on replacing the 'horizontal' democracy of the early French Revolution with a 'vertical' democracy based on the spontaneous emergence of a new élite, a new meritocratic aristocracy headed by an inspired leader. In a sense, then, fascism fuses the hierarchic elements of *ancien régime* absolutism with the democratic dynamic of revolutionary liberalism and socialism. It promotes the vision of a new state, a new leadership, a new political and economic order born of a revolutionary movement (and not a mere 'party') arising from within the people itself.

The ultimate goal of fascism: the creation of a charismatic national community

It follows from the above that the fundamental aim of any régime based upon fascism must be to bring about the rebirth of the national community. This involves the creation of the post-liberal and anti-Marxist 'new man' imbued with the vitalistic, heroic ethic which is presented as the polar opposite of the decadence encouraged by a 'materialistic' liberal or socialist society. The institutional implications of this programme are a series of structural changes designed to replace the rampant pluralism of liberalism with a structure sufficiently cohesive and centralised for ideological uniformity to be imposed on every aspect of society. This logically involves such measures as the abolition of liberal institutions (political parties, trade unions, basic freedoms, the separation of powers), the creation of single party State, the reshaping of the system of justice, the drafting of new laws of citizenship and nationality and the restructuring of economic institutions. Owing to its charismatic and hierarchical nature, a fascist régime naturally tends towards the introduction of the leader principle and the glorification of youth as the raw material of a heroic new generation. The fact that fascism emerged in the wake of the First World War also led to its bid to militarise civic society, as well as to celebrate the front-line soldier as a role model for the regenerated national community, because of his readiness to submit willingly to discipline and to sacrifice himself to a higher cause.

Apart from an extensive co-ordination and regimentation of society, a fascist régime has to resort to a centralised programme of social engineering, in order to encourage the conversion of the mass of the population to the palingenetic world-view which originally fuelled what started out as an 'extra-systemic' movement of a minority. In practice this means propaganda on a massive scale, the radical overhaul of education and academic life, and the reshaping of cultural life both at the level of 'high art' and of popular culture and leisure. Given the irreducibly pluralistic nature of modern society and the need to persecute alleged 'natural' enemies of the regenerated nation, 'actually existing' fascism also requires the creation of a terror apparatus to deter and punish deviation from the official world-view. Within the fascist mind-set, however, the apparent 'nihilism' of its persecutions, purges and violence are seen as the 'cathartic' destruction necessary as a prelude for any act of reconstruction and regeneration.

The 'totalitarian' thrust of the fascist revolution

Clearly, the régime described has every hallmark of a totalitarian one. Even so, an important consequence of fascism's nature as a revolutionary, populist and charismatic form of nationalism, is that a régime based on it does not try to regiment the masses simply in order to control them. Rather it does so as part of an elaborate attempt to bring about what is conceived as a *positive*, life-asserting, transformation of how they experience everyday reality and their place in history by enabling them to feel spontaneously an integral part of the nation and its 'higher' destiny. Not *all* the masses can be involved in this project, however, because the extreme emphasis which it places on enhancing national identity means that liberal concepts of human rights and citizenship are rejected, and nationality is redefined in exclusive historical, cultural or ethnic categories, though not necessarily using criteria derived from biological racism. The central emphasis on the affective and subjective sense of permanent revolution, of living through a historical sea-change, of belonging to a supra-individual reality, leads to an all-pervasive use of myths, symbols and rituals, designed to replace the primacy of individualism and reason by a transcendental community and faith. Expressions of this are the veneration of a mythicised version of national history, the invention of new heroes, traditions and ceremonies, the celebration of national achievements in the spheres of social programmes, technology, architecture and art, the cult of the leader, the myth of the New Man, and the infiltration of national symbolism (e.g. the Fascist Lictor's rod, the Nazi Swastika) into the most intimate aspects of everyday life.

The existence of only two fully fascist régimes

The consequences of applying our ideal type to comparative studies of inter-war régimes are fairly drastic. Of the scores of fascist movements which arose, only two proved capable of seizing power and hence set about implementing their myth of national resurrection from decadence; namely Fascism and Nazism. A handful of other fascist movements briefly formed governments, but either in an alliance with more powerful conservative autocrats (e.g. the Iron Guard with Antonescu in Romania), or as puppet régimes of the Nazis (e.g. Szálasi's Arrow Cross under the SS in Hungary), but none had the relative autonomy necessary to carry out their palingenetic programmes. In contrast, Mussolini and Hitler had sufficient autonomy to set about implementing transformations in the spheres of education, culture, foreign policy, economics, and demographic policy. These, for all the differences in the specific nationalist myths underlying them, point to radical attempts, not to restore past values or hold the fort against social collapse, but to enter a new age based on the regenerated national community endowed with a new hierarchy and with new myths by which to live. However, even in these two cases the translation of ideas into reality was a highly mediated and compromised process.

Under both the Third Rome and the Third Reich, fascism was forced into an alliance with conservative forces in order to gain and hold power, and there were from the outset several rival currents of fascism at work, all jostling to impose *their* vision of the new order on official policy-making. Also, the practical problems of creating a homogeneous national community out of a highly pluralistic modern nation-state meant that, in glaring contrast with the official propaganda of a totally co-ordinated régime, both countries remained polycentric and heterogeneous. In addition, even if the two leaderships had formulated a coherent vision of the ideal fascist order, their commitment to expansionist schemes of foreign conquest meant that the stability and colossal resources necessary for its full implementation never existed and never could have existed. Everything in the history of the two régimes, then, points to the gulf between Utopia and reality.

Meanwhile, to a greater or lesser extent, a number of autocratic conservative régimes deliberately aped some of the superficial aspects of the Fascist and Nazi apparatus and style of power (e.g. single party, youth movement, leader cult, corporatist economics, secret police, State terror, rhetorical commitment to a new State or new era). Portugal, Austria, Greece, Slovakia, Hungary, Bulgaria, Romania, the Baltic States, all provide examples of this *Ersatz* fascism, or what might be termed 'para-fascism'. Two other examples are provided by régimes covered in this volume; Franco's Spain and Vichy France. In all of these cases, although the façade of national regeneration was maintained, the State, as the representative of the interests of the traditional ruling hierarchy, repressed rather than encouraged those aspects of fascism which it rightly saw as threatening to its interests. These included the mobilisation of populist nationalism, the emergence of new élites through a genuine social revolution, or the diffusion of a heroic, tendentially pagan world-view incompatible with the strictures of Christian orthodoxy. This was done either by banning or repressing a genuine fascist movement (Chile, Brazil, Portugal), co-opting or marginalising it (Spain, Vichy France), or a mixture of both (Romania, Austria).

Implications of this ideal type for the study of 'Fascism and Theatre'

It should be clear from the above that the acceptance of 'palingenetic ultra-nationalism' as the definitional basis of fascism has major implications for a study of the theatrical culture in inter-war Europe. First, it means that only Fascist Italy and Nazi Germany provide case-studies in institutionalised theatrical practice under fascism, although there are a number of para-fascist régimes with theatrical traditions worth considering for comparative purposes. Indeed, the comparison offered by this book of the theatrical culture of the two genuinely fascist régimes with that of two para-fascist ones, Spain and Vichy France, provides some illuminating insights into the points of convergence between these two distinct types of political system, as well as the ideological gulf which separates them.

Second, the ideal type proposed throws into relief a defining trait of any theatrical practice which is consonant with fascist ideology, namely that it should set out to promote the rebirth of the national community (often symbolised in the experience of a representative individual) from the alleged decadence of liberal and socialist society in a spirit which goes beyond any purely conservative or restorationist goals. In fact, the predominance of the 'positive' palingenetic thrust of fascist myth over a 'nihilistic' anti-dimension (which is something all ideologies have as a corollary of their positive ideals, even liberalism) is corroborated by several scholars who have specialised in the theatre in Fascist Italy or Nazi Germany with no concern for the debate over generic fascism. For example, Pietro Cavallo sampled some of the 18,500 scripts voluntarily submitted for approval to the Theatre Censorship Office of the Ministry of Popular Culture in Rome between 1931 and 1943. He concluded that the basic scheme of these unsolicited (and therefore not in any straight-forward sense propagandistic) Fascist dramas is in essence 'an initiatic journey, of varying duration and involving various trials and tribulations. As in *rites de passage*, the new status is represented by entering a new experience of life(…) The progress towards fascism thus becomes – and I cite the linguistic terms which recur most frequently in the titles – the journey towards a "rebirth", towards the dawn of a new day.'[11]

Similarly Klaus Vondung, in his exhaustive investigation of the cultic aspects of Nazism, argues that central to Nazi theatrical projects in the narrowest and widest sense was 'metastatic faith', a phrase which clearly corresponds closely to what I term 'palingenetic myth', since it expresses itself in the belief in the imminent transformation of 'the old world into a new one'. He quotes the example of how Nazi liturgical drama transfigured Hitler's abortive putsch of November 1923 into an 'act of redemption', which had 'brought about a metastasis': 'the "old" world was thus "over", life had only now become truly real, while life before the metastatic event and the lives of those who have not responded to the new revelation, appears insubstantial and in the deepest sense of the word, not "real"'.[12]

Vondung goes on to show that translated into political terms this meant that all citizens of the new Germany were encouraged to experience transcendence of individual death through the permanent revolution taking place in national life. Because of the central stress in Nazism on the spiritual nature of the battle between 'health' and 'degeneracy', it was a revolution which was in many respects more subjective than objective, just as one of the major scholars of Nazism, Ian Kershaw, maintains.[13] Symptomatic of this core theme is the recurrent topos in Nazi theatre of renovation, renewal, rebirth (*Neugeburt*, literally 'new birth'). One example from the hundreds quoted by Vondung is a choral poem written for public performance in the Third Reich entitled 'The New City', which contains such lines as 'Thus everything new grows out of the new earth, The new human beings just like the new walls'.[14] It is precisely this theme of total renewal, rather than just the healing of the nation through the return to traditional values, which is missing from para-fascist theatre.

The role of the theatre in the creation of the new fascist man

It is the thesis of this chapter, then, that a truly fascist theatrical theory or practice will express itself in a central preoccupation with the victory over decadence by youthful new forces and the resulting birth of a new national community made up of a new type of 'man'. If it lacks these definitional elements it is not ideologically fascist. However, nothing in fascist studies is so straightforward. Even if this ideal type, with its built-in discriminating and simplifying function, *is* adopted, two factors complicate its application. Firstly, a para-fascist régime may well accommodate genuine fascists, who have projected onto it *their* own anti-conservative, radically palingenetic vision of a new order, some of whom may well promote cultural initiatives designed to forge a new national community from below as well as from above. Giménez Caballero is an outstanding example in Franco's Spain, and the attempts by the theatre director and theorist Jacques Copeau to foster a *théâtre populaire* which would act as a source of 'union and regeneration' likewise went some way beyond Vichy's ultimately reactionary programme.[15] What further complicates analyses of Fascism is that in Italy the reverse is equally true: it was heavily compromised by collusion with conservative forces (Church, army, monarchy, reactionary bourgeoisie) who continued to make their presence felt in the cultural sphere. Moreover, under Mussolini censorship was relatively lax, so that even after 1925 considerable pockets of cultural pluralism persisted which were unimaginable under Hitler. As a result, 'theatre under Fascism' was only to a limited extent 'fascist theatre'.

Another complicating factor is that both Fascism and Nazism suffered the fate of all revolutions: once they had seized power, the new régime they installed had to normalise everyday life for the 'people' as much as possible. This led to a paradoxical situation. A recurrent theme of State rhetoric was the imminent appearance of the heroic 'New Man', whose private existence would be totally subsumed within the higher organism of the national community. However, even in the public sphere considerable pockets of apolitical space remained available to people. In practice this meant that 'entertainment' was as important an ingredient of everyday life under Mussolini and Hitler as under any non-totalitarian régime. In fact, it would be highly ingenuous to assume that all art permitted under Mussolini or Hitler had an overt ideological or propagandist function: it could be argued that precisely because the bulk of magazine articles, books in print, films, radio broadcasts and plays were not overtly propagandist, the radical fascistisation of the spheres of life crucial to the hegemony of the régimes (institutions, news programmes, laws) could be more effective.

Thus, theatre under fascism in both countries continued to produce a large number of pre-fascist or non-fascist plays, whether classical or essentially escapist, as long as no expressly anti-fascist message could be read into them. It should be stressed that the Nazis went far further than the Fascists in applying social engineering to the arts: they devoted considerable energy to defining what was aesthetically 'decadent' (and hence anti-fascist), to carrying out a systematic purge of such 'cultural Bolshevism', and to encouraging a theatre practice designed to promote 'healthy' racial life. It is also worth bearing in mind that the New Rome and the New Reich could no more be built in one day than the old ones, and that inevitably there was a large degree of continuity between pre-fascist and fascist culture in both countries, both at the level of popular culture and of high art. Indeed, this continuity too, was a vital component of the normalisation of the régimes in the same way as the predominance of non-propagandistic art.[16] Finally, it should not be forgotten that the theatre was then, even more than now, a predominantly middle-class institution, while the fascist revolution was both ideologically and sociologically[17] a trans-class rejection of liberalism, including the bourgeois ethos (though not, of course, the institution of private property). The daily consumption of radio broadcasts, newspapers, and mass-circulation magazines were thus more central to fascist efforts in social engineering than the performing arts.

Thus there are a number of structural factors which point to the naïvety of assuming that even in a truly fascist régime the theatre would ever be transformed into a primary locus of total mobilisation, or that every play which the authorities allowed to be staged was necessarily a vehicle of indoctrination or an exercise in *agit-prop*. As with the cinema (a truly classless art form, to which fascist élites were bound to pay closer attention, as a vehicle for mass mobilisation or the normalisation of the régime, than to the theatre), the precepts of the New Order were promoted as much by the censorship of anti-fascist works as through the sponsoring of *pièces à thèse*. In any case, much more comprehensive and insidious exercises in winning hearts and minds were taking place off-stage.

The locus of fascist theatrical culture: civic life

To restrict studies of the aesthetics and politics of performance under fascism exclusively to what went on in public playhouses would clearly be woefully inadequate. It would be like writing a history of twentieth-century music which focused solely on concert halls, ignoring the way social space has become ever more saturated with pre-recorded non-classical music. In fact, one of the most important consequences of the fascist dream of creating a cohesive national State not only simultaneously democratic and aristocratic but *charismatic*, was the pervasive aestheticisation of politics.[18] As alluded to earlier, this expressed itself in the continual creation of a cultic social environment, both in the forging of 'sacred' spaces, through monumental public building schemes, and through the constant invention of public ceremonies and rituals imbued with symbolic significance for the regeneration of the national community, whether overtly political (party rallies, state funerals for national 'martyrs'), apparently apolitical (sporting events, art exhibitions), or quasi-religious (harvest festivals, solstice festivals, national feast days).

It is important to stress that the aestheticisation of politics under fascism did not stem purely from the demand for effective propaganda, as 'totalitarianism' theorists of structural-functionalist persuasion would have it. Instead, it resulted from a profound confusion within the fascist mentality of the inner world of Utopian longings, and of mythopoiea with the outer world of politics and history. This confusion is characteristic of all revolutionary movements: one only has to think of European millenarianism,[19] the French Revolution,[20] the Russian Revolution[21] or the Hippy counter-culture.[22] In this context, the transformation of political life into a continuous display of civic liturgy, staged by the poet Gabriele D'Annunzio as self-appointed regent of Fiume in 1920 can rightly be seen as a dress-rehearsal for what was to come under Mussolini,[23] but also as the first fully fledged expression of fascism in action. The most famous emblem of the synthesis of Utopia, ideology, manufacture of consensus and aesthetic politics to produce a 'political religion' is perhaps Leni Riefenstahl's *Triumph of the Will* (significantly Goebbels wanted the film withdrawn from cinemas because of its overtly propagandistic nature). Fascist ideologues themselves sometimes drew attention to the fusion of the aesthetic with the political so characteristic of charismatic politics. Thus Degrelle described Hitler, Mussolini and Codreanu as the 'poets of revolution',[24] while José Antonio declared that 'peoples have never been moved by anyone save poets, and woe to him who, before the poetry which destroys, does not know how to summon up the poetry which gives hope!'[25]

The recognition of the intimate link between fascism and an aestheticised, (liturgic, religious, dramatic) style of politics is common to many of the leading experts in fascist studies. According to George Mosse, the Futurist Marinetti's declaration that the economic hell of post-war Italy could be overcome by the staging of innumerable artistic festivals 'anticipates the success and function of much of the political liturgy of European fascism'.[26] Maria Stone's article on the Exhibition of the Fascist Revolution (which attracted nearly three million visitors between 1932 and 1934) argues that it aspired to 'turn the fascist assumption of power into a "public cult"', and that 'the ritualisation of the day on which fascism took the reins of government tied the participant to the experience on an emotional level, using the mystification of the historical event to create a common community'. Characteristically, she is prompted to use a theatrical metaphor to evoke fascism's aestheticised and charismatic style of politics, entitling her article 'Staging Fascism'.[27] Another academic reaches for the same metaphor in the analysis of the pervasively liturgic aspect of political culture in the Third Reich, talking about the 'stage-management of National Socialism'.[28] It thus seems only natural if in his highly influential typological definition of generic fascism Stanley Payne identifies as one of its traits 'the emphasis on the aesthetic structure of meetings, symbols, and political choreography, stressing mystical and romantic aspects'.[29]

Perhaps Emilio Gentile best sums up this dimension of fascism, as well as its intimate link with the myth of 'palingenesis' (Vondung's 'metastasis', or what he calls here 'metanoia') so central to fascist ideology in *Il culto del littorio*, which explores the cult of the Lictor's rod or the *fasces*, the symbol of Mussolini's New Italy. In the conclusion to an exhaustive analysis of the pervasive political aestheticisation and theatricalisation of public life under Fascism to date, he suggests that:

> ... movements like Bolshevism, Fascism and Nazism have asserted themselves as *political religions* and have intensified the sacral aura that has always surrounded power, appropriating from religion the function of defining the significance of life and the ultimate purpose of existence. Political religions reproduce the typical structure of traditional religions, articulated in the fundamental dimensions of faith, myth, ritual and communion, and propose to bring about, through the State and Party, a 'metanoia' of human nature out of which shall come forth a regenerated 'new man', totally integrated into the community.[30]

In short, fascism, if it can seize power, is able to remain true to its core myth and legitimate itself only by generating an elaborate civic liturgy (or a 'civic', 'secular' or 'political' religion) based on the myth of imminent national rebirth. In the two cases where it managed to conquer the State, it rapidly developed its own characteristic rites and ceremonial, its own iconography and symbology, its own semiotic discourse, aping (but only aping) any established Church. It is in this context of a general ritualisation and aestheticisation of political culture, shot through with palingenetic myth, that a new order was being born that the performing arts under fascism are to be studied.

The place of theatrical studies within fascist studies

It should be clear by now that the title of this paper, 'the staging of the fascist revolution', does not imply that the sense of participating in a benign revolution which both the Fascist and Nazi régime induced in so many of their subjects is to be dismissed as an elaborate piece of illusion, as when an audience is carried away by a skilfully staged open-air rock concert. To analyse dispassionately the experience of national revolution which fascism succeeded in conjuring up in its most ardent followers does not imply the absence of deeply held ideological convictions on the part of those responsible, any more than an analysis of the semiotics of faith in medieval Christian society would cast doubt on the convictions held in the Vatican (which, after all, bequeathed to the world the very term 'propaganda'). The 'myth' of fascism can only be perceived as such from outside, and the mechanics of the illusions it generated are transparent only to the agnostic. There is good evidence, for example, that Mussolini and Hitler were genuine believers in their private version of palingenetic myth, no matter how cynically their underlying scorn for the masses allowed them to manipulate their emotions with rhetoric and propaganda worthy of modern Princes.

Apart from stressing the need to take fascism seriously as an attempted political and cultural revolution, this essay has addressed two problems posed for researchers into theatrical culture in the age of fascism. The first is to distinguish fascist from non-fascist or para-fascist régimes, so that the operational environment of the theatre concerned can be established from the outset. The second is to know what aspects of a specific sample of theatrical culture might be considered fascist (whether produced under a fascist or non-fascist régime), and hence structurally linked to other samples of fascist cultural production. If the ideal type sketched out here is used as a heuristic device, then both problems can be resolved by paying close attention to the ideology, either of the political liturgy fostered by the régime, or of the performance aesthetics under consideration. In other words, attention must be paid to *which* Golden Calves the masses or the audience are being called upon to worship, to *which* Moloch they are expected to sacrifice individual conscience, critical detachment and humanist values. One central criterion should always be: are these the graven images of a *new order ruled by a new élite*, or merely old idols being worshipped in a revised, more 'up-to-date' form of service tailored to meet the demands of the modern age? Is the regeneration of the national community at stake, or simply the restoration of an older stage of society? Is the New Man, the Reborn National Community the hero, or is it the State, the Church, the Family, the traditional icons of conservative authoritarianism?

What has also emerged is that even when the application of this yard-stick has reduced the number of fascist régimes to two, and anticipated a paucity of overtly fascist *theatre* in both, any reduction of the field of study is more than compensated for by the over-abundance of *theatricality* in the sphere of public life. Social reality under Fascism and Nazism might be seen as an ongoing political miracle play punctuated by regular intervals of deliberately de-politicising leisure and light entertainment. Seen in this way, what might at first have appeared a neglected but navigable backwater within fascist studies becomes a truly oceanic topic. To study fascist theatre is to bring together the definitional, the methodological, the political, the social-psychological and the cultural-historical in a comparative perspective, and thus leads to an unusually sophisticated perspective on the fascist era as a whole.

Within this perspective certain texts, which might have been dismissed as empty rhetoric, acquire new significance as testimonies of an ideological faith which kept fascism alive for its followers. Here is an example taken from an article on 'magic realism,' published in Year 6 of Mussolini's New Italy (July 1928) in the Fascist modernist literary magazine 1900 (i.e. 'Novecento' or 'Twentieth Century') by one of the régime's most noted writers and literary critics, Massimo Bontempelli:

> There is a strange and spontaneous correspondence(...) between the theoretical ideals which 'Novecentism' espoused from the outset in a purely literary sphere, and the whole spirit in which Italian life has been renewed. We called for the deliberate creation of the myths for the new era: and is it not true to say that today the whole of Italy at every level, in every walk of life, in the most prosaic of activities, in politics and industry, in agriculture and fashion, is working as if intent on writing a mythic poem, with a precise sense of its rôle as the protagonist on the stage of a theatre, which is the theatre of history?[31]

Within this perspective the deeper logic behind certain fascist events also becomes transparent, such as the apparently perverse decision by Hitler's Minister of Armaments, Albert Speer, to destroy the call-up papers of the members of the Berlin Philharmonic in April 1945. At the very moment when the capital of the 1000 Year Reich was being reduced to rubble around his ears, he felt it appropriate that, rather than hold weapons they should take up musical instruments to play a final concert, the last ever performed in Hitler's Germany. It featured not only Beethoven's violin concerto and the Bruckner symphony, but Brünnhilde's last aria and the finale from *Götterdämmerung*. It was a programme which, as Speer himself boasted, was deliberately chosen for its pathos and melancholy and hence as a 'gesture pointing to the end of the Reich'.[32]

NOTES

1. Roger Griffin, *The Nature of Fascism*, London, 1991, 1993.
2. Roger Griffin, *Fascism*, Oxford, 1995.
3. See, for example, Lynn Hunt, *Politics, Culture and Class in the French Revolution*, Berkeley, Ca, 1984.
4. For an elaboration of this distinction see Roger Griffin, `Nationalism', in R. Eatwell and A. Wright (eds), *Contemporary Political Ideologies*, London, 1993.
5. For a more thorough exposition of these points see Griffin, *The Nature of Fascism*, ch. 2.
6 See Griffin, *The Nature of Fascism*, ch. 2, and the General Introduction to Griffin, *Fascism*.
7. The allusion is, of course, to the theory of fascism expounded by Ernst Nolte in *Three Faces of Fascism*, New York, 1964.
8. See Roger Griffin, 'Modernity under the New Order: The Fascist Project for Managing the Future', Oxford Brookes School of Business Occasional Papers, 1994.
9. Fascism is certainly not to be confused with 'politicised religions' such as Islamic fundamentalism, since it seeks to bring about a rebirth of the nation within human history, through human agency, legitimating itself through human authority. However, Emilio Gentile has convincingly demonstrated (e.g., in his *Il culto del littorio*, Rome, 1993) the value of the concept 'political religion' in the analysis of Fascism when it is used in a way which broadly corresponds to the concept 'civic religion' coined by Rousseau, i.e., a secular political system which generates elaborate civic creeds, rituals and liturgy in the attempt to integrate all citizens within the nation-state. As long as it is recognised that such 'civic religions' operate as *substitutes* for metaphysical religions based on tradition or 'revealed truth' (e.g. Holy Scripture), then this is a valuable heuristic device which is extensively compatible with the emphasis on 'palingenetic myth' so central to the ideal type applied in this essay. In his recent *Avant-Garde Florence: From Modernism to Fascism*, Cambridge, Massachusetts, 1993, Walter Adamson, also makes extensive and fruitful use of the term 'secular religion' in this sense.
10. For this distinction see Roger Griffin, 'Integration and Identification: Conflicting Aspects of the Human Need for Self-transcendence Within Ideological Communities', *History of European Ideas*, vol. 18, no. 1, 1994, pp. 11-23.
11. Pietro Cavallo, 'Culto delle origini e mito del capo nel teatro fascista', *Storia Contemporanea*, vol. 18, no. 2, 1987, pp. 302-3.
12. Klaus Vondung, *Magie und Manipulation*, Göttingen, 1971, pp. 164-5.
13. Ian Kershaw, *The Nazi Dictatorship*, London, 1985, p. 141.
14. Vondung, *Magie und Manipulation*, p. 174.
15. See Serge Added, *Le Théâtre dans les années Vichy 1940-1944*, Paris, 1992, pp. 235-42.
16. On this point see the chapter 'Public show and private perceptions' in Detlef Peukert, *Inside Nazi Germany*, Harmondsworth, 1989, pp. 187-196.
17. See Detlef Mühlberger, *Hitler's Followers*, London, 1991.
18. The phrase is reputed to have been first used by Walter Benjamin in his *Theorien des deutschen Faschismus*, vol. 3 of *Gesammelte Schriften*, Frankfurt am Main, 1977.
19. Norman Cohn, *The Pursuit of the Millennium*, London, 1970.

20. Hunt, *Politics, Culture and Class in the French Revolution*.
21. Richard Stites, *Revolutionary Dreams*, Oxford, 1989.
22. Theodor Roszak, *The Makings of a Counter Culture*, London, 1970.
23. George Mosse, 'The Poet and the Exercise of Political Power: Gabriele D'Annunzio', in *Masses and Man*, New York, 1980.
24. *Ibidem*, p. 257.
25. Quoted in Eugen Weber, *Varieties of Fascism*, London, 1974, p. 177.
26. George Mosse, 'The Political Culture of Italian Futurism: A General Perspective', *Journal of Contemporary History*, vol. 25, nos 2-3, 1990, p. 258.
27. Maria Stone, 'Staging fascism: The Exhibition of the Fascist Revolution', *Journal of Contemporary History*, vol. 28, 1993, pp. 215-241.
28. W. Benz, 'The ritual and stage management of National Socialism', in J. Milfull (ed.), *The Attractions of Fascism*, New York, 1990.
29. This is part of Stanley Payne's 'Typological Description of Fascism' under the heading 'style and organization' in *Fascism: Comparison and Definition*, Wisconsin, 1980, the most influential ideal type of generic fascism to date.
30. Gentile, *Il culto del littorio*, p. 309.
31. Quoted in S. Guglielmino, *Guida al novecento*, Milan, 1971, p. 236.
32. Albert Speer, *Inside the Third Reich*, London, 1971, pp. 618-619.

2

The Cultural Politics
of Fascist Governments

Reinhard Kühnl

Translated by Ann Requa-Dahl and Günter Berghaus

Fascist systems and their internal logic

F ascism as a political system was characterised by specific goals
that served as a basis for its policies, as well as by specific
methods with which it strived to achieve its objectives.[1] Parts of
the fascist system possessed a certain independence and inner
logic. However, these elements must be seen in the context of the
total system of control, for their essential features can only be
understood when they are analysed as integral elements of the
whole. This holds true for economic and social policy, as well as
for education, culture and the arts, including the field with which
this book is concerned, the theatre.

Since the cultural policies of fascist States were aimed at 'the
complete mobilisation for the intellectual struggle that is required
to reach the goals laid down by the politicians',[2] one needs to
examine with particular care the seemingly 'unpolitical' phenomena in the world of 'entertainment'. 'A good mood', according to
Reich's Minister of Propaganda Goebbels, was an 'instrument of
war', which 'under certain conditions could not only be important
for war, but even be a factor determining the outcome of war. (...)
It is therefore essential to keep the people in a good mood.'[3]

In order to analyse the key features of fascist cultural policies,
one has first to identify the main objectives of the political system

behind them. Secondly, one has to take into account the variations between fascist systems and the different logics operating within the various parts of the system (education, culture or, in this case, theatre). It can generally be observed that the more developed and powerful the State apparatus was, the stronger it could influence the various spheres of public life. In countries considered to be 'strongly' fascist, such as Germany, the goals of the 'totalitarian State' could almost be fulfilled, whereas individual freedom was less restricted in 'weak' fascist States such as Portugal and Austria.

The ability to centralise the apparatus of power and to attain political objectives depended upon the extent to which a society was industrially and technologically developed. Not only did bureaucracy and the military apparatus determine the course of history, but also the mass media. All three elements had to work in close co-operation with each other to achieve an effectiveness of the fascist system, as could be found in Germany. From end of the nineteenth century, Germany had been the strongest and most efficient industrial power in Europe. Part of this was due to Prussian militarism and monarchical bureaucracy, which influenced not only the structure of the State, but also determined the consciousness of the middle classes and social élite. However, this was in part also due to the pervasive acceptance of the ideas of duty and obedience that had been fostered by Protestantism (just as Confucianism had done in Japan).

The aims and objectives of fascist governments

Empirical research within the cultural, social and political sciences needs to ascertain how great were the relative freedoms in the individual parts of the system in any given fascist State. Fascist systems were marked by strong contradictions. The majority of the population was to be deprived of their civil rights, at the same time as being made enthusiastic about the régime that was limiting their freedom. People were to be placed under control, but at the same time to be motivated to voluntarily take part in the public life of their country. The combination of these diverging aims was not an easy task.

The policies of the fascist system were geared towards a systematic dismantling of the people's right to represent their interests and opinions in a democratic fashion. This applies especially to the working class, whose organisations had operated traditionally as a counterforce to the interests of the capitalists. Hence, one of the first political acts in every fascist State was to ban trade unions and socialist parties, to arrest their leaders and in many cases murder their representatives.

This also applies to the intelligentsia, whose political affiliations or sympathies tended to be oriented towards liberal or socialist parties, and who therefore represented an important impediment to fascism. But equally the middle classes and small entrepreneurs in the fields of trade, commerce and agriculture were restricted in their democratic rights, although at the same time they received numerous rewards for having lent important support to fascist movements.

As a result, all democratic forms of government were destroyed, a hierarchical system imposed in their stead, and military principles of order and obedience were imposed on the population. In the business world, the entrepreneur became the '*Führer* of the firm' and was equipped with wide-reaching authority over his employees. In Germany this was laid down by the Law to Regulate National Labour (*Gesetz zur Ordnung der nationalen Arbeit*) of 1934 and the State Security Law (*Staatssicherheitsgesetz*) of 1941; in Italy by the Charter of Labour (*Carta del Lavoro*) of 1927 and the anti-strike law of 1925; and in Spain by the Law of Labour (*Fuero del Trabajo*) of 1938 and in the Regulation of National Order (*Reglamento de Régimen Interior*).

The principle of authoritarian leadership was also applied to cultural institutions. Initially, this meant reserving access to public forms of exhibition to those works that fulfilled the aims and objectives of the political leadership. Secondly, it meant restricting the artists' control over the form and content of their cultural production.

In most fascist systems, and those similar to them, the main focus of power politics was directed towards defending the interests and privileges of the ruling élite. This holds good for Austria (after 1934), Portugal and Spain, as well as for the dictatorships in Greece (after 1967), Chile (after 1973), Turkey (after 1980), and so on. In countries that were within reach of becoming an imperial power (e.g. Germany, Japan and Italy), fascism also served to prepare for, and then to conduct a war of conquest. By comparison with developed Western States such as Britain, Holland and France, these countries had completed the transition to industrial capitalism and to a nation-state at a very late date, that is, at a time when the old empires had already divided up the world amongst themselves.

Consequently, the 'newcomers' on the political scene sought to strengthen their economic and military power and to create a strong and effective administrative system in order to pursue their imperialist objectives. The fascist systems erected in Germany, Italy and Japan marshalled the political, social, economic and ideological forces of the nation towards fulfilling the bellicose aims of their leaders. And in order to achieve this aim, all hindrances (of a material or human kind) had to be removed.

With the French Revolution the masses had taken a central position on the European political stage. In industrially developed countries, labour organisations had been formed which began to threaten the political power of the traditional élites. Under these conditions the policies of the Right-wing parties could no longer be implemented through mere repression of the masses. 'Mobilisation without participation' was the new maxim. This could already be detected before the First World War, but it became a pressing necessity in those States that were preparing for imperialist warfare. Here, the traditional forms of authoritarian rule were no longer appropriate. The masses had to be convinced that by identifying with the imperial policies of the government they would further their own interests.

Modern forms and methods of government were employed to attain intrinsically reactionary aims. The 'modern' needs of the masses had to be catered for, not only in political terms, but also in the spheres of social and cultural life. In this sense, the term coined by Jeffrey Herf, 'reactionary modernity',[4] takes on a precise meaning. It was exactly this new quality that distinguished fascism from conservative Right-wing movements.

Italian Fascism strove towards conquests in North Africa and in the Balkans. German plans for expansion required a particularly effective mobilisation of the masses if they were ever going to lead to a lasting subjugation of the European peoples from the Atlantic to the Urals. Ideological traditions had already paved the way for the 'new man', the 'blonde beast' who was destined to rule the world. However, this new 'master race' was only systematically created after 1933, through education and through intercourse with 'inferior beings' (Jews, Communists, Poles, Russians, etc.). Events such as the *Reichspogromnacht* of 9 November 1938 or the practices in the concentration camps can be regarded as a methodical application of this master-race ideology.

On the one hand, the goals set by the fascist régimes called for a brutal system of terror and control. On the other hand, they required sophisticated methods to influence the masses and to generate enthusiasm for the policies of the régime. What distinguishes fascist systems from traditional authoritarian régimes was their ability to establish a State apparatus that was able to mobilise a large part of the population, while at the same time eliminating systematically any oppositional forces. The relative success of the régimes depended to a large extent on how pronounced were the plans of conquest, how plentiful the resources, and how highly developed the communication technology of the country in question. In this regard, the dictatorships in Spain and Portugal represented transitional phenomena located somewhere between authoritarian and fascist régimes.

In those countries where a fascist system of government could be erected, a close alliance between the fascist Party, the military apparatus, the economic leadership and the State bureaucracy was required. The weight that each power-sharing faction carried, and the relationship between the Party and its conservative allies (nationalists, monarchists, ultra-conservatives etc.), differed from State to State.

In Germany, the NSDAP (*Nationalsozialistische Arbeiterpartei –* National Socialist Workers' Party) became particularly powerful, whereas in Italy and Spain traditional conservative élites continued to exercise considerable control in the running of the country. Between the power-sharing factions there were differences of opinion, conflicts of interest and battles for spheres of influence. In other words, 'pluralism' existed, but it was a pluralism that was strictly limited to the ruling élite.

The rôle of the arts in fascist States

Culture had a significant function in the process of creating a mentality that forced people to submit to the dictates of their fascist government. Furthermore, it was instrumental in persuading the masses to give active and enthusiastic support to the régime. The ultimate task assigned to art and other cultural activities was to offer ideological support to the ruling class, but also to prepare and mobilise the people for the war of conquest.

Fascist art and culture ran counter to the universal human values that had been proclaimed since the Enlightenment: individual freedom, equality, democracy, tolerance, and so on. Instead, they set out to legitimise the concept of the superiority of certain races and individuals, of a strict hierarchy of classes, nations and races. Fascism was strongly counter-revolutionary, in as much as it sought to eliminate the historical achievements of the French Revolution. German fascism, furthermore, aimed at obliterating the results of the November Revolution of 1918.

The concrete form of fascist cultural policies depended, on the one hand, on the national traditions of the respective country and on the other hand on the political and tactical objectives pursued by the régime. The ideological patterns and artistic forms of cultural production in a fascist State could therefore be extremely varied. They also changed during the course of development of a particular régime. In Germany and Italy, the fascist leadership tried to influence large sections of the population by means of theatre and the performing arts. Mass spectacles helped to forge a national community, whereas theatrical entertainment (farces, comedies, music-hall, operetta etc.) kept the population and the troops at the war front in a good mood (just as other actors had done in the past to entertain those working on the autobahn and the West Wall).[5]

In the cultural sector, the modernity of fascism came to the fore in the use of the most advanced mass media. Film and radio were made available to the whole community at low prices. At the same time, the régimes paid close attention to the tastes of the middle classes and approached the rural population and the petty bourgeoisie in small cities with other methods (e.g. folkloric dances, puppet theatre, religious drama and travelling comedy shows). They also employed theatrical forms that had proved to be effective with the working classes (e.g. the speech and movement choirs). In addition to the pluralism in the power cartel already mentioned, this variety of cultural forms could sometimes provide an opportunity for signalling oppositional attitudes (for example in productions of classical dramas). This, however, in no way impaired the overall effectiveness of the ideological apparatus.[6]

There existed a deep contradiction between fascists paying lip-service to the lofty traditions of bourgeois culture and their brutal destruction of the very core of humanist values, although it is possible that the two aspects were directed at different sectors of the population. Nevertheless, they were coincidentally, if not symbiotically related. German soldiers were morally educated with recitations of Goethe and Schiller. On the home front, classical music conducted by Furtwängler and Karajan lifted the spirits of the civilian population. In addition, the SS élite or the concentration camp commanders liked to relax to classical music after having performed their deadly duties all day. The way in which the supposedly unpolitical traditions of classical art and literature were employed to foster the barbaric intentions of the fascist leadership should be the topic of further investigation. There also remains the question as to why artists, intellectuals and scientists supported fascism to such a large extent.[7]

The outward appearance of the fascist message could vary considerably, since the concrete forms of presentation were tailored to the national traditions in each country. In Germany, for example, there dominated a *völkisch* nationalism that had its origins in the late-Romantic reaction to the French Revolution and, towards the end of the nineteenth century, had taken on an increasingly racist character. In Italy, on the other hand, there existed a much stronger bureaucratic nationalism that sought its legitimisation from the Ancient Roman Empire. In Spain, nationalism was also determined by the State, but here it was harking back to the Siglo d'Oro of Ferdinando and Isabella and the colonial empire in South America.

A second fundamental difference was that in denominationally unified countries, such as Italy, Spain, Portugal, Austria, Croatia and Slovakia, the Catholic Church could function as an ideological buffer. Although elements of fascist ideology such as anti-rationalism, anti-liberalism and anti-communism were also propagated by the Church, there were several countries (especially Spain) where the position of the Catholic Church proved stronger than that of the fascist Party. In countries divided in their religious beliefs, such as Germany, fascism could not attach itself to any one denomination without appearing to cause damage to 'national unity'. In this case, fascism was forced to search for other unifying factors, which it found in an Aryan and Germanic mythology (the 'positive Christianity' without 'denominational fixations' that was proclaimed in point 24 of the NSDAP programme of 1920, played only a minor part in the ideological struggle of the Party).

Tactical flexibility could take on many forms and have different purposes. Just as anti-Semitism could be fostered or discouraged by a régime, certain cultural forms could be in or out of favour. For example, the alternating valorisation of Shakespeare or Molière usually depended on how good or bad relations with Britain or

France were. Or certain theatrical traditions could gain official approval or discouragement depending on the régime's reliance on the good will of the social classes where the traditions had a popular following.

Summary

In different countries fascism developed varying degrees of efficiency in the way it propagated its ideologies and turned them into a social and political force. In the 1930s, Italian Fascism attained a high degree of consensus amongst the population. This, however, was a long way from the enthusiasm, fanaticism and active support that German fascism managed to generate in different social classes, after the terror of 1933/1934 had produced the fundamental preconditions for widely and efficiently propagating its ideology. German fascism was successful not only through its use of terror as a means of controlling the majority of the population, but also through finding ways of generating popular support for its ideology and politics. It is one of the most important tasks of research into fascism to explain these divergencies in different countries, and how particular historical, social, economic and cultural factors contributed towards the success, or lack of success, of a particular fascist movement.

NOTES

1. I have presented, justified and documented in more detail my interpretation of fascist systems in the following publications: *Faschismustheorien: Ein Leitfaden*, revised edition, Heilbronn, 1990; *Der Faschismus. Ursachen, Herrschaftsstruktur, Aktualität: Eine Einführung*, 2nd edition, Heilbronn, 1988; *Gefahr von Rechts? Vergangenheit und Gegenwart der extremen Rechten*, 2nd edition, Heilbronn, 1991; *Der deutsche Faschismus in Quellen und Dokumentation*, 6th edition, Cologne, 1987; article 'Faschismus', in *Europäische Enzyklopädie zu Philosophie und Wissenschaften*, vol. 2, Hamburg, 1990, pp. 53-62.
2. According to Theodor Blahut, Director of the German Academic Exchange Service (DAAD) in Rome, 1940. See Jens Petersen, 'Die Organisation der deutschen Propoganda in Italien 1939-1943', *Quellen und Forschungen aus italienischen Archiven und Bibliotheken*, vol. 70, 1970, pp. 513-555, here p. 520.
3. See Goebbel's diary entry of 27 February 1942. Peter Adam, author of the film,

Kunst im Dritten Reich, even maintains that 'art became one of the most important means of propoganda. Art and ideology were identical.' (Interview in the *Frankfurter Allgemeine Zeitung,* supplement to the issue of 12 February 1993).

4. See J. Herff, *Reactionary Modernism: Technology, Culture and Politics in Weimar Germany and the Third Reich,* Cambridge, 1984.
5. See G. Murmann, *Komödianten für den Krieg,* Düsseldorf, 1992.
6. Peter Reichel has published a systematic examination of all media and strategies of ideological manipulation employed by German fascism: *Der schöne Schein des Dritten Reiches: Faszination und Gewalt des Faschismus,* Munich, 1991.
7. See O. Rathkolb, *"Führertreu und Gottbegnadet": Künstlereliten im Dritten Reich,* Vienna, 1991.

3

The Ritual Core of Fascist Theatre
An Anthropological Perspective

Günter Berghaus

Introduction

The aim of this chapter is to elucidate the dynamic and reciprocal relationship between the rulers and the ruled during the
fascist era and to analyse one of the means that was employed to
foster the bond between them: ritualism. Fascist systems were
characterised by the invasion of the socio-political realm by cultic,
liturgic and religious elements. This chapter sets out to apply an
anthropological and psychological perspective to this relatively
neglected aspect of the two fascist régimes in the 1920s and 1930s.
The aim is to interpret, in a speculative and heuristic fashion, the
psycho-social framework in which fascist theatre operated, and
the functions which ritual performances could play in established
fascist systems.

Although I shall only make fleeting reference to the less successful fascist movements (and I do not enter at all into the debate
of what classifies as fascist, para-fascist, proto-fascist etc.), the
results of my analysis can be applied to any fascist 'mentality' or
predisposition whatever its degree of realisation. It therefore also
holds true of contemporary developments, where long-term factors (structural crises) accelerate into acute crises and call forth
regenerationist salvation movements with a neo-fascist thrust.

Fascist parties rose to positions of power by gaining mass support and winning democratic elections. Millions of people were
inspired by Mussolini and Hitler and developed a genuine enthu-

siasm for their politics, because they promised an answer to a need that was widely felt in different sections of the population. People were 'fascinated' by what fascism proposed in response to a crisis that affected the economic, social and cultural spheres of their lives. Political promises played a rôle in this, but the emotional appeal of the leaders and their programmes was probably stronger. Fascist leaders avoided the rational rhetorics typical of bourgeois politicians, and instead employed a performative language that had a captivating force unequalled by traditional means of propaganda.

A basic premise behind my analysis is that the individual's relation to his or her inner self is intimately connected to the individual's relation to his or her social surrounding. If a crisis affects the psyche of many individuals, it can give rise to a social crisis. Fascism has often been described as an illness of the body politic. This, in my view, is short-sighted, for fascism was rather an ill-advised cure for a deep crisis that affected individual and society. An illness requires a cure by responsible healers. But the fascist leaders exacerbated the pathological condition and exploited it for other, politically motivated, reasons. The outcome was an epidemic, and in Germany it reached catastrophic proportions.

Historians have chronicled and analysed the progression of this contagion from a political angle. I shall, in this essay, employ the methods of analytical psychology, the anthropology of performance and theatre studies to elucidate the political and psychological functions of the rituals that were used as an antidote to the crisis. In the first part of this chapter I shall discuss certain aspects of the psychology and anthropology of rituals which might help to explain the success of fascist systems in the 1920s and 1930s. In the second half, I shall analyse some of the rituals that became a dominant feature of fascist States, with theatre performances being only one form beside many others.

Ritualism and the crisis of the Body Politic

Rituals are a behavioural constant in the lives of animals and humans and are designed to co-ordinate conspecifics towards some social action that creates or re-establishes order. Their function is to control instinctual reactions to environmental, social, psychological change and to regulate transformations of an organic system, while at the same time preserving and maintaining its

integrity.[1] If the external change cannot be accommodated, a transformation of the system is required. The main function of rituals is
to ease this transition from one state into a new one. They serve as
a medium of equilibration, providing stability in change, allowing
the development and preservation of complex organisms.

More specifically, rituals are an adaptive technique of individuals and social groups faced with a situation of crisis. They are
evoked to provide 'an institutionalised way of coping with existential stress, a means of support and reassurance during identity-
crises (...) Ritual is about change, and the terrors and uncertainties
which surround change, but which must somehow be "accepted
into the system", both corporate and personal. It is about
mankind's fear of novelty, of unstructured situations and states of
flux, in which the old way is over and done away and the new one
has not yet really begun.'[2]

Human life is full of such crises and periods of change. This is
why rituals are so pervasive in both the private and the social
world. Effective participation in ritual as an adult requires the
learning of ritual practices in the early phases of life. Freud has
posited a structural parallel between the patterns of development
of the individual and those of the whole human race. Social
anthropologists have elucidated the connection between family
and social life. In addition, Jung's studies on the origins of culture
have suggested how dissensions in the political sphere are to a
large extent exteriorisations of conflicts in the individual's inner
constitution. In order to understand the emergence of fascist structures, these connecting lines between individual, family and State
need to be examined more closely.

The entry into the world is the first major crisis in the life of
each individual; adapting the demands of the pleasure principle
to the requirements of the reality principle leads to whole series of
further crises. As a result, the adult psyche is, under the best circumstances, a balance between an infinite number of potential
crises. Through unusual pressure from outside the balance can be
overturned and the crisis may erupt again. If many individuals are
affected by the same symptoms, a highly infectious psychic inflation of the masses sets in. Jung stresses that civilisation has only
occupied the last minutes in the long day of our development
from the animal world. The layers of culture are therefore
extremely thin in comparison to the basic store of the primitive
psyche.[3] Human civilisation is, psychologically speaking, still in
its infant years. In a crisis situation, adults may revert to mecha-

nisms one can still observe in every new-born baby. The psyche in its early phases of development is essentially collective. The differentiation between individual and parent/society has not yet set in. Even after individuation has been achieved, in moments of crisis the dependence on other members of the social group is once again activated as a necessary defence mechanism.

Recent research has proven that under the influence of extreme stress the adaptability and flexible operation of the psychological system is seriously reduced or inhibited.[4] Extreme stress affects the conceptual apparatus. The destruction of part of the system is interpreted by the victim as the breakdown of the entire system. He is stunned by a world of apparent total chaos. What an individual may experience after the loss of a limb or the death of a close relative, a social group perceives in a very similar manner. Wallace, who has analysed in great depth the social reactions to ecological and economic disasters,[5] has applied his resulting insights to the study of religion and has found that authoritarian revitalisation movements are a regular outcome of such crises.[6] The individual, overwhelmed by the chaos, no longer perceives traditional rituals and social structures as effective. The adult relives the experience of impotence as a young child, regresses to primitive instinctual behaviour and seeks for a parental figure. Any messiah who promises radical change, protection and the creation of a New Order will receive an attentive audience.

If the biological coping mechanism of an individual can be severely handicapped by neurophysiological factors such as stress, the same applies to social rituals normally employed to regulate human response to change. There are different reactions to crisis and hence different types of rituals.[7] Some act as a therapeutic measure or a means of 'social hygiene',[8] whilst others are pathological and ultimately can be destructive for the individual or society. Psychologists differ in their opinion as to how ritual should be viewed. Freud saw a close relation between neurosis and ritualism and demonstrated their common aetiology in the child's mind (see his *Obsessive Acts and Religious Practices* and *Totem and Taboo*). He viewed both the private rituals of a neurotic and their cultural elaboration in 'religion as a universal obsessional neurosis'[9] as protective mechanisms invoked in order to cope with an inner crisis. Jung, on the other hand, saw in rituals less a symptom of neurosis than a therapeutic force to release psychic energies and to overcome moments of crisis. Rituals have a reconciliatory, redemptive, healing quality when they remove individual anxieties and interpersonal tensions. However, when the crisis leads to uncontainable fears, the 'sane' half distances itself from the threatened part of the self, and schizophrenia, paranoia, projection of the phobic object onto imagined enemies take place. Jung repeatedly refers to this process as a dissociation from one's own 'shadow'. Melanie Klein has investigated this phenomenon further and has found that the 'paranoid-schizoid position'[10] can not only effect the individual, but a whole social group. By means of splitting and projective identification, the individual and group transfer the supposedly positive, parental functions onto the leader, and the unwanted, bad qualities onto an outgroup, perceived as 'the enemy'. Kleinian analysts have linked this process to crisis and fear of atomization:

> When the mechanisms of projection, introjection, splitting, idealization, denial and projective and introjective identification fail to master anxiety, and the ego is invaded by it, then disintegration of the ego may occur as a defensive measure. (...) Disintegration is the most desperate of all the ego's attempts to ward off anxiety: in order to avoid suffering anxiety the ego does its best not to exist, an attempt which gives rise to a specific acute anxiety – that of falling to bits and becoming atomised.[11]

In order to preserve the illusion of integrity and to fuel the fantasy of belonging, of being in control, pathological rituals are invented. A typical example of this is the subject of this study.[12]

Before we can examine fascist rituals and cultic theatre in more detail, we have to analyse some of the general features of rituals, in particular their performative structures, psychological effects and social functions. From there we can progress to an analysis of the specific character of the crisis to which fascism was reacting, and how the rituals of the régimes could be interpreted by contemporaries as a functional aid to quell the crisis.

> Ritual is a culturally constructed system of symbolic communication. It is constituted of patterned and ordered sequences of words and acts, often expressed in multiple media, whose content and arrangement are characterized in varying degree by formality (conventionality), stereotypy (rigidity), condensation (fusion), and redundancy (repetition). Ritual action in its constitutive features is performative.[13]

Performative anthropology has examined a whole range of rituals that are employed in periods of crisis and has shown how some patterns occur again and again in similar situations. 'Ritual and ceremonial behaviours develop in response to situations in which transition, ambiguity, conflict, or uncontrollable elements threaten a given structure of relations.'[14] According to Victor Turner, four key stages can be discerned in the development of such rituals: 1) the breach of norm, 2) crisis, 3) redressive or remedial procedure, 4) restoration of social peace.[15] Social dramas provide a motor for social development, and the rituals attached to them ensure that the change is not destroying the dynamic order of society. The most important aspect of ritual performances is the shared emotional experience that creates cohesion and unity of the celebrating mass.

Rituals regularly employ practices that have a strong neurophysiological effect on the brain (e.g. dancing, drumming, autosuggestion, hypnosis, drugs etc.[16]). Consequently, rituals lead to trance or possession states, which allow the individual to break through the normal state of consciousness and to go through a cathartic experience that serves as a safety valve to release the psychic tensions that have accumulated in response to the crisis.[17] They transform libidinal energy which otherwise may prove harmful to individual and society.[18]

As Munn has observed, ritual 'achieves its instrumental aims through its capacity to reorganize the actor's experience of the situation (…) Symbolic forms provide external templates for inner experience, and operations within the external, symbolic sphere are aimed (implicitly or explicitly) at adjusting internal orientations.'[19] Rituals are not grounded in logic but in feelings; they do not inform, but render experienceable and expressible what otherwise is repressed or inhibited. Rituals allow the community to act out their collective dreams and fears, and vice versa, through the numinous quality of the symbols the rituals can act as formative agents in the creation and fostering of communities. Rituals and their symbols are a reflection of the collective subconscious. The desires and anxieties are also objectified in other forms, e.g. dreams, myths, fairy tales. But in rituals they are acted upon.

Through rituals, the individual psyche becomes connected to the corporate psyche and experiences a mysterious sensation of wholeness and unity. Out of the ritualised interaction of bodies emerges a symbolic 'body' of society in its collective holism. Here, the individual has returned to a foetal state in the corporate womb of human society. The striving for such undifferentiated Being is automatically evoked in situations of crisis, when the integrity of self-hood is in danger of being ripped apart. Ritual performances produce a new equilibrium in the psychic household of both group and individual. They reinforce the individual's belief in the binding principles of order and makes him/her accept or endorse the values of society: 'Ritual, then, asserts and establishes social truth, truth about social obligations and expectations, social relationships, by public performance of an ideal social message.'[20]

Ritualism acts as a social bonding mechanism. It gives the individual a feeling of being connected to something larger than him/herself. This 'something' is both the group and the belief system that has brought the community together. Rituals are therefore essential tools for the creation and maintenance of social structures, corporate identities and collective actions (as well as exercising control and sanctioning power).[21]

The person in charge of the ritual acts as an agent of the community. He, or in some cases she, has been chosen for his or her psychic power, or has inherited the job and practises it in times of need. This magically effective figure channels the community's psychic energies and subconscious desires through the rituals. But frequently one finds that the medicine man or healer or shaman is abusing his or her position. The motive behind this may be financial, or a will for power.

The history of Western civilisation has provided many examples of messianic 'healers' and mass movements seeking a way out of crises by establishing a New Order: Christian religion born out the crisis in the Roman Empire; millenarian movements erupting in the first crisis of the feudal system; Protestantism after the second crisis of feudalism; the French Revolution after the final crisis of the feudal organisation of European society; fascism after the first crisis of capitalism and the liberal State.[22]

The use of ritual for political purposes is nothing new and was certainly not specific to fascism. In fact, the older traditions furnished much of the symbolism and performative models for the secularised religion of the régimes of Mussolini, Hitler et al.: the cult of the Roman Caesars, the pageants of medieval emperors, the *trionfi* and *feste teatrali* of the Renaissance princes, the cult of the Sun King in Versaille. Something new came into existence with the *fêtes révolutionnaires* of the French Revolution. They were celebrations *of* the people, not *for* the people. The masses who had toppled the *ancien régime* appropriated the older forms of celebrations and used them for a different purpose. But the bourgeois leadership was genuinely afraid of the power of the masses. This trend continued in the nineteenth century with the added characteristic that the festivities revolved around the notion of nationhood. They were centred around the symbol of national unity, the monarch, linking him to previous representatives of a historical or mythical age. But nationalism was very much an affair of the bourgeoisie, and the working classes generally abstained from lending mass support to the government. Participation in national celebrations could involve ten thousands of people, but they were, as Gentile points out, *folla d'occasione* and not *massa liturgica*.[23] For this reason, the rituals of nationalism alone could not function effectively as an integrating mechanism for the *whole* people. As long as the liberal State and capitalist market offered enough substitute pleasures, the cult of individualism could prevail. But around the turn of the century the situation began to change, or rather; conflicts that had been simmering for a while came to the fore.

Long before the fascist era, the symptoms of a pervasive crisis could be detected under a seemingly calm surface in many European States. During the nineteenth century, an order that had previously been provided by the Church, by social hierarchies and political figureheads, had become eroded by capitalism. The Industrial Revolution led to a mass migration from countryside to the cities. It uprooted millions of people and severed their traditional bonds with nature and their ties to family and social groups (the 'blood and soil' which Nazi ideology tried to re-establish). Through the break up of communal ties the individual became a cipher, an anonymous, atomised, interchangeable particle of a larger mass, but it was a mass without shape, cohesion or direction. Psychic alienation and social isolation in the urban conglomerations evoked instinctual fears of insecurity and disintegration.

The cult of rationality and the development of science as a rational means of controlling the world reinforced this process. The Enlightenment had dethroned the old Christian gods and had attempted to create a new human being 'released from his self-incurred tutelage' (Kant, *What is Enlightenment?*). But declaring the psyche a *tabula rasa* and constructing, with rational means and through appropriate education, a better person – the dream of Rousseauist philosophers and educationalists – did not abolish the primitive psychic constitution of the people. In fact, the Enlightenment accelerated the neuroses that had befallen early modern society since the second crisis of feudalism. One set of gods had been deposed, only to give rise to new ones. In an anti-religious age, the place formerly occupied by religion and the Church was absorbed by politics and a 'deified State'. The psychological impulses that in earlier societies had been externalised through religious and social rituals, in the modern age were projected onto politics.

The desire for a unifying stream to collect the isolated individuals was partially fulfilled by political groups and movements, who channelled the primitive and irrational drives of mass man. The demand for security and order, however, could only be partially fulfilled by the democratic institutions. They offered some outlet, but not to all and only insufficiently in times of acute crisis. In those States, where the capitalist process had been slow but steady over the last two-hundred years and had been accompanied by a maturing parliamentarian order, the fear of disintegration was counterbalanced by a learning process amongst the masses. They had generated an order from within to accommodate the loss of an order from without. But in the young national States, which had experienced a sudden capitalist development in the second half of the nineteenth century and had not developed any mature democratic structures (especially Italy and Germany), the cry for a strong figure of authority was greatest.

Around the turn of the century the situation became increasingly precarious and led to a new and pervasive phenomenon: the crisis of modernity. The lofty ideals of the nation-state could no longer hide the reality of the political and socio-economic condition of Italy and Germany. Many of the dreams that unification had promised to fulfil had gone sour. The result was a conservative backlash amongst the middle classes, and a revolutionary activism amongst the working classes. There was also a third group of intellectuals, who sought to create an amalgamation of both sources. They saw themselves as the avant-garde of a 'third way' between capitalism and communism. It was out of this group that the leading ideologues of fascism were recruited.

However, for fascism to emerge as a qualitatively new phenomenon, other 'stress factors' had to exacerbate the latent crisis that had befallen society in the nineteenth century. During the course of the first two decades of the twentieth century, European societies stumbled from one crisis into another: the First World War, the humiliating peace treaty, the *biennio rosso* in Italy and the *Inflationszeit* in Germany, the world economic crisis of 1929-1932. The accumulated effect of these events and the extreme anxieties that accompanied them completely disoriented people, and prevented them from reacting sensibly and flexibly to the situation. Incapacitated by the alarming scale of the crisis, considerable por-tions of the population slipped back into the collective psyche of childhood and primitive society. They asked for parental care, for a leader to take responsibility and alleviate the crisis. Individuals saw their salvation in the absolute State and thereby destroyed the last remnants of their individual power. A historical development that had begun with the installation of individual dignity and freedom led, paradoxically, to the destruction of the very same values it had once created. The lofty ideals of the Renaissance and Enlightenment – individual fulfilment, liberation from the bonds of the Church, abolition of fealty ties to the monarchy – were turned into their opposite: a new totalitarian order.

The desperate need for security in wide sectors of society was channelled by the fascist movements, who presented a seeming answer to the crisis of modernity: a return to the values of the past that had become eroded on an economic, political, social, spiritual level, and given way to the capitalist, liberalist, modernist spirit. They also offered a new *imago patris*: the Führer, Duce, Caudillo as a redeeming saviour figure, a man with healing power, a symbol for a new integration and unity. The masses of disoriented and economically threatened individuals could fall victim to messianic leaders, who promised to establish a 'new order' ('new', but still based on the traditional values for which people had a nostalgic desire), where the State would be again a 'universal provider' of emotional, social and economic stability and guarantor of discipline, order, security, etc. Hitler and Mussolini could make a bid for absolute power and achieve the total subordination of the individual under the State. In both countries, people projected the displaced paternal image once fulfilled by the Church onto the State, which could now claim the totalitarian authority of the old theocracy.[24]

A society that had turned 'psychotic' under the impact of intense crisis elected an equally pathological 'healer' to effect a cure by whatever means: 'Fascism must operate in this century as the skilful surgeon against all illnesses that threaten civilisation, family, religion, fatherland.'[25] Fascism can be interpreted as a pathological response to a severe ailment of the body politic. It was a politicisation of a neurotic reaction to an accumulated reservoir of inner and outer conflicts. It made individual pathology and political 'madness' merge. The fascist group or Party or State organised, under the guidance of a 'healer'/leader, 'therapeutic' practices – in the form of rituals – to alleviate the psychic tensions. Submersion in mass emotions (ecstatic possession) complemented the charisma (fascination) of the leader. The trance state allowed regression to the unconscious state of debilitating fragmentation. Exposure to the collective energy of the crowd provided an experience of wholeness and cohesion. Here, in the mass, the weak felt strong and they submitted to the strongest, the leader, who in return, found his confirmation through this contact with the masses. The cathartic experience bound the individual to the crowd (the fascist mass movement) and to the leader figure, who seemingly enabled the individual to overcome the fears and anxieties provoked by the crisis.

What distinguishes fascism from other animistic responses to crisis situations is that the healer who conducted the seances was not a responsible shaman, but a psychopath who was deluded by his own megalomania or who exploited the illness of the body politic for his own power and glory. The leader took over the parent function in the group, but being psychotic himself, he could not act as container of the split-off, unwanted emotions of the group. These had to be directed against external enemies. The cataclysmic result of this was the Holocaust and the Second World War.

Fascism and ritual theatre

Having established some of the basic patterns of people's ritualistic reaction to situations of crisis, we can now progress to an analysis of how fascism proposed to address the problem, what repertory of symbolic actions they drew on, and how the concrete forms of fascist drama and theatre relate to the general pattern of ritualism sketched out above. That way we can also explain the genuine hope fascism offered to many people (Party members as well as followers and voters in elections), the attraction of the fascist programme of renewal and regeneration, and the fascination exercised by the rituals and the purportive healers.

The crisis of identity and the intense feeling of insecurity that had affected Western society since the late nineteenth century led to an upheaval of psychic forces that could no longer be contained. Society, and the individual who had been ripped apart in the acute and pervasive crisis, had to be offered a way out of the situation. What we are concerned with here are not the political ideologies of Hitler, Mussolini or Franco, but the rituals that were invented to offer a healing experience, where the gaping wound could be stitched together and given a chance to recover.

Although the psychic conditions for the emergence of fascist movements were pervasive throughout Europe, peculiar local conditions and specific historical and cultural factors shaped the crisis in each country. Just as the specific afflictions that had befallen the masses in each country had to be matched with a fitting leader, so the spectacles organised by the fascist régimes had to be tailored to the subconscious needs of their nation. The repertoire of symbols, the mythical plots, the archetypal conflicts, the language of mysticism and magic, the stylised histrionic acts: all these elements formed part of a psychological strategy of persuasion finely attuned to the needs of the audiences. Hence, there existed different types of fascist theatre, but in principle terms, there were more similarities than differences between the performative languages employed by fascist régimes.

Although the propaganda of political programmes and ideological aims played a significant rôle in the formation of fascist mass movements, their leadership was fully aware that the press or radio were not sufficient means to elicit the desired response from the population. They had to appeal to the subconscious desires of the masses and give symbolic representation of the political system that promised to fulfil the dreams and aspirations of the population. Translating fascist ideology into a mythical language and actualising these myths through ritual performances was a far more effective way of producing consent and approval of the presented message than rational propaganda could ever hope to achieve. 'Theatre is one of the most direct means of arriving at the heart of the people,' Mussolini once said;[26] and he knew that once a presented message had been accepted emotionally, any critical response of the intellect would automatically be suppressed.

The symbolic language of drama and theatre was instrumental for turning ideology into a *living* force: 'With the fascist rituals, politics is transformed from abstract concept to human and living reality and becomes a dispenser of joy.'[27] The critic Peter J. Mellen summarised the spectacles in Nazi Germany:

> In these ritual dramas the Nazis employed dramatic narrative, symbolic gesture and elaborate staging techniques in order to arouse in the audience a willing acceptance of the irrational beliefs of the myth. Rituals were used to disseminate and win acceptance for the myth because the ritual's dramatic form allows the use of the logic of associated response, a felt logic which finds truth in

emotional response. Being highly charged, dramatically structured, narrative based events, the rituals elicited from the audience member, not only belief, but a desire to put those beliefs into action.[28]

The rituals and their underlying mythology were *created*, designed, and organised with specific psychological functions in mind. Whilst fascist mythology provided the ideas for the New Order, politics established the 'dogma' and rituals became the 'liturgy'. The fascist leaders were fully aware that well-staged rituals had the force to produce 'consensus and blind and global adherence; they set in motion the forces of feeling and will'[29] and 'constitute the motive force behind political action'.[30] They recognised the value of these rituals as a medium of political manipulation: 'Cultic rituals (…) lift the nation out of everyday anxieties into a holy state of festivity, transform the nation into a festive community, give expression to eternally true and binding values. They are therefore a process of highest political significance.'[31]

Indeed, ritual performance of fascist myths and ideology made the individual conform to 'something larger than oneself', in this case the plans and ideas of the fascist régime. Many reports on fascist mass meetings testify that the rituals did produce awe of, and willingness to submit to, the greater power of the fascist system and its leader: 'A symbolic figuration like the broad and solid base of a pyramid with a single, dominant persona at its apex: Mussolini'.[32] 'The demonstration rises to an immense religious rite of faith. It shows one people exalting itself in one Man and finding itself again in Him'[33] so that in the end there was only 'one people in perfect fusion with its leader.'[34]

A typical example of a person who found his spiritual salvation through theatre and who became one of the key architects of a fascist performance aesthetics was Hanns Johst. Like many intellectuals of his generation, he could not find a model for a new order in the bureaucratic State and political parties of the Weimar Republic, nor in the dogmatic system of the Christian Church. The impact of an existential 'despair and maddening affliction caused by exterior economic circumstances'[35] made them yearn for redemption through a 'secular religion', which would enable the 'rebirth of a spiritual community'.[36] A concrete realisation of such a community was to be anticipated in a new form of ritual theatre that would act as 'cultic place for giving shape to a people's yearning'.[37] The effect of such performances was thus described:

> We, without counsel and direction, visit the places that by their nature promise some mystical elation. As a restless and tormented community we form a chorus that is tortured by the adversities of fate and yearns for redemption. Full of child-like expectation and helplessness, we stay glued to the mouth of a speaker, who offers more than empty prattle and rhetorical phrases. (...) Theatre is the last refuge for an unprejudiced, elementary, living community. (...) This primitive psychic state has regained a fundamental significance today (...) We desire again to experience theatre performances that offer more than scenic actions and tableaux. We want to be put into contact with a *Weltanschauung*, with the metaphysical substance of the world. We want to ascend and follow the soaring flight of a soul that liberates us and instils a new, incomparable sensation of well-being in us. (...) We are all embroiled in a frantic whirlpool of an unfathomable fate. That's why we need this [theatre] experience as a confirmation of an alleviating and redeeming force, which in vain we have hoped for in our endless and exhausting fight for survival in our everyday existence. But in the theatre, in the community of like-minded, sympathetic brethren-in-faith, we can experience, as represented and predestined truth, this dream of a sudden dissolution of the afflictions, which shortly before seemed to be crushing our lives.[38]

Johst's reference to a 'primitive psychic state' and 'child-like helplessness', which foster experiences of ecstatic well-being in a soaring flight of fancy guided by a redeeming leader figure, describes the basic function of fascist theatre: redemption from the 'frantic whirlpool of an unfathomable fate', from an 'exhausting fight for survival' and the 'afflictions that seem to be crushing our lives'. It is a 'dream' represented as 'truth'. The new order has a semblance of life on a higher plane. It offers reprieve from the worries of everyday existence. But, because it is experienced in the community of 'brethren-in-faith', it generates ecstasy, trance and possession states and leads to a 'rebirth' of the individual's spiritual identity.

Johst's 'confession' is an exemplary description of what the creators of fascist theatre sought to achieve. To us it may appear like wishful thinking, escapism etc., but for them it was a formula to effect transcendence and the creation of an ideal New Order that has magical quality and could therefore influence reality. It confirms what Freud sketched out in *Totem and Taboo*:

> There is an intellectual function in us which demands unity, connection and intelligibility from any material, whether of perception or thought, that comes within its grasp; and if, as a result of special

circumstances, it is unable to establish a true connection, it does not hesitate to fabricate a false one. Systems constructed in this way are known to us not only from dreams, but also from phobias, from obsessive thinking and from delusions.[39]

To which one might add: from fascist ritualism and cultic theatre.

Fascism as a civic religion[40]

One of the first organisations to avail itself of these specific 'propagandistic' possibilities of theatre was the Catholic Church. In 1622 it instituted the *Propaganda Fide* and thereby bequeathed to the fascist leadership a concept of art operating 'like a religion, which also overcomes the divisions in people's principles and sympathies, and institutes – please forgive the comparison – a kind of parallel to the Pope's Propaganda Fide.'[41]

Many uninvolved contemporary observers were struck by the fact that the public rituals of fascist régimes were 'more than a gorgeous show; [they] also had something of the mysticism and religious fervour of an Easter or Christmas mass in a great Catholic cathedral.'[42] 'Is this a dream or reality', asked one of the visitors to the *Reichsparteitag* 1936 after the spectacle on the Zeppelinwiese and concluded: 'It is like a majestic church service (*Andacht*) where we have congregated to find new strength. Yes, it is the ceremonial hour of our movement, a service held to protect us in a sea of light against the darkness out there.'[43]

Speer said that Hitler canonised the formations, processions and celebrations so that 'they were almost like rites of the founding of a Church.'[44] Once he had worked out the right forms, he wanted to fix them as 'unalterable rites' that gave him the status of a 'founder of a religion'.[45]

The parallels between fascism and Christian religion were particularly apparent in Catholic countries. Here, a widely known repertoire of religious symbols were taken out of their originally Christian context and grafted onto political concepts. As we shall see, even in Germany – despite the purported recourse to Germanic cults – formal devices and structures stemmed predominantly from the Christian tradition.

Mussolini stated in 1923 that 'Fascism is a religious phenomenon of vast historical proportions'[46] and that fascism was 'a civic and political belief, but also a religion, a militia, a spiritual discipline, which has had – like Christianity – its confessors, its testifying witnesses, its saints'.[47] The Fascist Party was often described as 'a new Church' *(La nuova chiesa* is the title, for example, of a play by Caselli[48]) or as a 'religious and military order'. This is explained in the following manner: 'It is religious because it has its own faith and conscience. It is militant because to obey its orders defends the faith and risks sacrificing one's life for it. This is the mystic character of fascism. It is a militia of believers in a disfigured and cowardly world.'[49] If the fascist State resembled the Church, the Party as its militant spearhead was modelled on the Templars or the Società Jesu. Mussolini was elevated to the position of 'High Priest of the Fatherland',[50] if not a 'god'.[51] The Party was treated like a religious seminary where the apostles and militants of the fascist faith were educated and trained to become the leaders of a secularised *republica dei*. The principal rites of passage of the Party, the official meetings and public rallies were modelled on the religious ceremonies and liturgy of the Catholic Church. There were even temples erected in honour of the Fascist Revolution and its martyrs. Reviewing the Mostra della Rivoluzione Fascista, the journal *Gioventù fascista* (10 July 1932) declared: 'Fascism is a way of life, therefore it is a religion. A good fascist is a religious man. We believe in a fascist mysticism *(mistica fascista)*, because it is a mysticism with its own martyrs and devotees, and humbly unites a people around an idea.' Newspapers described the Mostra as an 'altar of the fascist faith' that could accommodate tens of thousands of 'pilgrims'. It was proposed to become a permanent 'reliquary of our fight so that, as in a church, the heart of the faithful and the fascist will each time overflow more liberally with enthusiasm and be recharged with hope'.[52] The exhibition did not present a historical picture of Mussolini's seizure of power, but a mythological interpretation of the Duce, his apostles and precursors. Garibaldi, d'Annunzio etc., were depicted as the prophets of the Messiah, to whom the *sanctum sanctorum* was dedicated. As in a religious reliquary, there were displayed for public veneration the *cimelia* of the Duce's life and actions. From there, the itinerary led to the hall with the Altar of Sacrifice, dedicated to the hundreds of *camicie nere* who had given their lives as Martyrs of Fascism.[53]

In Piazza Venezia, an Altar of the Fatherland was erected, which became the focus of many 'sacred pilgrimages' undertaken by Mussolini and the fascist leadership[54] to commemorate the resurrection of the New Italy in the First World War, an event that was viewed as the 'symbol of the redeeming martyrdom for the religion of Italy, equal to the symbol of the cross in the religion of Christ.'[55] In fact, all *Case del Fascio* (local centres of the Fascist Party) were furnished with bell towers and considered 'churches of our faith' and 'altars of the religion of the Fatherland'.[56] Members of the Fascist youth organisations were exhorted: 'After the Credo in God, recite every morning the Credo in Mussolini.'[57] Gentile reports what the *Credo Fascista* consisted of:

Q: What is the Credo of Fascism?

A: It is the Credo given to us by the Apostles of Italy and of Fascism.

Q: How many articles does it consist of?

A: Twelve, in the following order: I believe in Eternal Rome, mother of my Fatherland, and in Italy, her first son – Who was begotten from her virginal womb by the grace of god – Who suffered under the barbarian invaders, was crucified, died and was buried – Who descended into the grave and rose again from the dead in the XIX century – Then ascended to heaven in the years 1918 and 1922 – And sits on the right hand of Mother Rome – From whence it shall come in glory to judge the quick and dead – I believe in the genius of Mussolini – And in our Holy Father Fascism – And in the communion with the martyrs – And in the conversion of the Italians – And in the resurrection of the Empire – Amen.[58]

Amongst the common people, religious sentiments that had been fostered by the Catholic Church were projected onto Mussolini. He became the object of magical veneration. He was treated as an idol; his portraits were worn as talismans; his voice on the radio was believed to have occult powers.[59] An unprinted report of a visit of Mussolini to Trieste described people 'with eyes sparkling with emotion and that indescribably joyous anguish' that made their bodies tremble as they kissed the hand of the man who 'seemed like a god'.[60] Another document describes how a woman anticipates the Duce's visit with 'trepidation and anxiety which makes the heart beat with unrestrainable force. It is the Father we are expecting, the Messiah who comes to visit his flock of goats to give them new faith (...) Duce! This magic word makes the heart beat as if an electric flash went through it.'

Documents of this kind indicate that the fascist rituals could indeed be like magical rites that led to trance and possession states. At the core of the Fascist revolution was 'a holy madness', which 'in its sublime and irrational greatness is felt and accepted by the heart and the spirit'[61] However, such ecstasy and fervour did not square too well with the requirements of an ordered State. Therefore, with the establishment of Fascism as a régime, it had to be canalised into clear structures that also offered guidance to the masses. Institutionalising the initial revolutionary impetus and religious sentiments led to the rigid structures of a Fascist 'Church', complete with a credo, a doctrine, a hierarchy of priests and acolytes.

However, what distinguished Fascism from Catholicism was that the former attempted to establish 'the most glorious reign of God *on earth*'.[62] Fascism was not a belief system that sought redemption in the World of Beyond, but a political cult where the magic was supposed to have effect on the here and now. Whilst Catholicism preached a metaphysical religion, Fascism promised to establish Paradise on earth. (Hence the emphasis on Mussolini as a *divinità terrestre*, of the Party members as *archangeli mondani*, and of Fascist Italy as *il regno di Dio in terra*, etc.)

The chiliastic doctrine that Christ will reign on the earth for one-thousand years was equally employed by the Nazis to transfigure Hitler's régime into the *Tausendjährige Reich* that will finally bring 'the thousand years of the Vale of Tears to an end and turn the world into heaven'.[63] However, contrary to Medieval millenarian belief, which projected the erection of a *republica dei* into the celestial future, the Nazi Reich was posited as historically immanent. Hitler was portrayed as the redeemer who opened the door to an eternal reign of *terrestrial* happiness. The official view was that the fight between good and evil had principally been won in 1933 and that the transformation of the old world into a new one had already begun. But, because the process had not yet reached its conclusion, the ideal State still needed to be evoked and represented in the form of cultic theatre and liturgical drama.

Fascist cultic theatre

Fascism established an alternative religious practice through a) plays of a cultic, mystical, magical quality, and b) through festivals and rituals that regulated the life of the individual and the community. These could take the form of either seasonal festivals, life cycle rituals, or ceremonies related to the fascist movement. In all these cases, the performances were festive events, a communion of believers, where the play/ritual served as the liturgy, the leaders acted as the high priests, and the spectators formed the congregation.

The journal *Neue Gemeinschaft* offered a poignant characterisation of this cultic theatre: 'The aim of our festivities is the creation and consolidation of the *Volksgemeinschaft*. One of our most important tasks is to integrate the celebrants into the celebratory action and to turn them into the immediate protagonists of the festivity. The confessional force of our festivities can be significantly enhanced by making the *Volksgemeinschaft* confess themselves, at significant climaxes, to the represented ideals and principles.'[64]

The most common form of cultic drama were the choric plays written for political gatherings and open-air festival arenas.[65] These plays were meant to offer a 'mystic transcendence of the myths of our new times which will be sublimation and choric elevation of the conquests and truths of our age. It is not reality in the naturalistic, documentary, holographic sense of the nearly-true *tranche de vie*, and does not fulfil a chronistic function which is nowadays reserved to cinema and radio, but seeks a creation of the Hero who personifies the Myth and purifies our life and society in a tragic catharsis'.[66]

A comparable rôle was played by historical dramas. They aimed at a similar 'lyrical transfiguration of the days we live in'[67] and had, in fact, little to do with history, but with a mythical elevation of historical figures and events. The distinction between myth and history was broken up, or rather, both were regarded as two different aspects of the same process. Myth was seen as the further end of history, which reaches at its opposite pole into the here and now. History is rooted in myth, and myth sums up accumulated history. Through myth we are given access to the eternal aspects of Being. Fascist mythology drew on archetypal experiences, but was also composed, structured and 'manipulated'. Fascist mythopoeia offered 'a partly moulded, partly unconscious representation of the world',[68] i.e., a world as seen and experienced by the mythmaker. It became a vehicle to present Fascism in the context of a wider historical and metaphysical reality.

Fascist mythopoeia employed and utilised the cyclical time concept of religion[69] and irrational philosophy (such as Nietzsche's doctrine of Eternal Return). A good example of this was Hitler's concept of the Aryan race or Mussolini's recuperation of the myth of *romanità*. Roman mythology, as well as selected inci-

dents of the history of the Roman Empire, were employed to visu-
alise the rebirth of a nation. The mythical past was resurrected in
order to restore an Italian identity. With Caesar and Augustus
reborn in Mussolini, the *civitas romana* was reborn as *civitas fascista*.
As the *Mostra Augustea della Romanità* of 1937, organised in parallel with the *Mostra della Rivoluzione Fascista*, tried to underline:
under the guidance of Mussolini, Rome can fulfil its historic mission in the modern world. The ancient and the modern world are
once again linked and brought together under the banner of Fascism. Hence, the *Prima Mostra Romana 1923* was commemorated
with a coin that was inscribed: 'Incipit vita nova'.[70] It followed
that a new calendar be introduced to complement and, ultimately,
to replace the Christian datation system (starting with 1923 as
Anno I).[71] However, it must be stressed that this myth of 'Rome
reborn in Fascist Italy' was not determined by nostalgic veneration of the past. Mussolini was conscious of 'utilizing the Roman
patrimony'[72] and presenting a new and original concept of Roman
modernity, a 'Roma del ventesimo secolo'.[73]

This 'back to the future' concept applies equally to both drama
and ritual. Myth stands to ritual as playscript does to theatre performance. Acting out fascist myths means giving concrete shape,
visualisation and dramatisation to an otherwise abstract concept
of the world. As to the forms of these rituals and dramas, the fascists again tried to transform the old traditions rather than slavishly copy them. Giménez Caballero's concept of *renacimiento del
teatro*, for example, is entirely based on *servirse* and *utilizar* the
'liturgical, hieratic, mystical and therefore mysterious' master-
works of the past that can inspire, as 'symbolic models', a new and
authentic theatre of the future.[74] Similarly, the German *Thingspiele*
were no authentic copies of the cultic rituals of the Germanic peoples, but only rather vaguely inspired by them.

Beside the dramatic theatre of the fascist régimes there were
other, more participatory forms of cults and rituals, which were
aimed at incorporating the wider community into the fascist State.
These celebrations were 'an enlightening meeting and enthusiastic declaration as well as a regular covenant and festive appeal to
the emotional forces of every Party member and *Volksgenosse*.
Having confirmed his faith in the regularly repeated communal
confession he can let his convictions flow into the collective of the
people, overcome the half-heartedness of his surroundings, and
reinforce the energy of the nation.'[75] The basic idea behind these
festivities was to make public and relate to the fascist State what

had hitherto been a private affair. Secondly, the fascist leadership was fully aware that the majority of the population remained attached to the Church and that even amongst Party members the percentage of atheists was small. Therefore, competition with the Church could only be won if a parallel cult could take over the functions that gave the Church such strong roots in society.

Fascist open-air rallies and pageants made conscious use of Christian rituals and ceremonies and employed a symbolic repertoire and dramaturgical patterns that were derived from such traditions as the Corpus Christi processions, the *Festa di San Giovanni*, *autos sacramentales* or miracle plays. The marching to the sound of drums and trumpets and the singing of songs had a heroic and unifying quality. The purpose of such participatory elements was apparent: 'The marching of singing columns is a truly liturgical gesture of immense power. It is a physical exercise which better than any solicitation or demand implants the will to conquest and the victorious confidence of faith in the flesh and blood of everyone down to the smallest child.'[76]

In Italy, a new festive calendar fixed by the Gran Consiglio was introduced to create an annual cycle of rituals, which aimed at transforming the individual and turning the masses into an instrument of the State (*plasmare le masse* and *fare gli italiani*, Mussolini used to call this.) The rituals were 'destined to generate collective states of mind' and a 'collective life, directed towards giving the nation a sense of united existence.'[77] The same applies to the German calendar of public celebrations. New holidays were introduced to supersede the Christian feast days. Furthermore, *Morgenfeiern* were held in order to replace the traditional church services, or so-called *Lebensfeiern* to supplant the Christian rituals of baptism, confirmation, marriage and burial (now re-named *Namensweihe, Verpflichtungsfeier, Eheweihe, Totenfeier*).

As far as indoor meetings were concerned, Vondung has shown how closely their structures were again modelled on church services. The linguistic and musical symbols were either directly taken from or constructed in parallel to Christian liturgy. The texts used stylistic devices and formulae such as heroic metres and rhyme forms, repetition of words and phrases to give them a sacred and heroic character, and direct borrowings from church genres such as the responsorium, intercession, confession and invocation were employed to increase the 'mysterious' aura of the rituals. The music was chosen to 'flood the hall with a powerful sound and to permeate it with an enchanting atmosphere and mystical resonance.'[78] The architecture of the meeting places imitated Christian churches or ancient temples, and the décor emulated the interior design and requisites of chapels and church houses.

During these rituals, the gospel of fascist ideology was preached and the followers of the cult entered into a mystical communion with their leader. However, just as the Christian priests of the past had found performative means of illustrating the Bible, so was the reading from 'fascist scriptures' (*Mein Kampf, La dottrina fascista, Il primo libro del fascista*) meant to be supplanted or complemented by more effective means of confirming belief in the fascist 'faith'. The doctrine had to be given dramatic representation, or even better, to be turned into participatory rituals. The most astounding of these rituals were those of the fascist 'faithful', e.g., the initiation rites of the Partito Nazionale Fascista (PNF), the consecration of banners and standards in the *Fasci di Combattimento*, the hieratic rituals of the SS and Totenkopforden. They provided a bonding ritual for the members of the organisation and helped 'to establish a National Socialist community feeling through emotional experiences', as one of their originators, Alfred Rosenberg, explained.[79]

The fascist community: The leader and his followers

Hitler gave a vivid description of the aim and function of rituals in a fascist State:

> Mass meetings are a necessity because the individual (…) who feels isolated and easily succumbs to the fear of loneliness, is given here an idea of a greater community. (…) When he as a seeker is swept along by the mighty effect of the ecstasy and enthusiasm of three to four thousand others, when the visible success and agreement of thousands confirm to him the rightness of the new doctrine (…), then he will submit to the magic spell of what we call 'mass suggestiveness'. The will, the longing, as well as the power of thousands of people are accumulated in every individual. The man who entered such a meeting doubting and wavering leaves it with an inner conviction: he has become a member of a community.[80]

Mussolini was equally aware that rituals were the most effective means of creating 'the new connective fabric which firmly keeps the organism of our civil society united.'[81] The formation of a cohesive and harmonious collectivity was an ambitious project of the fascist State which no form of rational propaganda would have been able to achieve. The fascist answer to the outcry of an anguished people for a protective shield against the effects of crisis was basically a ritualistic one. Rituals were employed to integrate a geographically and socially splintered society, to mobilise the masses, to orchestrate collective sentiments, to conquer their consent, and give them a direction. 'The people: sons of the same soil united in their vibrant love for their common Fatherland. The people: all of them sons of Magna Mater (…) The whole Italian people finding themselves united, for the first time maybe, under the colours of the banner of the Fatherland, in a spiritual unity which finally renders them worthy of their victory and their most splendid aims.'[82]

Theatrical performances in playhouses, public rituals, festivities and ceremonies were designed to foster communal experiences. Both open-air and indoor performances were intended to overcome the traditional stage-audience relationships and to unite actors and spectators so that 'the whole theatre would become one single song'.[83] A precise definition of the psychological function of fascist theatre is given by the critic W. Kurz in his aptly entitled essay, *On the Overcoming of the Ego Through Theatre*: 'The last and most important function of the theatre is the redemption of the Ego, the liberation from the captivity of individual narrowness and individual anxieties, and the surrender into the universe, the whole, the community.'[84] Consequently, fascist playwrights evoked a large number of situations that indicated a return to a united people. They propagated a new ethics that was aimed at overcoming egotism, uniting one individual with other individuals, creating a firm bond between them, making them identify with the aims of the fascist State and submit to the orders of the leader. The redemptive virtue of this submission to a superior principle was demonstrated in many plays. To quote one example, M. Federici's *Lunga marcia di ritorno*: 'For years I've travelled the world in search of a superior harmony. I have dreamed of war, of the time when we were in the trenches (…) I always hoped. I was in a crisis (…) And then, you see, from time to time a man comes forward, one of our men, and he makes himself our leader.'[85] The conduct of this leader was modelled, of course, on the historical examples given by the Führer, Duce, Caudillo. Or rather, one should say, on the way these historical figures were mythisised, legendised and sanctified in fascist hagiography.

In this literature, two basic tendencies can be observed: first, the stylising of the leader into a messiah and founder of a new religion, and secondly, presenting him as a redeemer, saviour, healer, shaman. Hitler promised the re-establishment of the mythical Aryan community as the brotherhood of Germans, a harmonious *Volksgemeinschaft* without any class barriers. The SS catechism taught: 'Why do we believe in Germany and the Führer?' – The answer: 'Because we believe in God, we believe in Germany which He created in His world and in the Führer, Adolf Hitler, whom He has sent us'.[86] I mentioned above the Fascist Credo which the Ballilla had to say every morning. In Germany a similar phenomenon could be observed. Mosse reported that in Cologne school children began and ended their lunch with the following prayer: 'Führer, my Führer, bequeathed to me by the Lord, protect and preserve me as long as I live! Thou hast rescued Germany from deepest distress, I thank thee today for my daily bread. Abideth thou long with me, foresaketh me not, Führer, my Führer, my faith and my light.'[87]

Cavallo has shown that the stylisation of Mussolini as 'a leader whom Providence has sent' or 'the new Moses' who leads the Italians to the promised land[88] was expressed in dozens of plays penned by Fascist playwrights in Italy. Mussolini's divine mission was thus expressed in one of them: 'And God looked at our Fatherland, and to liberate us from our foreign enemies, he sent us Mussolini of the Redshirts, and to liberate from our inner enemies, he sent us Mussolini of the Blackshirts.'[89] Another of these plays ends with the protagonist exclaiming: 'I believe in him, son of the people and our brother, illuminated by the divine light (...) He gives fecund inspiration to the creative minds so that they may achieve new harmony. He is our renewer who reforms the people who have fallen in disgrace (...) He guides the march of the people thirsting for light and song and he leads them to the accession of the Holy Trinity: Faith, Peace and Labour (...) Thank thee, oh Lord, for having sent Him to remodel our spirit and body.'[90]

This grafting of the Christian redeemer and saviour image onto a historical person was a postfiguration technique often employed in the Christian drama of the Baroque period and was ultimately derived from medieval theology.[91] Both Hitler and Mussolini were well versed in the literary traditions of Christian religion and were fully capable of adopting their conventions. Hitler helped the transformation of his own person into an archetypal, divine redeemer figure through his mythological biography, *Mein Kampf*. The broad outline of the classical saviour figure emerges from many stylised incidents in the book: the call from above that takes him out of his family, the crossing of the threshold and the passage into the new world, the descend into the abyss, the wrestling with the satanic powers, the ordeal with the opponents who need to be slain, the resurfacing from the lower depths, the calling of apostles, the triumphant progress of his message through the world. And at the nadir of his career the union with the supreme principle (God, the People).[92]

However, the stylisation of own's own biography is not enough to provoke reactions such as the one Dorothy Thompson reported from a woman at the Oberammergau Passion Play: 'When they hoisted Jesus on the cross, she said, "There he is. That is our Führer, our Hitler!" And when they paid out the thirty pieces of silver to Judas, she said: "That is Röhm, who betrayed the Leader."'[93] For Hitler or Mussolini to be venerated as Messiahs, some previous emotional experiences must have taken place in the souls of their followers. Thousands of reports on fascist rituals confirm that Hitler's or Mussolini's hypnotic qualities kept people enthralled and took complete possession of them. In primitive societies, people fall under the magic spell of the shaman. The rituals he conducts sweep them into a state of trance. In this ecstatic and emotionally intoxicated condition they act as if under hypnosis. The compelling effect of the ritual produces these states of altered consciousness; but equally important is the shaman's mana, his divine power and inner force that makes things move and brings about restoration of health.[94] The fascist leaders have also been described as possessing the magnetic spell of a shaman: 'He is simply a sort of great medicine man. He literally is that, in the full sense of the term. We have gone back so far toward the savage state that the medicine man has become king among us (...). It is the shaman's drum which beats round Hitler (...). Cults and bewitchment are the true element of his spell, and furious dances to the point of exhaustion. The primitive world has invaded the west.'[95]

The redemption of mankind from the evils of the world may ultimately be the task of the Messiah, but there is no Saviour without his Apostles. Similarly, the fascist leader gathers around himself a flock of faithfuls to cure society from the effects of the crisis: '[Mussolini] went to the country where the socialist-masonic fight was raging, and he won apostles for the new doctrine, men of the people who tomorrow, in the days of need, stand ready with a faith worthy of the new government.'[96] Together, they spread 'the new Gospel'[97] and engage in a fight against those who are held responsible for the chaos, and the 'false prophets' who seek to seduce the people with their erroneous solution to the disorder of the capitalist/liberalist world. Healing metaphors abound in the plays that describe their fight against this 'odious Muscovite contagion'[98] and 'that infectious Communist disease'.[99] Another metaphor for this fight was that of a war of religion. In truly millenarian fashion the fascists were depicted as the army of God, whilst the socialists appear as 'occult forces sprung from the bosom of Satan'.[100] Other playwrights compared this 'holy battle' with the Christian crusade against the infidels: 'Save Europe from Communist barbarity like many centuries ago Europe was saved from the Moors and Turks'.[101] Or they proclaimed: 'We have to show to the Red Mammeluks that the Italian Catholic youth is strong and pure (…) and ready to give their lives for the greatness of Italy and for the salvation of Christian civilisation.' Others again equated the Bolsheviks with the hordes of Tartars over-running the Occident, or with the Goths and Langobards destroying the ancient Mediterranean culture.[102]

Out of this 'purifying bloodbath' and 'regenerating violence' the fascist New Man and New Order would be born. Hitler reported in *Mein Kampf* how the First World War made him 'see the light of truth' and how he overcame his early infatuation with socialist doctrines. Similarly, Mussolini had to undergo the conversion from Socialist to Fascist during the war before he could engage in his preordained task of setting up the *Fasci di Combattimento*. These rites of passage, from socialist to fascist, were often depicted in plays and were compared with the conversion of Saul into Paul. The dramaturgical pattern was usually sinning – recognition of the truth – perdition – salvation.[103] In this apocalyptic fight between Good and Evil, many of the Apostles lose their lives, and many of them know so in the hour of their conversion. For example, in the play *Risorgi e cammina*, the protagonist is lying in his barracks and suddenly 'hears a silver voice: "Get up", it said, "and join the national army. You will die, but you will be resurrected."'[104] Or in G. Magrone's *Risorgi e cammina* a socialist experiences his 'Damascus' in a similar manner: 'You have heard this voice, the voice of the Fatherland's God. You have seen an image surrounded by a halo of celestial light that led you onto the path of death, which was also the path of resurrection.'[105]

This 'resurrection' of the martyrs of the fascist movement took place in commemorative rituals celebrated by both the German and Italian régimes. During the annually repeated 'Feier des

Sieges und der Auferstehung' the names of the sixteen Nazis who died in the Munich Beer Hall Putsch of 9 November 1923 were summoned and the Hitlerjugend answered to each with 'Here!' to symbolise their resurrection. The ceremony was not a simple memorial service in honour of the 'Blood Witnesses', but a reactualisation and transfiguration of the historical events through ritual, i.e. a procession with the sacred symbols and holy relics of the putsch, the firing of sixteen cannon shots, the consecration of the martyrs' bodies in their 'temple' at the Königsplatz, sermons, prayers, hymns etc. The ritual, performed annually in Munich, elevated the sixteen Nazi thugs to the status of saints and martyrs who had sacrificed their lives in the apocalyptic fight between good and evil. Their death became integrated into a *Nazi Heilsgeschichte* and was interpreted as a sacrifice that contributed to the redemption of mankind: 'We feel enriched / by the blood of those who fell / so that their banner pure and bright / shall give us revelation of the Reich / (...) / With your fame our life begins.'[106]

Summary

In this chapter I have discussed public celebrations and other forms of ritual theatre, invented and devised by fascist régimes in response to psychic needs that had arisen in large sections of the population in reaction to a profound crisis affecting both the individual and society. The psycho-social mechanisms of ritual practices were exploited to serve the political aims of the régimes. Ritualism was believed to be an effective tool to foster a fascist community, to instil a fascist ideology in the people, and to win support for fascist political actions. As to the actual efficacy of these rituals, a few provisos need to be added.

My analysis has tried to elucidate why fascism could gain mass support and generate genuine enthusiasm for its political programme in the population of many European States. However, not *all* citizens fell for the compelling power of fascist ritualism, and not all performances in fascist States qualify to be designated 'fascist ritual theatre'. It is not within the scope of this essay to analyse non-fascist rituals, such as the bourgeois ritual of visiting traditional dramatic performances in their municipal theatre, or the rural population holding *sagre* or village fêtes. The régimes, who were so alert to the usefulness of ritual practices, did not want to be seen as a destabilising agency and rarely interfered with such relief-giving traditions. As a result, a good ninety per cent[107] of theatre performances in fascist States were non-fascist in form and content, although their function was firmly integrated into a wider fascist concept of ritualism.

If rituals can be considered a means to generate enthusiasm, belief, order, security, a feeling of community, etc., there is also plenty of evidence that some people found fascist ritualism exceedingly tedious, or after some initial interest grew tired of it. This is where the *fascinum* of the theatre had to be complemented by the *fasces* of the military apparatus. The magic spell of the rituals may have compelled people to carry out, *voluntarily*, actions that filled them with horror after the war. But to others, the rituals were not conducive to a wholesale surrendering to their internal logic; so the coercing force of the *fasces* was required to make these people toe the fascist line.

As a result, fascism entered into the chronicles of this century as the bloodiest and most destructive reaction to a pervasive crisis. To prevent any repetition of history, the 'fascinating' force of fascist ritualism has to be fully understood, since without this *fascinum* the terror system of the *fasces* would not have worked.

NOTES

1. See James D. Shaughnessy (ed.), *The Roots of Ritual*, Grand Rapids/MICH, 1973; Adolf Portmann, *Animals as Social Beings*, London, 1961, pp. 193-218; Eugene G. d'Aquili et al. (eds), *The Spectrum of Ritual: A Biogenetic Structural Analysis*, New York, 1979.
2. Roger Grainger, *The Language of Rite*, London, 1974, pp. 87, 115.
3. See C.G. Jung, 'The Role of the Unconscious', in *Collected Works*, vol. 10, London, 1964, p. 12.
4. See R.S. Lazarus, *Psychological Stress and the Coping Process*, New York, 1966; J. Cullen et al. (eds), *Breakdown in Human Adaptation to Stress*, Boston, 1984; A. Monat & R.S. Lazarus (eds), *Stress and Coping*, New York, 1985.
5. See Anthony F.C. Wallace, *Human Behaviour in Extreme Situations (Disaster Study Series*, vol. 1), Washington, 1956 and N.J. Demerath & A.F.C. Wallace, *Human Adaption to Disaster. Special Issue of Human Organization*, vol. 16, no. 2, 1957.
6. See A.F.C. Wallace, *Religion: An Anthropological View*, New York, 1966.
7. See C.D. Laughlin Jr. & E.G. d'Aquili, 'Ritual and Stress', in d'Aquili et al., *The Spectrum of Ritual*, pp. 280-317.
8. See Mary Douglas, *Purity and Danger*, Harmondsworth, 1966.
9. S. Freud, *Standard Edition of Collected Works*, vol. 9, London, 1959, p. 127.

10. See Melanie Klein, 'Notes on Some Schizoid Mechanisms', in M. Klein (ed.), *Developments in Psycho-analysis*, 2nd edition, London, 1989, pp. 292-320, and 'On Identification', in M. Klein (ed.), *New Directions in Psycho-analysis*, London, 1955, pp. 309-345 (p. 311).

11. Hanna Segal, *Introduction to the Work of Melanie Klein*, London, 1988, pp. 30-31.

12. For Jung's views on fascism see his *Aufsätze zur Zeitgeschichte*, Zurich, 1946, translated as *Essays on Contemporary Events: Reflections on Nazi Germany*, London, 1947 (reprinted in his *Collected Works*, vol. 10, London, 1964).

13. S.J. Tambiah, 'A Performative Approach to Ritual', *Proceedings of the British Academy*, vol. 65, 1979, p. 119. For a detailed analysis of these performative structures see Ronald L. Grimes, *Beginnings in Ritual Studies*, Lanham/MD, 1982, Victor Turner, *The Anthropology of Performance*, New York, 1986, Richard Schechner, *Performance Theory*, London, 1988, Eugenio Barba (ed.), *A Dictionary of Theatre Anthropology*, London, 1991, E. Barba, *The Paper Canoe: A Guide to Theatre Anthropology*, London, 1995. Some biological and ethological foundations of human performative behaviour have been pointed out by Jean-Marie Pradier, 'Towards a Biological Theory of the Body in Performance', *New Theatre Quarterly*, vol. 21, 1990, pp. 86-98.

14. Terence S. Turner, 'Transformations, Hierarchy and Transcendence', in S.F. Moore & B.G. Myerhoff (eds), *Secular Ritual*, Assen, 1977, p. 60.

15. See Victor Turner, *The Ritual Process*, London, 1969; *Dramas, Fields and Metaphors*, Ithaca, 1974; *From Ritual to Theatre*, New York, 1982.

16. See the essays on the neurobiology of rituals by Lex and d'Aquili/Laughlin in D'Aquili et al., *The Spectrum of Ritual*.

17. See Thomas J. Scheff, *Catharsis in Healing, Ritual and Drama*, Berkeley, 1979.

18. See C.G. Jung, 'On Psychic Energy', in *Collected Works*, vol. 8, London, 1960, pp. 3-66.

19. Nancy Munn, 'Symbolism in a Ritual Context', in John J. Honigmann (ed.), *Handbook of Social and Cultural Anthropology*, Chicago, 1973, p. 605.

20. Grainger, *The Language of Rite*, p. 87.

21. See Tom Burns and Charles D. Laughlin, 'Ritual and Social Power', in d'Aquili et al., *The Spectrum of Ritual*, pp. 249-279; Moore & Myerhoff, *Secular Ritual*; Max Gluckmann (ed.), *Essays on the Ritual of Social Relationships*, Manchester, 1962 and *Politics, Law and Ritual in Tribal Society*, Manchester, 1965; R.D. Fogelson & R.N. Adams, *The Anthropology of Power*, New York, 1977; S.L. Seaton & H.J.M. Claessen (eds), *Political Anthropology*, The Hague, 1979; Georges Balandier, *Political Anthropology*, London, 1970; E.R. Leach, 'Ritual', in D. Sills (ed.), *International Encyclopedia of the Social Sciences*, vol. 13, New York, 1968, pp. 520-26; Bruce Lincoln, *Discourse and the Construction of Society: Comparative Studies of Myth, Ritual, and Classification*, New York, 1989.

22. For the application of the crisis concept to historical sciences see, for example, Perry Anderson, *Passages from Antiquity to Feudalism*, London, 1974 and Leopold Génicot, 'Crisis: From the Middle Ages to Modern Times', in *The Cambridge Economic History of Europe*, vol. 1, Cambridge, 1966. On the pervasive forms of millenarianism see Sylvia L. Thrupp (ed.), *Millenian Dreams in Action*, The Hague, 1962, Kenelm Burridge, *New Heaven, New Earth: A Study of Millenarian Activities*, Oxford, 1969 and Bryan R. Wilson, *Magic and the Millenium*, London, 1973.

23. Emilio Gentile, *Il culto del littorio*, Rome, 1993, p. 23; On the national celebrations in nineteenth-century Germany see also Julius Petersen, *Geschichtsdrama*

und nationaler Mythos, Stuttgart, 1940; Klaus Sauer & German Werth, *Lorbeer und Palme: Patriotismus in deutschen Festspielen*, Munich, 1971; George Mosse, *The Nationalization of the Masses*, New York, 1975; Wolfgang Hartmann, *Der historische Festzug: Seine Entstehung und Entwicklung im 19.und 20. Jahrhundert*, Munich, 1976; Dieter Düding (ed.), *Öffentliche Festkultur: Politische Feste in Deutschland von der Aufklärung bis zum Ersten Weltkrieg*, Reinbek, 1988.

24. Roger Griffin develops some similar thoughts in chapter 7 of his study, *The Nature of Fascism*, London, 1993.

25. F. Papa & R.M. Bonanno in their play *Il mito della razza*, quoted in Pietro Cavallo, *Immaginario e rappresentazione: Il teatro fascista di propaganda*, Rome, 1990, p. 233, n. 24.

26. Letter to Gastone Monaldi of 22 June 1927, quoted in Cavallo, *Immaginario e rappresentazione*, p. 213, n.5.

27. Nazzareno Padellaro, *Fascismo educatore*, Rome, 1938, p. 154.

28. Peter J. Mellen, *The Third Reich Examined as Dramatic Illusion of Ritual Performance*, Ph.D. Thesis, Bowling Green State University, 1988, pp. 335-336.

29. Giovanni Gentile, *Fascismo e cultura*, Milan, 1928, pp. 48-49.

30. Art. Razza, in *Dizionaria di politica*, vol. 4, pp. 23-29.

31. Erich von Hartz, *Wesen und Mächte des heldischen Theaters*, Berlin, 1935, p. 79 f.

32. Massimo Scaligero on the mass celebration of the tenth anniversary of the March on Rome, 'La folla', *Gioventù fascista*, 10 November 1932.

33. Report on one of the rituals in Piazza Venezia printed in *Il popolo d'Italia*, 24 March 1932.

34. Report on the 1926 anniversary of the March on Rome in the PNF *Foglio d'ordini*, no. 11, 15 October 1926.

35. H. Johst, *Ich glaube*, Munich, 1928, p. 73.

36. *Ibidem*, p. 36. Johst's artistic and political development has been analysed by Helmut F. Pfanner, *Hanns Johst: Vom Expressionismus zum Nationalsozialismus*, The Hague, 1970.

37. See the chapter 'Kultstätte für die Gestaltung einer völkischen Sehnsucht' in Johst, *Ich glaube*, p. 73.

38. H. Johst, *Ich glaube*, p. 73.

39. S. Freud, *Standard Edition of Collected Works*, vol. 13, London, 1955, p. 95.

40. Much has been written on Fascism as a 'civic' or 'secular' religion. See in particular Erich Voegelin, *Die politischen Religionen*, Vienna, 1938; Oskar Söhngen, *Säkularisierter Kultus: Eric sicut deus*, Gütersloh, 1950; Hans-Jochen Gamm, *Der braune Kult: Das Dritte Reich und seine Ersatzreligion*, Hamburg, 1962; E.B. Koenker, *Secular Salvations*, Philadelphia, 1964; Klaus Vondung, *Magie und Manipulation: Ideologischer Kult und politische Religion des Nationalsozialismus*, Göttingen, 1971; Christel Lane, *The Rites of Rulers*, Cambridge, 1981, pp. 267 ff.; Jean-Pierre Sironneau, *Sécularisation et réligions politiques*, The Hague, 1982; Claude Rivière, *Les liturgies politiques*, Paris, 1988; Emilio Gentile, *Il culto del littorio*, Rome, 1993.

41. Basilio Cascella, Unprinted report presented to Mussolini on 14 February 1930, quoted in Gentile, *Culto del littorio*, pp. 203-204; see also Ernesto Giménez Caballero's religious definition of propaganda in his study *Arte y estado*, Madrid, 1935, p. 84.

42. William Shirer, *Berlin Diary*, New York, 1941, p. 18.

43. *Niederelbisches Tageblatt*, 12 September 1937, quoted in Gamm, *Der braune Kult*, pp. 55-56.

44. A. Speer, *Spandau: The Secret Diaries*, London, 1976, p. 262.
45. *Ibidem*.
46. Speech in Cremona, 17 June 1923, in Mussolini, *Opera Omnia*, ed. Susmel, vol. 19, p. 274.
47. 'Un rito fascista', *Il popolo d'Italia*, 13 December 1923.
48. See Cavallo, *Immaginario e rappresentazione*, p. 258, n. 65.
49. 'Santa Milizia', *I fasci italiani all' esterno*, 2 May 1925.
50. 'Sacerdote della Patria', *L'idea nazionale*, 23 August 1923.
51. 'Il fascismo è una religione, religione che ha trovato il suo Dio.' This sanctification of the Duce appears in an official document on the Mostra della Rivoluzione, quoted by Gentile, *Culto del littorio*, p. 271.
52. Report of 1933, quoted by Gentile, *Culto del littorio*, pp. 234-35.
53. See the official, illustrated guide to the exhibition, edited by Dino Alfieri and Luigi Freddi (*Mostra della rivoluzione fascista: Guida storica*, Rome, 1933).
54. See 'Il sacro pellegrinaggio', *Il popolo d'Italia*, 24 May 1923.
55. 'La commovente adunata di Redipuglia', *Il popolo d'Italia*, 25 May 1923.
56. *Il popolo d'Italia*, 9 & 30 October 1923; on the rituals carried out in the *case* see Piero Zama, *Fascismo e religione*, Milan, 1923.
57. From a command sheet of the Federazione Fascista di Ascoli Piceno, 22 August 1936, quoted by Gentile, *Culto del littorio*, p. 127.
58. Quoted in Gentile, *Culto del littorio*, p. 143, n. 89.
59. See Cavallo, *Immaginario e rappresentazione*, p. 249, n. 57.
60. Quoted in Gentile, *Culto del littorio*, p. 287.
61. Pietro Misciattelli, 'La mistica del fascismo', *Critica fascista*, 15 July 1923.
62. Paolo Orano, *Il fascismo*, vol. 2, Rome, 1939, p. 144.
63. 'Das Reich zum Himmelreich machen' was Hanns Johst's clever wording in *Die Dichtung im Kampf des Reiches: Weimarer Reden 1940*, Hamburg, 1941, p. 14.
64. See the journal *Die neue Gemeinschaft*, 1942, p. 330.
65. On the *chorische Dichtungen* in Germany see Vondung, *Magie und Manipulation*. On the Thingspiele see Stommer, Gadberry, Zortman, Eichberg in the bibliography at the end of this volume. An excellent interpretation of the metaphysical dimensions in these choric plays is offered by Uwe-Karsten Ketelsen, *Heroisches Theater: Untersuchungen zur Dramentheorie des Dritten Reichs*, Bonn, 1968. It is worth mentioning that they tie in neatly with Sultana Wahnón's observations in this volume on the aesthetic of heroic tragedy as it was propagated by the Falange.
66. A. Vigevani, 'Problemi del nostro teatro: Attesa del mito', *Gerarchia*, no. 8, August 1937, pp. 571-72.
67. A. Vesce, 'Stato e teatro', *Il dramma*, no. 310, 15 July 1939, p. 20.
68. Art. 'Mito', in *Dizionario politica del PNF*, vol. 3, Rome, 1940, p. 186. See also G. Neri, 'La tradizione mitica che ritorna', *Il popolo di Lombardia*, 23 February 1924.
69. See Mircea Eliade, *Patterns of Comparative Religion*, London, 1958.
70. See *Il giornale d'Italia*, 4 April 1923.
71. For a discussion of the whole complex see Dino Cofrancesco, 'Appunti per un'analisi del mito romano nell'ideologia fascista', *Storia contemporanea*, vol. 11, 1980, pp. 383-411; Peter Bondanella, *The Eternal City: Roman Images in the Modern World*, Chapel Hill/NC, 1987; Romke Visser, 'Fascist Doctrine and the Cult of the Romanità', *Journal of Contemporary History*, vol. 27, no. 1, January 1992, pp. 5-22.
72. 'Un patrimonio ch'io cerco d'utilizzare' was his wording; see Emil Ludwig,

Colloqui con Mussolini, Milan, 1932, p. 193. The English edition translates this as: 'The virtues of classical Rome, the doings of the Romans of old, are always in my mind. They are a heritage which I try to turn to good account'. *Talks with Mussolini*, London, 1932, pp. 193-194.

73. Speech on the Capitol on 21 April 1924, in *Opera Omnia*, XX, 235. Similarly, Bottai spoke of 'il ritorno a Roma, provocato dalla Rivoluzione delle Camicie Nere è (...) un rinnovarsi dell'idea di Roma nella coscienza dell'italiano moderno; non una restaurazione, ma una rinnovazione, una rivoluzione dell'idea di Roma (...) rifacendola nostra, conferendole nuova originalità nel mondo moderno.' G. Bottai, 'Roma e fascismo', *Roma*, October 1937.

74. See the chapter 'El teatro vuelve al misterio' in Giménez Caballero, *Arte y estado*, pp. 161-176.

75. *Die neue Gemeinschaft*, 1942, pp. 595 ff.

76. Wilhelm Stählin, *Vom Sinn des Leibes*, Stuttgart, 1934, p. 161.

77. U. Bernasconi, 'Vita di masse', *Gioventù fascista*, 1 May 1934.See also K.C., 'Concezione Mussoliniana del teatro', *Bibliografia fascista*, November 1933, pp. 829-830.

78. *Die Neue Gemeinschaft*, 1942, p. 510.

79. *Weltanschauliche Feierstunden der NSDAP*, Munich, 1944, p. 7.

80. A. Hitler, *Mein Kampf*, Munich, 1936, pp. 535-36.

81. Mussolini, 'La celebrazione', *Il popolo d'Italia*, 23 April 1925.

82. Luigi Freddi, 'Le sagre della rinascita', *Il popolo d'Italia*, 26 September 1922.

83. E. de Martino in the didascalia of his play, *Donde vieni mio soldato*, quoted in Cavallo, *Immaginario e rappresentazione*, p. 230, n. 146.

84. *Bausteine zum deutschen Nationaltheater*, vol. 1, 1933, p. 83.

85. Quoted in Cavallo, *Immaginario e rappresentazione*, p. 236, n. 60.

86. Heinz Höhne, *The Order of the Death's Head*, London, 1969, p. 148.

87. Quoted in G. Mosse, *Nazi Culture*, New York, 1981, p. 241.

88. Gabriele Giuseppe, *L'ultima freccia*, Alberto Lucini, *28 Ottobre*, quoted in Cavallo, *Immaginario e rappresentazione*, pp. 143, 75.

89. Bartolomeo di Filippo, *Dalle camicie rosse alle camicie nere*, quoted in Cavallo, *Immaginario e rappresentazione*, p. 75.

90. G. Bertinetti and L. Bernatto, *La veggente*, quoted in Cavallo, *Immaginario e rappresentazione*, pp. 246-247.

91. See Erich Auerbach, 'Figura', *Archivium Romanicum*, vol. 22, 1938, pp. 436-489; E. Auerbach, *Typologische Motive in der mittelalterlichen Literatur*, Krefeld, 1953; Günter Schöne, *Säkularisation als sprachbildende Kraft*, Göttingen, 1968, pp. 87-91, 274-287.

92. See the detailed analysis of the composition principles in *Mein Kampf* by Mellen, *The Third Reich Examined as Dramatic Illusion*, pp. 128-192 and Erik Eriksen's examination of its fairy tale quality in 'The Legend of Hitler's Childhood', in his *Childhood and Society*, New York, 1950. See also Werner Maser, *Hitler's Mein Kampf: An Analysis*, London, 1970 and Cornelius Schnauber, *Wie Hitler sprach und schrieb: Zur Psychologie und Prosodik der faschistischen Rhetorik*, Frankfurt/M, 1972.

93. Quoted in John Toland, *Adolf Hitler*, New York 1976, p. 359.

94. See Mircea Eliade's classic study, *Shamanism: Archaic Techniques of Ecstasy*, London, 1964.

95. Hermann Rauschning, *Voice of Destruction*, New York, 1940, p. 259.

96. Alberto Lucini, *28 Ottobre*, quoted in Cavallo, *Immaginario e rappresentazione*, p. 86.

97. Sebastiano N. Fabbianini, *Giovinezza in marcia*, quoted in Cavallo, *Immaginario e rappresentazione*, p. 85.

98. Battista Ardau Cannas, *Falange straniera*, quoted in Cavallo, *Immaginario e rappresentazione*, p. 136.

99. F. Papa and R.M. Bonanno, *Il trionfo della razza*, quoted in Cavallo, *Immaginario e rappresentazione*, pp. 54, 233.

100. Libero Pilotto, *Guida alla sbarra*, quoted in Cavallo, *Immaginario e rappresentazione*, p. 149.

101. Quoted in Cavallo, *Immaginario e rappresentazione*, pp. 124, 137.

102. See Cavallo, *Immaginario e rappresentazione*, pp. 133-34.

103. See the many redemption plays analysed by Cavallo, *Immaginario e rappresentazione*; e.g., *Redenzione* by Farinacci, *Redenzione* by Birga & Masi, *Redenzione* by Pini, *Redenzione* by Collina, *Redenzione* by Vallauri & Bertazzoni, *Terra di redenzione* by Finzi, *Alba di rinascita* by Zuccaro & Amadei, *Risveglio* by Razzolini, *Pasqua di risurrezione* by dal Maschio.

104. Quoted in Cavallo, *Immaginario e rappresentazione*, p. 123.

105. Quoted in Cavallo, *Immaginario e rappresentazione*, p. 123; see also the dedication of *Arriba* by Magistri, quoted in *ibidem*, p. 256, n. 37.

106. Herbert Böhme, 'Kantate zum 9.November', in H. Böhme, *Gesänge unter der Fahne: Vier Kantaten*, Munich, 1935, pp. 38, 44.

107. This assessment is primarily based on my analysis of the the annual statistics published in the *Bausteine zum Deutschen Nationaltheater* and Dino Alfieri's report, *La vita dello spettacolo in Italia nel decennio 1924-1933 (II-XI dell'era fascista)*, Rome, 1935.

4

The Theatre of Politics in Fascist Italy

Emilio Gentile
Translated by Kate Rickitt

Political theatre and the theatricality of politics

In classical Greece, the term *theatron* could mean either a place for dramatic performances or one for civic gatherings and public orations. Similarly, in modern mass society there is a theatrical dimension to politics, understood in the dual etymological meaning of the term. Since the time of the French Revolution, mass political movements have exercised considerable influence on politics and have experimented with a new form of political theatre. Ideologies were given representation in performance, which became an instrument of propaganda and a weapon in the political struggle. Political theatre has not always been successful though, owing to its artistic quality or the extent to which it was able to attract a mass audience. There is, however, another aspect of the connection between theatre and politics which is intrinsic to politics as such. I am not talking here about a type of theatre that serves politics, but rather the form of politics that enters directly onto the stage. Politics assumes a performative character when it unfolds by means of mass spectacles, such as political meetings, processions, parades, festivals, ceremonies and rituals. These events dramatise the myths and ideologies of political movements and régimes, and involve the public both as spectator and actor. This *theatricality of politics* has acquired, particularly in contemporary society, an important and enduring collective dimension and has become an integral part of mass politics.[1]

Of all the political movements of this century Fascism has been, from its very inception, the one to give the greatest boost to the theatricality of politics. Fascism attempted to create a truly political theatre. In 1933 Mussolini, himself the author of plays about historical characters and events,[2] launched the idea of the creation of a 'mass theatre'. However, the actual result did not live up to the Duce's expectations.[3] The real 'political theatre' of Fascism cannot be found in the experiments with propagandistic theatre, but rather in the creation of a Fascist liturgy for the masses, in the theatre of political rites at meetings, celebrations and festivals.

The importance of theatricality in the mass politics of Fascism did not escape contemporary observers. The French historian, Paul Hazard, visited Italy at the beginning of the 1920s and was struck by the overt ritualism of the *Fasci di Combattimenti*.[4] In the mid-1920s, the American scholar Schneider attached great importance to what he defined as 'the new fascist art of secular celebrations'.[5] And yet, in spite of these perceptions, the question of a specifically Fascist theatricality of politics has been neglected by historians. Up until now, the tendency has been to view mass spectacles either as the more ridiculous and grotesque face of Fascism, or as a mystifying instrument used to deceive and manipulate the masses. This attitude has not completely disappeared in recent studies, in which the theme of Fascist mass spectacles is analysed using Walter Benjamin's concept of the 'aestheticisation of politics'.[6] When the *aesthetic* element is foregrounded to the detriment of the *political* element, the theatricality of Fascism becomes viewed as being only a surrogate of the dearth of political culture and ideological coherence. This, however, does not suffice.

Certainly, the theatrical aspects of Fascism can often appear grotesque and as purely instrumental in the mystification of the collective. Mussolini was not in the habit of hiding the fact that mass spectacles had a manipulatory function. Nevertheless, an analysis conducted along these lines is, in my view, too limiting and misleading, above all because it undervalues the consistent link between the *theatricality* of Fascism and its culture as a totalitarian movement and modern political religion.

The 'aestheticisation of politics' is certainly an important aspect in the relationship between theatricality and Fascism. The crucial point though, is to arrive at a clearer understanding of the nature of this relationship. In so doing, one inevitably discovers another typical aspect of Fascism, the *sacralisation of politics*. This, in my opinion, is an essential ingredient of the political theatricality of

Fascism, whether in the form of performances of political theatre or mass spectacles. Both shall be dealt with in this chapter.

The liturgy of a modern political religion

Fascism was a political religion with a coherent system of beliefs, myths, rites and symbols, with a 'sacred history' and a vision of mystical community. Its most conspicuous symbolic and dramatic representation was the Lictorian cult. Here, 'sacred' and 'secular' stood side-by-side and more often than not intermingled to disseminate and reinforce faith in the Fascist religion.[7] Fascism's greatest ambition was to achieve the rebirth of the Italian population, to create the 'New Man' and a 'New Civilisation', which would confirm Fascism's historic mission:

> The Fascist era will really have commenced the day on which Fascism has moulded the whole population by uniting it in the Fascist faith (...). Men of the Fascist Revolution have to perform the work of Titans: all artistic works and cultural trends of the past must be closely examined by the Fascist eye. With political religion and by means of the political religion, which we practise every day, we must recreate the world as we feel and experience it. The reality of the past must be subdued to fit the reality of our times: to be loftier, brighter and more profound, because it is a part of us and nearer to us, because it is our true self.[8]

The theatricalisation of politics, in the form of 'sacred' rites and 'secular' spectacles, was considered necessary to fulfil this aim, to shape the spirit of the masses and to obtain their consent. This, however, was not to be attained through free and critical approbation, but rather through mystical participation in the cult of a lay religion. In this sense, one can view the Fascists as degenerate disciples of Rousseau. Although rejecting the ideology of the French Revolution, they nevertheless followed its example in their attempt to construct a new lay religion.[9]

In his drawing up of a Fascist political liturgy, Mussolini followed a logic that was consistent with his own concept of the masses. There was an awareness of the collective function of symbols, rites and festivals. The author of a treatise on the Fascist concept of the State maintained that the masses 'need spiritualism, religiosity, catechism, rite.'[10] Mussolini saw politics as the art of moulding the masses; he therefore made use of rites and col-

lective ceremonies to implant Fascist ideology in the heart of the
population:

> For me, he masses are nothing but a herd of sheep as long as they
> are unorganised. I am nowise antagonistic to them. All that I deny
> is that they are capable of ruling themselves. But if you lead them
> you must guide them by two reins, enthusiasm and interest. He
> who uses one only of the reins is in great danger. The mystical and
> the political factors condition one another reciprocally. Either
> without the other is arid, withered, and is stripped of its leaves by
> the wind.[11]

According to Mussolini, the Fascist Revolution: .

> creates new forms, new myths, and new rites; and the would-be
> revolutionist, while using old traditions, must refashion them. He
> must create new festivals, new gestures, new forms, which will
> themselves in turn become traditional. (...) The Roman greeting,
> songs and formulas, anniversary commemorations, and the like –
> all are essential to fan the flames of the enthusiasm that keep a
> movement in being.[12]

This concept led Fascism to assert the supremacy of mythical
thought in mass politics. *Il popolo d'Italia* maintained that the true
force of a political movement came from the suggestive potency of
its myths, which would propel people to live and die for it.[13] The
Fascist leadership was fully aware of the connection between
myth, symbol and rite as a necessary precondition to instil and
keep alive a collective faith. The Fascists had probably learnt the
lesson of Le Bon, an author much admired by Mussolini: 'A religious or political belief is based on faith, but without rites and
symbols, faith would not last.'[14] They knew that the masses could
be more enthused by 'a beautiful symbol than a mediocre reality
of fact'.[15] The dramatisation of myth by means of collective ceremonies was therefore essential to the politics of Fascism, which
primarily aimed at moulding the Italian masses and transforming
them into a *community of believers*:

> In its celebration of solemn rites in accordance with austere, simple
> and strong forms, which themselves have so much fascination sim-
> ply through their single exterior appearance, Fascism itself, even
> before Art, has given aesthetic expression to the new myth by
> which it shall speak more profoundly to hearts and minds. (...) But
> today, when classical mythology is perhaps more than ever a sign
> of cultural dilettantism and artificial symbolism, a whole new
> mythology adorns the immense Pantheon of our faith.[16]

The rites of communion of the Fascist action squads

From its very inception, Fascism developed its own political style and placed particular emphasis on the theatrical aspects of its public events. The Fascists boasted that they had restored the so-called 'art of mass ceremonies'. On the eve of the March on Rome, *Il popolo d'Italia* proclaimed:

> Public demonstrations before Fascism were extremely anti-aesthetic. Fascism has returned to Italian cities that *art of human movement and group gathering* which is referred to in the Statutes of Fiume. Our processions, winding their way through the streets, passing under the arches, standing in formation in the town squares around the belfry and towers, are worthy of our cities, and their beauty increases that of the stones and marble.

Fascism spread amongst the people 'the unifying love of *civic festivals*, which as such is a love of the city, tradition and therefore of the country' and reawakened 'the love of improvised singing and choral concerts. Fascist celebrations are *great choral celebrations*.'[17] In 1923, Margherita Sarfatti, an authoritative interpreter of Fascist aesthetics, wrote that the true art of Fascism was 'the beauty of its outward displays – I would go as far as to say that its rituals are new and ancient, simple and solemn, stately and war-like'.[18]

The Fascist liturgy possessed a highly militarist character. It was used to glorify the privileged status of the Fascist Party as an 'army of the nation' and to assert the pretensions of Fascism as a charismatic movement, invested with the mission to regenerate the nation and erect a new State. All the ceremonies and public displays carried out by the Fascist action squads – the forays of challenge and conquest, the processions, demonstrations, funerals, consecration of the colours, the occupation of cities – were staged with the declared aim of conveying 'the tangible and real sensation of the power of our movement and the indestructible fate of its future'.[19] Public ceremonies of the Fascist action squads were organised according to precise choreographic plans. Stylised gestures and movements were designed to externalise the squads' war-like spirit in 'a military formation that marches behind its leaders, behind its pennants, in step, singing hymns of war and songs from the trenches'. It was 'an exercise in discipline and pride', which contrasted with the 'badly designed white or red demonstrations based on insults, offensive posters, drunken choirs and shouting down the opposition'.[20]

The Fascist *war of symbols* against the 'enemies of the nation' entailed a variety of formal devices and performative elements. There were the devastating forays of the action squads, the impressive processions, the inauguration rites of the pennants of the Fascist action squads, the display of the tricolour on civic buildings, as well as the reconsecration of squares and streets in honour of the country's new religion. A triumphant theatricality of terror transformed the brutality of Fascist violence into a crusade for the redemption of the country. The political struggle was symbolically represented as an epochal clash between Good and Evil, between the black Fascist knight and the red Communist dragon. On the victorious completion of an action squad's expedition against the representatives of a socialist city administration, the Fascists would carry out a ritual display of the national flag or bless the action squad pennant in the main square. Such ceremonies functioned as purification rites to redeem the place and the crowd from the contamination of Bolshevism and to baptise them in the name of Fascism.

The Fascists compared themselves to the first Christians, who spread the word amongst the pagans, ready to brave martyrdom for the triumph of the new faith. The close connection with Christian martyrology became most apparent in the celebration of funeral rites, which, from the era of the action squads onwards, played a central rôle in the Fascist cult. Careful preparation ensured the prevalence of an extremely emotive atmosphere, which would leave a deep impression on the public spectators assembled in the 'sacred space' specially decorated for the occasion. A procession, made up of thousands of people, was grouped according to the locality of the action squads, each with their own pennant. There were representatives from the different local branches, from the national leadership and the patriotic associations, as well as from the Fascist youth movements. The processions were characterised by hierarchical unity and military discipline, and the whole ceremony was designed to conjure up a picture of ordered and lasting strength, effected by the country's new religion. However, these rites also had other functions. After the procession to the roll of drums and the playing of funeral marches by the Fascist bands, the rite would culminate, amongst the colours of hundreds of pennants and black flags, with a funeral oration by a Fascist leader and the slow march of the action squads past the coffin, silently honouring the dead with the Roman salute. Then the leader would call out the names of the fallen heroes, to which the action squads would respond 'present!'. At his command, they would kneel in silence for a few minutes; then, when commanded to rise, they would shout out 'alala', invoking the names of the martyrs.

The presentation of the Fascists as defenders and martyrs of a national religion continued a tradition well-known from Christianity, the Risorgimento and the Great War. The set for the funerals was designed to symbolically represent this ideal continuity, integrating Catholic liturgy into the lay Fascist ritual. In these death rites, Fascism always emphasised the link with life: the spirit of the fallen heroes is resurrected in the Fascist cult, united with the action squad community, and consecrated to the immortal memory of the Fascist faith, so that finally they can ascend to the Fascist Pantheon, where they keep alive the spirit of the Fascist Revolution.

Furthermore, the funerals were celebrated as *rites de passage* for the Fascist youth, thereby turning them from *death rites* into *rites of life*. The ritual was no 'lugubrious ceremony of death', but rather 'a serene rite of faith and youth, which unfolds before the glory of the sun, in a floral celebration, in the benediction of a whole multitude in a melancholy gathering, in the offering of the tears of women and young girls.'[21]

The symbolism of the rite and the theatricality of the performance are effectively evoked in typical description of a Fascist funeral by *Il popolo d'Italia*:

> The Milanese Fascists march past, bare-headed and silent, in martial step, to the rhythm of fanfares. They file past, austere and proud, without a sound, sorrow written on their faces, but with an expression of strength, dignity and pride. The gallant battalions march between two dense bands of people, who know not how to hold back their admiration. Old and new faces pass by. There are all the old Fascists, those of 1919 [i.e., the founding members who gathered in Piazza San Sepolcro], the first formidable, faithful nucleus of men, who have experienced all the battles of Fascism, always staying on the road, through sad and happy times, through the bitterness of disappointment and the joy of triumph. And now with them are all the new and newest recruits, forming a phalanx of men equal in pride, courage, enthusiasm and faith to the Fascists of the old guard, those who are unforgettable.
>
> The pageant is impressive: the battalions march in an admirably ordered and disciplined fashion. Who, or what has been able to so perfectly discipline the Italian population? How has it been possible to attain such a miracle, to organise responsible and strong-

willed, audacious and generous individuals, to go so far as to make an army out of them, an army that has nothing in common with the old processions, with the formless pageants of time past, gatherings of uncontrolled and incontrollable crowds? What, if not the profound, undefinable, infinite Fascist faith? It is the new awareness, the new virile and war-like pride of our race, which returns to the Roman spirit by virtue of Fascism. The Fascist battalions march past: here they are, joined together in martial rhythm, disciplined into perfect ranks; here passes the most handsome, the noblest, the most generous section of our population. Young men with open and intelligent faces, with sparkling and vivacious eyes, side-by-side with old men, who do not show any sign of weariness despite the fast pace of the march. Workers with modest clothing and employees, who have all relinquished their Sunday afternoon siesta to respond to the call. Fighters from all the army units and front lines proudly display their war decorations and march with the same pride as when they left the trenches. They glorify the dead, extol victories, strengthen the spirit by paying homage to the martyrs and heroes, thereby preparing themselves for new victories, new glories. (...) Strong and wonderful peasants from our countryside, with severe male faces, bronzed faces of youths, decorated with ribbons for bravery in war, handsome in their bearing, which emphasises their appearance as strong, healthy workers. It is in these strong men, who carry the signs of hard daily labour, that one discovers the immense, everlasting and historic value of the Fascist miracle: to have returned to the People, who are the backbone of the nation and who seemed to be carried away by the Bolshevik madness, but are now the healthy conscience of the Nation and an inextinguishable pride to our Race.[22]

The exultation and choreographic display of youth and symbolic unanimity beyond divisions of sex, age or class prefigured the image of the New State and the *rebirth* of the country from the ruins of the Liberal State.

The Lictorian Cult

One of the principal aspects of the 'Fascist religion' was the institutionalisation of a State liturgy, not only for the Party activists, but for all Italians who, willingly or unwillingly, were involved in the periodic celebration of the régime's rites. Fascism entrusted to the State the task of realising the ideal of a mystic community, involving Italians of every class and every age, in an experiment of collective regeneration. The theatricality of politics was funda-

mental to the mass pedagogy of the totalitarian State and dominated every aspect of public life for millions of men and women.
Italians became actor-spectators in an succession of 'sacred' and
'secular' mass spectacles, distinct but complementary displays of
the mass liturgy of the Fascist religion. Herman Finer, one of the
more perceptive observers of Mussolini's Italy in the 1930s, rightly
stated that the mass spectacles were the main industry of the Fascist régime.[23] Artists and architects were summoned to construct
temporary or durable monumental sets, which played host to the
'sacred' and 'secular' displays of Fascism's political theatricality.

Immediately after the Fascists came to power, they renewed
and enriched the calendar of State lay-festivals and established
procedures for celebration.[24] The régime set a calendar which
articulated the annual rhythm of mass ceremonies and the ritual
celebration of great events in the 'sacred history' of the Italian
race. For example, there was the celebration of the Birth of Rome
(21 April), the anniversaries of the 'rebirth of the nation', such as
the entry into the Great War (24 May) and the Victory (4 November), and the dates fundamental to the Fascist Revolution, such as
the birth of the Fascist combat groups (23 March), the March on
Rome (28 October) and the Foundation of the Empire (9 May).

The First World War played a central rôle in the symbolic legitimisation of the Fascist government. In the first years of the
régime, the anniversary of the entry into the war was celebrated
with great solemnity in the capital and in other cities. There were
many participants: the armed forces, servicemen's associations,
associations for the disabled, for invalids, for mothers of the fallen,
for widows and orphans of war and, naturally, the Fascist Party
faithfuls. Everywhere, public and private buildings were
bedecked with flags, bands played patriotic songs, monuments
were unveiled, orations held to praise the revived country and the
new national government. Over the years, the rites for the 'rebirth
of the country' were incorporated into the Lictorian cult and
became less spectacular. In many cases, the ceremonies consisted
of a single rite, the cult of those who died for the country and of
those who died for the Fascist Revolution. Speaking in Enna on
the anniversary of Italian victory in the First World War, at the
unveiling of a war memorial on 4 November 1932, the Under-Sec-
retary of State, Ruggero Romano, described 'how in the Decennial
of the Régime, the victims of the War and the Revolution have
returned to us, wrapped in the same flag.'[25] The typical ritual for-
malisation of the anniversaries of the Great War, after the incor-

poration of the Lictorian cult, is summed up in a report by the Prefect of Padua, dated 4 November 1932:

> This provincial capital – after morning mass celebrated in the cathedral – present: civil and military authorities, organisations of the Party, armed troops, representatives of servicemen and war-disabled – gathered together from all provincial towns – formed an impressive procession which went to the monument to the fallen to lay wreaths and assist in the blessing given by the Archbishop – procession re-established – then reached the Park of Remembrance – singing of patriotic songs – great applause when victory bulletin, naval bulletin and reasons for granting war cross to this city were read.
>
> This afternoon – this municipal theatre – present: city authority, organisations, associations, and large general public – local Fascist combat squat has effectively re-evoked victory, eliciting enthusiastic and impassioned response – manifestations of consensus and devotion to the House of Savoy, Duce and régime.[26]

The start of the Fascist year was 28 October, the date of the March on Rome. In 1923, Mussolini wanted to celebrate the first year of his accession to power in a solemn and spectacular manner and decreed five days of ceremonies and mass rituals. On the morning of 31 October, an impressive procession, accompanied by four-hundred aeroplanes circling the skies, formed in the streets of Rome. It was headed by the Duce, followed by Party leaders and cadres from all over Italy, representatives of associations for servicemen, the war-disabled, mothers and widows of the fallen, the militia, as well as representatives from political parties, trade unions and Fascist youth organisations. For about five hours, the pageant wound its way through the centre of the city, retreading the route taken by the columns of action squads during the March on Rome. Accompanied by singers and bands and passing through streets bedecked with flags, it made its way from the Piazza del Popolo past the Altar of the Country in Piazza Venezia, where homage was paid to the Unknown Soldier, to the Quirinal to salute the king.[27]

The ceremonies commemorating the March on Rome were a spectacular review of force, which aimed to glorify the Fascists and reinforce in them a sense of unity around Mussolini. Moreover, the exhibition of the Party's strength, and the public display of consensus granted to the Fascist government by the institutions and the population served both to make an impression on the sympathisers of Fascism and to intimidate its opponents. In 1926, the anniversary of 28 October was included into the State calendar of celebrations as a public holiday.[28]

Another annual mass ceremony of particular solemnity was the celebration of conscription: a young man's rite of passage from the Fascist youth organisation to the ranks of the Party. The rite took place at the same time in all provincial centres before the eyes of the Fascist faithful and the general public. Naturally, the most solemn ceremony was staged in Rome, in the presence of the Duce, either in the Colosseum or in the Mussolini Forum. The representatives of the various ranks of the youth organisations would stand to attention. After the swearing in, the rite of passage would be symbolically carried out. The young Fascist conscript would be given a gun by a soldier of the Fascist militia; the Fascist youth would then present the Vanguard Rifleman with a scarf in the colours of Rome. Following this, the Balilla would receive white braids from the Vanguard, and the Wolf-Cub would be given a blue scarf from the Balilla. The whole intricate ceremony would be concluded with an embrace and a salute to the Duce. Comparable to confirmation in the Catholic Church, conscription was a rite of passage to admit the youth into the Fascist community. This perennial renewal of the symbolic bond of spiritual continuity between the old and young soldiers of the Fascist religion found its most conspicuous representation when the new generation of faithful pledged to consecrate body and soul to the Duce and to Fascism.

The Fascist rites and festivals took place at different times of the year in order to distinguish the 'sacred' from the 'secular'. The *rite*, which was generally celebrated in the morning, included religious and martial ceremonies. Rites with a religious function included those in memory of the victims of the Great War and the Fascist Revolution. The Party ordered that the ceremonies had to be 'marked by the greatest severity and sobriety' debarring banquets and sumptuous receptions. The oratorial part was restricted to the reading of messages from the Duce, or a Party Secretary conveying solemn descriptions of the glorious achievements of the Fascist Revolution.[29] Party members were obliged to wear black shirts, and in the evenings were expected to meet in their headquarters for 'confidential displays of fraternity' in memory of the fallen heroes. The place of honour was reserved for the mothers of the fallen, the decorated, the war-disabled, volunteers and servicemen. After a religious function in memory of the victims of war and revolution, which would be held near a war memorial, a

Park of Remembrance, or a sanctuary dedicated to the martyrs in every branch of the Fascist Party, a procession would form and move to a recently completed public building, where they affixed the symbols of the Fascist Revolution to the façade. The whole ritual was interpreted as renewal of the 'oath of faith' to the Duce and to Fascism.[30]

The military rites consisted predominantly of parades which sought to convey to both participants and spectators 'the idea of a formidable company of forces which rests at the basis of the Fascist Revolution and protects the life and development of anyone who is part of it.'[31] The ceremonies combined both traditional and modern symbols: public buildings were illuminated and decorated with flags, the bells of civic towers were rung at full peal for half an hour, Fascist insignia and inscriptions praising the Duce were hung in town squares and streets, torch-lit processions paraded through the city, and in the evening fires would be lit on mountain summits.

Festivals, on the other hand, took place in the afternoon and included holiday outings, dances, singing and musical entertainment. The performance of choral songs was present in both the 'sacred' and 'secular' ceremonies. They were meant to give symbolic representation of the spiritual unity of the masses and to enhance the solemn atmosphere of this feast of Fascist communion.

Naturally, the most important national celebrations of the Lictorian cult took place in the capital, in the presence of the Duce. They were performed against the backdrop of Ancient monuments such as the Colosseum or the Capitol. Piazza Venezia, situated between the ancient Roman and Italian temples and housing the Altar of the Country and Mussolini's residence, was the 'sacred centre' of the Fascist religion. It was the '*piazza* of the Revolution, synthesis of all *piazze* in Italy', destination of pilgrimages and assemblies of vast crowds, which would 'call upon the Duce to appear [on the balcony of Palazzo Venezia] and speak, which always rises tension to an absolute high.'[32] In addition to the ritual processions and the Duce's speeches, ceremonies in the capital sometimes included other extraordinary acts. In 1928, for example, on two Roman altars taken from the Diocletian Baths and erected in front of the Altar of the Country, the Duce carried out the symbolic burning of National Debt notes to the value of 140 million Lira as a 'symbol of the offering of the Italian people to the National Treasury.'[33]

The best-known and most grandiose events in the history of Fascist mass rituals were the vast assemblies which occurred during the Ethiopian campaign. It was perhaps at this point that the régime and the Italian population came closest to a state of mystic communion, which Mussolini would have liked to be a permanent state of the nation's collective life. On 18 December 1935, during the Ethiopian campaign, a 'Day of Faith' was held throughout Italy: Italian women donated their gold wedding rings to the country in exchange for rings of steel. In Rome, the rite was symbolically carried out on the Altar of the Country, where the Queen and a group of war widows threw their wedding rings into the burning fire. As a communiqué of the French embassy in Rome reported, the whole celebration had 'the solemn character of a new mystical marriage between the Régime and the Nation (...) The impression was clearly theatrical, as is almost everything in this country, but it was not less moving, nor less thrilling for it.'[34]

The 'New God' and His Faithful

Enthusiastic mass gatherings celebrated the Ethiopian victory and the declaration of the Italian Empire. The successful campaign led to a veritable deification of the Duce, who now rose to the rank of 'the new god of Italy'.[35] The glorification of Mussolini became the principal activity of the 'factory of consensus',[36] which worked ever more intensely to spread the myth and cult of the Duce amongst the masses, making his image omnipresent. Mussolini's continued encounters with the masses, during public festivals or on his visits throughout Italy, played a major rôle in sustaining and feeding the cult of the Duce amongst the population. Mussolini was the first Italian Head of State to have visited the length and breadth of Italy only a few months after coming to power. Moreover, he visited regions and cities where his predecessors had never ventured. He established direct contact with the ordinary 'man in the street' and gave to him the feeling of being closer to power and of being heard and answered by the Duce. Many of the speeches were also broadcast on radio. They often announced important decisions for which the Duce asked the people's consent, thereby giving them the impression that they were involved in his decision-making process.

Mussolini's encounters with the crowd were an important ingredient in the theatre of Fascist politics. Careful preparation ensured that the right conditions prevailed to create a highly charged emotional atmosphere and to elicit collective enthusiasm which, at the climax of the ceremony, would lead to a 'mystic' union of leader and crowd. It was a symbolic dramatisation of the unification of the nation through its leader. The stratagem of the 'factory of the consensus' was to produce a collective trance state in the congregation. Mussolini's visits were *cult events* with two protagonists: *Dux et popolo*, or the leader and the led.[37]

The meetings between deity and crowd were carefully designed to synthesise all aspects of the Fascist liturgy and mythology: the sacred and the secular, the modern and the traditional, the national and the regional. In general, the visits were preceded by an *invocation*, made by the Prefect or provincial Party Secretary, to the population to receive the visit of the Duce. Then followed the *announcement* by the Duce himself. However, it was not unusual that a few years would elapse between the invocation, announcement and visit, so that the feeling of expectation was all the more intense. For example, on 9 July 1934 Mussolini answered the invocation of the Genovese Fascists, who, after eight years, wanted to see their leader again, and announced that he would visit Genoa in 1936. However, he only arrived in May 1937, but this helped to make his reception even more fervent.[38] As with a pilgrimage, people rushed from all over the province to be present at the *appearance* of the Duce. On arrival, the Duce stopped at the memorial chapel for Fascist martyrs, close to the Fascist Party headquarters, and paid his respects to the fallen heroes. Then followed his address to the general public. Lined up in a large square were the forces of the Party and the army, together with representatives from patriotic associations and the local government. The Duce arrived to the sound of trumpets, volleys of machine-gun fire, bellringing and Fascist hymns. A high podium, dominated by a gigantic letter 'M', the name 'Dux' and the Roman eagle, towered over the crowd assembled in the piazza. The stage was surrounded by pennants, banners and flags and assumed the symbolic character of an altar, which presented the deity to the crowd of believers:

> The multitude is stupefied for a moment. The eyes of the faithful multitude are fixed on His face. The podium is, now, an altar. The delirium is immediate: there is an outburst of voices and gestures, the loud ringing of fanfares. Flags, pennants, ensigns stretch forward in a wonderful agony of offering (...) There are many minutes

of rejoicing (...) Now everything is given up to the Leader, down to the last breath and drop of blood.[39]

Before beginning his speech, Mussolini gazed, obviously delighted, at the exultant mass shouting 'Duce, Duce, Duce'. His oration was scattered with tags and *sententiae*, and occasionally interrupted by jubilant ovations, which took on the character of an impassioned dialogue between the Duce and the crowd. At its conclusion, as after a very successful theatre performance, the Duce was recalled to the podium many times by the cheering crowd. The visit then continued with the inauguration of public works, the laying of foundation stones for new buildings, visits to factories and agricultural centres, and so forth. During his journey the Duce stood upright in his car and received the tribute of the crowd, who exhorted him to extend his stay or to pay a return visit.

Celebrations of the 'harmonious collective'

Fascist civic religion not only embraced the political rites of the régime, but also the popular festivals. By means of syncretistic assimilation, Fascism incorporated the whole complex of existing displays of collective life into the Lictorian cult and, vice versa, introduced its own system of myth, symbols and rites into traditional festivities. In this way, the Fascist cult was divested of its most overtly political features and as such was made more suited to influence the lives of those individuals still diffident or resistant to the Fascist message. For example, the agrarian 'Feast of the Grape', celebrated on the last Sunday in September, was relaunched by the régime to 'publicise amongst the masses the consumption of the exquisite and wholesome fruit of life' and to help the Italian wine industry.[40]

The Feast of the Grape became an occasion for celebrating the Roman spirit of Fascism and restoring 'the healthy traditions of earth and fertility', which 'defeat time and reunite the new races, who create and restore those ancients of the Mediterranean, whose law it was to construct and produce'.[41] As with other rituals linked to agricultural production and peasant labour, this festival was not only 'a colourful and joyous folklore display, but the healthy and vigorous expression of life in the fields, of the serene joy of agricultural work, of the luxuriant fertility of our vineyards.'[42]

Although Fascism encouraged a certain cult of nature, it did not follow the mystic 'religion of nature'[43] as it was practised in National Socialist Germany. In the Lictorian cult, nature is tamed, redeemed and fertilised by the labours of man. For example, in 1931 a procession of 207 floats took place in Rome, in the presence of Mussolini, to celebrate the Feast of the Grape. The Lictorian concept of the 'work of redemption' found expression in one of the first groups of carts, depicting the malaria-infested marshland of Maccarese. The following carts showed the various stages of progress towards land reclamation, with the last one offering 'the wonderful vision of a grape harvest cheered by the opulence of bunches of grapes and the festiveness of large casks.'[44] The Fascist régime promoted the wine festival as a 'joyous and solemn rite'. The festival added 'high symbolic value' to the commercial importance of viticulture and, as the 'great autumn festival for the whole nation', it played an important part in the liturgy of the 'harmonious collective'.[45] Nature as such was not part of the Fascist religion, but served as a backdrop for the celebration of Fascist rites: 'The new life of the new Italy must be taken out of the enclosure in which it once grew weak and mouldy. It must be brought into the fresh and sunny air. For many people, physical improvement will mean spiritual improvement.'[46]

The mixture of modernism and traditionalism helped to raise the image of Fascism as the modern heir of the Roman spirit. The invocation of the past in the production of public celebrations was a mythical appeal to the 'sacred history' of Fascism, and was used to summon the people in the drive towards the future. Aircraft circling over the town squares during the solemn meetings between the Duce and the crowd introduced an element of modernity into the setting of monuments from Italy's past. Mussolini would often arrive at public gatherings by air, himself at the controls. In Fascist mythology, the machine was a modern instrument of power and well-being. Together with the traditional elements of popular culture, folklore, craftwork and regional costume, it was employed to enhance the image of Fascism as an integrating and harmonising force linking the leader and the masses, man and nature, past and future.

The Fascist glorification of all forms of outdoor collective life encouraged the development of gymnastics and sport, which at mass spectacles were put to the service of the 'propaganda of the faith'. The gymnastic and sporting displays aimed to represent the Fascist community and 'to stir up that authentic service and civic duty', which 'the good Fascist citizen' had to practise in order to 'be a truly integral part of that population, which the DUCE has proclaimed to be *the body of the State* and dynamic coefficient of that State which is, by the same high definition, *spirit of the body*.'[47] The régime made use of its fiscal resources to widen the practice of gymnastics and sport and to finance the construction of gymnasia and stadia. Practising the cult of physical health was integral to the Lictorian cult; it was an essential component of the education of the masses and the creation of the 'new Italian'; it prepared the physique and tempered the character of a virile and virtuous citizen, a believer in, and fighter for, the fatherland.

One of the first 'temples' of this new sports cult was the Littoriale in Bologna. It sprang up in 1927 through the initiative of Leandro Arpinati, the local Fascist leader, who was described by *Il popolo d'Italia* as a 'visionary and practitioner, the most suitable champion of lay religions.'[48] An equestrian statue of the Duce held a prominent position at the entrance to the Bolognese amphitheatre, to immortalise the discourse of 1926 held by the Duce from horseback, to fifty-thousand blackshirts gathered 'in the bare, elliptical interior of the Littoriale, scarcely laid out, like the ancient Roman population in the design of a city of the future'.[49] In the most grandiose architectural sporting complex constructed under Fascism, the Mussolini Forum, the vast entrance square was dominated by a large marble monolith, inscribed with the name of the Duce in order to 'project into the future, the epoch and name of Mussolini'.[50] Renato Ricci, president of the Fascist youth organisation, Opera Nazionale Balilla, had designed even more grandiose projects to glorify the Lictorian cult. For example, he wrote to Mussolini of a large bronze statue to Fascism, which would have made 'the memory of the legendary Colossus of Rhodes turn pale'. The statue, called 'Arengo of the nation',[51] would have taken up an area five times the size of Piazza Venezia and would have been three times higher than the Statue of Liberty; it would have stretched over 120,000 square metres and held 300,000 people. The project was commenced, but had to be abandoned as a result of the demands of the Ethiopian war.[52] The Mussolini Forum became a 'sacred space', a place to celebrate the cult of the Duce. It was a space for gymnastic displays accompanied by choral singing, which together represented the strength, health and faith of the new Italians. Fascism promoted sport in order to 'create passion amongst the masses and not just champions'.[53] It was an essential component of the totalitarian project of collective mobilisation, by means of which Fascism aimed to overcome the mentality of private isolation and to imbue the masses with a sense of 'human communion'.[54]

As a final example of the mass spectacles designed to spread the Fascist faith I would like to mention the exhibitions organised to celebrate the great achievements of Rome, Italy and Fascism. On the occasion of the tenth anniversary of Mussolini's seizure of power (the so-called *Decennial*), a vast array of ritual activities and mass ceremonies were organised to glorify the first ten years of Fascist government and to counteract the effect of the 'great crisis', i.e., the growing signs of discontent that were spreading amongst the Italian population. Numerous exhibitions were organised, from agrarian mechanics to land reclamation, from fruit farming to bread production, from anniversary celebrations for the death of Garibaldi to an exhibition on the Fascist Revolution, all inspired, as *Il popolo d'Italia* explained, by one single criterion, 'the work of national education, which has been taken on by the Fascist State and is being developed by schools, sports clubs, youth organisations, after-work groups, all diverse initiatives'.[55] The inauguration of exhibitions in the Duce's presence almost always took on a cultic character, in which the 'sacred' and the 'secular' were intertwined. The visits turned into 'pilgrimages' undertaken as part of the Lictorian cult.

A particularly illuminating example of these ritual representations of the 'harmonious collective' was the opening and closing ceremonies of the exhibition of the Fascist Revolution, held in 1932 to re-evoke the 'sacred history' of Fascism.[56] The exhibition itself was an extraordinary cult event, with the museum designed as a 'sacred space' and the visitors serving as a liturgical mass. Different groups took turns to perform the changing the guard, and the public assisted in the rites that took place in front of the entrance: marches, singing, music and chanting in praise of the Duce and Fascism. At the opening ceremony, on 28 October 1932, Mussolini and the upper ranks of the Party were welcomed by a Fascist hymn sung by a military division, riflemen, 180 consuls from the National Voluntary Security Forces lined up with their legions' standards, the Quadrumvir and the national directorate of the Fascist Party. At the entrance, where the Fascist oath was silhouetted on an illuminated wall, a young Fascist posed the traditional question, 'Do you place your oath?', to which the division shouted their response. Having walked through the halls accompanied by his retinue, Mussolini reached the memorial chapel to the martyrs, where he silently paid his respects to the fallen Fascists.[57] Throughout the two years of the exhibition, the changing of the guard was carried out many times a day. It was performed not only by regular soldiers, but also by representatives of the fallen, the crippled, the ex-servicemen, the workers, the professionals and the mercantile community. An official columnist commented that this participation of different elements of Italian society turned the performance into 'a profoundly symbolic act showing the close spiritual union between the people and Fascism, between the citizen and his government, between the well-being of the individual and that of the fatherland'.[58]

On 28 October 1934, the exhibition was closed with an even more solemn public ritual. It started in the morning, when the tri-colour and the black flag of Fascism were raised up onto the façade of the entrance hall, where throughout the day they were protected by a guard of honour. In the evening, Mussolini arrived, accompanied by the Secretary of the PNF and members of government. He returned to the memorial chapel, where he stood to attention for a few minutes and gave the Roman salute. He then approached the crowd, preceded by the standard of the Party carried by a group of Men of the First Hour (*sansepolcristi*). Mussolini stood alone at the top of the flight of steps, illuminated by the huge Lictorian emblem on the façade. Achille Starace, the First Secretary of the PNF, launched the 'salute to the Duce', to which the crowd responded with 'to us!'. Immediately afterwards, a Balilla went up to the Duce and, after giving the Roman salute, swore an oath, to which the crowd responded in chorus. Starace then declared the exhibition closed and ordered the guard of honour to file off. The flag was lowered, trumpet blasts and volleys of gunfire made everyone stand to attention, and to conclude the event, there was a *son et lumière* spectacle with choirs of young Roman girls singing patriotic and Fascist hymns amongst the multi-coloured blaze of torches and flares.[59]

Faith and manipulation

All 'sacred' and 'secular' Fascist mass spectacles were instruments to manipulate public opinion, to enforce obedience and to obtain consent by appealing to people's emotions, fantasies and desires. In the period of greatest economic crisis, the mass spectacles compensated for the privations suffered by the lower classes of society.

The mass spectacles concealed the régime's difficulties behind a façade of order and efficiency. They distracted public attention from the problems of foreign policy and gave them reassurance with a joyous picture of the 'harmonious collective'. As spectacles of power they served to reinforce a sense of identity within the Fascist movement and to project to the outside world an image of unity, solidarity and force, which would fascinate the masses and intimidate enemies.

The theatricality of Fascist politics also aimed at propagating faith. The rituals dramatised the myths of a political religion. Liturgical devices glorified the sacredness of the State and surrounded the Duce and the Party with an aura of 'numinousness', evoking devotion and fear. Fascism proclaimed itself to be a new religion, and those who had to compete with its magnetic power on the masses – e.g., the Catholic Church – became very aware of the religious aspect within the political theatricality of Fascism. The Vatican did not underestimate – as many historians have done – the impact the totalitarian experience had on the population, especially through the institutionalisation of the Lictorian cult.[60] In 1940 *Civiltà cattolica* wrote: 'In this way, politics is turning into a lay religion, which demands the complete devotion of the whole human being, and prevents him from using his rational faculties.'[61]

In this chapter we have seen only a few significant examples of the theatrical aspects of the Fascist experiment. I have attempted to illustrate some connection between mass spectacles and Fascist political culture. The area of research remains open for more detailed analysis of the nature and function of the theatre of politics in the lay religion of Fascism. Every conclusion can only be but provisory.

NOTES

1. On the intimate connection between theatre and politics see R.M. Merelman, 'The Dramaturgy of Politics', *Sociological Quarterly*, vol. 10, no. 2, 1969, pp. 216-241; Ferdinand Mount, *The Theatre of Politics*, New York, 1973; James Rosenau, *The Drama of Political Life*, North Scituate/MA, 1980; Georges Balandier, *Le Pouvoir sur scène*, Paris, 2nd edn, 1992; Gautam Dasgupta, 'The Theatricks of Politics', *Performing Arts Journal*, vol. 11, no. 2, 1988, pp. 77-83; Murray Edel-

man, *Constructing the Political Spectacle*, Chicago, 1988; Art Borreca, 'Political Dramaturgy: A Dramaturg's (Re)View', *The Drama Review*, vol. 37, no. 2, 1993, pp. 56-79.

2. See Mario Verdone's essay in this volume.
3. See Pietro Cavallo, *Immaginario e rappresentazione*, Rome, 1990, and his contribution to this volume.
4. See Paul Hazard, *L'Italie vivante*, Paris, 1923.
5. Herbert Wallace Schneider, *Making the Fascist State*, New York, 1928, p. 222.
6. See, for example, R. Golsan (ed.), *Fascism, Aesthetics, and Culture*, Hanover, 1992.
7. See E. Gentile, 'Fascism and Political Religion', *Journal of Contemporary History*, vol. 25, nos. 2-3, 1990, pp. 229-251, and my recent study, *Il culto del littorio*, Rome, 1993.
8. Salvatore Gatto, *1925: Polemiche del pensiero e dell'azione fascista*, Rome, 1934, p. 62.
9. In 1922, Mussolini's paper made explicit reference to the festivals of the French Revolution. See Volt [i. Vincenzo Fani], 'Pareto e il fascismo', *Gerarchia*, October 1922. A French journalist, who visited Rome in 1924, was struck by the apparent similarities between the symbols, ceremonies and rites of the French Revolution and the Fascist Revolution. See R. de Nolva, 'Le mysticisme et l'ésprit révolutionnaire du fascisme', *Mercure de France*, 1 November 1924.
10. Guido Bortolotto, *Lo stato e la dottrina corporativa*, Bologna, 1930, p. 35.
11. Emil Ludwig, *Talks with Mussolini*, London 1932, p. 122 (Italian edition, pp. 121-122).
12. *Ibidem*, pp. 70, 123 (Italian edition, pp. 72, 122. See also *ibidem*, pp. 193-194).
13. See F. di Pretorio, 'Il nostro mito', *Il popolo d'Italia*, 5 July 1922.
14. See Gustave Le Bon, *Aphorismes du temp présent*, Paris, 1919, p. 96.
15. Camillo Pellizzi, *Problemi e realtà del fascismo*, Florence 1924, p. 116. See also Ludwig, *Talks with Mussolini*, p. 191 (Italian edition, p. 190). Many years later, Pellizzi returned to the subject and wrote a highly informative treatise on the function of symbols, myths and rites in political liturgy. See his *Rito e linguaggio*, Rome, 1964, esp. chapter VIII.
16. Roberto G. Mandel, 'Mitologia fascista', *L'assalto*, 25 November 1922.
17. 'Le opinioni degli altri sul fascismo', *Il popolo d'Italia*, 5 May 1922.
18. Margherita Sarfatti, 'Nei dodeci mesi dall'avvento: L'arte', *Il popolo d'Italia*, 22 October 1923.
19. 'Superba dimostrazione a Milano', *Il popolo d'Italia*, 4 October 1921.
20. Ernesto Daquanno, *Vecchia guardia*, Rome, 1934, p. 218.
21. *Il popolo d'Italia*, 8 August 1922.
22. *Il popolo d'Italia*, 4 October 1922.
23. See Herman Finer, *Mussolini's Italy*, London, 1935, p. 404.
24. See the material in the Archivio Centrale dello Stato in Rome, Section PCM, 1924, file 2.4.1.996.
25. See the telegram of the Prefect of Enna, dated 4 November 1932, in the Archivio dello Stato, MI, DGPS, 1932, cat. C4, Sez. 2a, b. 58.
26. See the letter of the Prefect in the same file (Busta 58).
27. See the reports in *Il popolo d'Italia*, 30 October to 1 November 1923.
28. Royal Decree no. 1779 of 21 October 1926, transformed into Law on 6 March 1927, no. 267. See Archivio Centrale dello Stato, PCM, Gabinetto 1926, fasc. 2.4.1. no. 3904.

29. See *Foglio d'ordini*, 15 October IV (1926).
30. *Foglio d'ordini*, 7 November IV (1926).
31. *Foglio d'ordini*, 9 October IV (1926).
32. Ottavio Dinale, *La rivoluzione che vince*, Foligno, 1934, pp. 57, 69.
33. 'Il rogo simbolico', *Il popolo d'Italia*, 28 October 1928.
34. Archives Ministère des Affaires Etrangères, Europe 1918-1940, Italie, vol. 258, communiqué of 19 December 1935.
35. See Gentile, *Il culto del littorio*, pp. 263-297.
36. See Philip V. Cannistraro, *La fabbrica del consenso: Fascismo e mass media*, Rome, 1975.
37. Mario Appelius called this mystic union a 'dramma epico con due protagonisti: Mussolini e la moltitudine'. See his article, 'Il Duce e il popolo', *Politico sociale*, August 1937.
38. See the material preserved in the Archivio Centrale dello Stato, PCM, 1937-1939, fasc. 20.2., no. 946. This visit, as well as others to Trieste and Venice in September 1938, was also well-documented in the contemporary press and the cinematic news reels.
39. *Il popolo d'Italia*, 25 May 1930.
40. See the article 'L'uva', in *Il popolo d'Italia*, 27 September 1931.
41. M.S., 'Spirito rurale', in *Gioventù fascista*, 30 October 1932.
42. 'Il Duce alla festa dell'uva a Roma', *Il popolo d'Italia*, 29 September 1931.
43. See R.A. Pois, *Nationalsocialism and the Religion of Nature*, London 1986
44. 'Il Duce alla festa dell'uva a Roma', *Il popolo d'Italia*, 29 September 1931.
45. See Rustico, 'Vendemmia in città', *Il popolo d'Italia*, 21 September 1932.
46. A. Toni, 'Il littoriale polisportivo', in *Il popolo d'Italia*, 29 August 1926.
47. R. Nicolai, 'Sport', in *PNF Dizionario di politica*, vol. 4, Rome, 1940, p. 343.
48. Toni, 'Il littoriale polisportivo'.
49. *Ibidem*.
50. C.R. Maccaroni, 'La colonna del Duce verso il mare di Roma', *Il Carlino della sera*, Bologna, 16 January 1929, quoted in S. Setta, *Renato Ricci*, Bologna, 1986, p. 159.
51. The Arengo was the 'parliament' of the medieval city republics in Italy.
52. See Setta, *Renato Ricci*, pp. 162-165.
53. PNF, *Atti: 1931-1932*, Rome, 1932, circular of 16 May 1932.
54. P.L., 'La coscienza della collettività e lo sport', *Bibliografia fascista*, no. 2, 1933, pp. 108-110.
55. 'Lettere romane', *Il popolo d'Italia*, 6 July 1932.
56. See Gentile, *Il culto del littorio*, pp. 212-235 and the recent study on the exhibition by O. Ghirardo, L.A. Andreotti and J.T. Schnapp in the *Journal of Architectural Education*, February 1992.
57. See 'La ceremonia inaugurale', *Il popolo d'Italia*, 30 October 1932.
58. Francesco Gargano, *Italiani e stranieri alla Mostra della Rivoluzione Fascista*, Turin, 1935, p. 266.
59. *Ibidem*, pp. 715-723.
60. See Gentile, *Il culto del littorio*, pp. 135-146.
61. A. Messineo SJ, 'Il culto della nazione e la fede mitica', *Civiltà cattolica*, vol. 3, 1940, p. 212.

5

The Organisation, Fascistisation and Management of Theatre in Italy, 1925-1943

Doug Thompson

Theatre in pre-Fascist Italy

Fascism inherited a confused, uneven situation so far as the organisation, the types and rates of development of theatre were concerned; a legacy which still largely reflected the various regional customs and practices of pre-unification Italy. Andrea Camilleri speaks of 'obvious dissatisfaction with the way theatre was organised' during the second half of the nineteenth century,[1] while Emanuela Scarpellini indicates that 'from the closing decades of the nineteenth century, a breakthrough from the early, pre-industrial phase' in the direction of 'a somewhat more complex, "industrial" kind of organisation' took place.[2] This latest phase was represented primarily by the entrepreneurial initiatives of a few theatre companies, initially in Milan and Rome. They formed trusts, which soon controlled almost all the major theatres in the larger cities, and were thus able to impose their own conditions and rates of remuneration on all categories of theatre workers.[3]

By the beginning of the 1920s, this kind of development had given some sort of stability to the theatre as a profession, but it had also created very real tensions as a result of the frequently conflicting claims of artistic excellence and commercial viability. Unfortunately, the late and, geographically speaking, unevenly distributed take-off of industry, coupled with the slow accumulation of capital available for public spending, meant that State-supported education had hardly begun to expand by the time of the outbreak of the First World War. Thus even secondary – to say nothing of higher – education was still comparatively rare over much of the peninsula. The modernisation of theatre organisation was therefore not matched by any noticeable increase in the intellectual and linguistic sophistication of theatre audiences.[4] Their demand was chiefly for variety shows and low-to-middle-brow comedy, preferably in their local dialect. The small theatre-going public was limited mainly to the middle classes since lack of education, together with the depressed level of average wages and the comparatively high cost of theatre tickets, excluded the lower social orders. Thus, theatre managers generally followed a policy of giving their audiences what they wanted.

The theatre, dictated effectively by the conservative tastes of the lower-middle classes, had thus little room for intellectually demanding plays (although foreign, particularly French, plays commanded a better market than the home-made products), while the avant-garde survived precariously only in Rome and Milan. Not surprisingly, playwrights, critics and those concerned with theatre as a social and intellectual force, were frustrated and dismayed by this static state of affairs. Silvio d'Amico, the most prominent critic of his day, argued strongly that theatre 'was no longer in touch with the spiritual reality of the nation'.[5] Aware that the commercial argument was overwhelmingly against them, they sought to strengthen their tenuous position by using the national-cultural argument to persuade the Fascist government to provide guaranteed financial support for 'good theatre' and for the creation of a National Theatre following the French, German and Russian models. It was an argument which should have appealed to Fascism with its insistence on *italianità* and a strong sense of national identity.

Fascism and the idea of a National Theatre

Prior to 1925/1926, Mussolini's government was far too preoccupied with securing its political future in the face of opposition from the old constitutional parties of the Left and Centre, and from intransigent, grass-roots Fascists in the regions, to have much time, energy or will, let alone financial resources, to deal seriously with what was, after all, only a minority concern. Admittedly, early in 1924, Gentile had suggested that the State might well be pleased to contribute, along with local authorities, to support a State theatre.[6] Indeed, in the same year, Mussolini himself had hinted at a future policy for the arts (among which theatre was specifically named) 'to educate taste and sensibility, to keep alive a sense of wonder, to refine the highest, most powerful gifts of the spirit'.[7] However, when approached with specific proposals for the creation of a National Theatre, he rejected them on the advice of his Finance Ministers, on the grounds of prohibitive cost and more pressing needs for the State's limited financial resources. Perhaps not wholly unsympathetic to the needs of the theatre, Mussolini commissioned Paolo Giordani and Luigi Pirandello to explore other means of creating such a national organisation, but in the end nothing was to come of it.

The idea of a National Theatre persisted, however, and was strongly revived in the wake of Silvio d'Amico's cogently argued case in his 'La crisi del teatro' (1931). Readers of *Scenario*[8] would have been much heartened by the article, which appeared in the journal's very first number in February 1932. It enthusiastically outlined the main features of d'Amico's imaginative and far-reaching proposal, only at the very end introducing a salutary note of caution:

> How, we wonder, are we to pass from idea to realisation? Which points of the programme should we insist on as a matter of urgency and which, on the other hand, should we be content to see evolve gradually? For the moment no one can say. In the first instance that will be the job of the Corporation,[9] and only after that the task of those responsible for directing the new theatre. For the moment it would be indiscreet, indeed terribly premature, to make any pronouncement on that score.

As we learn from the article itself, a year had already passed and yet the realisation of the proposal still awaited its 'first step'; this in itself was ominous. d'Amico was later to suggest that the project was sabotaged by the Directing Council of the Corporation itself, which was dominated precisely by those commercial interests which would have been most damaged by it. However, Scarpellini argues that the real, insurmountable stumbling block, once again, was Mussolini himself. In his reply (dated 27 May, 1932) to Bottai's request for funds to construct two theatres, in Rome and Milan, as the permanent homes for the National Theatre, he curtly refused:

> No new theatres (…). It's the usual materialistic-positivistic mistake to think that new *modern* buildings will rescue the theatre. It's the endless confusion between the extrinsic and the intrinsic that Fascists should no longer entertain. It's what authors create that will

save the theatre, bring back the audiences, not the technical wizardry of theatre engineers (...) It is not the right moment, either psychologically or economically speaking, for building *new* theatres, when both old and new theatres are empty – and often rightly so.[10]

This point of view was in any case to be substantially reversed less than a year later, with the Duce's prognostications about the causes of the crisis in the theatre and its salvation through the creation of a 'theatre for the masses'. The second part of the 1932 argument was on much firmer ground. The world economic recession was still not over, and with so many Italians out of work and very many more living on or below the poverty line it would, indeed, have seemed insensitive, to say the least, to launch the National Theatre project (L'Istituto Nazionale del Teatro Drammatico) with two new, purpose-built theatres.

Whilst favouring the use of theatre and the other arts to spread the unifying Fascist gospel throughout Italy, Bottai knew well enough that authentic art comes only from contemplation of the individual's encounter with lived reality. A State-prescribed, formularised art must inevitably be superficial and false, because it is not 'felt' (except as obligation) by its author. It is doubtful whether Mussolini entertained such a view. What he and the majority of policy makers sought, although with no apparent urgency, was an art which would itself be a vehicle of mass fascistisation. Bottai may well have realised that serious theatre, even if, for the moment, not particularly Fascist in sentiment, must nevertheless be protected and nurtured, since the national culture would be much poorer without it. He was dismayed by the Duce's rebuff.

Mussolini's views on theatre and its functions

In contrast to Bottai, Mussolini regarded theatre as essentially a vehicle for strong emotions, as 'one of the most direct means of getting through to the hearts of the people'.[11] This view was to be reiterated and further elaborated in his 1933 speech to the Società Italiana Autori ed Editori, which was to be the source of so much debate and policy-making for the theatre. Mussolini argued on that occasion that the theatre was much more efficacious as an instrument of popular education than was the cinema. Thus, it 'must be directed at the people, and for that reason, theatre productions must provide what the people need.' This sentence alone embodies his popularising vision and programme for the theatre. Its 'wide appeal' was to be essentially emotional in character, for the theatre 'must arouse great collective passions.' If 'collective passions *are* given dramatic expression', he told his audience, '*then* you'll see the theatres filling up.'[12]

It is ironic that the support and protection which proponents of serious theatre had sought from the State (in the face of the commercial philistinism of the powerful, private trusts), should have opened the floodgates to what amounted to a State policy of perhaps even greater debasement of theatre, for political ends. Mindful of this, Lucio d'Ambra scornfully dismissed the popularising Fascist vision as 'il teatro UPIM'.[13] At the Convegno Volta, a conference which took place between 8 and 14 October 1934, Silvio d'Amico argued, as had Pirandello before him, that a new theatre, expressing the new, Fascist times, could not come either from decrees or from theses, but rather from 'a deep faith, from boundless feelings'. The State, he argued, should subsidise the theatre but not seek to impose themes or styles of presentation upon it. If there was indeed a new spirit abroad, then playwrights would inevitably give expression to it anyway. It is difficult to judge whether d'Amico was expressing a modicum of doubt with that 'if'. Others, however, holding positions of political power and influence in these matters, were not willing to take the risk, perhaps because they, despite their habitual rhetoric to the contrary, lacked the necessary 'faith' in Fascism's ability to bring about real 'spiritual' change among the Italian people.

Theatre and *Italianità*

According to Arnaldo Mussolini, a tight political discipline was required in the theatre and the other arts, to regulate what the public saw, to foster the expansion of art and to create awareness of the new Italian spirit abroad.[14] Paternalism and an accompanying xenophobia were hallmarks of Italian Fascism. Both implied exclusion (including, of course, censorship), since both were probably expressions of a deep-seated fear of the inadequacy of what Fascism itself offered the Italian people at the material and spiritual levels. Dino Alfieri, who had succeeded Galeazzo Ciano as Minister for Popular Culture in July 1936, argued that the government's propaganda was 'intended simply and exclusively to facilitate knowledge of the truth, objective expression of the Fascist reality as opposed to the bad faith of its opponents, to clarify what seemed unclear'. In short, its aim was to implant its own 'truths' in the minds of 'the people' – which was merely another manifestation of the extreme paternalism that characterised the régime in the 1930s.

What then did Fascism seek to convey as opposed to withhold? It has long been argued that its ideology (as opposed to its organising principle) contained nothing that was original. After its initial, revolutionary phase, when it organised around an absolute rejection of all existing political creeds and parties in favour of the national principle of *italianità*, the régime settled into an eclectic mixture of elements, which came precisely from those previously anathematised ideologies, in support of that same principle. Whatever it was, it did not constitute a new ideology, but rather a means of organising a nation around an exaggerated awareness of its own identity and importance.

It is in seeking to identify the individual components of *italianità* that one is made aware of the strength of its negative, as opposed to positive, principles. Fascism is defined more by what it rejects than by what it proposes. At its centre was an ideological vacuum which the mystique, the faith, the *credere*, were intended to cover. The only positive principle was national unity, perceived as a source of limitless, unassailable strength. If this ideological simplicity proved effective as a political spur, it certainly did not make for engaging theatre.

The poverty of the ideology to be conveyed by Fascist theatre should not be allowed to mask the much more effective, elaborate, framework constructed to control theatre in all of its aspects. Alfieri admitted as much (although with different emphasis) in his speech to the Camera dei Fasci e delle Corporazioni, reported in the June 1939 issue of *Scenario*. There, he argued that the State had tried to provide an infrastructure which would guarantee a viable theatre in most Italian cities, and to 'facilitate artistic output worthy of our traditions and our times.'[15] His conclusion, despite its understatement, was clear enough: 'However much one might point to the infrastructure, the theatrical results have not always been proportionate to the generosity of the State'.

As was suggested earlier in this chapter, the theatre was primarily the domain of the middle classes. In its exclusiveness, guaranteed by its prices, its customs of dress and behaviour, even the intimacy of its ambience, and especially its repertoire, it symbolised resistance to the all-embracing goals of mass-based fascism. Its preferences were overwhelmingly for those kinds of theatrical experience which reinforced its own sense of identity. For these reasons, Bontempelli proclaimed that it was the principal task of theatre to 'de-bourgeoisify the bourgeoisie, which coincides precisely with the principal task of the ongoing Fascist revolution'[16] and that the State should mount an aggressive campaign against dialect theatre in particular (which it soon did). Gherardo Gherardi went a good deal further in his idealistic version of *'andare verso il popolo'* (going out to the people). In an article commemorating the recently deceased Pirandello, he confessed that:

> ...we authors have to find the words which synthesise and define so that [the masses] can understand. Up to now we have spoken to the narrowest and most selective of audiences, who did not represent reality. Reality is this: an immense stream of peasants and labourers who, from their daily contact with the forces of nature (with which they work, live and struggle all the year round), assume a mysterious, mythical, essential spirituality. We must start with that raw material, transfigure it and exalt it.

His article concludes with his own expression of 'faith' in the outcome – 'we must attempt to create the tragedy, the political mystery, in which the lives and the adventures of the people-as-hero are exalted.'[17] The 'people-as-hero' was to be both the protagonist and the recipient of this new theatre, which would effectively function as 'a mirror held up to nature'. In practice, whatever they proclaimed in public, few playwrights shared Gherardi's views.

The creation of a legal and institutional framework for theatre and the performing arts

It was not until 30 March 1931, when the very first Corporation (which happened to be the Corporazione dello Spettacolo) came into being, that the State seriously set about creating a legal and institutional framework for theatre and the performing arts.[18] Initially, it was intended that the Corporation would be the keystone in the State's policies for, and administration of, these arts. However, with the establishment of the Ministry for Popular Culture, under Ciano, in 1935, it became virtually redundant.[19]

Censorship

Censorship, which had been on the statute books long before Fascism came to power, was made much more efficient and was more widely used under the régime. At the beginning of the 1930s, manuscripts began to be examined by the Minister of the Interior, whereas previously the task had been in the hands of local prefects. The law which brought about this change in policy (No. 599 of 6 January 1931) aimed at much greater consistency in the application of the relevant criteria and at much greater rapidity in reaching decisions than had (notoriously) been the case until then. It also made provision for a standing commission to undertake the task, but this was never to come into existence. Bocchini, the Chief of Police, appointed a civil servant from the Ministry of the Interior, Leopoldo Zurlo, to the post of censor and, in practice, it was he who made the final recommendation about whether or not any play (new or old) was suitable for public performance. Copies of all theatrical works had to be presented to the censor within thirty days of their publication or of their intended performance. The law decreed that all such works submitted had to have printed on their covers (or frontispiece) the name and surname of the author, the title, the names and addresses of the publisher and printer, and the year of publication, while translations must, in addition, indicate the language of the original. Each of these requirements was aimed at making it easier to identify writers and others involved in the production of play scripts, who might show subversive or critical tendencies towards the régime and its policies.

Zurlo's criteria were both political and moral. They not only provide close insight into the cultural policy of the régime, but also demonstrate that rarely anything new, much less revolutionary, was introduced by Fascism. Indeed, the underlying ideology in most censorship decisions was that of the Catholic Church. Thus, it was extremely unlikely that plays would be accepted if they hinged on or dealt with adulterous relationships, illegitimacy, breakdown of the family, abortion, suicide, or if they used sexually explicit or suggestive language. The 'new' drama (which, in truth, never emerged) was thus pushed towards social idealism, as conscious object lessons for the theatre-going public, parting company with the portrayal of any reality with which that public could identify.

When, in the mid-1930s, Fascism embarked on its warring adventures and, towards the end of the decade, drew closer to

Nazi Germany, criteria of a more overtly political nature gained much greater prominence. Respect for the police and the armed forces, the unacceptability of non-European or Jewish characters and 'situations', of anything at all which might upset Italy's political allies – even the treatment of dictators, past or present – were the kinds of criteria used in the evaluation of plays by the censor. By the beginning of the 1940s, the whole dramatic repertoire of certain nations such as Britain, France and the United States were excluded. Once Italy was at war with Greece (from late 1940), this principle of general prohibition was even extended to the theatre of classical Greece!

From the beginning of the 1930s, however, pressure was exerted on companies to include a very high proportion of Italian plays in their seasons. Although seen as patriotic and in the interests of national unity, such a policy did the Italian theatre little good, either artistically or commercially. There were simply not enough plays being written by Italian authors that were worthy of performance, and therefore this policy led to a further decline of theatre audiences at a time when the theatre was already deep in crisis. Companies often found themselves faced with a dilemma in that the government's policy of promoting competitive subventions rather than guaranteed funding (which would, of course, have cost a great deal more) meant they had to tread warily when balancing Italian against foreign plays in their repertoires, and indeed, in many other matters too. When applying for subsidies, companies had to provide very detailed information about the works they would present, the names of all those who would be employed in whatever capacity, of other sources and likely levels of funding, predicted income and expenditure, and so forth. Other important criteria were the presentation of new Italian works, the engagement of young Italian directors and/or actors, and intended venues – if the season or part of it was to be given in towns which were not normally a part of the professional circuit, this would be likely to count in the applicant's favour. Furthermore, and most importantly, the company had to prove that its various personnel were complying with all the legal obligations (including hiring through the government employment agencies) laid down by the *sindacato*.

As if this were not enough, further investigation of a company applying for a subsidy was likely to be carried out through the prefect's office or from police surveillance records, particularly where actors or directors of unproven Fascist sentiment were involved. The subvention system was itself an indirect extension of censorship since it was extremely difficult for companies to survive, let alone mount ambitious programmes, without substantial financial assistance from government sources. They tended, therefore, to comply rigidly with all legal obligations and directives – official, unofficial or merely rumoured. The end result was a rigorous process of self-censorship, which led to a safe but frequently dull repertoire.

The Theatre Inspectorate

The introduction of a Theatre Inspectorate in 1935 was yet another powerfully oppressive factor which Fascism brought to the theatre industry. The appointed inspector, de Pirro, whilst certainly believing in the need for widespread discipline and organisation, was also both knowledgeable about, and sympathetic towards, the artistic aims and potential of the Italian theatre. Although much of what he attempted to achieve in that role was resented by many, his approach was not that of a disinterested bureaucrat but of one who genuinely had the interests and future of the theatre at heart.

Among the duties mapped out for the inspector, were those of overseeing the modernisation of antiquated theatre buildings; strict controls over the formation of new companies; the establishment of a State Academy of Dramatic Arts which would give instruction in all aspects of theatrical production; keeping a careful watch over playwrights and their output; the aforementioned 'Italianisation' of the repertoire; striking a just balance between artistic and commercial interests; and the creation of a National Theatre. Funding for the Inspectorate was to come from several ministries, some of whose responsibilities the new Ministry for Press and Propaganda was taking over, and also from radio licence fees, 6.17 per cent of which were earmarked for the purpose. The funds, however, were exceedingly small when set beside the prescribed objectives.

Other forms of State intervention in the world of the theatre included extensive powers given to prefects, including the right to close down plays and theatres if, in their judgement, public morality was likely to be offended or a public disturbance might occur; competitions and competition prizes; the creation and operation of the theatrical employment agencies; the publication of new laws affecting the theatre in journals such as *Scenario*; as well as control over foreign companies in Italy and tours by Italian companies abroad. The range and depth of control and management were impressive and generally quite effective. It would be misleading to give the impression that these factors, despite their irritants, were not widely appreciated by those working in an industry in which the livelihoods of many had traditionally been precarious. State intervention brought a stability which had hitherto been largely lacking; it regularised wages, sickness benefits and pensions, and whilst it often legitimised injustices, theatre workers nevertheless had a much clearer view of their rights than before.

The Corporazione dello Spettacolo and the trade unions

Much of the work of the Corporazione dello Spettacolo was delegated, from the very outset, to a variety of specialist commissions, so that in the first two-and-a-half years of its existence it met fewer than ten times. There were very real doubts about the ability of the Corporation to deal adequately and efficiently with the many problems of an industry in crisis. For one thing, it was hamstrung by its legal obligations to other bodies (such as the Federation of Industrialists and that of the Theatre Workers, as well as to the National Council of Corporations) whose consent it had to secure before it could issue regulations or grant subsidies it had agreed upon. Almost invariably, it encountered opposition, indecision and inevitable delays, so that its achievement was modest indeed.

Another area of difficulty during the first two years of operation was uncertainty about the precise nature of the relationship between the Corporation and the unions it purported to link, co-ordinate and advise. Theoretically, the much greater degree of centralisation it represented was to guarantee greater efficiency and unity in the theatre. There was much resentment in the ranks of the *sindacati* not only about their subordination to what they saw as merely a new tier of bureaucratic control, but also about their emasculation as effective economic representatives of their particular categories of workers. Indeed, the Corporazione dello Spettacolo had come into being against a background of wage cuts in the order of five to twenty per cent (1930). Increasing rivalry from both cinema and radio – new industries both in a vigorous expansionist phase – fuelled unemployment in the theatre by poaching its audiences and thus reducing takings at the box office. Unfortunately, despite Bottai's idealism, promises and good will, the Corporation itself had autonomy neither as a planning organisation nor as a body exercising economic management of the theatre. Consequently, it merely added further complication and control in an economic sphere which was already complex and precarious.

With all their limitations, the *sindacati* continued to do a useful job so far as regulation of work relations and working conditions in the theatre were concerned. From the employers' point of view, they were a calming hand inside the industry as well as a means of lobbying public bodies for the furtherance of their sectorial aims. As far as theatre employees were concerned, they frequently established favourable collective agreements with management for all categories of workers and particularly those whose positions had traditionally been weak. To some degree they safeguarded the rights of their members against abuse by employers, and set up health insurance, pension and financial assistance schemes where none had existed before. From the government's point of view, the unions had not only brought all categories of theatre personnel under control, but had also been instrumental in curbing the speculative activities of private entrepreneurs who had effectively lost control of an industry they had previously dominated.

The President of the Corporation, Gino Pierantoni, reported on its activities towards the end of 1932, when it had been in existence for less than two years. The tone of his address (to a Conference in Venice) was, with the benefit of hindsight, somewhat over-optimistic, yet it is clear from what he said on that occasion that the Corporation had by no means been idle since its inauguration in March 1930.

The Corporation had hitherto been fully occupied with the discipline and regulation of foreign companies performing in Italy and of Italian companies applying to undertake tours abroad; the setting up of registers of singers and musicians; of insurance schemes for all categories of theatre workers; the just regulation of work relations between employers and employees; the fitting out of performance spaces; with problems relating to the film industry; the staging of particular plays; and with the administration of popular opera seasons. Additionally, Pierantoni reported that the State had granted long-requested reductions for travel and transportation of theatre equipment by rail; it had sanctioned an increase in the cost of radio licences to subsidise different theatrical enterprises; and it had granted subsidies totalling more than one million lire for the opera seasons in the smaller, provincial theatres. Work had progressed on the proposed creation of the Istituto Nazionale del Teatro Drammatico (National Theatre

Organisation), and government-approved theatrical employment agencies had been in operation since October of that year.

Nevertheless, solid achievement was a good deal less than this catalogue suggests. The Corporation was cumbersome in its operations and generally out of touch with constituent associations. It failed singularly to quell the jealousies and disagreements between associations; it lacked initiative and was generally perceived to be too closely associated with the private sector (notably the Suvini Zerboni trust), so that it was suspected of suppressing or subverting measures which would run counter to the interests of the latter. It was also dependent on the close personal support of Bottai, and with his transfer to the Ministry of Education, it lost a powerful and knowledgeable champion.

Owing to its multifarious activities and connections in the private sector of the industry, the Corporation could never become the instrument of the totalitarian policy that Mussolini's government aspired to. This was not the case with the Ministry for the Press and Propaganda, which was suddenly transformed into the Ministry for Popular Culture in 1935. As a consequence of this, government pressures on the theatrical sector during the second half of the 1930s were considerably greater than they had been when the Corporation was still the leading government agency for the theatre. Effectively, with this transfer of power, the theatre ceased to be controlled by people who had a genuine interest in its future. From this point on, it became the responsibility of bureaucrats who were much more interested in efficient systems than in the well-being of the industry.

The popularisation of the theatre

The government pressed ahead with its popularisation of theatre for 'educational' purposes, encouraging at minimal cost the creation of the *Carri di Tespi*, the Carri Lirici (travelling theatres, dramatic and operatic) and other forms of open-air theatre. The performance of classical-historical dramas in restored Greek and Roman amphitheatres was a form greatly favoured by Mussolini, not least because it served to strengthen the myth of the legitimate and ideological continuity of the régime with the cultural and political glories of classical Greece and Rome. The very notion of open-air theatre was thus seen by Fascist ideologues as a quasi-religious, mystical experience. It is questionable, however, whether this idea of popular theatre permeated down to the lower levels of society which, by and large, remained impervious to the régime's efforts to reach it, particularly with this kind of 'intellectual' entertainment.

The *sabato teatrale* (by analogy with the *sabato fascista*, the 'Fascist Saturday') met with greater popular success and approval. This was probably as a consequence of the government-imposed reductions in the cost of tickets and even greater reductions for block bookings from the *dopolavoro* (working men's clubs) and *filodrammatici* (amateur theatrical) organisations, which made even the greatest and most opulent theatres accessible to all sections of society. Nevertheless, it still tended to be the lighter, intellectually less-demanding forms of music-hall entertainment which appealed to the masses. The régime had already entrusted the task of the 'spiritual' control and education of the peasant and factory workers to the *Opera Nazionale Dopolavoro* (OND – National Federation of Working Men's Clubs), through management of welfare benefits, sporting and other recreational facilities. That mandate was extended to include the use of the *dopolavoro* organisation to inculcate a practical interest in live theatre among workers. To this end, many new amateur theatrical clubs (*filodrammatici*) were created. Although their usual fare was the light-hearted and the comical, they nevertheless served their 'educational' purpose by stimulating active cultural experiences and promoting a sense of discipline. As in the professional theatre, a predominantly Italian repertoire was favoured. Royalties for the performance of foreign plays were, in any case, usually so high that most amateur organisations simply could not afford them.[20] The activities of the *filodrammatici* did not stop, however, at the production of plays at the local level. Through the Provincial Federations of the OND, enthusiasts were able to participate in theatre courses and workshops, make use of theatre libraries, attend festivals and competitions as well as lectures and conferences. It must be acknowledged that the OND was highly successful in promoting the idea and the reality of theatre among the working classes, where hitherto it had been the exclusive preserve of the better-off.

The *Carri di Tespi* and Carri Lirici grew directly out of the OND's work with the *filodrammatici* towards the end of the 1920s. The intention was to take theatre to the remoter parts of Italy where it was rarely, if ever, seen. The Technical Office of the *filodrammatici* demonstrated a prototype of a travelling theatre, which could be assembled or dismantled in an hour, at the Fiera di

Milano in 1928. Giovacchino Forzano was entrusted with the organisation of the whole venture at the beginning of 1929, and the first performance of the Carri was given in Rome, in the presence of Mussolini, on 4 July of the same year. The first summer season followed immediately, with plays being mounted in no fewer than forty-two different towns throughout southern Italy to something in excess of 300,000 spectators. This success led to the repetition of the experiment in the following year, only this time with three companies touring, so as to be able to cover the whole of Italy. Forzano also introduced the idea of the Carri Lirici and their first short season also took place in 1930. Initially, the companies were made up of professionals, and there can be no doubt that they successfully extended theatre into geographical areas and to social groups which had not previously experienced it. The Carri had the added virtue of alleviating the high level of unemployment in the theatre. They created many new jobs, and since their season exceeded that of the more conventional theatres by several weeks, they provided a longer period of employment.

The major problem faced by the Carri, one of whose major functions was propagandistic, was that of putting together a suitable repertoire. As has already been indicated, 'Fascist' plays of an adequate artistic standard were simply not forthcoming. Thus, it was not so much what appeared on stage, but rather the very presence of the Carri themselves which provided the opportunity for publicising concrete evidence of the 'caring' State. It was a far cry, however, from the 'educative' function which Mussolini had originally envisaged with his theatre for the masses (*teatro di ventimila*).

A National Theatre, had it been created, would have deflected from this policy of *andare verso il popolo* by virtue of the huge cost involved and the narrow social base of its audiences. In political terms, the comparatively small funds made available by the régime for the promotion of theatre were much better spent in making it available also to the lower classes. The extension of theatre to the masses, against a background of deep economic recession and at so little expense, must be accounted a positive achievement of the régime, as indeed must its concern (whatever its real motivation) to include the whole of Italian society in its own cultural heritage. Silvio d'Amico points out, however, that the commercial and artistic success of the Carri Lirici did not usually extend to the *Carri di Tespi*. Their professional talents were often quite modest. Instead of setting up their theatres in remoter settlements they often operated in towns which were already well catered for, frequently in competition for limited audiences with more 'permanent' companies, themselves sometimes also subsidised by the government.[21]

Yet it is doubtful whether the theatre, despite its rigorous organisation, played any significant role in the fascistisation of the masses. It may, from time to time, have appealed to a fairly shallow, sentimentalised national pride, but even in this it was hugely eclipsed by Italy's achievements in the sporting world. Perhaps the main reason for the failure to produce a truly Fascist theatre lay deep within the very nature of Fascism itself. Successful theatre is always concerned with tensions and conflicts which it seeks to explain and resolve. Between the March on Rome and the invasion of Abyssinia there were few tensions and conflicts which could be openly acknowledged in Italian society. They existed – as writers in exile (external, internal or 'hermetic') such as Ignazio Silone, Alberto Moravia, Carlo Levi and Eugenio Montale demonstrated – but virtually all overt opposition had been silenced. The 'battle for wheat', land reclamation, the 'demographic battle', and so on, did not inspire the kind of theatre the 'continuous revolution' required. Even after 1935, when once again real battles were being fought in real wars, the many attempts to turn them into theatre ended in failure. Totalitarianism always expects its art to be celebratory, eulogistic, paternalistic, monumental. This requirement derives from the fundamental absolutism which drives the régimes. The division of the world into opposing pairs, simplistic in the extreme, removes the essentially human problems of not knowing where one stands or where one is going. Such a division is based on certainties, whereas human uncertainty would seem to be a *sine qua non* of all good art. Even in 1935, eight years before the fall of the régime, Silvio d'Amico was openly acknowledging the failure of 'Fascist' theatre and the reasons for it:

> Anyone like me who samples the manuscripts which the endless drama competitions produce, knows what the situation is. An ever-increasing percentage insist on patriotic, war-like or Fascist themes; even the best of them are nothing if not didactic, presenting a world conventionally divided between villains and heroes, with a moralising conclusion. In the very unlikely event of such works ever reaching the stage, they wouldn't even score any marks as propaganda, while the theatre, for its part, would surely die the death as a result of final and total abandonment by its audiences.[22]

At the moment of the fall of Fascism in July 1943, the editorial of *Scenario* observed that:

> ...the theatre will now once again be able to resume its function of interpreting collective feeling through the sensibility of its poets (...) despite everything that has been done by those responsible for the theatre, it is very clear that they have never managed to achieve the sort of theatre they wanted – political, propagandistic, belonging to the régime. It has been, if not the only sector, almost the only sector, at which tremendous political pressure has been directed without obtaining the desired results.[23]

There appears to be no reason to disagree with this judgement, in so far as it refers to the type of theatre exhibited under Fascism, but it is far from correct if applied to the theatre industry as a whole. The government was not able to create a Fascist theatre repertoire, but on the other hand it was able to ensure that the theatre did not become the voice of social and political discontent. It did this through taking control of every conceivable aspect of the industry, through continuous vigilance with regard to organisations and individuals, and by providing a career structure with proper pensions and other financial benefits for all categories of theatre workers. It went well beyond control of the purely professional theatre, however, providing the means and the organisation for practical and spectator interest at the amateur level, whether in the OND-sponsored *filodrammatici* or, on a different intellectual plain, the *Littoriali della Cultura e dell'Arte* (national student competitions which were held for seven years between 1934 and 1941). Whatever its motivation, more was done under Fascism to promote theatre than ever before in the short history of united Italy. Unfortunately, the amounts of finance made available to theatre by the government were exiguous and the industry had to survive as best it could. Nonetheless, for the theatre worker it was now the law and much less the whim of an individual entrepreneur which governed professional life. Ironically, despite the many shortcomings of the system, the great majority had some reason to be grateful to Fascism's forceful intrusion into the life and work of the theatre.

NOTES

1. Andrea Camilleri, *I teatri stabili in Italia (1858-1918)*, Bologna, 1959, p. 7.
2. Emanuela Scarpellini, *Organizzazione teatrale e politica del teatro nell'Italia fascista*, Florence, 1989, p. 1.

3. Scarpellini *ibidem* notes (pp. 3-4) that the Società Anonima Suvini Zerboni was established on 7 September 1905 and very soon gained control of many theatres in Milan and neighbouring cities. A virtual monopoly was sealed by agreements made with rival theatres in Rome, Bologna, Turin and Genoa. By 1925, Giordani and Riboldi had taken over the Suvini Zerboni empire, the former already owning the Società Italiana del Teatro Drammatico (Sitedrama). Additionally, Giordani was also largely responsible for importing much foreign drama into Italy – yet another field in which he had a virtual monopoly. In May 1926, Suvini Zerboni gained controlling shares in Sitedrama. These shares proved extremely lucrative, so much so that they figured regularly on the stock market. As a result, wide and important areas of professional theatre were controlled by people whose primary interest was not the theatre but the financial gain they could make from it.

4. It should be remembered that Italy had been unified only in 1861, and that even after sixty years the cultures and dialects of the regions (formerly separate states) were still largely dominant over the national culture. In general, only secondary and higher education gave adequate lasting contact with the national language for it to supplant, or at least co-exist with, dialect. Of course, only a very small minority of Italians could afford to progress beyond a rudimentary education.

5. Silvio d'Amico, *Il teatro non deve morire*, Rome, 1945, p. 14.

6. See Scarpellini, *Organizzazione teatrale*, p. 90.

7. See Benito Mussolini, *Opera omnia*, E. and D. Susmel (eds), vol. XX, Florence, 1951-1962, p. 276.

8. *Scenario* was published between 1932 and 1943. Until 1935, it was directed jointly by Silvio d'Amico and Nicola de Pirro, thereafter by the latter alone. De Pirro was to become the single most important figure in the organisation of theatre under Fascism, being by turns the secretary and then director of the Associazione Nazionale della Federazione degli Industriali dello Spettacolo. In 1935, he became the first Theatre Inspector. Perhaps owing to his close involvement with government policy for the theatre, *Scenario* became arguably the most influential and authoritative of theatre journals in Italy.

9. The Corporation was a socio-political system which organised society around occupational groupings. It was intended to eradicate class conflict and foster class co-operation for the greater good of the nation. In Fascist Italy the system was created piecemeal over a period of fifteen years but never functioned successfully, principally because it was subverted by powerful interest groups, as well as by Mussolini himself.

10. See Scarpellini, *Organizzazione teatrale*, p. 149.

11. Letter from Mussolini to Gastone Monaldi, 22 June 1927, quoted by Pietro Cavallo, *Immaginario e rappresentazione: il teatro fascista di propaganda*, Rome, 1990, p. 213, n. 5.

12. R. Forges Davanzati, 'Mussolini parla agli scrittori' in *Nuova Antologia*, f. 1468, 16 May 1933, p. 191.

13. UPIM (Unico Prezzo Italiano di Milano) was, and remains to this day, a popular department store, not unlike Woolworth's in its range and quality of goods.

14. 'Arte ed artisti', *Il Popolo d'Italia*, 10 April 1928.

15. Dino Alfieri, 'Il teatro italiano', *Scenario*, 6 June 1939, p. 247.

16. See Reale Accademia d'Italia, Fondazione Alessandro Volta, *Convegno di lettere, 8-14 ottobre 1934: Il teatro drammatico*, Rome, 1935, pp. 45-6.

17. Gherardo Gherardi, 'Proposti d'un drammaturgo italiano', *Scenario*, February, 1937, p. 57.
18. In reality, the Corporation had begun life much earlier in the theatre (as the Corporazione Nazionale del Teatro) in January 1922, some nine months before Fascism came to power. In line with unfolding Fascist socio-economic policy in the early years of the régime, it underwent several transformations and revisions in terms of function and representation until it emerged, in 1931, as the guinea pig for the whole corporatist system. It remained the only Corporation in existence until 1934.
19. The primary function of the Ministero della Cultura Popolare was the definition, diffusion and suitable 'packaging' of the *realtà fascista*. The ministry began life as the government Press Office, but under Galeazzo Ciano it underwent a rapid expansion in functions and importance so that within a year of his taking charge, it had already become the Under-Secretariat of State for the Press and Propaganda (6 September 1934). This phase was quickly left behind when its propagandistic functions were divided into separate categories (including the creation of the Theatre Inspectorate in April 1935). It became a full Ministry on 24 June 1935.
20. However, Scarpellini writes (*Organizzazione teatrale*, p. 106) that 'in spite of all of this, the foreign repertoire did not disappear altogether, since even during the early thirties, according to data furnished by the Italian Society of Authors and Editors (SIAE) the picture was as follows: in 1932, the OND was responsible for 7,511 performances of which 5,497 Italian, 1,566 dialect and 488 foreign; while in 1933, out of 7,303 performances, 4,939 were Italian, 1,894 dialect and 470 foreign.'
21. S. d'Amico, *Il teatro non deve morire*, p. 40.
22. S. d'Amico, *Invito al teatro*, Brescia, 1935, p. 16.
23. Editorial (author unstated), 'Tempi nuovi', in *Scenario*, 8 August 1943, p. 257.

6

Theatre Politics of the Mussolini Régime and Their Influence on Fascist Drama

Pietro Cavallo

Translated by Erminia Passannanti and Günter Berghaus

Fascism and theatre

During the years of Fascism, Italian theatre was characterised by complex and contradictory features. Against all expectations, the 'official' theatre of the time avoided subject matters inspired by the 'new time' and 'new spirit' of Fascist Italy. This lack of commitment was often commented on and condemned by intellectuals close to the régime, by Ministers of the *Cultura Popolare* and, of course, by the Duce himself. Mussolini had complete faith in the educational power of the stage: 'Theatre is one of the most direct means of reaching the heart of the people'.[1] In 1933, he coined the ambiguous expression *teatro di massa* (theatre of the masses), which implied that the traditional theatre, due to its limited seating capacity and antiquated repertory, was inadequate to rally people under the banner of Fascism. Soon, the expression became the object of (often contradictory) interpretations. On 28 April 1933, on the occasion of the fiftieth anniversary of the Società Italiana Autori ed Editori, Mussolini delivered a speech at the Teatro Argentina and declared:

> I've heard that theatre is going through a crisis. This crisis does exist, but it is mistaken to believe that it is in any way connected to the rising popularity of cinema. We must take into account both the spiritual and the material aspects of this crisis. The first concerns the authors, the second the number of seats. We have to make plans for a theatre of the masses, a theatre with a capacity of 15,000-20,000 seats (...) The art work of the stage has to possess the wide-ranging

appeal that people are asking for. It must stir great collective passions and must be imbued with a sense of vivid and deep humanity. It has to present matters that truly count in people's spiritual life and that reflect their aspirations. We have had enough of the obsession with this ill-famed 'theatre of adultery'! The spectrum of these 'triangular' complications has at last been exhausted. Allow the collective passions to find dramatic representation, and you'll see the stalls crowded with people again.[2]

And yet, the Duce's warning went unheard. Italian dramatists remained ultimately deaf to the appeal, despite their respect for a government that seemed to hold them in great esteem and, for the first time in Italian history, showed an interest in promoting the theatrical arts. Throughout the years of the Fascist régime and even during the Second World War, they clung to innocuous themes, especially to that 'ill-famed triangle' the Duce had castigated and rebuked.

Although there is clear evidence that many people in show business endorsed Fascism, they made little attempt to deal with subject matters directly related to Fascist myths and ideology. Throughout the Fascist era there were few signs of a truly Fascist theatre as envisaged by intellectuals and students close to the régime. At several congresses they demanded a theatre that would give expression to the 'new spiritual climate' Italy was experiencing, a theatre innovative in form and content, capable of revealing both the ideals and ethics that were already inspiring the 'faith' and behaviour of the masses.[3] However, a theatre of this kind would have implied an overcoming of Fascism itself; or, to be more precise, the superseding of the traditional and reassuring values, which for large strata of the Italian society – especially the petit and middle bourgeoisie in urban centres, who formed the social basis of the régime – represented the main reason for lending their support to Fascism. It was, in other words, an overcoming of the tranquillity and certainties so effectively summed up in a popular song of 1937 that spoke of 'one-thousand lira a month', the 'modest job', the 'little cottage in the suburbs' and the 'pretty, young wife'.[4]

There was a general tendency for dramatists to comply with the taste of their audiences (who showed no interest in experiments with new themes and forms of presentation). Therefore, playwrights continued to deal with traditional topics and employ popular formats. In addition, when a first attempt was made to create a theatre for the masses (with *18 BL* on 29 April 1934 at the opening of the *Littoriali del Teatro*[5]), it failed abysmally. The same 'catastrophic'[6] results – to quote an expression used by the stage censor, Leopoldo Zurlo – could be observed at the première, given at the Teatro Lirico in Milan, of *Simma*, a drama in which Francesco Pastonchi outlined the conflict between spirit and materialism so dear to the régime. Despite Mussolini's support for the production, and in fact, for several others to follow, little popular enthusiasm could be generated for spectacles of this kind. There was even active opposition in Fascist circles to such plays. For example, between February and March 1935 the Compagnia del Nuovo Teatro of Fernando de Cruciati staged two of the most emotionally charged Fascist plays in Rome: *La lunga marcia di ritorno*, by Mario Federici, and *I tre atti*, by Marcello Gallian. The message behind the first play was that because the First World War had not lived up to expectations, the soldiers' 'march' had to be taken up again,[7] whereas the author of the second play exalted the revolutionary spirit of the early Fascists and contrasted this with the petty quibbles and narrow horizons of the middle-classes.[8] The productions of these two plays were organised under the auspices of the *Ispettorato del Teatro* with the aim of promoting a Fascist youth theatre.[9] However, the reactions were so violent that Zurlo felt bound to intervene, noting that the opposition to the production 'seemed to be organised by someone who either had not viewed the plays or had done so with a deplorable lack of attention'.[10]

However, there was another form of Fascist theatre, mainly produced by amateurs (teachers, journalists, lawyers, but also workers, housewives, unemployed people). Their plays hinged upon situations, characters, plots and slogans more or less dear to the régime. These dramas were far more popular than one would imagine: thousands of scripts were submitted to the censor, who with unrelenting dedication sifted through every piece of dramatic writing to be performed on stage (irrespective of whether the boards were erected in a rural hamlet, a small parish, a *Casa del Fascio*, or a major playhouse). Hence, there are hundreds of files that can still be consulted in the Central State Archives in Rome, giving us a detailed insight into the dramatic aesthetics of dedicated Fascists.

Fascist theatre came into existence soon after the March on Rome. Salvator Gotta claimed in *Comoedia* his right of primogeniture,[11] staking a claim for having written the first example of Fascist drama with *Il convegno dei martiri*. It was performed at the Teatro Argentina in Rome, on 21 April 1923, and dealt with the tragic destiny of a young Fascist, Gustavo Doglia, who had died in Turin in a clash with left-wing partisans just before the March on Rome.

The régime showed a rather ambivalent attitude towards such openly propagandistic theatre. Although striving to foster new dramatic writing with competitions and prizes awarded by Fascist organisations such as the *Dopolavoro*, it did not create any structured network of performance spaces, where the stream of new and Fascist plays could be performed. As far as the *Carri di Tespi* and the *Dopolavoro* amateur dramatic companies were concerned, they had a repertory which resembled that of the normal theatre and show business. Genuinely Fascist theatre lacked even the kind of support which the Catholic theatre movement (founded by Don Giovanni Bosco in the second half of the nineteenth century) had enjoyed during the first post-war years.[12]

Much of this was due to the fact that the régime preferred to entrust its propaganda to newspapers, magazines, cinema and radio rather than to the theatre. This choice was determined, perhaps, not so much by the failure of the practical experiments made with a Fascist theatre for the masses, but rather by the unsatisfactory quality of the scripts submitted to the censor or the juries of important national competitions.

A typical example of this situation was Renata Mughini's *I figli*, a play infused with the Fascist spirit of the time, which won the San Remo Prize in 1938. As Zurlo noted, this altogether mediocre work offered an ending which was 'too contradictory to be logical'.[13] Equally tangible were the other weaknesses of the play, and they had not escaped the members of the jury, Marinetti, Rosso di San Secondo, Simoni and d'Amico, or its chairman Ettore Romagnoli. In their final verdict, they emphasised the freshness and lack of rhetoric in the play: 'Even though the play does not reach a high artistic standard, as a typical juvenile work it seems to embrace at least the spirit our time'.[14] This episode is quite remarkable, for among the 177 competing plays there were those such as *Chilometri bianchi*, by Mario Federici – who also wrote the already mentioned, and often fiercely criticised, play *Lunga Marcia di ritorno* – which put themselves in the wrong by presenting anxieties and doubts, rather than certainties or reassuring realities. *Chilometri bianchi*, which was put on at the Teatro delle Arti in Rome and published in *Il dramma* a few months later, portrays the anguish of a survivor who, returning from the war after having wandered through half of Europe, no longer feels inside himself the old love for his Fatherland. For this reason, his wife persuades him to avoid meeting their children:

> We, who love our children so dearly, could hurt them in their purest sentiment, their unshakable faith. Even though they are good boys, they would start having doubts, they, who never had any doubts. Maybe we wouldn't even notice it immediately. It's terrible, Marco, it's like a hidden illness for our poor children! They would start wondering how you, their hero, has been able to lose yourself. And they would start thinking that the love people feel for their country is not as absolute as they thought.[15]

In all the drama competitions, the quality of the plays which drew their inspiration from Fascist mythology fell short of expectation. Zurlo himself came to realise this when he was correcting, often at the explicit request of the author, both the grammar and syntax of the scripts submitted to him. It is probable that these dramas found their only attentive reader in this scrupulous officer!

Furthermore, Fascist theatre experienced the hostility of Silvio d'Amico, one of the 'High Priests' of Italian theatre. He resolutely opposed didactic theatre as practised in Soviet Russia or Nazi Germany. In October 1934, at a congress organised by the Fondazione Volta on the state of Italian drama, he declared:

> A theatre with didactic aims might be expected to be alright for the working class, but it falls outside the realm of art. Posters displayed on school walls are fine to impress and move our pupils. So, in a sense, they do work, but who would dream of showing them in an exhibition among genuine works of art?[16]

The following year, d'Amico placed his ban on the theatre of propaganda, which for some authors had become their only chance to achieve popularity:

> Those who have to scrutinise the flow of scripts submitted to drama competitions, which succeed each other almost incessantly, know well that an increasing number of plays deal with patriotic subjects like soldiers, Fascists, and so on. They are, in the best cases, nothing but mere didactic compositions with edifying endings, conventional pictures of a world inhabited by heroes and villains. If, by an absurd coincidence, these plays would ever reach the stage, propaganda would gain no profit from it and theatre itself would decline, forever deserted by its audience.[17]

Confined as he was to a logic still anchored to a canon of traditional aesthetic standards, d'Amico could not understand that the criteria he was applying to that form of theatre had to be extended. As a matter of fact, the points he objected to were indeed the key features of those plays. They tried to communicate, as efficiently as possible, a simple message which could not be misinterpreted by the audience. Such avoidance of any ambiguous touches led to a rather Manichean character divide into good and evil, with a positive hero often identifiable from the very beginning of the play (even when he initially fought on the side of the enemy). As a result, the plots of these dramas were of the most predictable and elementary kind, and the dialogues full of slogans and apodeictic phraseology. ('In a work of art, nothing is more anti-fascist than irony!' Salvator Gotta rightly affirmed[18]). In short, this form of theatre was aimed at confirming and strengthening the convictions of a public that was already tuned into the author's feelings. In some plays, the dividing line between fiction and reality was entirely dismantled: the actors addressed their speeches straight to the audience, or mingled with the spectators in the auditorium. Along with this new mannerism came the habit of resorting to strongly symbolic or allegorical characters. Some scripts ended by displaying either the Fascist insignia or a portrait of Mussolini. For example, M. Dorta advised in the final stage direction of his play *Ritorno* (1935): 'The scene remains in the dark – while against the sky the Duce's figure appears, surrounded by applauding young Blackshirts'.[19]

This, however, must not lead us to the conclusion that Fascist theatre was erected on the same principles as left-wing militant theatre. Formal devices such as direct addresses to the audience or symbolic characters were rarely exploited in an inventive fashion. Compared to the traditional bourgeois theatre, *agit-prop* introduced remarkable innovations in staging technique (for example, when performing in the courtyards of working-class tenements, in front of factories, in the streets, or even on tramways[20]). Fascist theatre, however, remained rooted in the schemas of nineteenth-century dramaturgy and stage design. The plays possessed a traditional beginning, a linear development of the chosen theme, a peripetic climax and a conflict-resolving finale; the stories imitated real-life events; the characters embodied, except in some rare cases, real people. Left-wing *agit-prop*, on the other hand, turned 'characters' into 'stereotypes' that schematised some fundamental characteristics of the various social classes.[21] It must be emphasised that *agit-prop* theatre made its 'debut' in a revolutionary period during which the cultural patterns of the nineteenth century were breaking down and a fruitful dialectic relationship was established between political innovators and creative intellectuals. Fascist theatre, on the other hand, appeared on the scene after the March on Rome, when the 'revolution' had already taken place; therefore, its task was not so much to mobilise the masses against the constituted order, but rather to reinforce an already established system.

Fascist theatre from the March on Rome to the African War

As one would imagine, the first years of the Fascist movement assumed a significant position in the drama and theatre of the régime. Since the birth of Fascism had been closely linked to the experience of the First World War, the movement regarded itself as the direct heir of the ideals that had been kindled by the conflict. For example, in *Retaggio di trincea*, an ex-serviceman alludes to the Fascists by saying:

> These 'hot-heads' are our followers, our only heirs, to whom we trustfully hand over the weapons still stained with the blood we have shed on the fields of Glory. In so doing, we will make them continue the never-ending march of our people towards a goal that is afar, but not unattainable for our legions.[22]

Often enough, the principal characters in Fascist dramas were either ex-servicemen wearing the old scars of war, or people too young to have taken part in the conflict, but who had nevertheless suffered the loss of a father, brother or uncle. To have been involved in the war – either personally, or vicariously through a close relative – became the distinctive sign of an hero (an hero who, to begin with, did not necessarily have to be a Fascist). It was a common trait of the plays to show, at the outset, the main character to be a Socialist and how he, after a period of crisis and reflection, would abandon his Party in order to join the opposite side. The official blessing of the hero's conversion or, to use the term favoured by most authors, 'redemption', came through his death. To die for a good cause was presented as the hero's ultimate liberation and purification from his previous faults.

At times, the clash between Fascists and Socialists was reduced to a troublesome relationship between members of the same family. Naturally, the conflict ended by having the character who initially displayed an hostile or sceptical attitude towards the 'new ideas' being converted to Fascism. Here too, the death of a loved one (a relative or a friend) represented a prime cause for redemption.

As for the plots, they principally revolved around three basic and constantly recurring topics: Socialism, Fascism, sacrificial death. If the starting point was not Socialism, but something similar (like, for example, an intemperate and licentious life style), the ending was still more or less geared towards the protagonist's conversion to Fascism.

Such story developments can ultimately be interpreted as *rites de passage*. The journey of initiation can be long or short, easy or fraught with obstacles. As in any initiation rite, the new status is exemplified by reaching a new stage in the life cycle, where the experiences of the previous life are subsumed. In most cases of Fascist *rites de passage*, this 'previous experience' was the First World War. The hardship and feelings endured at the front had formed the hero's ethical and moral values. He had felt what it meant to be part of a whole – a whole that had a precise name: Fatherland. In the trenches, the individual merged with a group that knew no social distinctions or barriers. In these plays, war was presented as a unique opportunity to overcome the alienation, egotism and materialist thinking that characterised human life in the industrial age.

Socialism had proven itself to be as materialistic as capitalism, and not to be substantively different from the society it pretended to fight against. In *La morte degli eroi*, Romano, a young man who had volunteered for war service and who, in the end, dies while defending the *casa del fascio* from the 'Reds', confronts his father, an industrialist who has profiteered and grown rich from the war, as follows:

PROSPERO: Say what you like! But your motivations are as abstract as those of the poets you read.

ROMANO: No, they are firm realities, but realities you can't grasp because you only talk, act and think in the name of your personal interests. Of course, for you they are the only things you consider worth saving in this chaos.

PROSPERO: Yes, you're right, they are very important, at least for me! –

ROMANO: You're living by instinct!

PROSPERO: How else should I live then? Please tell me!

ROMANO: Through your spirit! –

PROSPERO: Do you really think it's worth ruining both your health and career for the sake of ideas which nobody understands?

ROMANO: Who says that nobody understands them? Stepping into the trenches is enough to be able to feel that you are a small but necessary part of a whole. (...) There reigns a sublime unselfishness, down there! – But here, you can only find shameful egotism! – Daddy, I will go back to the front immediately!

PROSPERO: You dramatise the simplest things!

ROMANO: You haven't seen them dying; that's why you speak like that! – Sacrifice exalts life. Have the dead no meaning to you? And their crying mothers? – No, they mean nothing to you! For you, nothing is of importance but money. It's your strength and your shame! – The soldier despises you, but he is a great man: he suffers and gives his life away, also for you! – Down there, we learn to love each other more than we ever thought we were capable of! – That love will be our invincible weapon against the enemy, against you. Our will-power is inexorable. We are the new world![23]

The Fascist hero did not confront his enemies with any sophisticated or definite programmes: he simply suggested a way to 'spend' one's existence, a way that can give meaning to life (and death). He was ultimately professing a 'faith', a willingness to listen to his heart rather than just following the dictates of his 'belly',[24] as both the Socialist and the bourgeois characters do. There was a willingness to believe that life cannot be determined merely by material interests and that the engine of history keeps on going by virtue of the same ethical and moral forces that had brought about the final victory in 1918. In *Retaggio di trincea*, the Fascists are accused of being nothing but 'mad dreamers', which prompts the main character to respond:

You just can't see. A bank note is covering your eyes – money has clipped the wings of your soul. You can't fly in the name of Glory, as we do, across the clear skies of Thought and Action (...) Shut up! Don't look at us, you can't understand us.[25]

In plays like these the difference between the Fascist hero and his antagonists is primarily indicated through language ('you do not understand us'). Although both may use the same vocabulary, the meaning of their words is radically different. Their import is not based on their content (the 'signified'), but on the language itself (the 'signifier'). Their main referent is an attitude towards life, acquired through the conquests, but also the sacrifices and suffering endured during the war period. Words assume, in this way, a symbolic charge and a power to eliminate – or, at least, to weaken – their conceptual referent, or 'meaning'. Words no longer count for what they designate in common speech, but for their evocative power. The rational, compared to the symbolic, content of a verbal proposition is only of minor significance. Logical reasoning was in fact precluded, because the Fascist characters confront their opponents only with 'faith', a sentiment that can only be instinctively apprehended. They never present political programmes or precise and articulate aims, but rather a set of symbols to guide people through their lives and to act as models for concrete actions. But these 'actions' possessed symbolic meaning rather than clearly defined objectives. Their value primarily consisted in being 'action', in providing the pleasure of forming part of a wider 'battle':

> The élite of the trenches (*il fior fiore delle trincee*) together with those who were too young to take part in this war, do not have the pleasure of knowing you, yet they also fight and die for you. In the game of life they play the desperate card, only because it gives them ultimate pleasure.[26]

What we discover here is the contradictory nature of Fascist theatre. Although regarding the stage as a medium of propaganda, the Fascist playwrights did not present explicit political programmes, but transmitted myths and symbols designed to shape a new, a *Fascist*, mental attitude which embraced each and every aspect of life. Thus, the Fascist hero became representative of the values and symbols that had shown the 'way to victory' in the Great War. In a sense, the main reason for joining the Party was not so much to participate in a political association, but to express one's love towards the Fatherland. The decision to become a member of the PNF was often attributed to instinctual and sentimental feelings rather than to any rational motivation. For example, in *Alba di rinascita*, Nino explains to his brother the reasons why he has become a Fascist supporter:

> There is something new in me, Riccardo, something I can't explain! It's a strange sensation! It is both an urge to fight and to sacrifice ourselves. It makes us love life with no fear of death. It makes us look into the future whilst keeping in mind what we leave behind. I can't tell what came over me, but when they asked if I wanted to join the Party, I immediately answered: yes! That 'yes' sprang from my heart, not from my mind. My lips uttered it long before my brain had ordered them to do so.[27]

The motivating force was more than a political doctrine; it was life experience elevated almost to the status of religion. In *Mistica fascista*, a character says of the Blackshirts:

> Their belief has religious significance. It stands for something that is far more than a method: it is a way of life, mystical in its sources, palpitating, restless, and heroic in its deeds.[28]

This attitude generated a pronounced tendency towards adopting a linguistic code and discursive style borrowed from the Catholic tradition. For example, Claudio, the priest in *Giovinezza*, asserts about Mussolini:

> It is as if He had to climb another Calvary, a kind of new 'via crucis', which leads to His resurrection. Aided by our faith we will go beyond our limits! Its powerful echo will squash the interests of Plutocracy. Our helmsman knows very well what needs to be done. I, who have the honour of often staying close to His side, know what fruits His sleepless nights bear for us.[29]

The Catholic idiom was the only language available to those authors who wished to translate into widely intelligible form the force and intensity of the hopes people placed both in the Fascist movement and in Mussolini. There was the recurrent use of terms such as 'redemption', 'deliverance', 'ascent', 'salvation'; the frequent declaration of being ready to offer one's blood for the salvation of 'sinners' (i.e., those who had not yet joined in the Fascist Party); the elevation of Fascists, who had been killed by the 'Reds', to the status of 'martyrs'; the designation of the Fascist doctrine as 'the New Gospel'; and, finally, the figurative assimilation of Mussolini's image with that of Christ.

The Fascist movement was born out of the wish to renew those 'natural' and 'immutable' values the war had temporarily depressed. These values were mainly connected to a rigidly hierarchical society, where each person had a definite function and occupied a fixed position. Socialism was accused of having pushed the country into chaos by upsetting this 'natural order' and by suppressing the legitimate distinctions among the social classes. In *I ritornati*, a play of 1934, a character speaks of 'the shame of social equality' and explains this by saying: '"Social equality" is a beautiful, high-sounding word! It's even rather seductive. But tomorrow, I am sure, people will have to suffer the unpleasant consequences of that equality.'[30]

In *Ha 'tama* (a play on the subject of the African War), de Robertis translated the need for inequality onto the international scene:

> Yes, Pinuzza! There are human beings in this world whose fate it is to give, always to give, just as history shows us that there are countries whose destiny is exactly the same: to give, always to give! – Nature rightfully makes them stronger than anyone else, to let them withstand all the tribulations Man and Fate unrightfully inflict upon them. They are the strongest, Pinuzza, indeed they are! It's their distinctive characteristic! This means that it is Nature who does not want to throw things into confusion, neither amongst those poor souls nor among the nations. All this fuss about abolishing the frontiers and putting everyone on the same footing is just like levelling all the distinctions between the souls![31]

At the basis of these arguments we can discern a profound lack of confidence in the people's ability to govern their own lives and the fate of their country. In *Fiamme nere* it is stated: 'People wish to be wisely guided; only in this way can they enjoy freedom.'[32] The leaders (either of the earliest Fascist squads, or of the subsequent public and private organisations of the régime) impose themselves by virtue of either their skills or merits. Consequently they become the 'new aristocracy' and take the place formerly held by the aristocracy of blood or wealth.

This trend becomes most obvious in the scripts based on the African War, which was the culmination of an historical process that began at the outbreak of the First World War. The Ethiopian War was meant to reveal to the 'new Italy' and the 'new Italians' their hidden energies and abilities and to bring to light a new élite of diligent and conscientious leaders. The plays dealing with this subject matter often have as their protagonist an engineer, whose rôle it is to show that Nature can be tamed to serve the people and the Nation. Such an educated, energetic, adventurous and determined élite had to take the place of the old aristocracy without, however, severing its popular roots, but proudly holding claim to them. This is exactly what Giovanna, the female protagonist in *L'eroica barriera* (1937), a play about the opposed love-affair between a common girl and an aristocrat's son, does:

> I am a daughter of the working-class, and this is my noble lineage. These hands of mine have endured work since I was a little girl. These tired eyes of mine have stayed open during the long hours of night. This back of mine has been bent by the never-ending labour that earned the daily bread for our family. This heart of mine still bears all the anxiety and suffering of a troubled soul. –

Aren't they the sign of a higher nobility than anything to be found in your dark world?[33]

Thus, appealing to a distinctive *topos* of popular romances – the opposed love-affair between characters belonging to different social classes – these dramas emphasised two closely connected assumptions: aristocracy is no longer a question of blood; and nobility can only be valiantly earned through fighting (e.g., in the First World War or in the African War). However, those who perform their duties in peace time also deserve to be given elevated status and honour. The human qualities that had guaranteed victory in war were placed on equal standing with the sacrifice, risk taking and boldness required in civil society. Personal gifts replaced the caste privileges of the old order: 'We must keep on working. This is the only path towards a better life. The nobility of labour will replace the nobility of blood.'[34]

The plays of the period gave testimony to the emergence of new social classes on the national scene. Nevertheless, these texts must be interpreted as symbolic rather than actual data of contemporary social realities in Italy. The frequent attacks on both the aristocracy and the upper-middle class, who had always sanctioned individualism, hedonism and wealth as means to attain a higher social standing and who had for a long time prevented the birth of a real national community, gave expression to the desire for a social life beyond egotism and personal interest. In other words, this critique was aimed at those who, by following the life style of the enemy countries – especially England – were jeopardising the unity and social harmony, which the Nation was to achieve under the 'attentive and far-seeing guidance' of the Duce (whose image was increasingly overshadowing that of the régime itself). The Ethiopian war was meant to reflect what, supposedly, had already happened within the country: it metaphorically represented the military side of a coin, which on its reverse was displaying the civil achievements of the Fascist régime.

Epilogue: The Second World War

Fascist theatre reached its widest radius of diffusion during the years 1936 to 1940. Exemplary figures pointed out the correct form of behaviour to the Italians and acted as rôle models for the development of the country. This, naturally, produced a celebratory rather than polemical type of theatre, which became fully apparent at the outbreak of the Second World War. The lack of victories that could be exploited for war propaganda forced dramatists to indulge in episodes which epitomised singular feats of civil or military heroism. Already during the second year of war, episodes which were actually defeats began to proliferate in the plays, marking in this way the wretched conditions of both the soldiers and the civilians. No wonder the censors judged these plays to be counter-productive in terms of propaganda.[35]

By reading these plays, one gets the impression that, initially, the armed conflict was no traumatic experience for the Italians. People continued to treat it as a remote event which did not interfere with the 'normal' course of their daily lives. In 1940, the censors recorded a dearth of suitable plays based on war topics. The following year, the percentage of 'performable' scripts had increased considerably, but they progressively lost their peculiar ideological features and, step-by-step, revealed the intrinsic horrors of war. This is not to say that there was a linear progression from enthusiasm to condemnation of the war. Public opinion oscillated just as much as the view points expressed in the plays, although by winter 1942-1943 eloquent signs of disapproval could be heard everywhere in Italian public life.[36]

From the scripts preserved in the censorship archives one indisputable fact emerges: for a large number of Italians, the war was gradually causing serious disruption to the fixed pattern of everyday life. The plays I have been able to analyse display a considerable variety of attitudes and dramatic narratives, and such heterogeneity was more pronounced than one would normally expect to find in this type of theatre. In short, clear and authoritative patterns that could be used to interpret the war events were vanishing. The images of armed conflict conveyed by the authors (mourning and suffering caused by the bombings, food shortages, restrictions of every kind that were imposed on civilians) were more and more often based on real-life experiences rather than on the official war propaganda.

From 1942 onwards, the stage functioned as more than a medium to broadcast phrases and slogans imposed from 'above'. It turned into one of the few channels authors could employ to express personal anxieties, even to question the reasons for fighting the war. Although some of these doubts may have been purely rhetorical and were ultimately aimed at reinforcing the official Party line, they nevertheless offered unexpected answers to the questions civilians and soldiers were asking themselves during those years.

Let us take, for example, *Sulla Manica visibilità discreta*, a play by a young student of the Genoese GUF[37] Federico Pescetto, staged at the Teatro Sperimentale dei GUF in Florence. The main character is a war pilot, Mietti, who does not have enough courage to face the enemy. Mocked by his comrades, he finds in the captain of the squadron his only friend and confidante. Having understood the drama of the young pilot, the officer comes to his aid, explaining that to be brave does not necessarily mean to be reckless, but to be capable of overcoming one's fear. Mietti does find the strength to hurl himself upon the enemy, but only after seeing his captain's aeroplane being shot down. Only then does he find an answer to his sceptical self-questioning: 'Why must I kill other men and be killed by them?'[38] So, Mietti fights and dies as an hero not for ideological, but purely personal reasons. The human sentiment of pity and compassion pushes the ideological world of propaganda into second place.

It is of some significance that only a few of the plays produced after 1942 were concerned with the actual front-line battles (and it must be underlined that the Russian front, which alone amounted to a large-scale tragedy, completely disappeared out of sight), but with the soldiers' return to their family and home towns. The scripts were crowded with survivors, exhausted, wounded, blind, at times proud of having sacrificed themselves in the name of their country, but more often utterly distressed because of their disablement. For example, the main character in *Famiglie eroiche* cries out: 'No! – Don't uncover my eyes! I could horrify you. Make me strong enough to bear my misfortune, my God! Oh, unlucky mother of mine! (...) Why didn't I die? Much better to die hundreds of times than to live such a disgraceful life.'[39] In a way, this play can be regarded as emblematic of the Fascist stage during the last years of war. That which in this play started off with unbounded enthusiasm for Italy's entry into the war, progressed in the third act to 'palpable sadness'[40] and ended in the last act with a gloomy air of despair.

Plays of this last period were increasingly characterised by a dreary and agonising atmosphere, which emphasised the gap between the author's purpose and the effect the play actually had on the audience. Zurlo was more and more often compelled to forbid those performances which could cause 'bitter thoughts provoked by the display of innocent victims', and he felt obliged to ask: 'How can it be desirable for a play that purports to exalt war to show at its beginning an ambulance out of which the desperate cries of both the mothers and the wounded can be heard?'[41] In a letter to Pavolini he stated: 'I can't deny that I fully support a glorification of war; however I also find it most inopportune to offer a realistic reproduction of it. Too many hearts in the audience would bleed when the dangers, sufferings and pains of war are demonstrated on stage.'[42]

Zurlo's remarks reflected the vision of the war that was, albeit often unintentionally, projected by the scripts submitted to his office. In *La rinuncia,* for example, the author relates an ordinary day in a girl's school. The pupils talk about their innocent dreams, their elevated hopes, their love affairs, etc. They discuss their like or dislike for this or that teacher, but this garrulous atmosphere soon comes to end, and the uncertain life in war-time rises to the surface. Erminia, one of the students, learns that her fiancé has been killed at the front. In order to avoid reminding her of her sorrow, the other girls ask their boyfriends not to come and meet them by the school gates. This 'renouncement' is suggested by an old spinster, who went through the same pain in her youth: 'I can still remember – them happily walking off with their boyfriends, and me, alone, standing in the middle of the road and feeling so bewildered and unhappy. I could have died staring at the house from which he was never to appear again. I would have given anything to escape looking at their happiness, which only multiplied my torments.'[43]

Fascist theatre concluded its trajectory by giving evidence to needs that hardly corresponded to the imperatives of the régime (it is no coincidence that the shows promoted by the Dopolavoro delle Forze Armate [the Armed Forces Recreational Service] were primarily escapist comedies and music-hall entertainment). While the régime's propaganda machinery continued to deal with war topics, promising more justice, a new redistribution of wealth among people and nations, and a new social and moral order, the playwrights confronted the burning emotional issues that were on most people's minds. Initially they interspersed them with official ideological rhetoric, but eventually these slogans were almost completely supplanted by evocative descriptions of the soldiers' experiences in the trenches and those of their brides, mothers and children suffering at the front-line.

This is to say that the war, depicted in the early stages of Fascist drama as a collective event, had slowly been transfigured into a

merely individual and private matter. The symbolic system of sig-
nification, on which Fascist theatre and drama of the 1920s and
1930s relied so heavily, had entirely collapsed. The supremacy of
Fascist ethics over the real and existential needs of the people had
collapsed. The events of the war had underlined the fact that
human virtues, such as the courage and the strength to endure
sacrifices and suffering (i.e., the 'blood' which the régime had
always placed in opposition to the forces of 'money'), could no
longer suffice to triumph over the enemy's (i.e., the plutocracy's)
indisputable technological superiority.

This situation caused dramatists to change direction in their
plays written after 1942. The authors had basically two choices:
the first was to base their works on values alien to both Fascist culture and propaganda. In this case, the word 'faith', having lost its
polysemous significance, assumed again a merely religious con-
notation and re-established prayer – especially the one addressed
to the 'Madonnina' – as the only possible medium to escape the
atrocities of war and to instil hope for a better future.[44] The alternative was – in a desperate attempt at re-affirming the natural
desire to live – to operate with common values even though they
had by now learned that these values were by no means the
engine of history, nor could they lead to victory: 'It's wonderful to
fight like this', it is stated in *Il labirinto*, a script dated 1942, 'with
no hope of escaping: no hope of winning. The only thing we can
do is to hold out, to hold out to the last.'[45]

NOTES

List of abbreviations

ACS	= *Archivio Centrale dello Stato di Roma*
	= Central State Archives in Rome
SPD	= *Segreteria Particolare del Duce*
	= Special Secretariat of the Duce
MCP	= *Ministero della Cultura Popolare*
	= Ministry of Popular Culture
cens. teatr	= *fondo censura teatrale*
	= censorship archive
C.O.	= *carteggio ordinario*
	= ordinary collection of documents

c.r.   = *carteggio riservato*
         = secret collection of documents
b.   = *busta*
         = envelope
f.   = *fascicolo*
         = file
sf.   = *sottofascicolo*
         = subfile

1. Mussolini in a letter to the actor Gastone Monaldi, founder and director of the company *Il teatro del popolo*, dated 22 June 1927. ACS, SPD, c.o., b. 1018, f. 509.103/1.

2. See Roberto Forges Davanzati, 'Mussolini parla agli scrittori', *Nuova Antologia*, no. 1468, 16 May 1933, p. 191. For a report on the meeting see 'Il Duce partecipa alla celebrazione del cinquantenario della Società Autori ed Editori', *Il Popolo d'Italia*, 29 April 1933.

3. See Pietro Cavallo, *Immaginario e rappresentazione: Il teatro fascista di propaganda*, Rome, 1990, pp. 15-38.

4. 'Se potessi avere/ mille lire al mese, / senza esagerare, sarei certo di trovare / tutta la felicità! / Un modesto impiego, io non ho pretese, / voglio lavorare per poter alfin trovare / tutta la tranquillità! / Una casettina / in periferia, / una mogliettina / giovane e carina, tale e quale come te.' 'If I could earn / one-thousand lira a month / I'm sure it would give me, / – I am not exaggerating – / all the happiness in the world! / A modest job, my demands are small. / I want to work to get in the end / what I need most: my tranquility / a little cottage / in the suburbs, / a young and pretty wife / just like you!' (C. Innocenzi, S. Innocenzi-Sopranzi, 'Mille lire al mese', *Il canzoniere della radio*, n. 5, p. 13). The song was taken from the homonymous film, directed by Massimilano Neufeld.

5. See G. Salvini, 'Spettacoli di masse e 18BL', *Scenario*, no. 5, May 1934, pp. 253ff.

6. L. Zurlo, *Memorie inutili: La censura teatrale nel ventennio*, Rome, 1952, p. 22.

7. M. Federici, *Lunga marcia di ritorno*, ACS, MCP, cens. teatr., f. 8214, 1935

8. M. Gallian, *I tre atti*, ACS, MCP, cens. teatr., f. 6591, 1935.

9. See *Rapporto dell'Ispettorato del Teatro per S. E. il Sottosegretario di Stato*, 11 March 1936, ACS, MCP, cens. teatr., f. 6591 as well as *Relazione di Zurlo sulle rappresentazioni della compagnia De Cruciati al Teatro Eliseo nel Febbraio-Marzo XIV*, in the same file.

10. *Relazione di Zurlo sulle rappresentazioni della compagnia De Cruciati al Teatro Eliseo.*

11. S. Gotta, 'Teatro fascista', *Comoedia*, no. 5, May 1934, p. 6.

12. S. Pivato, *Il teatro di parrocchia: Mondo cattolico e organizzazione del consenso durante il fascismo*, Rome, 1979, p. 7.

13. Zurlo, *Memorie inutili*, p. 186.

14. The report is enclosed in Renata Mughini, *I figli*, ACS, MCP, cens. teatr., f. 9960, 1938.

15. M. Federici, 'Chilometri bianchi', in *Il dramma*, no. 319, 1 December 1939, p. 17.

16. Reale Accademia d'Italia, Fondazione Alessandro Volta, *Convegno di Lettere. 8-14 ottobre 1934: Il teatro drammatico*, Rome, 1935, p. 323.

17. S. d'Amico, *Invito al teatro*, Brescia, 1935, p. 16.

18. Gotta, 'Teatro fascista', p. 7.

19. M. Dorta, *Ritorno*, ACS, MCP, cens. teatr., f. 11074, 1935, p. 24.

20. See G. Buonfino, 'Agitprop e "controcultura" operaia nella repubblica di Weimar', *Primo maggio*, nos. 3-4, February – September 1974, pp. 100-101, 114-115.

21. E. Casini-Ropa, *La danza e l'agit-prop: I teatri-non-teatrali nella cultura tedesca del primo Novecento*, Bologna, 1988, p. 151; C. Hamon, 'Formes dramaturgiques et scéniques du théâtre d'agit-prop', in D. Bablet (ed.), *Le théâtre d'agit-prop de 1917 à 1932*, vol. 2: *L'URSS – Recherches* , Lausanne, 1977, pp. 62-71; B. Lupi, 'L'agit-prop: Une culture politique vécue', *ibid.*, vol. 3: *Allemagne, France, U.S.A, Pologne, Roumanie – recherches*, pp. 40ff.

22. M. Massagrande, *Retaggio di trincea*, ACS, MCP, cens. teatr., f. 1020, 1935, Act I, p. 7.

23. L. Borghi, *La morte degli eroi*, ACS, MCP, cens. teatr., f. 4968, 1937, Act II, pp. 13-15

24. The expression is used in Farinacci's *Redenzione*, which was published in 1927 and staged at the Teatro Manzoni in Milan. The PNF expressed itself rather sceptical about the play, as is apparent from General Carini's letter to Turati, dated 13 December 1927, where he maintained that 'the literary value of the script is faint' and that 'it will do nothing but spread the idea that Farinacci is a rather uneducated and slipshod fellow who likes to improvise his affairs. But in the end it is only Fascism that will lose its face!' ACS, SPD, c. r., b. 42, f. 'Farinacci Roberto', sf. 22.

25. M. Massagrande, *Retaggio di trincea*, Act I, p. 7.

26. B. Zanelli, *Aurora*, ACS, MCP, cens. teatr., f. 7649, 1939, p. 12.

27. L. Zuccaro, G. Amadei, *Alba di rinascita*, ACS, MCP, cens. teatr., f. 4489, 1935, Act III, p. 18.

28. G. Solimene, *Mistica fascista*, ACS, MCP, cens. teatr., f. 760, 1940, p. 111.

29. G. Murri, *Giovinezza*, ACS, MCP, cens. teatr., f. 2489, 1942, p. 36.

30. R. Melani, *I ritornati*, ACS, MCP, cens. teatr., f. 1006, 1934, Act III, p. 2.

31. F. de Robertis, *Ha 'tama*, ACS, MCP, cens. teatr., f. 11032, 1936, Act III, p. 8. De Robertis, some time later, became the director of the film, *Uomini sul fondo*. See Marcia Landy, *Fascism in Film: The Italian Commercial Cinema, 1931-1943*, Princeton, 1986, pp. 222-225.

32. G. Bucciolini-M. Foresi, *Fiamme nere*, ACS, MCP, cens. teatr., f. 4879, 1934, p. 32.

33. L. Bellosi, *L'eroica barriera*, ACS, MCP, cens. teatr., f. 1219, 1937, Act I, p. 5.

34. G. Ruffini, *La scelta*, ACS, MCP, cens. teatr., f. 1224, 1937, p. 19.

35. 'Should I, in my rôle of censor, pretend not to recognise the depressing effect your script produces on the audience? Your play is undoubtedly full of noble and impartial sentiments, but it also presents all the dark nuances of the war.' Thus was Zurlo's charge in a letter to Sergio Motroni, who was the author of *Vento del Nord*, a play that was meant to show, according to the author's Foreword, the 'Italians as they really are', devoid of any 'vain rhetoric'. Zurlo to Motroni, 18 August 1942, ACS, MCP, cens. teatr., f. 2693.

36. See A. Lepre, *Le illusioni la paura la rabbia: Il fronte interno, 1940-1943*, Naples, 1989; A. Lepre, *L'occhio del duce: Gli italiani e la censura di guerra 1940-1943*, Milan, 1992; S. Colarizi, *L'opinione degli Italiani sotto il regime, 1929-1943*, Rome, 1991.

37. GUF was the Fascist student organisation, the *Gruppi universitari fascisti*.

38. F. Pescetto, *Sulla Manica visibilità discreta*, ACS, MCP, cens. teatr., f. 6451, 1941, p. 56.

39. G. M. Giuliani, *Famiglie eroiche*, ACS, MCP, cens. teatr., f. 9711, Act III, p. 1.
40. Stage direction to the third act of Giuliani, *Famiglie eroiche*.
41. Report by Zurlo, s.d., attached to the script by C. Magliulo, *Ritorneranno*, ACS, MCP, cens. teatr., f. 9977, 1943.
42. Zurlo to Pavolini, 6 February 1942, ACS, MCP, cens. teatr., f. 3993. The answer given by the Minister is of some interest: 'Your observations are right, especially those about the bombings (indeed, in a work of art they are more touching than in reality). It is all a question of the right measure. Generally speaking, I do not object to the fact that war is given a direct representation in the play. One must take into account that the audience, especially after having been shown the horrors of war in those German documentary films, has become less sensitive in these matters. In a way, everyone has become accustomed to them.' Pavolini to Zurlo, 9 February 1942, *ibidem*.
43. G. Ammirata-L. Capece, *La rinuncia*, ACS, MCP, cens. teatr., f. 5048, 21941, p. 20.
44. This play by a front-line soldier who had fought in the African War employed the form of a prayer as a medium to connect civilians and soldiers. It was meaningfully dedicated 'To the Virgin Mary, so that she may protect all the soldiers' (see C. Basilico, *La preghiera dei piccoli*, ACS, MCP, cens. teatr., f. 5271, 1943). Another example of a play using the prayer format was A. Lenzi's *Ma se brilla una stella* (ACS, MCP, cens. teatr., f. 2590, 1943). It is about a large rural family whose father left for the front and never returned home. It was awarded a prize in a competition organised by the Federal Headquarters of the GIL of Florence.
45. A. Angeli Coarelli, *Il labirinto*, ACS, MCP, cens. teatr., f. 2831, 1942, p. 46.

7

Mussolini's 'Theatre of the Masses'

Mario Verdone
Translated by Isabella Madìa

Theatre for the 'New Age'

It is well known that the theatre policy of the Fascist régime aimed at re-educating the population, and particularly the younger generation, by offering them new types of theatrical performances that were in line with the 'new spirit' of the times. Authors were encouraged to write plays imbued with Fascist sentiments, and theatre directors were given the means to develop new staging methods in order to present these dramas to a wide array of audiences.

Part of this drive towards a 'mass-theatre', initiated in 1929, was the institution of so-called *Carri di Tespi*, circus-like organisations that were to perform plays and operas in remote or small cities, which in the past had been excluded from the circuits of major or minor touring companies. Other forms of reaching new audiences in the lower strata of society were attempted by instituting 'Theatrical Saturdays' (*sabato teatrale*), where performances were given at very low prices, or by encouraging the foundation of amateur companies run by the Opera Nazionale Dopolavoro, the national agency for after-work entertainments.

In order to promote the idea of education through theatre, an Experimental Theatre of the Fascist Associations of University Students (Teatro Sperimentale dei Gruppi Universitari Fascisti) was created in Florence. Young authors were encouraged by national drama competitions (the *littoriali*) and by the creation of *Teatri-GUF*, in analogy with the *Cine-GUF*, to write and produce a body of revolutionary, Fascist drama. However, neither the theatre nor the film section of the GUF fulfilled the hopes the régime had placed in them. They managed, on the whole, to remain independent of political influences and to pay little more than lip-service to their ideological mission.

As far as the professional theatre world in Italy was concerned, it is a well-known fact that it was entirely governed by commercial interests and by the conservative tastes of the predominantly middle-class audiences. The acting profession did not possess any public training institutions and was often suffocating in the age-old formulae of histrionic rhetorics. In order to ameliorate this situation, in 1935 the Accademia d'Arte Drammatica was created in Rome by Silvio d'Amico, the leading critic of his time and certainly not a Fascist. This institution injected new energies into the Italian theatre. It was here that Vittorio Gassman, Alessandro Brissoni, Ettore Giannini, Luigi Squarzina, Orazio Costa, Luciano Salce, Vito Pandolfi and other leading actors and directors of the post-war period received their training.

Apart from fostering a new type of acting, the régime also showed an interest in promoting a modern art theatre. At that time, there were only two theatres in Italy that operated on a line similar to the Moscow Art Theatre or the Munich Künstlertheater. Mussolini repeatedly showed his esteem for Anton Giulio Bragaglia and gave public funding to his Teatro degli Indipendenti and, through the Confederazione Artisti e Professionisti, financial assistance to build the Teatro delle Arti in Via Sicilia in Rome.[1] The Teatro d'Arte of Luigi Pirandello was also given generous support by the Fascist régime. However, none of the many new plays that were performed in Pirandello's theatre had anything in common with Fascism,[2] whilst Bragaglia's cosmopolitan repertoire included Brecht's *Threepenny Opera* and, at the time of international 'sanctions' against Fascism, plays by Shaw, Wilde, Wilder, O'Neill, Synge, O'Casey and Yeats (pretending they were all 'Irish' or 'of Irish origin'). He also presented Futurist, Dadaist, Surrealist or Expressionist authors in his theatre, rather than performing dramas with nationalist or patriotic tendencies.[3]

Two Fascist playwrights: Forzano and Pastonchi

As regards the professional authors, the most successful writers (amongst whom was Aldo de Benedetti, a man of Jewish extraction) concentrated on romantic comedies and on *grotteschi*, which had nothing to do with the new political situation. When Luigi Pirandello accepted to join (formally) the Partito Nazionale

Fascista (probably in order to avoid losing public subsidies for his Teatro d'Arte), it was hoped that his works would be in keeping with the new political climate. However, not one line of the theatrical writings by Pirandello makes the least allusion to Fascism.

An author who undoubtedly represented Fascist theatre *par excellence* was Giovacchino Forzano (1883-1970). On 18 December 1930, the Teatro Argentina in Rome staged the play *Campo di maggio*, jointly written by Forzano and Benito Mussolini.[4] Vittorio Mussolini (son of Benito) said to film critic Dario Zanelli: 'My father enjoyed working with Forzano on theatrical projects, because theatre belonged to his cultural background and therefore interested him more than movies'.[5]

In 1929, Mussolini expressed the idea of writing a drama about the end of Napoleon and gave Forzano several sheets of notes. He trusted this writer, who was the author of traditional dramas with pseudo-historical settings. They were not particularly refined by our standards, but well-liked by the public of the time. *Campo di maggio* was a drama of anti-parliamentary propaganda. The Duce used to intervene, both with suggestions and then with amendments to the text that Forzano was submitting to him for approval, as he was writing the play. The result of this collaboration, signed by Forzano alone, who had faithfully executed the Duce's instructions, was published in 1931 (it was only in the French, English and German translations that Mussolini agreed to have his name appear as co-author on the title-page[6]).

The play was a major success in many Italian theatres: 'Applause began early, after the first dialogue; it was warm and persistent and continued until the last scene', wrote Renato Simoni after the performance given by the Compagnia Za Bum in Milano at the Teatro Olimpia. He continues: 'This drama shows the most touching part of Napoleon's life: the tragedy of the hero, when his contemporaries lose the sense of his greatness'.[7] The 'conflict between a giant and the pigmies' runs throughout the play, but is particularly emphasised in the scenes depicting Napoleon's departure from Elba, his landing in France, his enthusiastic reception by the soldiers and the people, his defeat at Waterloo and the fight between Parliament and Emperor.

From this time on, Gioacchino Forzano was the Fascist playwright most frequently staged in Italy. He was also appointed director of the above-mentioned *Carri di Tespi* initiative.

On 15 December 1931, the Teatro Lirico in Milano staged *Villafranca*, another patriotic drama by Forzano, dedicated to the memory of the deceased brother of the Duce, Arnaldo Mussolini. Again, the drama was initiated by the Duce who, after the success of *Campo di maggio*, had continued his exchange of opinions on the theatre with Forzano and had suggested a play dealing with the political manoeuvres against Camillo Cavour, the hero of the *risorgimento* and first Prime Minister of the unified Italy.[8]

Another major success was *Giulio Agricola*, premièred on 27 April 1939 at the Teatro Argentina in Rome in the presence of Mussolini. In this *pièce à clef*, Forzano extolled the greatness of Caesar and, by analogy, that of Mussolini. The Emperor's grandiose schemes to reclaim swamp-land and to cultivate newly conquered territories in Africa bear more than a superficial resemblance to Italy's colonisation of Abyssinia, whereas his generous treatment of treacherous patricians and his pardoning of enemies who deserve capital punishment alluded to the Duce's 'magnanimous' predisposition.

All stage designs of the productions mentioned above (in the theatre as well as in their film versions) were the work of Antonio Valente, a regular collaborator of Forzano's. For the Opera Nazionale Dopolavoro he built the *Carri di Tespi*, and his film décors include *Camicia nera*, directed by Giovacchino Forzano and shot in Cinecittà in 1933. In 1943 and 1944, they worked together on the film *Piazza San Sepolcro*, which was intended to become a commemoration of the creation of the Fascist Party. However the film was never distributed, possibly not even completed.[9]

The poet Francesco Pastonchi (1874-1953) was also engaged in writing drama during Mussolini's régime. His *Simma* was written in 1935 and was an experiment in Fascist poetic theatre, a kind of tragedy of supermen and heroes, written in high-sounding language and rhetorical hyperbole, not dissimilar to the style of Gabriele d'Annunzio. Pastonchi was an old-fashioned 'poet' rather than a man of the theatre (he is not even mentioned in the *Enciclopedia dello Spettacolo* edited by Silvio d'Amico).

Simma was inspired by the cities that the new Italy was to erect in an imaginary and Utopian future. Pontia is a mountain town built by the visionary architect Pietro Brea, with a Temple that should defy the centuries. Although the play is set in a mechanised world, constructed in the style of the Futurist architect Antonio Sant'Elia and bravely addresses avant-gardistic themes, the poetic language spun around the rickety plot (the exiled Simma returns to Pontia, when the inhabitants are about to inaugurate the Temple; he foretells its collapse and goes mad) is extremely distant from Futurism. The 'tragedy' was given a rather controversial reception. The Fascist leadership did not like its symbolism – which they regarded as nebulous and conceited – despite the fact that the Temple of Pontia boasted four *fasci littori* (the well-known symbols of ancient Rome, adopted by Fascists). The drama expresses desire for transcendence, exaltation of a creed, of a new political and social order. The symbolic Temple of Art is due to collapse, and old Brea has taken the initiative to have it replaced with a new one. But Simma does not believe in the project and in vain tries to dissuade the others from it. Finally, a new hero takes over: Aeli, an inspired, pure, artist, who is not looking for perfection and will combine tradition with modernism. The text is full of tags and *sententiae* (for example, 'Everything comes from the people and goes back to the people' or 'The time of the tragedy is today, and perhaps tomorrow'). Even so, under the rhetorical bombast and poetic bathos the author's message remains cryptic, unclear and confused. When the play was first performed (on 27 January 1936), Renato Simoni appreciated the religious sentiments expressed in the production, but found it otherwise to be of little dramatic value.[10]

Theatre of the Masses Italian style: 18 BL

The most notorious production of a play tailored to fulfil all key criteria Mussolini demanded of the new 'theatre of the masses', was *18 BL* by the film director Alessandro Blasetti (who also shot the Fascist film *Vecchia guardia* in 1935). *18 BL* was indeed theatre for the masses and theatre of the masses, inspired by Josef von Fielitz's *Spartacus* spectacle in Leipzig and Evreinov's *Storming of the Winter Palace* in St Petersburg (both performed in 1920). It was produced in 1934 by the music festival Maggio Musicale Fiorentino and presented in an open-air location in Florence, in the park Le Cascine.[11]

What does '18 BL' mean? It was the logo of a Fiat truck that had carried soldiers to the river Piave (just as the Parisian taxis had conveyed French soldiers to the Marne). The trucks had also been employed to transport the Fascists on their 'March' on Rome (which was not, in fact, a walk on foot but a journey on Heavy Goods Vehicles). Alessandro Blasetti, who a year previously had shot the much-appreciated war film *1860*, had turned the Florence production into a 'mass battle', excavating trenches and building earthworks in the area between Le Cascine and Albereta del-l'Isolotto. Engines were roaring, muskets and machine-guns were crackling, bombs and mortars exploded. One could hear the *Marcia del Piave* (a song from the First World War), the stanzas of *Giovinezza* (a well-known Fascist song) and music by Renzo Massarini. The words of some actors (among whom Ugo Ceseri) were delivered through loud-speakers. The script had been written by a large group of writers and playwrights: Luigi Bonelli, Gherardo Gherardi, Nicola Lisi, Riccardo Melani, Alessandro Pavolini, Corrado Sofia, Giorgio Venturini, Luciano de Feo. There must have been insufficient consultation between them, for the resulting script lacked coherence and all too often amounted to little more than a collage of independent scenes to be acted out in various locations.

Why was the performance such a prime example of 'theatre of the masses'? Mainly because large numbers of soldiers and farmers acted out the drama on the vast terrain near the river Arno, in front of an even larger audience of approximately twenty-thousand spectators. The national and regional federations of the P.N.F. had organised collective trips (this was the time of 'trains for the people') and had recruited spectators in several Tuscan cities and villages. I, myself, went to Florence with other students (*balilla* and *avanguardisti*) from Siena, my hometown. During the performance, when it had become dark, and military searchlights were being switched on (as well as lights on boats moored on the river Arno), there was a terrible dust storm and, to be honest, one could not see or understand very much, especially if one had been allocated one of the cheaper seats. It is therefore not astonishing that the audience showed little enthusiasm after this 'exemplary' mass-spectacle, and that the negative reception in the Fascist press[12] persuaded the authorities to relinquish the plans for more high-flying productions in the 'theatre-for-the-masses' mould.

NOTES

1. See Alberto Cesare Alberti, *Il teatro nel fascismo: Pirandello e Bragaglia. Documenti inediti negli archivi italiani*, Rome, 1974.
2. See Richard A. Sogliuzzo, *Luigi Pirandello, Director: The Playwright in the Theatre*, Metuchen/NJ 1982 and Alessandro d'Amico & Alessandro Tinterri (eds), *Pirandello Capocomico: La Compagnia del Teatro d'Arte di Roma, 1925-1928*, Palermo, 1987.

3. See the fundamental study by Alberto Cesare Alberti, Sandra Bevere and Paola di Giulio, *Il Teatro Sperimentale degli Indipendenti (1923-1936)*, Rome, 1984, and my writings on Bragaglia: *Anton Giulio Bragaglia*, Città di Castello, 1965; 'Anton Giulio Bragaglia', in Pontus Hulten (ed.), *Futurismo e Futurismi*, Milano, 1986; *I fratelli Bragaglia*, Roma, 1991; *La casa d'arte Bragaglia, 1918-1930*, Rome, 1992.

4. See Renato Simoni's eulogising review in the *Corriere della Sera* of 30 December 1930, reprinted in his *Trent'anni di cronaca drammatica*, Turin, 1951-1960, vol. 3, pp. 372-373.

5. Renzo Renzi (ed.), *Il cinema dei dittatori: Mussolini, Stalin, Hitler*, Bologna, 1992, pp. 43-47.

6. See *Les cents jours (Campo di maggio): Trois actes et treize tableaux tirés d'un scénario de M. Benito Mussolini par M. Giovacchino Forzano*, Paris, 1932; *Napoleon: The Hundred Days. A Play by Benito Mussolini and Giovacchino Forzano*, London, 1932; *Hundert Tage (Campo di maggio). Drei Akte in neun Bildern, von Benito Mussolini und G. Forzano*, Berlin, 1933. For the Italian text of Mussolini's plays see *Mussolini autore drammatico, con facsimili di autografi inediti*, Florence, 1954.

7. See Renato Simoni, *Trent'anni di cronaca drammatica*, vol. 3, p. 372.

8. Both plays were also turned into films, *Villafranca* in 1933 and *Campo di maggio* in 1935. One of the scenes of *Villafranca*, after being published in the magazine *Signal*, no. 17, December 1940, was reprinted in the chapter 'Mussolini scrittore di teatro' in Renzi, *Il cinema dei dittatori*, pp. 67-9.

9. Valente also built several film studios, as well as the building of the Centro Sperimentale di Cinematografia. Several of his sketches for Forzano's plays can be found in the volumes of Barbera Edizioni in Florence, who published the texts of *Campo di maggio* and *Villafranca*. See also Giovanni Isgrò, *Antonio Valente: Architetto scenografo e la cultura materiale del teatro in Italia fra le due guerre*, Palermo, 1988.

10. See Simoni's review published in the *Corriere della Sera* on 28 January 1936 and reprinted in *Trent'anni di cronaca drammatica*, vol. 4, pp. 270-2.

11. See Mario Verdone, 'Spettacolo massa,' in *Futurismo oggi*, nos. 9-12, 1986, and 'Spettacolo politico e "18 BL",' in Renzo de Felice (ed.), *Futurismo, cultura e politica*, Turin, 1988. See also the chapter '"18BL" di Alessandro Blasetti: Un spettacolo di massa' in Franca Angelini, *Teatro e spettacolo nel primo novecento*, Rome, 1988, and Silvio d'Amico, *Invito al teatro*, Rome, 1935, pp. 185-94.

12. See Pietro Cavallo, *Immaginario e rappresentazione: Il teatro fascista di propaganda*, Rome, 1990, pp. 27-8, 221.

8

Censorship in Nazi Germany
The Influence of the Reich's Ministry of Propaganda on German Theatre and Drama, 1933-1945

Barbara Panse
Translated by Meg Mumford

The Theatre Section of the Reich's Ministry of Propaganda

On 13 March 1933, the Reich's Ministry for Enlightenment of the People and for Propaganda (REPP) was founded. Only one month later the Theatre Section of the Department for Propaganda came into being, and in August 1933 Rainer Schlösser was appointed to the post of *Reichsdramaturg*. The Reich's Theatre Act, passed in May 1934, formed the legal basis for his work as Chief Inspector and Censor. However, it was Goebbels who assumed ultimate responsibility for all the German theatres: he was granted the legal authority to intervene in their repertoire and to order or ban performances.[1] Within the space of a year and in quick succession, the pre-requisites for controlling the German theatres were established.

By 1934 Goebbels had managed to rid himself of all rivals. Even his strongest competitors, Rosenberg and Göring, were not capable of disputing the decisions of the Reich's Minister for Propaganda (Göring controlled the Prussian State Theatres of Berlin, Wiesbaden and Kassel, for whom all the laws, decrees and censorship regulations passed by the REPP were likewise valid). Goebbels' instructions[2] and his diary records[3] as well as the memoranda of the Theatre Section reveal the wrangling over respective areas of responsibility by individual Reich's governors or important local Party figures. The records verify that most of the clashes in the battle for power and spheres of influence occurred in the first two years of the régime. After that, Goebbels' supremacy was unchallenged. The disputes that arose in the ensuing period amongst the inner circle of NSDAP leaders concerned individual plays (for example, *The Sword* by Curt Langenbeck[4]) and a number of authors (such as Eberhard Wolfgang Möller[5]). In terms of theatre politics, however, the disputes were hardly of any consequence, merely serving to confirm and strengthen the path already taken towards rigid control and censorship of the theatre repertoire through the REPP.

Goebbels' rapid and sustained success is also attributable to the theatre managers, directors and *dramaturgs*, who immediately after 30 January 1933 adapted to the new balance of power. All remaining theatre managers[6] bowed down to pressure from above and followed, without showing open resistance, the directives of the NSDAP's local leading figures, thanks to whom their posts had been confirmed. Even in the first months after the so-called 'seizure of power', while the Theatre Section of the Department for Propaganda was still being constructed, many of these managers already practised a type of self-censorship and celebrated the Führer and his Party in speeches of homage. The majority of those who were dismissed in the first months of 1933 (and were not of Jewish ancestry, or did not belong to the Communist or Social Democrat Party) found a new engagement at other theatres in Germany, often as soon as the very next season. And after suffering the shock of dismissal, they went along, probably all the more keenly, with the political line demanded by the Nazi authorities. When in the summer of 1933 the Theatre Section began to operate in Berlin, the theatres' seasonal plans had to a great extent already been adapted to the new situation: plays that could possibly incur disapproval – owing to their political or aesthetic qualities, or because their authors were known to be Jewish – had been withdrawn by the theatre managers from their repertoire. Consequently, the Reich's Minister for Propaganda and his officers had no difficulty at all in submitting the theatres, who had given such evident proof of their compliance, to the apparatus of control and direction adopted in the interim.

Within a year, the REPP's Theatre Section had found the practical ways and means – which were used from then on until the closure of the theatres (on 31 August 1944) – to bring the repertory, as quickly and inconspicuously as possible, in line with the requirements of the political concerns of the day. Control, direction and censorship instructions were put into motion and carried out via the Stage Publishers' Union, the publishing companies, the authors and theatre managers. In addition to this vertical plane, in which the Theatre Section operated as the leading authority of directives, there was a horizontal plane of action, where the inter-connected and interdependent institutions and individuals con-trolled and denounced each other. The Theatre Section supported this interlinked system of control for two reasons: firstly, its own rôle as the supreme authority of censorship remained to a large extent hidden from the uninitiated public; and secondly, through these channels it could receive new information about the authors kept under surveillance and about their plays.

The REPP imposed the rule that before each season all theatre programmes had to be sent to Berlin for assessment. Thereby a method was found, as simple as it was effective, of keeping tight control over all theatre managers in the government's realm of power. Year after year, the censors in Berlin examined the pro-gramme lists submitted; neither the far-flung theatres in the remote provinces, nor the well-known theatres of the Reich's cap-ital city were excluded. Amongst the first to be removed were plays by tolerated or acceptable authors, which due to internal or external political considerations were no longer deemed to be appropriate for presentation. The extant programme lists provide no indications that a theatre ever attempted to include a work in its submitted plan by an author known to be banned. Only occa-sionally did theatre managers venture to make timid inquiries about whether this or that play might again be performed. How-ever, after receiving a clear 'piece of advice' from the Theatre Sec-tion, none of the theatre managers dared insist further!

The publishing houses specialising in dramatic literature pro-vided an important link between the theatres and authors and were, in turn, despotically organised within the Stage Publishers Union. The Union functioned as a second instrument for dis-creetly guiding and censoring the theatre repertoire from a central observation point. Following the instructions received from the Theatre Section, the Union allocated certain plays only to selected theatres. Due to internal political considerations these were either not allowed to be performed in large cities or only in a particular region. In addition, the Union sanctioned both the textual correc-tion, undertaken in accordance with the orders received from Rainer Schlösser and his officers, as well as the production of new versions. In the end, it was this organisation which held ultimate responsibility for checking that only the censored play versions went to the theatres.

The implementation of concrete censorship instructions from the Theatre Section was also delegated to the publishers. They passed on the REPP's comments to their authors (to change certain text passages, for example, or to completely rewrite a play) and conveyed to the respective theatres any advice on performance matters (e.g., to withdraw or give particular emphasis to certain passages from the questionable play).

Only in a few cases did the Theatre Section send its orders, formulated as 'comments', directly to the authors. In addition, it was usually only in correspondence addressed to prominent authors that reasons were given, and these in a more or less roundabout fashion, for why the play under question did not meet the political or aesthetic standards and how it should be rewritten. If internal or external political considerations dictated that the drama was no longer 'performable', the prominent authors were instructed to withdraw it from the market. In cases where the author was less well-known, the ban simply went into force. In the extant files of the Theatre Section there is no indication that an author refused to comply with the 'requests' of the censorship authorities in Berlin. On the contrary, a number of authors rewrote their plays several times in order to adapt them to the changed political situation. Even so, in the majority of cases, even these concoctions did not escape the censor.

The influence of the censor on the repertoire of German theatres

The result of this censorship practice was a radical break with existing theatre traditions and one with far-reaching effects. In several theatres, approximately half of the plays that had had a firm place in the repertoire prior to 1933 were banned.[7] Two dates mark the development of severe measures by the Nazi apparatus of control: the period after 30 January 1933 and that after 1 September 1939. From 1933 onwards, all authors and plays which, so it was claimed, did not fit the National Socialist world view, were removed from the repertoire. Aesthetically unpopular and politically undesirable texts alongside all Jewish authors were put on the 'Index'. After the outbreak of the war, dramas by authors from the so-called 'Enemy Countries' were also forbidden.[8]

How restrictive these theatre politics were can be gauged by two interrelated features: the drastic alteration of the programmes after 1933 and the tough judgement of all plays by the Theatre Section. Not only contemporary drama, but also works from antiquity right up to the twentieth century were subject to the criterion of ideological usefulness. These assessments were crucial for selecting opportune dramatists and for determining the ideological-propagandist rôle of plays in the Nazi theatre repertoire.

In the period prior to 1933, the National Socialists were already labelling the contemporary leftist and liberal drama as 'degenerate, Jew-infested asphalt art'. It was a declared aim of the programme planners after 1933 to expel these contemporary authors from Germany or to silence them, to ban their plays once and for all. Within a few months, this goal was achieved: barring a few exceptions, the German-speaking drama of the 1920s and early 1930s had been 'eradicated' from the German stage.

How brutal this blood-letting actually was, is illuminated in the following statistics compiled by Thomas Eicher:[9] The performances of German works written in the 1920s and early 1930s constituted, percentage-wise, the greatest part of the repertoire during the period 1929 to 1933. Their share per season amounted on average to 30 per cent of the total programme. After the 'takeover', and by the first 'National Socialist' season of 1933/1934 it sank to 5.56 per cent due to the prohibition of numerous works. These plays were particularly hit by the Nazis' censorship measures. How radical the break brought about by the ban was, can be gleaned from the statistics of the first seasons after the take-over: in the second half of the season 1932/1933 (after 30 January 1933) the share amounted to almost 16 per cent (191 performances); over that entire season it just reached 35 per cent (473 performances), the highest figure in the period under investigation. Beginning with the season 1933/1934 (5.56 per cent) the percentage share in the total programme sank continuously: in 1937/1938 it fell short of the 2 per cent mark (48 performances) and in 1943/1945 it reached its absolute low at 1.49 per cent (25 performances).

The place of the outlawed was now taken up by 'patriotic' and *völkisch* authors, who to some extent were already represented in the repertoire of the Weimar Republic. The performance share of their plays rose considerably in the ensuing years: incorporating the dialect folk plays, farces and comedies, it stood on average at

58 per cent in the entire programmes of all theatres. After 1933, the share of 'accepted' contemporary German-language drama doubled in comparison to the seasons from 1929 to 1933.

A characteristic feature of this drama is its confinement to historical subject matter. Apart from a few exceptions, from 1934 onwards none of the 'serious drama' allowed to be performed was set in the present. Several explanations can be found for this phenomenon. In the understanding of all Nazi ideologists, contemporary drama was causally linked to the Führer State, and its producers were envisaged as bringing about the 'New Age'. Every play was to uphold the professed ideological models and principles, and to either instil or reinforce them in the consciousness of the German people. Historical conflicts and situations were to be portrayed in such a manner that they could be seen as mile stones on the way to the creation of the German Nation State. Additionally, the centre of attention had to be those mythically transfigured and often tragically foundering Führer characters. They were supposed to have been a driving force in the unification of Germany and the struggle against the 'racially inferior' foreign peoples and States. These characters, who represented central figures in German national history, were placed in a paradigmatic situation that could be used to legitimise the National Socialist claim to power. For only now, according to the omnipresent message, would the 'mission' of the exemplary Führer characters and the connected fate of the German nation be completed.

However, the closer the historical events depicted in the plays came to the immediate present, the more difficult it was for the authors to invent a believable version of that favoured monumental hero. It is not any economic or social position that pre-determines the hero to become a fighter; rather it is sheer will power or commitment to the concept of the 'supra-individual' – that is, to the race, the people, the nation – that forces him into action. All attempts to portray the complicated turmoil of the post-war period or of the Weimar Republic had, by 1934/1935 at the latest, been declared failures by the Theatre Section and were subsequently stalled and prohibited. This was due to the fact that the playwrights had not sufficiently exorcised social reality from their texts, in the main written shortly before or after Hitler's take-over. Although they distorted historical events by giving them an ideological gloss, some of the actual historical reality was still discernible and could be interpreted in its political significance for the course of the most recent German history. They presented, at least, real people of the time, individuals who, although they acted in exemplary fashion, were not mythically transfigured heroes (and the audience members could always, by means of their own personal experiences, verify the truthfulness of the plays by comparing them with the real events and people depicted in the works). Moreover, given such themes, the authors were unable to avoid bringing the political opponent onto the stage. Albeit distorted for demagogic purposes, the enemy's triumphs, aims and slogans were nevertheless reported. Herein lay the central problem with these plays, for after 1933 political opposition was no longer allowed in Germany. The anti-Nazis of the late 1920s and early 1930s had been murdered, had fled abroad, sat in concentration camps, or, and this was the most important factor, had gone over to Hitler's side. Why remind us – so went the argumentation of the censors – that in the years of turmoil Germans had fought one another? Why recall that in the fifteen years of the Weimar Republic the German people were divided amongst themselves by deep political trenches? In terms of propaganda nothing could be gained from it. Now the majority of the German population stood united as never before, behind their Führer (less so behind his Party). German industry flourished – which manifested itself in full employment – and in foreign politics Adolf Hitler scored one success after the other. Through the propagation of the 'national community', every reminder of the previously ubiquitous class struggle had been silenced. Why now, of all times, open up old wounds?

From 1935 onwards, even the plays about the First World War by conservative or National Socialist authors only rarely passed the censor. Written in many cases before 1933, they told of the violence of war, the horror of the battles, and the heroic courage of individual soldiers faced with death. These dramas did not conceal that the Great War had demanded a terrible toll of lives (two million German soldiers had been killed or were regarded as missing); that the period afterwards was determined by post-war chaos, 'the diktat of Versailles', inflation and world economic crisis. This approach no longer fitted in with the ideological plan of the programme directors, who knew that, with regard to politics and propaganda, the Führer now had other objectives. In 1936, universal conscription was introduced and the Third Reich started to mobilise. Hitler was already planning the next war. From now on, plays which glorified the war in a new, symbolic, way were called for: the focal point was not the personal fate of the individual soldier, but rather the 'supra-individual' sacrifice for the people's community.

The Theatre Section also banned or censored all plays which referred to the immediate present, in which Adolf Hitler or other well-known leaders in the NSDAP as well as so-called martyrs of the 'movement' (e.g., Horst Wessel) were mentioned by name or made an appearance as dramatis personae. In addition to this, neither uniforms of the Wilhelmine Empire, the Reichswehr, the SA, the SS nor the Wehrmacht could be worn on stage. Barring the first two seasons after 1933, these prohibition orders were rigidly administered.

An exception to this rule was Dietrich Loder's drama *Boom* (*Konjunktur*) subtitled 'Comedy of the Revolution 1933'. The play begins in January 1933 before Hitler's appointment as German Chancellor (30 January 1933). It is then set in March after the Reichstag Election (5 March 1933) and ends around the time of the Enabling Act (23 March 1933). *Boom* is a scornful satire of the so-called 'March victims', who are all presented as opportunistic members of the upper class, only interested in their own economic advantage. In addition, a Jewish 'man of letters' enters the scene, a speculator, who at the end of the play is put under 'protective custody'. At the centre of attention is a positive hero in the figure of a selfless SA officer, to whom the fate of Germany is everything and his own career (in the civil service) nothing. *Boom* was first performed on 19 June 1933 at the Munich Residenztheater, and in the season 1933/1934 it was performed fifty times. Barely two years later, on 2 January 1936, it was again produced, this time at the Saarbrücken Stadttheater; after that the play was presented once more in the season 1936/1937.

The 'new' drama of the Nazi period

Many of the plays by new authors that were admitted into the repertoire after 1933 gave expression to the political objectives of the Nazis. Excessive nationalism, glorification of war and military death, rejection of democracy and a declaration of belief in the Führer State were characteristic of these 'serious dramas'. Many similarities in the choice of thematic emphasis can be discerned in the most frequently performed plays. Ideological concepts such as the 'Führer Idea', heroic sacrifice for the 'people's community' and the inevitability of the 'racial struggle' played a major rôle. Historical dramas that put the conflict between the Reich and the Vatican at the centre of the scenic debate took pride of place. The hegemonic strivings of the Catholic Church, which over the centuries had obstructed the establishment of the 'Greater German Reich' – the final historical aim of all Germans – were subjected to pillory. In many works, 'Lutheran' is assigned to the positively regarded pair of concepts Germanic/irrational, while on the other hand 'Catholic' stands for Romance-speaking/rational.

Plays such as *Thor's Guest* (62 performances) by Otto Erler or *Uta von Naumburg* by Felix Dhünen (109 performances) describe the Teutons' conflict-ridden conversion to Christianity. Both authors extol the struggle for freedom of the proud Germanic warriors against fanatical Catholic priests. Führer characters, all of them experienced fighters, free from the torments of doubt are, thanks to their racial qualities, victorious over the degenerate representatives of Rome, or willingly sacrifice their own lives. Other playwrights turned historical defeats into victories of 'the people'. The plays *Gregor and Heinrich* (twenty performances) and *Heroic Passions* (seventeen performances) by Erwin Guido Kolbenheyer, both set in the Middle-Ages, present Führer characters who fearlessly challenge the power of the Catholic Church. In the former, the German Emperor Heinrich IV, after a long battle and terrible casualties, 'triumphs' in Canossa over his adversary Pope Gregor VII. With this victory, young Germany – so runs the author's message – had for the first time broken the hegemony of Rome. In the second play, the protagonist Giordano Bruno publically opposes the intellectual supremacy of the Catholic Church. An exemplary Führer figure, Bruno heroically sacrifices his own life for his convictions. In doing so, according to Kolbenheyer, Bruno gained the all-important 'spiritual victory' over his opponents.

Not historical figures, but mythical Führer characters, are central in other dramas. A 'rider' in Heinrich Zerkaulen's eponymous play, *Der Reiter* (ninety-nine performances), rescues a German girl from certain death at the stake. This theme emerges in many works. Naïve girls and women of 'natural' femininity (character types that were declared specifically German) are always at the mercy of witch hunters. In contrast to the pathological and perverted henchmen, the Führer character, Paroli, offers a 'shining light'-type figure. In Eberhard Wolfgang Möller's *The Franconian Game of Dice* (nineteen performances) it is likewise a rider, though this time in black armour, who prevents the execution of Austrian farmers at a time when the Counter-Reformation was beginning to flag and the farmers were to be forcibly converted to the 'true faith' (Catholicism). They are in a hopeless situation until a Führer is found in their midst. When he enters the scene, the day of judgement has come for the Papist Kaiser and his followers. Irrespective of whether the battle is lead against fanatical Catholic priests or against secular rulers, these mythical Führer characters always act in accordance with a 'higher law'. In Zerkaulen's play, the Kaiser grants the rider the authority to act in the name of the Reich against injustice. In Möller's drama, there is no longer anyone who stands above the almighty Führer figure. He alone embodies law and order.

In other lands and ages too, model heroes struggle or beat the drum for the idea of a great 'Reich'. In *Isabella of Spain* by Hermann Heinz Ortner (ninety-four performances) and *Thomas Paine* by Hanns Johst (seventy-four performances) they ultimately die a sacrificial death for their national ideals. Ortner also condemns the Catholic Church, which wants to subordinate an entire country – in this case Spain – to its political influence. The Church's instrument of power is the Holy Inquisition, and it is this tool that Rome uses to pressurise the Spanish Queen in 1492. When a young aristocrat appears at court, the power struggle enters a new phase. Only one thought inspires this ardent patriot: to conquer the Americas for the glory of Spain. It is the mission of the State, according to the ideology represented here, to subjugate foreign lands. Ortner shows that Rome fails to recognise this 'natural law' of State politics, and that instead it attempts to assert its particular, religiously based, interests. The intrigues of the Church dash the hero's greatest hopes, and in the end he chooses sacrificial death. Before doing so, however, the Führer figure indignantly rejects the help of a Jewish merchant. The protagonist is presented to the spectator as an heroic example: he would rather die than play a part in the shady dealings of 'world Jewry'.

In Hanns Johst's play, Thomas Paine is the ideological Führer of the American War of Independence. He, too, upholds the notions of colonisation and conquest. With the propagandistic slogan, 'America needs land', he seeks to mobilise the exhausted and hungry insurgent army so that they venture to take the path into the unknown, to victory or death. His appeal to faith and comradeship forges the 'racially worthy citizens' (*völkisch wertvollen Glieder*) of America into a nation. In this play, the life of the Führer character also ends tragically; but his mission is fulfilled: the 'national idea' has come to fruition.

Another theme favoured in Nazi drama is the fate of the exemplary German Führer figure abroad. Many plays foreground the idea of a German hero tragically foundering in a foreign world that is hostile, corrupt, decadent and immoral. These 'leaders without followers' are stylised as visionary precursors and pioneers, whose mission is 'to relieve the northern race, exhausted by centuries of struggling to assert themselves',[10] but who fail in their preordained task.

This ideological thrust is exemplified in plays such as *The Minister's Fall* by Eberhard Wolfgang Möller (thirty-four performances), *Struensee* by Otto Erler (thirty-four performances) and *Petersburg Crowning* by Friedrich Wilhelm Hymnen (twenty-one performances). In *Struensee*, the eponymous doctor hero is unsuccessful as a minister in Denmark, just as the fortress civil engineer Münnich does not achieve his self-devised purpose. The idea being conveyed here is that the reformation of the Russian State and the restructuring of its economy along the lines of the German example cannot be accomplished by one individual alone. Both protagonists become tragic martyrs for the people's cause and ultimately die.

The situation is somewhat different in Friedrich Bethge's *The Veteran's March* (fifty-five performances). The drama is set in Napoleonic Russia, and the sovereign Führer character is a Prussian officer. Through his realistic decision-making – testimony to the fact that he was trained in the Prussian State under Frederick the Great – the Governor-General of St Petersburg forces corrupt Russian ministers and large-scale landowners to their knees. For the simple Russian soldiers, who in the war against Napoleon were reduced to cripples, and who are now provided neither with honour nor a bearable existence, the Prussian becomes a Führer, the bearer of hope. Bethge's message to the spectator is: only through Prussian discipline can the terrible conditions in the vast realm of Russia be changed.

As from the beginning of the Second World War, Bethge's play was no longer performed. There are two reasons for the ban: firstly, the Theatre Section feared that the ever-present image of the crippled victims of war, eking out a miserable existence, would compromise the German war propaganda. Secondly, after the declaration of war against the Soviet Union, the thrust of German propaganda concerned with Russia changed abruptly. In 1942 and in connection with the banning of Hymnen's play, *The Petersburg Crowning*, *Reichsdramaturg* Rainer Schlösser wrote to

Goebbels: 'It can no longer be the task of a German loner as Führer of the Russian people to pursue an exclusively Russian politics. This Asiatic bloc of millions can only be taken into hand correctly when you have Frederick the Great behind you.'[11]

In February 1943, a general ban on all contemporary plays dealing with Russian themes came into effect.[12] Only Herbert Reinecker's *The Village by Odessa* (75 performances) was expressly excluded. This drama is a special case in the contemporary German-language drama, for it is set in the present during the summer of 1941 in a Bessarabian village near Odessa. The German troops find themselves ten kilometres from the town, whose inhabitants feverishly resist being liberated from the 'Bolshevik yoke'. Suddenly, a straggling commissar appears in the village who, with the help of the Russian supervisor and just before his own downfall, wants to rekindle the flames of merciless terror. Reinecker shows how the defenceless villagers, faced with a hopeless situation, eventually triumph over the despotism of the Russian. The heroic sacrifice of two young Germans leads to the village community being saved.

Even in this topical play, the names of neither Hitler nor Stalin are mentioned; the Russian commissar wears no uniform, and German soldiers do not make an appearance. Similarly, the contrast between National Socialism and Bolshevism remains superficial and the question of why Germany is at war with the Soviet Union is never raised. In this way, Reinecker cleverly circumnavigated all obstacles placed by war-time censorship and managed to slip in numerous allusions to the daily political happenings, and in particular, to the current war events. Instead the author argued in a political and philosophical way: the opposition between Germans and Russians was fundamental and insurmountable mainly due to the 'racial-national' superiority of the Germans. The conflict between the village community and the Russian commissar is presented as a 'racial struggle'. The play's finale resounds with the overtones of Goebbels' exhortations to endure: no peaceful agreement can be arrived at with 'subhuman creatures', only 'ultimate victory' guarantees the survival of the German people. In turn – and Reinecker demonstrates this in exemplary fashion – the struggle can only be won, when all Germans are unconditionally willing to sacrifice themselves.

Prussian history is a theme dealt with in many contemporary dramas. Concurring with the official propaganda in the Third Reich, the Prussian State, its virtues and military code are interpreted as presaging National Socialism. The two most frequently performed plays of this kind, *Katte* by Hermann Burte and *The Eighteenth of October* by Walter Erich Schäfer, were produced in many theatres even before 1933: *Katte*, first performed 1914, was presented at sixteen different theatres in the seasons 1929/1930 to 1932/1933, and by ninety theatres after that. *The Eighteen of October*, given its première in February 1932, had reached seventy-one performances by January 1933, and from then onwards achieved a total of sixty-two performances. Burte gave an account of the famous conflict between Frederick William I and his son, which is resolved in accordance with the Prussian ethos of duty. Katte is the main protagonist, who must give up his life for the successor to the throne. The Prussian officer confidently faces his death, for, as Burte formulates it, he conceives of himself as 'a martyr to the creation of the Prussian State'. Schäfer's *The Eighteenth of October* is set in 1813 shortly before the beginning of the Battle of the Nations at Leipzig. Here, the centre of attention is a German regiment which is supposed to fight on Napoleon's side. A young Prussian officer obstructs the fratricidal war between Germans. After the sacrificial death of their commander, the regiment unanimously goes over to the Prussian side.

In contrast to these works, Hans Rehberg's plays with a Prussian theme elude the obligatory heroic transfiguration, supposedly a defining characteristic of Prussian history. Rehberg also deals with the expansionist power politics of the Prussian kings, which as a natural consequence demanded that any human stirring must be repressed in favour of the idolised State. However, the author manages to present realistic and multifaceted characters. Reared on Shakespeare, he broke through the clichéd character typing to be found in other Nazi dramas. In *The Seven Years War*, for example, Frederick the Great is a sensitive person, deeply disturbed by the horror of war, but never forgetting his historical task: Prussia's victory over external and internal enemies. Even though the productions of Rehberg's plays at the Berlin Staatstheater directed by Jürgen Fehling and Gustaf Gründgens were important theatre events in the Third Reich, his works continued to raise controversy.

The Seven Years War is also a rare example of a National Socialist historical drama in which Jewish characters are not portrayed in an obviously anti-Semitic way. As early as 1935, plays which assigned to Jews the rôle of protagonist were suppressed by the Theatre Section.[13] In terms of internal politics such texts were superfluous, for the German population – partly overtly and partly tacitly – accepted the anti-Jewish laws. It was feared that a public discussion of the delicate theme might lead off in an incalculable direction. After 1935, any play in which Jewish figures appeared was an historical play. Faceless and nameless caricatures of the 'eternal Jew' always operate on the fringe of the events without having any connection to the central conflict. 'The Jew has been like this for centuries, and this is what he did to the German nation': such is the characterisation that occurs, for instance, in the following plays: *Panama Scandal* (fifteen performances) and *The Downfall of Carthage* (fifteen performances) by Eberhard Wolfgang Möller; *The Lonely Man* (forty performances) and *Prophets* (thirteen performances) by Hanns Johst; *Isabella of Spain* (ninety-four performances) by Heinz Hermann Ortner.

One exception is Möller's *Rothschild Triumphs at Waterloo* (34 performances), for here a Jew, the banker Nathan Rothschild, is the protagonist. Nevertheless, a characteristic feature of the work is its penetrating anti-Semitic tendency, perceptible in every line. It is not astonishing, therefore, that contemporary critics celebrated Möller's play as a contribution to 'the national reckoning with the Jewish cast of mind'.

Only a few 'blood and soil' plays (i.e., those dealing with the idea of the unification of race and territory) achieved such a high number of performances as Sigmund Graff's *The Homecoming of Matthias Bruck* (111 performances) or Richard Billinger's *Titan* (forty-four performances). In Graff's play, first performed in 1933, the rural world is represented as a solid bastion of natural, unspoilt life. The archaic existence of the villagers, exemplified by their elders, is glorified as typical of the ideal. The farmers subordinate themselves unconditionally to the 'eternal law of blood and earth'. Anyone who is no longer suitable for the 'duty' to the soil or who does not fit into this world view is cast out. Even the protagonist, a disturbed and late homecomer from the First World War, internalises this 'natural law'. Placing the welfare of the rural (national) community above his own life, the farmer goes to his death.

In Richard Billinger's *The Titan*, first performed in 1937, the rural world has a more modern appearance: there are no dull hill-billies here. The protagonist is a skilful, world-experienced farmer, the owner of a large flourishing agricultural estate in Moravia. In this play, danger threatens from the negatively characterised city Prague and from the Czechs, who attempt to undermine the 'racial superiority' of the Germans. Despite the thematic differences, in Billinger's play the sentence passed on the outsider who betrays her native soil is exactly the same as in Graff's drama: the farm girl is expelled and goes to her death. Only thus can she expiate her guilt.

The censorship criteria of the REPP

Internal and external political reasons dictated that between 1933 and 1944 the Theatre Section censored a list of works by contemporary German-speaking playwrights. Entire thematic areas, regarded before 1933 as the preferred domains of nationalist or National Socialist authors, were increasingly banned from production. The internal political situation and the external political manoeuvres of the Third Reich always provided the guide lines for the draconian decisions taken by the programme makers, resulting in oscillating and at times almost contradictory censorship directions issued between 1933 and 1944.

Several contemporary plays, which made reference to or were set in Czechoslovakia, Austria, Poland, France, Britain and the Soviet Union, were subjected to a particularly tough assessment by the Theatre Section. If the relations between the Third Reich and these countries had been settled – temporarily or through formal treaty – to Hitler's satisfaction, all contemporary plays that inveighed against the humiliating Treaty of Versailles, and thereby showed the ally in a negative light, were indexed. Likewise, a prohibition was placed on texts which denounced the 'humiliating' treatment of border-zone Germans and of German minorities in foreign countries, or which aggressively called for their *Anschluß* or 'return home to the Reich'. Those historical dramas which, for the purpose of analogy, moved the military conflicts of the past into the centre of attention, were taken out of the repertoire. However, when foreign relations had deteriorated and Hitler was threatening his former allies with the imposition of war sanctions, then plays which supported a friendly co-existence between the nations were censored. After the outbreak of the Second World War, the censorship measures became even more stringent. Dramas set in the aforementioned lands had to be rewritten or were immediately banned.

No less restrictive was the censorship practice based on internal political considerations. After 1933, plays dealing with war, aviation, espionage and counter-intelligence, written in many cases during the 1920s and early 1930s, were surveyed not only by the Theatre Section but frequently also by the headquarters of the Wehrmacht and by the Reich's Ministry of Aviation. The majority of the plays came up against considerable reservations on the part of these censors. They had to be rewritten or were withdrawn from the repertoire. As of 1939, the Theatre Section exercised systematic control over all texts which in any way referred to an historical armed conflict or to the present war situation. Only in a few instances did Schlösser and Goebbels establish and duly push through other ideological propagandistic priorities. The two known exceptions are both set during the Second World War: despite the reservations on the part of the Wehrmacht's Supreme Command, the Theatre Section released Edgar Kahn's play *The Eternal Chain* (eighteen performances).[14] Although armoured soldiers provide the background, the play actually deals with a family conflict which is resolved in a 'soldierly' way. Just as in Herbert Reinecker's *Village by Odessa*, the war is omitted from the stage. Curt Langenbeck's *U-Boat Soldiers*, commissioned by the admiralty, fell through because of Goebbels' veto.[15] A skilful propagandist, the minister did not wish to tax the audience with a realistic scene – a reminder of the victims of war – in which the entire crew of a German submarine is sent to the bottom of the ocean.

NOTES

This chapter reviews some of the results of the research project 'Structural History of the German Theatre 1933 to 1945', which was carried out, with the support of the German Research Foundation, at the Institute of Theatre Studies at the Free University, Berlin from 1987 to 1992.

1. Reichsgesetzblatt 1934 (IS), pp. 411 ff.; quoted in Jutta Wardetzky, *Theaterpolitik im faschistischen Deutschland*, Berlin, 1983, pp. 260 ff.
2. In terms of the scope of the research project the extant files of the Theatre Section of the REPP, held in the Federal Archive Potsdam, were extensively analysed.
3. Elke Fröhlich (ed.), *Die Tagebücher des Joseph Goebbels: Sämtliche Fragmente, Teil I, 1924 to 1941*, 4 vols, Munich, 1987.
4. Federal Archive Potsdam, ProMi, file 230, pp. 12 ff.

5. Federal Archive Koblenz, PS 11/23 a; Hans W. Hagen, 'Ästhetische Leichenschändung', in *Die Weltliteratur*, no. 7, 1941, p. 191; Günther Rühle, *Zeit und Theater*, vol. 3, Berlin, 1980, p. 790.

6. In Part I of the publication, resulting from the research project *Strukturgeschichte des Deutschen Schauspieltheaters 1933-1945*, Henning Rischbieter presents an overview of the institutional and personnel changes that occurred in all German theatres of the period.

7. See Part II of the research project: Thomas Eicher, *Spielplananalyse der deutschen Schauspieltheater 1929-1944*, unpublished dissertation, Free University Berlin, 1992.

8. See Part III of the research project: Barbara Panse, *Autoren, Themen und Zensurpraxis: Zeitgenössische deutschsprachige Dramatik im Theater des Dritten Reiches*, unpublished postdoctoral thesis, Free University, Berlin, 1993.

9. Eicher, *Spielanalyse*, chapter on 'Deutschsprachige Dramatik der 20er und frühen 30er Jahre'.

10. Eberhard Wolfgang Möller, 'Struensee im Drama', *Deutsche Bühne*. Edition Ortsgruppe Chemnitz, 1937/8, pp. 2 ff.

11. Federal Archive Potsdam, ProMi, file 231, p. 514.

12. Federal Archive Potsdam, ProMi, file 231, p. 273.

13. Federal Archive Potsdam, ProMi, file 73, p. 280.

14. Federal Archive Potsdam, ProMi, file 700, pp. 163, f. and file 234, pp. 165 f.

15. Federal Archive Potsdam, ProMi, file 230, pp. 217 ff.

Illustration 8.1

Please see pages 299-303 for descriptions of illistrations.

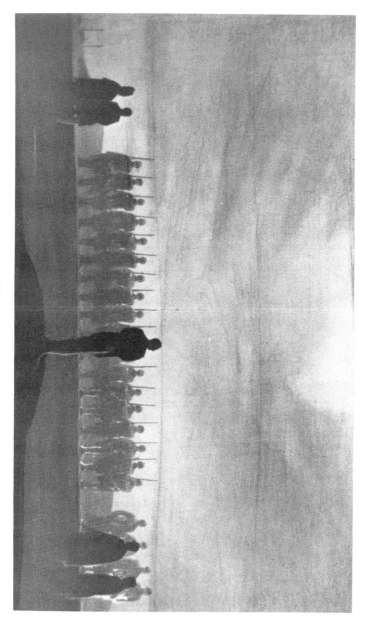

Illustration 8.2

Illustration 8.3

Illustration 8.4

Illustration 8.5

Illustration 8.6

Illustration 9.1

Illustration 9.2

Illustration 10.1

Illustration 10.2

Illustration 10.3

Illustration 12.1

Illustration 12.2

Illustration 12.3

Illustration 13.1

Illustration 13.2

Illustration 13.3

Illustration 13.4

III CAMPEONATOS NACIONALES DE GIMNASIA FEMENINA

Illustration 13.5

Illustration 13.6

Illustration 15.1

Illustration 15.2

Illustration 15.3

Illustration 15.4

9

The Municipal Theatre in Frankfurt-on-the-Main

A Provincial Theatre under National Socialism

Bettina Schültke

Translated by Laura Tate and Günter Berghaus

Introduction

Most existing publications on theatre in Nazi Germany are to a large extent based on, or influenced by, self-portrayals of theatre artists, who were actively involved in productions during the Third Reich and who sought to whitewash their past in the form of memoirs, interviews, or 'confessions'. Consequently, a lot of myths were perpetuated in the 'critical' literature published during the post-war period. A significant factor in this delayed critical examination of Nazi theatre was the rôle that leading theatre scholars, such as Heinz Kindermann, Hans Knudsen, Otto Carl August zur Nedden and Carl Niessen, played during the Third Reich and the position they continued to occupy in the university departments of theatre studies after 1945.

The autobiographical material published after the war was soon complemented by historiographical studies, which took the Nazi declarations on their theatre policies at face value, rather than examined to what extent the central directives were actually implemented in the playhouses and productions. The first serious attempts at putting research on Nazi culture on a sounder factual footing were undertaken in the 1960s. Joseph Wulf's five-volume collection of documents on Nazi theatre, film, literature, fine art, music, press and mass media[1] is still fundamental for the present-day scholar. Hildegard Brenner's study on the artistic policies of the National Socialist régime revealed how politicians were able to manipulate artists for their political aims. Ilse Pitsch,

in her dissertation on theatre as a means of directing public opinion, showed (and often over-estimated) how artists practised an
active or passive resistance against the régime. And Wolf-Eberhard August demonstrated in his study of the acting profession in
the Third Reich how cunning and manipulative both politicians
and actors were in their interactions.

However, it must be emphasised that these studies were heavily biased towards the theatres in the capital of the Reich. Many of
their findings have to be reconsidered when one analyses the situation in the provincial theatres, where directors and managers
possessed much less artistic licence than Gründgens or Hilpert
had in Berlin.

It was only in the 1980s that a more complex picture of the
contradictions between artistic policies decreed from above and
their actual implementation in the theatres began to emerge.[2]
Three of the most significant studies, all supported by extensive
documentary evidence, were published by Jutta Wardetzky,
Bogeslaw Drewniak and Konrad Dussel. They examined in great
detail the legal and administrative framework of National Socialist theatre politics and demonstrated the principal objectives
behind the decisions taken by the Reich's Ministry of Propaganda, the Reich's Chamber of Theatre, the Reich's Office of Dramaturgy, Rosenberg's Militant League for German Culture, as
well as Göring's influence through his position as Prime Minister
of Prussia. However, none of these studies fully assessed the efficiency of these offices or the actual control they exercised over the
theatre practitioners and managers. Many more detailed analyses
are required before a comprehensive history of German theatre
during the Third Reich can be written. Only then will it be possible to understand how the ideological or personal rivalries
between the political authorities in Party, administrative and theatre positions affected the running of companies and the productions of plays.

As to the drama of these years, literary studies have dwelled
virtually exclusively on the *volkish* plays, their predecessors and
ideological intentions.[3] No scholar has assessed their position
within the overall repertoire of German theatre between 1933 and
1945, and consequently a highly distorted picture of German the-
atre-life during the Nazi period gained ground. It is only with
Thomas Eicher's recent statistical analysis of 40,267 productions
(carried out as part of the research project 'Structural History of
German Theatre 1933-1945', directed by Henning Rischbieter at

the Free University Berlin) that we can fully assess the changes in the German repertoire of the period and the rôle played within it by distinctly National Socialist drama. Further elucidation is provided by his colleague, Barbara Panse, whose *Habilitation* thesis examined the themes and ideological content of these plays (a summary of her findings is contained in her essay published in this volume).

The changes in provincial theatres during the Nazi period

It is common knowledge that many leading National Socialist politicians and functionaries were unsuccessful artists; it is not so widely known that they declared politics to be the one and only true art. The Municipal Theatre in Frankfurt opened its 1933/1934 season with a commemorative speech that begins with a statement by the *Reichspropagandaminister*, Joseph Goebbels, on the close links between art and politics:

> As politicians we also think of ourselves, so to speak, as artistic people. I would go so far as to say that politics is the highest form of art, for the sculptor shapes only the dead stone, and the poet shapes only the word, which is also dead in itself. But the politician shapes the masses, gives the masses law and skeleton, so that from the masses the Volk may emerge. This captures the essence of art so succinctly, that from now on the discussion will be closed once and for all.

Accordingly, the politician surpasses the director – who shapes the actors in his productions – because as 'super-creator' he models all mankind according to his imagination, like a modern Prometheus. Art was no longer allowed to be a medium of reflection; instead, artistic forms of expression were deployed at National Socialist mass events and marches to bring the masses into alignment and overpower them. By means of theatrical devices the National Socialists succeeded in a cultic aesthetisation of politics.

The dichotomy of pure art and everyday politics, which was generally insisted upon within the theatre community, was hardly appropriate when dealing with the totalitarian strategies of the Nazi régime. National Socialism was characterised precisely by its meshing of culture and terror, which reached its bizarre and gruesome climax in the concentration camps, when inmates' orchestras had to accompany the extermination by day with classical music and entertain SS guards in the evening with otherwise forbidden jazz. The public nature of theatre work ruled out any 'inner emigration' of the type claimed by the fine artists and writers who chose to remain in Germany until 1945. The allegedly unpolitical nature of the theatre could not be maintained in the raging storm of the time, and Gründgen's attempt to preserve the Prussian State Theatre in Berlin as an artistic 'island'[4] in a brown sea was doomed to fail.

The effects of National Socialist totalitarianism on the theatre in general are best demonstrated through the example of a specific theatre. I have chosen to present the case of the Municipal Theatre in Frankfurt-am-Main. In order to include all institutional and aesthetic aspects and changes, its organisational structure and repertoire will be analysed.

The most noticeable change in the German theatre world after 1933 was one of centralisation. Individual towns lost responsibility for their municipal theatres and control passed to the new Ministry of Propaganda, headed by Joseph Goebbels. The creation of a second authority parallel to existing State institutions and controlled only by the Party led to an intertwining of State and Party political power. There was no dualism of State and Party, as most representatives of State authority were exponents of the NSDAP and no longer an independent arm of government. However, since tasks were never clearly allocated, horizontal and vertical disputes over respective areas of responsibility became unavoidable. Power struggles took place both between and within the local, regional and central departments. The new apparatus of central control, comprised of the Ministry of Public Information and Propaganda, the Reichstheaterkammer and the Prussian Theater Commission, assumed responsibility for Frankfurt's theatre. In the regional area, the *Gau* (Nazi administrative unit) of Hessen-Nassau, the theatre was responsible to the *Gauleiter* and the *Gaupropagandaleiter*.

The director of the theatre was answerable to the mayor or his appointed cultural administrator. Before 1933, the Municipal Theatre committee was a democratic body, which reflected the composition of the town parliament. Under the National Socialists, its responsibilities were systematically curtailed and passed to the mayor, in keeping with the National Socialist principle of leadership.

Frankfurt am Main had the highest proportion of Jews in the Reich after Berlin (five per cent compared to the national average of under one per cent). More than half the patrons of the Municipal Theatre and of the Art and Museum Societies were Jewish. The mayor, the cultural administrator, and the directors of both the opera house and the municipal theatre were all dismissed in 1933 on racial grounds.

The phases of discrimination

On 30 January 1933, ten SA men stormed the Municipal Theatre and hoisted the Swastika on the roof of the opera house. At the end of March, municipal administrative departments reported all Jewish and 'unpatriotic' employees. The Municipal Theatre 'blacklisted' seventeen people. Apart from applying the label 'Jew' or 'half Jew', the list took note of membership – lapsed in many cases – of left-wing parties or organisations. For example, under the name of a choral singer the remark 'greeting a stage-hand with the communist salute' was added, followed, in brackets, by 'clenched fist'; an actress is alleged to have given 'un-German' performances; opera director Herbert Graf is said to have disseminated Communist ideas in his productions 'without having been a member of the KPD (Communist Party) or actively working for the KPD'.[6]

With the Act of Restoration of the Civil Service (*Gesetz zur Wiederherstellung des Berufsbeamtentums*) of 7 March 1933, suspensions could legally be turned into discharges. Since administration officials were concerned about making the dismissals as cheap as possible for the municipal treasury, they recommended firing Jewish theatre company members under section four of the Act (which dealt with politically incriminated persons and allowed dismissal without notice). This meant that no severance payments had to be made, as would have been the case with a discharge based on section three ('non-Aryan'). After all, the appearance of legitimacy had to be maintained!

The fates of patriotically minded members of the theatre community were tragic and absurd. *Generalmusikdirektor* Hans-Wilhelm Steinberg, suspended in 1933, emphasised in a letter of complaint (25 May 1933) that he had worked all his life as a German artist, and that his family had resided for many hundreds of years in Germany. Nevertheless, he was dismissed for financial reasons under section four. The new *Generalintendant* reduced his monthly severance payments on the grounds that the full salary would provide Steinberg with an easy income and weaken his incentive to look for a new occupation. Supplementary sources of income were deducted. The executive director regularly checked whether Steinberg was living in his apartment. In April 1934, a city official questioned the grounds of the discharge under section four. 'Political unreliability' was not legally tenable in the case of a director of music, he argued, because a musical performance could not be alien to German nature or be offensive to the national sensibility, as a conductor is always bound by the composition.

In reaction, Steinberg reiterated his claim to the full salary. Six weeks later, he was turned down on the insidious grounds that 'Steinberg relinquished any claim to more money by having accepted the lower income for months, although the legal status must have been known to him'.[7]

Private disputes or rivalries which had been intensifying for years often became coloured by political motivations. Denouncements and accusations, however difficult to confirm, could lead to dismissals. A Jewish orchestra musician's letters illustrate his naïve disregard of the genuine peril he faced: 'Not too long ago the orchestra musician Meinel said: "I'll send a couple of SA-men to his house sometime." I regret that they have not come yet; whoever is guilty of nothing, has nothing to fear.'[8] The musician was killed in 1942 in Auschwitz.

Following the introduction of the 'Nuremberg Laws' in 1935, theatre workers with Jewish spouses were also given notice. The National Socialists laid off a total of over forty employees of the Municipal Theatre – from stage-hands on up to the director. Members of the theatre community dismissed for political reasons emigrated as quickly as possible, whereas many of those dismissed on racial grounds clung to their illusions until as late as the November pogroms of 1938. The artists who remained in Frankfurt were deported and killed.

In August 1942, retired opera singer Richard Breitenfeld asked the mayor for assistance:

> I found out today that the residents of our apartment house at 7 Hansa-Allee must leave Frankfurt on the next transportation, probably in eight to ten days. I had heard from prominent figures that, in recognition of my thirty years' service with the Frankfurt opera, I could remain in Frankfurt in the event of an evacuation of the Jews. At the same time I found out from Berlin that I am on *Staat-*

srat SS Hinkel's[9] list, which records the Jews who are not required to leave their place of residence. In the community no one knows anything about it. Would you, esteemed Mayor, be able to help me and my wife? Of course only if it can be done without causing you any trouble. Otherwise I will submit to the inevitable. I am 72 3/4 years old and a city pensioner.[10]

The Municipal Theatre did not act on Breitenfeld's behalf. At the end of August, Richard 'Israel'[11] Breitenfeld wrote that he and his wife were to be taken to Theresienstadt on a 'Jew transport'. He asked again: 'What is going to happen to my pension?' A city administration memorandum notes two days later that nobody in Berlin had been reached by telephone. A municipal office assistant ascertained that Breitenfeld's apartment had been cleared out. The subsequent bureaucratic orders were carried out without delay: Hans Meissner, who had been appointed *Generalintendant* by the National Socialists in 1933, stopped Breitenfeld's pension the same day. Breitenfeld died in December 1942 in Theresienstadt.

The Other Side of the Coin

Whereas Jewish theatre people became unemployed in 1933, many Party members of the NSDAP either received a boost to their careers, or were given their first theatre engagements.

Hans Meissner, who always took the path of least resistance, became the new *Generalintendant* of the Municipal Theatre. During the Weimar Republic he had run a touring company of the 'people's theatre movement' in Hessen, and in 1930 he had been offered a position as director in Stettin. For Meissner, a member of the Social Democratic Party, things came to a head in March 1933. His National Socialist friend, Friedrich Krebs, had in the meantime become acting mayor of Frankfurt and had arranged a position for Meissner at the Municipal Theatre. Meissner left the SPD and, on 10 April 1933, joined the NSDAP.

The city had no say in the appointment of *Chefdramaturg* Friedrich Bethge. Bethge, a playwright, had been a Party member and SS man since 1932 and was sent from Berlin to the Municipal Theatre. With him the theatre received its own official Party post (which he demonstrated by wearing an SS uniform at work). Such placements of authors loyal to the Party in senior dramaturgical positions represented an attempt by the National Socialists to gain influence in predominantly leftist or liberal theatre circles. The careers of these dramatists, who had been com-pletely unknown before 1933, ran parallel to their rise in the NSDAP, SA or SS.

A fervent Germanisation of the names of theatrical profes-sions and seating areas was a sign of the take-over of the theatre. A *Regieassistent* (assistant director) became a *Hilfsspielwart*, an *Inspizient* (stage manager) a *Bühnenwart* and a *Souffleuse* (prompter) an *Einhelferin*. The audience no longer sat in a 'French' *Parkett* (stalls), but rather in a 'German' *Erdgeschoß*. This alteration of the 'foreign-language seating designations' cost the Municipal Theatre five thousand Reichsmarks in 1938. Similarly, the pro-gramme brochures were systematically brought into line with the new régime: the '*Blätter der Städtischen Bühnen*' was rechristened '*Der 30. Januar: Die Braunen Blätter der Städtischen Bühnen*'.[12]

By order of the Ministry for Public Information and Propa-ganda, the Municipal Theatre, like all other theatres, organised special events and ceremonies on new National Socialist holidays such as 30 January ('Day of the Seizure of Power'), 20 April ('Birthday of the Führer') and 9 November ('Day of the Novem-ber Putsch').

The Frankfurt repertoire during the Third Reich

The decrease in foreign authors in the Frankfurt repertoire of 1933 is noticeable at first glance. Anglo-American dramatists such as Robert Cedric Sherrif, Eugene O'Neill, Elmer Rice and Noel Cow-ard were dropped, while the share of German-language authors climbed to almost eighty per cent. However, some, such as Arthur Schnitzler, Frank Wedekind, Friedrich Wolf, Georg Kaiser, Carl Zuckmayer, Bertolt Brecht, Arnold Zweig, Fritz von Unruh, or Ferdinand Bruckner, were excluded.

The new *Intendant* Hans Meissner especially castigated the political repertoire of the 1920s:

> That time serves as a warning to us. Krankheit der Jugend, Ver-brecher, Revolte im Erziehungshaus, Brülle China, Cyankali, Para-graph 218 and similar plays swept like poison gas through many German theatres and announced the domination of baser instincts. Putting into practice the demands of such plays would have had to lead to anarchy where everybody – man being the foe of every other man – would give free rein to his desires. Art and culture do not stand in the service of the sub-human, the animal existence.[13]

The National Socialist authorities rejected both the Naturalistic drama of the late nineteenth century and the topical political theatre of the Weimar Republic. In their view, race was the central determining factor of human behaviour, and not the social environment (which the political authors of the preceding period had always presented as changeable). Plays such as those mentioned by Meissner stood in marked contrast to the assumption that art and theatre had to propagate eternal values and had to show human life being governed by the conflict between heroic perseverance and tragic death.

Half the Frankfurt repertoire between 1933 and 1944 consisted of plays by contemporary authors. On average, four premières were staged per season. Scores of amateurish playscripts were submitted by Party comrades. Owing to their local positions of power, the theatre critic of the National Socialist *Frankfurter Volksblatt*, the wife of the Frankfurt Chief of Police, and the *Gaupropagandaleiter* of Hessen-Nassau, Wilhelm Müller-Scheld, all succeeded in having their inferior plays staged at the Municipal Theatre. *Reichsdramaturg* Rainer Schlösser[14] personally ordered a pseudonym for the latter author. He wrote: 'As a general rule, one can hardly deny creative writing to those who choose to serve our cultural policy.'[15] As to the artistic quality of such plays, the statistics speak for themselves: two-thirds of the plays which were premièred in Frankfurt from 1933 to 1944 were never staged again.

It is striking that the Berlin authority, the *Reichsdramaturgie*, rarely imposed explicit bans on theatres. Managers often tried to anticipate objections, rather than explore their room to manoeuvre. Regulations were regarded as conservative guidelines in deciding what was potentially objectionable, so that even among National Socialists uncertainty existed about which plays were now allowed, particularly desirable or forbidden. For example, in the summer of 1943, *Generalintendant* Meissner and *Chefdramaturg* Bethge argued over whether it was opportune to stage Schiller's *Jungfrau von Orleans*.[16] The changing political climate had to be taken into consideration when deciding on the new repertoire.

The new National Socialist drama and the productions of NS touring companies had a distinctly deterring effect on the predominantly conservative middle classes. Attendance figures for the 1933/1934 season dropped by around thirty per cent. The Jewish audience, who had accounted for half the season-ticket sales, no longer attended. Although the city of Frankfurt reduced admis-

sion charges by around fifty per cent and attempted to drum up
support with slogans such as 'Attending the theatre is a duty for
officials!', the attendance figures fell even further.

Chefdramaturg and Writer-in-Residence Friedrich Bethge

Frankfurt's most important author was *Chefdramaturg* Bethge,
who had seven of his plays performed at the Municipal Theatre. A
first version of his anti-Polish tragedy, *Rebellion um Preußen*, had its
première on 20 March 1939 and eight further performances.

The main conflict in the play, which is set in the fifteenth century, is the dispute between the High Master of the German Order,
Heinrich von Plauen, and the leader of the Order Council, Michael
Küchmeister, about their policy towards the Polish king, Jagiello.
Plauen wants to defend German soil to the last man by force of
arms, while Küchmeister advocates a policy of peace and reconciliation. The Treaty of Thorn is referred to as 'the Eternal Treaty of
Thorn' in a pejorative allusion to Versailles, and Küchmeister is
denigrated as an appeaser.

Despite the historical disguise, the reviewers regarded *Rebellion
um Preußen* as a topical political commentary: 'Historical accuracy
is not of paramount importance, the conflicts are conflicts of our
time', wrote the *Neueste Zeitung* on 21 March 1939. Bethge himself
had described his play in an interview as a *pièce à clef*, whose
supreme art consisted in concealing the topical intent.[17]

To Bethge, all Poles are 'subhumans' who appear only in groups,
in 'Tartar hordes', murdering and scorching. A characterisation of
Jagiello in Meissner's production notes shows that the director
supported Bethge's intention: 'Jagiello must be presented as mali-
cious, greedy, cunning, sly – ambition – good enunciation, posture
stooped, sitting on the throne like a beast of prey, ready to spring,
sword like a sickle, scythe.'[18]

After the German attack on Poland, Bethge reacted to the
changed political situation by re-writing the play. This new version was premièred on 29 October 1939. He wrote to the *Reichsdramaturg*: 'How unexpectedly "timely" the theme has become
due to Poland!'[19] and prefaced the revised text with a dedication:
'To the home of my ancestors, East Prussia !' These areas had
fallen into German hands again. The newly added prologue
immediately gave the audience an inkling of the new direction of

Hitler's power-politics. Bethge expanded and intensified the anti-Polish sentiments of the play, for example by having Plauen refuse an offer of peace by Jagiello and proclaim the warring slogan: 'My hand and this sword will not tire until Prussia is rid of the Tartar hordes! – To God and the Virgin Mary!'

The production in Frankfurt took recourse to a whole gamut of theatrical trickery in order to inject life into this ceremonious and static drama. Director Meissner employed an expressionistic acting style, sophisticated speech-choirs and choreographed mass-scenes to counteract the lack of character development and dramatic action. An effective lighting design and a spectacular décor were devised to add visual spectacle to the ponderous and stilted monologues. To facilitate the audience's understanding of the play, projections of geographical maps, names and dates were employed to provide important historical information. The simultaneous use of multi-levelled rostra framing a central row of choir stalls and a large cross suspended from the flies emphasised the power and cultic significance of the Knights' Order. Even so, the spectators were hardly able to comprehend the action which, as critics unanimously asserted, was far too slow in this four-hour long production.

In an essay of 1944, entitled 'The Rebellious Marshal', Bethge referred once again to the play:

> The theme treats the origin of the events of 20 July as seen through the parallel example of the fall of the brilliant Master of the Order, Heinrich von Plauen, caused by his rebellious Marshal of the Order, Michael Küchmeister, and elucidates the consequences of this deed. I was inspired to write this essay by the remarkable fact that von Witzleben attended the première of this Plauen-Küchmeister tragedy here in Frankfurt, thereby experiencing a piece of subsequent autobiography.[20]

General Field Marshal Erwin von Witzleben was the highest-ranking officer in the circle of men involved in the plot to kill Hitler on 20 July 1944. On 8 August he was hanged in Plötzensee.[21] Unscrupulously, Bethge used the execution of Witzleben to further his own career, presenting himself as a visionary, who had poetically foreseen this 'treason'.

Productions of German classical drama

German *Sturm und Drang* classics accounted for about a tenth of the repertoire in Frankfurt, both before and after 1933. However,

Schiller replaced Goethe as the most frequently produced author. In 1933, to inaugurate his directorship, Hans Meissner produced Schiller's early work, *Die Räuber*. The programme notes cite a statement by *Reichspropagandaminister* Joseph Goebbels: 'If Schiller had lived in our times he would unquestionably have become the great poetic champion of our revolution.'[22] The *Frankfurter Zeitung* mentioned the changed composition of the audience: 'Members of the Militant League for German Culture filled the seats, leading dignitaries appeared, uniforms set the tone of the audience.'[23]

The reviews described the selection of this play as a political decision. Meissner shortened the piece to two-and-a-half hours and brought the heroic-revolutionary aspects to the fore. The evening began with a declaration by the protagonist Karl: 'This ink-soiled century turns my stomach'. The audience took the youthful hero's anger at a dissolute world to be a criticism of the Weimar Republic. The press also underscored the play's topical references:

> Today, a young man does not become a thief, but rather a disciplined SS man. The youthful energy of the boys in the play is uselessly dissipated, because nobody calls on them to put their lives to good use. It is a tragedy of adolescence, destroyed by its own intoxicating vigour, and the neglect of the nation.[24]

Only one critic objected to the adaptation and warned against the glorification of the thieves: '*In tyrannos* – Yes, why not challenge the ruined century? Certainly. – But where anarchy begins, the right to revolution ends. A fury, which is not capable of acting according to laws, was disapproved of by the young revolutionary Schiller.'[25] Producer Meissner only saw the band of thieves in a positive light. In the programme notes he wrote: 'The exuberance of youth is an eternal sign of the drive to unconditional self-fulfilment, to freedom above the law and beyond reality, to stormy rage against all that has been, to passionate yearning for all that is to come; *in tyrannos*!'[26]

It would surely be an over interpretation to see Meissner's production as a blind glorification of the acts of violence of National Socialist bullies. However, by emphasising and celebrating the thieves as a youthful, heroic mob, he captured the mood of the times in 1933 and the discussion on the completion of the 'national revolution'.[27] No critic mentions whether the role of the Jewish character Spiegelberg was presented in an anti-Semitic fashion.

The last phase

Attendance figures began to rise again after the outbreak of war. Theatres responded to the public demand for amusement and diversion with performances of comedies.

In August, before Goebbels closed the theatres with the 'total war' declaration on 1 September 1944, the Municipal Theatre achieved its highest ticket sales since 1933. On an auxiliary stage a variety show, entitled 'Immortal Germany' was offered. Quotations from Hitler's speeches alternated with classical music, readings from fallen soldiers' letters, poems by German classical authors and National Socialist writers. The programme closed with Franz Schubert's *Victory* song. *Reichsdramaturg* Schlösser travelled repeatedly to Frankfurt to ensure that the Municipal Theatre was keeping to the decreed course of holding out to the end. His last speech before the ensemble was printed by the *Offenbacher Zeitung* on 15 November 1943:

> We will face up to everything with cold determination, come what may. The cultural policy maker and the artistic person must have the courage to see the situation clearly, free of heady passions. Once again, the primacy of politics demands of us a resolute willingness to make sacrifices. We know only one thing: a German victory, even at the cost of every castle, opera-house and theatre.

It was at the cost of Frankfurt's theatres. In March 1944, the opera house, the theatre, the administration buildings and most of the temporary entertainment halls were destroyed.

NOTES

1. For detailed references to these studies see the bibliographical appendix to this volume.
2. See Uwe-Karsten Ketelsen, 'Kulturpolitik des Dritten Reichs und Ansätze zu ihrer Interpretation', *Text & Kontext*, vol. 8, 1980, pp. 217-242; Hans Dieter Schäfer, *Das gespaltene Bewußtsein: Über deutsche Kultur und Lebenswirklichkeit 1933-1945*, Munich, 1981; Hans-Ulrich Thamer, *Verführung und Gewalt: Deutsch-*

land 1933-1945, Berlin, 1986; Volker Dahm, 'Anfänge und Ideologie der RKK', *Vierteljahreshefte für Zeitgeschichte*, vol. 34, 1986, pp. 53-84; Norbert Frei, *Der Führerstaat: Nationalsozialistische Herrschaft 1933-1945*, Munich, 1987; Peter Reichel, *Der schöne Schein des 3.Reichs: Faszination und Gewalt des Faschismus*, Munich, 1991; Uwe-Karsten Ketelsen, *Literatur und Drittes Reich*, Schernfeld, 1992.

3. See Uwe-Karsten Ketelsen, *Von heroischem Sein und völkischem Tod*, Bonn, 1970; Bruno Fischli, *Deutschendämmerung*, Bonn, 1976; Erwin Breßlein, *Völkisch-faschistisches und nationalsozialistisches Drama*, Frankfurt/M., 1980.

4. See Gustaf Gründgens, *Briefe, Aufsätze, Reden*, Munich, 1970, p. 16.

5. See 'Städtische Bühnen', in: Magistratsakte 1100/204, vols. 1 and 3; Municipal Archives, Frankfurt/Main.

6. *Ibidem.*

7. H. W. Steinberg, personal files, Municipal Archives, Frankfurt/Main.

8. Moses Slager in a letter of 20 July 1933 to director Staubesand. See 'M. Slager', personal files, Municipal Archives, Frankfurt/Main.

9. Hans Hinkel (1901-1960): 1921 joined the NS movement; 1933 State commissioner in the Prussian Ministry of Science, Art and Public Education; 1934 notorious special emissary for the surveillance of all Jews active in the cultural life of the Third Reich; 1944 *Reichsfilmintendant*; 1943 SS *Gruppenführer*; 1945-1952 interned.

10. Magistratsakte 6140, Municipal Archives, Frankfurt/Main.

11. After 1 January 1939, Jews were forced to add 'Sara' or 'Israel' to their Christian names.

12. 30 January 1933 was the date of Hitler's appointment as chancellor; 'brown', of course, related to the Nazi colours.

13. Hans Meissner, 'Kulturarbeit: Gegenwartsnähe der Deutschen Klassik', *Die Braunen Blätter*, 1934/1935, p. 85. The cited plays by Ferdinand Bruckner, Peter Martin Lampel, Bill Bjelozerkowski, Friedrich Wolf and Carl Credé had been produced under Meissner's predecessors at the Municipal Theatre.

14. Rainer Schlösser (1899-1945), critic and author: 1933 appointed *Reichsdramaturg* by the Nazis to keep the repertoire of individual theatres under surveillance; from 1935 to 1944 also leader of the theatre section in the Ministry of Public Information and Propaganda; from 1944 to 1945 leader of the propaganda ministry's cultural section.

15. Documents of the Ministry of Public Information and Propaganda 50.01, no. 6070/172, Central State Archives, Potsdam.

16. Magistratsakte 6112, vol. 2, Municipal Archives, Frankfurt/Main.

17. *Frankfurter Volksblatt*, 12 June 1937.

18. Estate of Meissner, University Library, Department of Music, Theatre, Film, Art and Media, Frankfurt/Main, file no. 18.

19. Documents of the Ministry of Public Information and Propaganda 50.01, no. 226, Central State Archives, Potsdam.

20. Berlin Document Center, documents of the *Reichskulturkammer*, personal file on Bethge.

21. See Reiner Pommerin, 'Erwin von Witzleben', in R. Lill and H. Oberreuter (eds.), *20 Juli: Portraits des Widerstands*, Düsseldorf, 1984, pp. 349-361.

22. *Blätter der Städtischen Bühnen*, no. 34, 1938/1939, p. 437. The quote is taken from an older speech.

23. Rudolf Geck in the *Frankfurter Zeitung*, 3 October 1933.

24. *Rhein-Mainische-Volkszeitung*, 3 October 1933.
25. Siegfried Melchinger, *Frankfurter Generalanzeiger*, 2 October, 1993.
26. *Die Braunen Blätter*, no. 3, 1933, p. 2.
27. As the SA called for a 'second' revolution in 1933, Chief of Staff Ernst Röhm and other persons out of favour were murdered in June 1934 by the SS and the Gestapo.

10

The Orchestration
of the National Community
The Nuremberg Party Rallies of the NSDAP

Hans-Ulrich Thamer
Translated by Ann Taylor

To contemporaries, the Nuremberg rallies of the NSDAP[1] were the perfect example of the unfolding glory and power of the Third Reich. They became a symbol for mass orchestration and mass fascination, as well as for the pseudo-religious character of the National Socialist movement.

National Socialist propagandists celebrated the yearly reviews of their Party as a 'magnificent military parade', which they claimed was 'more glorious than the pageantry of the old emperor'. In September every year hundreds of thousands of Party functionaries, men from the SA and SS, the Labour Service, the Hitler Youth, and girls from the 'Bund Deutscher Mädel' came to Nuremberg to be protagonists or supernumeraries in the ornament of the masses or to form an applauding audience. Officers, diplomats and journalists from both home and abroad observed and admired the monumental show of power which aimed to demonstrate the strength and unity of the régime and the aura of Adolf Hitler's leadership.

The principle objective behind these massive spectacles was to offer visual evidence of the German community united behind its leader. The ritualised rally of all National Socialist organisations was carefully stage-managed to present an impressive image of mass support for the new régime. The rally site formed the stage for the production of a Führer-cult. Hitler was not only leading actor and point of reference for both the architecture and the processions; he was also director and high-priest of the event, symbolically bringing the people together in an emotionally elating, communal experience. The ritualistic and symbolic actions characterised the National Socialist aestheticisation of politics and gave emblematic representation to the intimate connection between seduction and power – a fundamental feature of National Socialist rule.

Festivals and politics

The Nuremberg Party rallies were part of a long tradition of bourgeois public celebrations. Since the Enlightenment and the French Revolution, modern political festivals have served as a medium to create a politically minded public and differed from the representative public of the corporate systems of the early modern age. Modern political festivals were a seismograph of a political culture and gave expression to political and social values by means of their transparent forms of communication.

The highpoints of bourgeois festival-culture in the nineteenth century were the national celebrations, which after German unification had increasingly lost their oppositional, liberal-democratic characteristics. In the monarchic nation-State they became festivals led 'from above'. They offered dynastic representation and were characterised by their militaristic form and content. They were no longer occasions for fraternalisation and integration of the masses but were instituted in order to foster loyalty, chauvinism and military spirit.

How then, can we define the historical place of the political festival in National Socialist Germany? On the one hand, they continued the bellicose tradition of the Prussian State through their military pomp and circumstance; but on the other hand they created, through their mass rituals, a new and no longer monarchically based legitimisation. The National Socialist festivals served to enhance the charisma of the government and to generate universal consent, if not submission, to the will of the leader.

Any investigation into political festivals has to elucidate their basic forms and structures, their symbols and codes, and finally their reception. In the case of the Nuremberg Rallies we will concern ourselves firstly with the planning and the objectives of the Party rallies, then analyse their rituals as an expression of political aims and as a means of influencing the masses, and finally enquire as to what effect they had on their participants and audiences.

Nuremberg: Centre for the Party Rallies

Why did Nuremberg of all places become the scene for the NSDAP rallies? There were different reasons for this choice, but it was not primarily because Nuremberg was a particularly 'brown' town. In fact, the city had a reputation for being a 'red' stronghold with a social-democratic majority. Only in the region of Franconia were the election successes of the NSDAP above the average for the rest of the country. The reputation and powerful position of the leader of Franconia, Julius Streicher, and his administrative district organisation were significant, but above all it was the following facts which determined the decision to move the third rally in the still young and turbulent history of the NSDAP to Nuremberg. In March 1927, the ban on Hitler's public appearances in Bavaria was lifted, and Gareis, director of Nuremberg police appointed by the Bavarian State government, was favourably disposed towards the activities of the political Right, including the NSDAP. Added to this was the possibility of using the historic and romantic scenery of Nuremberg to construct a visible continuity from the 'Reichstag Town' to 'Rally Town'. Furthermore, Nuremberg was particularly suited to national mass events thanks to its convenient geographic position in central Germany.

After the success of the 1929 Nuremberg rally there seemed to be no alternative to Nuremberg. Following his seizure of power in 1933, Hitler sought to accentuate the still young festival tradition of the Party, which had been interrupted in 1930 and 1931 by the town fathers' refusal to make schools, halls and stadia available to accommodate the Party delegates and provide them with meeting places. In 1933, it was still necessary to overcome the reservations of the municipal government, which had in the meantime converted to National Socialism, yet was still opposed to having a monumental, self-contained building erected solely for the purpose of Party rallies in the south of the town. On 21 July, during a fringe gathering at the Bayreuth Festival, Hitler requested that representatives from Nuremberg decide quickly, 'whether every two years for the next hundred years they want to accommodate the Party rally and its several hundred thousand participants in their town', or whether, for the sake of preserving 'a number of old trees', they were willing to sacrifice the business advantages which would ensue from this event.[2] He also informed them that Stuttgart was applying to stage the future rallies. In a memorandum of 24 July it was stated that at the instigation of Hitler, *Gauleiter* Streicher and mayor Liebel, the desired site around the Leopoldhain was to be made available. During the opening of the rally on 30 August, Hitler announced 'that our rallies will take place in this town now and forever'.[3] Soon afterwards the town was designated as the 'Rally Town' of the National Socialist movement.

At this time there was neither far-reaching nor precise planning as to the extent of the events. The Third Reich in no way began with a unified and qualified concept even as regards propaganda and political cult. The rally of 1933 differed from its predecessors only in its high number of participants and the utilisation of all State resources; the scene and scenario still matched those of the 1929 rally.

From improvisation to professionalism

Following the stabilisation of the régime, a monumental architectural backdrop based on the eternal nature of the 'Thousand-Year Reich' was erected, and improvised planning gave way to an increasing canonisation regarding the form and content of the rituals performed during the rally. The heroic style and dramaturgy of the event were fixed on celluloid by Leni Riefenstahl in her film *Triumph of the Will* (1934). Much more than simply a documentary, this film foregrounded the symbolism and liturgy of the ceremonies and established their pattern for the years to come. At the same time, the film disseminated the mass spectacle of Nuremberg throughout Germany. It was a 'production of a production' and thereby a reduplication of the 'mass appeal' of National Socialist political aesthetics.[4] *Triumph of the Will* turned the military parade of the National Socialist movement into a platform for the Führer-cult. Film and architecture supported the development of an outsize image of the Führer and thereby moulded the public image of National Socialism.

In 1934, the basic sequence of events and propagandist elements of the National Socialist rallies were established. In the following years, they underwent only modification and expansion, primarily through the gradual completion of the rally buildings which were constructed in great haste between events. From 1933 onwards, the great rallying calls of National Socialism ran under mottos which reflected the political situation and the pretensions of the Third Reich: 'Rally for Freedom' (1935), 'Rally of Honour' (1936),

'Rally of Labour' (1937) and 'Rally of a Greater Germany' (1938). In September 1939, the motto was 'Rally for Peace'. This rally, however, was never to take place, for at the time of its planning in the spring of 1933 Hitler had already set in motion the preparation for the military expansion of his Reich. He thereby destroyed the false façade of the 'Rally for Peace' that was intended to camouflage his aggressive policies, which up until then had successfully been hidden behind the glamour of the public celebrations.

Rallies as *Gesamtkunstwerk*

The National Socialist direction of public life demonstrated the full scope of the régime's organisational and propagandist abilities. Mass rallies and hours of commemoration, appeals and parades, military show-manoeuvres and public entertainment alternated with each other in the Nuremberg festival, which at first lasted four, then seven and finally eight days. The magic of the flags, banners and torches, of the mass rituals and the Führer-cult, the transfiguration of death and the oath of allegiance numbed the senses and satisfied 'the age-old lust for horror'[5] as much as the desire for sensation and the need for community. The monumental size of the surrounding architecture heightened these emotions; the most modern media, radio and film, broadcast the monumental event into the last corners of the Reich. All forms of communication and propagandist elements were summoned up to create a *Gesamtkunstwerk* (Total Work of Art) under the guidance of a political aesthetic that replaced rational forms of discourse with vague and emotional appeals to the audience's fears and aspirations. The rallies were not forums for discussion, but rather a cultic representation of the régime's self-image and pretensions. The fusion of aesthetics and politics found its expression in the ritualised mass events, the symbol-laden liturgy and the monumental scenery of the architecture. The Nuremberg Party rallies were the pinnacle of achievement and the most powerful examples of the political aesthetics of National Socialism and the artist-politician Adolf Hitler. With hindsight it is clear that the National Socialist mass spectacles were the most conspicuous and highly developed form of the political-ideological mass cult that was gaining ground in many European countries during the inter-war period.

Although Fascism in Italy fostered a political style infused with ritual and myth, Mussolini's régime, unlike German National Socialism, did not develop into an all-embracing political cult penetrating all areas of life. Rather, it found its limits where the Catholic Church and other traditional powers were able to claim their autonomy. In terms of the scale and accomplishment of the political cult, National Socialism proved itself to be the more radical variant of fascism. Whereas the strongly bureaucratic Italian Fascism concentrated on the emotional self-portrayal of the State, the National Socialist cult sought to influence the everyday life of the people. Besides regular national Party and State celebrations at administrative district, constituency and local group levels, there were also National Socialist life-cycle celebrations glorifying birth, marriage and death; there were flag hoistings and morning celebrations of the Party on Sundays. The National Socialist festival year followed a clear pattern and rhythm that affected the life of everybody.

The National Socialist cult thereby filled the vacuum that had been left by the modern State as it had separated itself from all things religious, and had confined itself to the organisation of worldly and political affairs. Time and again since the French Revolution there have been political movements which, through the mobilisation of the masses, have sought to establish political and spiritual authority and thereby assure their political control all the more thoroughly and permanently. George Mosse has accurately characterised this process as 'the nationalisation of the masses' in response to the emergence of the political mass market:

> Such mass movements demanded a new political style which would transform the crowd into a coherent political force, and nationalism in its use of the new politics provided the cult and liturgy which could accomplish this purpose.[6]

The most important element of this new political style, which was later to be deployed to such cruel ends, was, according to Mosse, aesthetics:

> The political aesthetics of the National Socialist régime was a force that connected myths and symbols with the emotions of the people. The evil purposes, for which they were eventually misused, were masked by a certain feeling for beauty and form. The new political style affected large segments of the population through its ability to capture their dreams and longings. The aesthetic formulae objectified people's dreams of beauty, joy and order, whilst at the same

time they brought the audiences into contact with the supposedly immutable forces outside the course of everyday life.[7]

National Socialism was without doubt the apotheosis of this new political style. The National Socialists incorporated everything which for a century had been developed in different political mass movements as an alternative to the political rhetoric of parliamentary democracy, and perfected it. The political style of National Socialism was popular, not least because it was founded on familiar traditions, but also because it revitalised and adapted them to suit the majority taste in a technical era. National Socialism brought together both the ancient and the modern.

The Artist-Politician creates his own liturgy

The purpose of the ingeniously thought-out liturgy was for Adolf Hitler, the ultimate creator of the National Socialist mass cult, to prolong the political system of National Socialism beyond his death and to establish a 'Thousand-Year Reich'. Albert Speer, co-creator and executor of this concept, informed us that it was Hitler's aim to restrict the significance of the single personality of the head of State or Party leader within the ritual, and to put in its place a course of events which in itself was capable of impressing the masses. This idea arose from his observation that, in all probability, his successor would not be person with the same mass appeal. Therefore, the ritual had to predominate and a system be installed where even a 'small political goblin' would be able to bring a certain fascination to bear on the masses. This 'fascinating power' was more or less generated by mass choirs and parades of flags, in solemn demonstrations – such as the march from the memorial in the Luitpold arena back to the platform – so that the actual address was only a part of the proceedings which, even if it did not achieve the highest possible impact, would still be an impressive and effective manifestation.[8]

According to Speer's testimony, Hitler directed his particular attention towards perfecting the ritual of the Party rallies at Nuremberg. During a meeting after the rally of 1938, Hitler reviewed every part and day of the event. 'Some demonstrations', he judged, 'have already found their definitive form.'[9] Amongst these he included the parade of the Hitler Youth, the assembly of the Labour Front, the night-time parade of political leaders on the Zeppelinfeld, as well as the remembrance of the dead from the SA and SS in the Luitpold arena. Hitler, the fallen Catholic and artist-politician, revealed that he understood the appeals, marches and consecrations not simply to be a 'propagandist revue', but rather a celebration of a political cult and a means of stabilising his rule:

> We must keep the procedures for these events fixed so that they will become unalterable rites while I am still alive. This means that no one will be able to mess these things up later on. I fear the urge for innovation on the part of my successors. Perhaps future leaders of the Reich will not be able to achieve the effects I can, but this framework will support them and lend them authority[10]

Even the subordinate organisers sought to perfect the further development of the mass events at Nuremberg. The leader of the German Labour Front, Robert Ley, appealed, with a clarity peculiar to him, for the overhaul or replacement of sacred forms by the political cult of the régime. At a meeting where the outcome of the 1937 rally was discussed, he demanded that the celebration should become bigger and more beautiful so that 'participants stream to these celebrations and festivities in ever greater numbers, gradually staying away from the churches by their own choice and, from the experience thus gained, come to the conviction that at these festivals National Socialism provides them with much more intense experiences than the sermons of the priests in the churches'.[11]

The structure of the political liturgy of the Nuremberg rallies

The glory and power displayed during the histrionic events of the Nuremberg Party rallies surpassed all other occasions in the National Socialist calendar. The series of celebrations in the National Socialist festival year began on 30 January, the day of the seizure of power, and ended on 9 November, commemorating the martyrs of the movement. In between came a wealth of remembrance hours, consecration feasts and demonstrations. The National Socialist festival year was to some extent determined by the ecclesiastical calendar of the church and sought both to overcome and to replace this. In the number and sequence, as well as in the arrangement, of the festivals it soon became as canonised as its church counterpart, which in many ways was also imitated in its liturgy.[12]

The stylistic elements of the pageants and theatrical shows at the Party rallies had, like National Socialist ideology, a syncretistic character. They united many forms of the political cult that had emerged from various patriotic celebrations in the German Empire, from the commemoration and festival forms of the youth movement, and from the early fascist forms of demonstration and rally in Italy. The uniformed groups and their marches, the cult of the martyrs of the movement and the consecration of the flag in the form of a religious ceremony with a concluding address, came from their own Party history. The use of the historic background of Nuremberg as a framework for the rallies heightened the emotional effect and justified the organisers' claims that they were preserving and vitalising that which had been handed down to them.

Each day had a canonised course of events within the liturgical programme of the Party rallies and served to represent the specific features of a particular branch of the Party.[13] The mass ritual was celebrated in a space specifically created for it, and the Führer was always at the centre of the complex agenda. Again and again we find a threefold basic scheme within the course of events, adapted from Christian, particularly Protestant, liturgy: march in and call up, address and pronouncement, confession and closing communal song and march out.

The first day bore the imprint of the Führer's celebratory entry into his town – a ritual that was obviously adapted from the early modern historical entry of leaders and which was further intensified and interpreted in Riefenstahl's film, through the motif of the saviour descending from the clouds to the old Franconian town in a glittering masterpiece of German aircraft technology. There were iconagraphical references to the entries and pageants of medieval emperors, now reproduced by means of modern technology. To the sound of the ringing town bells, Hitler marched to the council chamber. There he was welcomed by the town fathers in front of the imperial regalia, brought from Vienna in 1938 – a symbol of regained imperial glory. The conclusion of the day was the festival production of an opera. Wagner was the natural choice.

The second day began with a march by the Hitler Youth past Hitler's hotel. This was followed by the opening of the Party congress in the Luitpold Hall, a former machine shed from an industrial exhibition in 1906, renovated by Speer in neo-classical style in accordance with the taste of the times. The ceremony again followed the pattern of a church service: the marching in of the banners led by the 'Blood Flag', an emotional opening address by

Hess leading up to *Gauleiter* Wagner proclaiming Hitler Führer of the Nation, closing with a remembrance and honouring for the fallen heroes of the movement. According to one report, participants were 'filled with almost religious emotion'.[14] In the evening there followed a cultural conference during which the 'German National Prize for Art and Science' was awarded as an alternative to the Nobel Prize.

The third day belonged to the Labour Front. Fifty thousand chanting men assembled on the Zeppelinfeld in front of the Führer's rostrum. The climax of the ceremony was a huge choral celebration with dialogue, a genre which Gabriele D'Annunzio had developed as *commandante* in Fiume in 1919 and which had been incorporated into the new political style of Fascism. During huge open-air events he had whipped up his black-uniformed volunteer corps and roused the people of the town into euphoric responses to his speeches. During the assembly of the Labour Front in Nuremberg, the choral dialogue was integrated into a pseudo-religious liturgy. The ceremony concluded with a 'Celebratory Song of Labour', which finished with the words: 'May the work of our hands succeed/ for every cut of the spade which we perform/ should be a prayer for Germany.'[15] After this the 'Spade Bearers' marched out singing, and strode towards the Deutscher Hof, Hitler's hotel.

The fourth day, Community Day, was dedicated to shows of sporting prowess and mass exercise, again taking place on the Zeppelinfeld. In 1937 this was supplemented by the laying of a foundation stone for a gigantic German Stadium, which in the future would become home to the Germanic World Festival, a replacement for the Olympic Games. In the evening, in a great torchlight procession, the political leaders filed past Hitler, who greeted his officials from the hotel balcony. Once again, rally ground and town were theatrically bound together.

The fifth day continued with special meetings of individual Party organisations and Party congress sessions. The main event was the nightly hour of commemoration at the Zeppelinfeld in the brilliantly stage-managed 'cathedral of light', the highpoint of pseudo-sacred mass fervour. Flags, fire and light were united in the image of a church, cutting off the assembled community from the darkness of the hostile world outside. As Hitler arrived at the main rostrum, the beams of one hundred and fifty gigantic searchlights shot into the night sky and created an enormous shining cupola of rays above the quarter of a million spectators. Even the

British ambassador, Sir Nevile Henderson, was impressed: 'The effect, which was both solemn and beautiful, was like being inside a cathedral of ice.'[16]

A rampart of flags and beams of light shielded the inner circle from the darkness of the outside world, a symbolic expression of the Manichean conception of the National Socialist world. Hitler appeared on the floodlit altar-stage as a charismatic healing figure, the high priest of a new cult. Once again there followed an honouring of the dead, a short address from Hitler and a ceremonial song of commemoration. The communal singing of the national anthem brought events to a close. Through this the 250,000 assembled people became emotionally involved in the cult, and the message of a united and strengthened nation was successfully conveyed to the audience.

Then came two days that demonstrated the military character of the régime, both in the form of the parading Party formation and the corresponding Wehrmacht (armed forces of the Reich). The sixth day belonged to the SA and SS who, organised and concentrated in huge blocks according to their standards, assembled in the Luitpold arena on either side of the so-called 'Führer Street'. After his ceremonial arrival and cult-like invocation, to the accompaniment of mournful music, Hitler walked from the Führer's pulpit to the memorial on the other side. The chief of staff of the SA and leader of the SS followed him, like ministrants, at a respectful distance and laid the 'Blood Flag' across the Führer's wreath. Whilst the remainder of the flags were lowered, the Führer stood silently in front of the 'Blood Flag', a scene clearly expressing his cult status.

Hitler then walked back from the memorial to the rostrum, followed by the bearer of the 'Blood Flag'. As high priest of the Party, the Führer brought the flag from the memorial to the dead across to the youth movement and then, surrounded by a sea of flags, consecrated the new flags and standards with the 'Blood Flag', salutes being fired at every touch. The sacrificial death of the National Socialist martyrs was understood to give incentive to the Party followers to consecrate themselves to the NSDAP and its leader. The image of aggressive determination in the service of the National Socialist cult was then strengthened by the following procession past Hitler. This consisted of 120,000 people marching for several hours against the backdrop of the town's main market and the Frauenkirche, with the black columns of the SS and the *Leibstandarte* (Hitler's personal guard) as the rear formation.

The eighth day began with a great reveille in the town. This was the day of the Wehrmacht, with mock-battles and a parade of the three Wehrmacht divisions on the Zeppelinfeld. This show of military strength was later transferred to a purpose-built parade ground at the end of the rally site. The Wehrmacht had its own ceremonial tradition which kept it apart from the pseudo-religious cult of National Socialism and the Party army. In the afternoon the final appeal took place in the old Congress Hall, celebrated by Hitler as the conclusion and ultimate manifestation of an 'ideological-national creed'.

The propagandistic elements of the Party rallies

Three fundamental aspects of propaganda and consecration were blended together in the mass events at Nuremberg. The monumental aspects within the celebratory style and the places where events took place, political symbolism and political myth, and Hitler, political symbol and figure of integration, whose mythical status was also established and intensified by the stage-management.

The concord between the architecture and mass scenes characterised the specifically National Socialist dimension within the political aesthetics of the fascists. The architecture of the 'Titanic Forum' – the name reverently given to the pulpits and halls of the rally site in Party circles – reiterated the message of the political liturgy and heightened the emotional effect on the audience. The architecture functioned as *architecture parlante* or, as Hitler put it, as 'the word of stone [which is] more convincing than the spoken word', because, according to Hitler again, when people enjoy inner experiences of great emotional intensity, then they are desirous to mould the outer world in the same vein.[17]

The political utopia of National Socialism and its aspirations to world domination were realised and indeed anticipated in Nazi architecture. Its monumental, if not megalomaniac, style was partly developed by Albert Speer, under the constant supervision of Hitler himself. No costs were spared in order to ensure that these buildings were 'immortal substantiations' that were going 'to tower, like the cathedrals of our past, into the millenniums of the future.'[18] For only 'great monuments of civilization made from granite and marble', were regarded by Hitler as a 'truthful, calming influence on the fleeting world of appearances'.[19]

The architecture of the rally site must therefore be regarded as an expression of National Socialist ideology. Speer articulated its thousand-year long, imperialist intentions in his 'Theory of Ruin Value', which was keenly picked up by Hitler. By making use of particularly enduring materials, buildings should still bear witness to the greatness of the Germanic Empire even when they had fallen into a state of ruin. Hitler was filled with enthusiasm for this idea and incorporated the 'ruin principle' as the basic concept for all building in his Reich. Speer had to submit drawings which illustrated the state of decay in which the respective building would find itself after five hundred, one thousand and two thousand years. The building should bear witness to the greatness of the Germanic Empire in the years to come, to transmit its spirit to posterity and to speak to the conscience of a future Germany. At the same time, they were designed 'to lend enhanced cultural expression to the inner value of life and the nation's will to live in an age of restricted political power'.[20]

At the laying of the foundation stone for the German Stadium, Hitler again claimed eternal value for his imperial architecture:

> It is to fortify this authority that these structures are being built! (...) One day it will be understood with utmost clarity how very great the blessing is which shines forth throughout the centuries from the tremendous edifices of this history-making age. For they above all will help, in a political sense, to unify and fortify our *Volk* more than ever before; in a collective sense, they will – for Germans – become part of a proud feeling of belonging together; in a social sense, they will prove the ridiculousness of any other differences of this world in comparison to these tremendous, gigantic witnesses of our sense of community.[21]

Instead of erecting functional multi-purpose halls, Hitler sought to develop cult gathering places, which aspired to the eternal and the classical. For this reason he turned down the plans drawn up in 1933 by the Nuremberg city councillors, who took into consideration the varied functions of the Party buildings and did not want to use them for only eight days a year. Hitler, on the other hand, understood the buildings to have a symbolic function and to underline the message of the ceremony. They served as an appropriate spatial frame for a political cult, which a contemporary art historian explained thus: 'The whole planning and structuring of the individual buildings and groupings was determined by a relationship fundamental to the National Socialist order, the relationship between the Führer and the people.'[22]

The architectural emphasis of the Führer's rostrum made his status omnipresent. It always faced the assembled Party and the mass of his followers. The main platforms of the Zeppelinfeld and of the incomplete new Congress Hall, modelled on the Colosseum at Rome, but intended to surpass it in size, raised the new political élite above the mass of the audience. The dual conception of the Luitpold arena matched the liturgical course of the funeral and redemption ceremonies. The Führer's long route through the ornament of the masses allowed a solemn progression through the assembled masses and emphasised the processional nature of the event. The gathered masses were nothing but window-dressing for the colossal architecture which only then unfolded its aesthetic effect. It was not the masses who were at the centre of the events, but the intoxicating geometry that drew the attention. The massive use of flags not only served to intensify the emotional experience of community, but also to brighten up the architecture and convey a feeling of unity. An additional heightening of the magical backdrop was finally brought about by enhancing the night-time events with fire and light.

Flags, fire and death

Three elements circumscribed the most important political symbols of the National Socialist cult: the standards and flags (especially the 'Blood Flag'), the flickering torches symbolic of fire, the sacred character of the cathedral of light. For National Socialists the burning flame meant purification, symbolised brotherly community and reminded Party members of the 'eternal process of life'. Over and above this, the flame was a symbol of 'eternal reincarnation'. However, it was not life that was celebrated in the cults, but rather its inherent components, struggle and death. The honouring of the dead and the veneration of death always held a central position in the political liturgy, as did the preference for night-time rituals. Through his central role in the celebrations, Hitler was again and again transfigured as a saviour and a death-conquering hero. The National Socialist followers were integrated into the redeeming function of the Führer by participating in such ceremonies.

The Führer as mythical hero, who through his actions and edifices gave shape to the eternal values of the nation, was the central reference point of the celebrations. The Führer-myth united the different rituals and endowed Hitler's charisma with supernatural powers, making him the integrating and legitimating force of the National Socialist régime. The identification between leader and mass following as the propagandist core of plebiscitary rule was expressed in the liturgy of the Party rallies. It is no coincidence that it was in Nuremberg that Hitler phrased his claim to power in almost classical terms: 'That is the miracle of our age – that you have found me among so many millions! And that I have found you, that is Germany's good fortune!'[23]

The magical quality of the cultic celebrations turned the Nuremberg rallies into an ideal instrument of manipulation. Architecture, scenery and lighting design were synchronised to proffer a shield against the actualities of everyday life in the Third Reich. The festival constructed a second reality which distracted from the political and social conditions in which Germany found herself. The cathedral of light and the sea of flags served two functions at the same time: they were emotionally elating *coups de théâtre*, but they were also meant to conceal the blemishes that did not fit into the celebrants' dream world.[24]

The management of the irrational

Nothing was left to chance in the stage-management of the Nuremberg rallies. Every stylistic device had a purpose. The flags were determined in number, size and position; shortcomings in the urban development and gaps in the old town fortifications were covered up by scenery. Everything was subjected to the meticulous plans of the bureaucratic and technical apparatus. The men in charge of the cult were cool-headed technicians, sons of a rational era. Yet they were also theatrical wizards who knew intuitively how to exploit age-old cultic practices for their political aims. It was exactly this link between irrationality and technical rationality, between atavistic ideology, mystical ceremony and the modern age, which helped to eliminate all critical reasoning in both, audience and participants.

It would be self-deceiving to play down the propagandist effect of these mass celebrations. The fascination which sprang from the lavish and cunning display of power, order and festive spirit, from the management of the people and light, as well as the magical quality of the geometry and monumental size of the architecture has been described many times. Films document the euphoria of the people, and even independent observers and diplomats were astonished by the atmosphere of general enthusiasm. It is no surprise to discover that foreign fascists, such as the French authors Brasillach and Drieu la Rochelle, who on several occasions went on pilgrimages to Nuremberg, were enthused by the monumentality and believed that they had seen the new man, the *homme hitlerien*, there.

Even the 'Reports about Germany' of the exiled SPD confirmed the mass enthusiasm which the rallies generated. Initially, they refused to admit this and pointed out the function of the event as diversion from the conditions within Germany. As late as 1935 they stated that 'such celebrations are simply worn out and cannot deceive the masses about the real situation in Germany'.[25] However, in 1937 they admitted that in the early years of the régime the Nuremberg rallies had not missed their target. In the meantime, however, even the participants themselves were no longer filled with enthusiasm and shied away from the strain of the endless assemblies and marches.

Situation reports from the various Party districts in the years 1937 and 1938 confirm this.[26] The tensions caused by rearmament and mobilisation gradually reduced the willingness of Party comrades to participate actively in the celebrations. When the Party leadership noticed the flagging enthusiasm of the rank and file of the followers, they sought to whip it up by increasing the monumentality of the festivities.

Emotiveness of the cult and the everyday life during the rallies

In spite of the perfect stage-management of the Nuremberg rallies, an increasing gulf between claim and reality, between cult pathos and ordinary everyday existence, began to emerge, as has often been attested by observers. Various reports from National Socialist local and district groups make it very clear that the political leaders from administrative district divisions revealed themselves to be anything but a political élite. One is also made aware of the freewheeling nature of the eight days, the excessive alcohol consumption, hooliganism and acts of vandalism in the camps. Indeed, it was not only the behaviour on the fringe of the celebrations, in the lodgings and guesthouses of the town, which stood in clear contradiction to the pretensions of order and cleanliness of National Socialism. Even during the march of the political leaders a lack of discipline led again and again to embarrassing slips. The torchlight parade past the Führer, regarded as a 'reward for the political leaders for arduous years of work',[27] turned into a torch-lit jog as the administrative district of Weser-Ems sought to close a large gap in the marching order, to the amusement of the spectators. The Führer greeted the district standard, but then disgraced the district by turning his gaze away from them. Instances such as these reveal how small the dividing line between the sublime and the ridiculous can be.

Yet the decoration of the stage and the charismatic power of the hero was believed to counteract the negative impressions. The parade of the political leaders under the cathedral of light was, according to a report from Bremen, 'an act of worship in its truest sense'.[28] In another report the effect of the Hitler-cult was described: 'For everyone the most uplifting experience was to be able to look the Führer in the eye from close by. This experience was a powerful incentive to get people involved in the movement.'[29] The Führer-myth as the propagandist core of the rally distracted from the political reality of Party as well as everyday life and became the most important means of stabilising the rule of the Nazi Party. The dream world conjured up by the events manipulated consciousness and created a second reality, which of course could not change the outside world, but could counteract and control it.

The ultimate aim: War

The political cult of the National Socialist régime, which produced such fascination amongst the masses, was aimed at creating a national community and at instilling the values of the fascist leadership in the population. The pronouncement of the Nuremberg Laws at the 1935 rally were a means of achieving National Socialist domination and were an important step on the way to depriving Jews of their civil rights and preparing for their extermination. It was not by chance that values such as obedience, willingness to make sacrifices, heroic death and struggle were celebrated in every ritual, not by chance that visions of death were conjured up. Two days before its opening in August 1939, the 'Rally for Peace' was cancelled. Something deadly serious had emerged from the heroic style of the rallies. Even during preparations for the Russian campaign in the summer of 1941, Hitler did not hold himself back from further monumental building projects. He turned down Speer's suggestion that during the advance into Russia building projects not specifically important to the war effort be stopped. Instead, he insisted on the realisation of his architectural Utopia, the Party buildings in Nuremberg and the project for a capital city for the world, Germania. However, in 1942 the huge building projects in Nuremberg were halted until 'peacetime'. The huge tower-cranes were used in the construction of the IG paint factory at Auschwitz.[30] The outbreak of the Second World War revealed what the double face of the National Socialist régime had been hiding for so long – seduction and violence.

NOTES

1. See Hans-Ulrich Thamer, 'Faszination und Manipulation: Die Nürnberger Reichsparteitage der NSDAP', in U. Schultz (ed.), *Das Fest: Eine Kulturgeschichte von der Antike bis zur Gegenwart*, Munich, 1988, pp. 352-368. For further bibliographical references see the notes to this short essay, which as been revised and expanded for the English version in this volume.
2. See Jost Dülffer, Jochen Thies, Josef Henke (eds), *Hitlers Städte*, Cologne, 1978, p. 214.
3. Quoted in Karl Arndt, *Baustelle Reichsparteitagsgelände 1938/39: Edition zum Film G 142 des IWF*, Göttingen, 1973, p. 31.
4. See Peter Reichel, *Der schöne Schein des Dritten Reiches: Faszination und Gewalt des Faschismus*, Munich, 1991.
5. See Joachim C. Fest, *Hitler: Eine Biographie*, Frankfurt, 1973, pp. 698 ff.
6. George L. Mosse, *The Nationalization of the Masses: Political Symbolism and Mass Movement in Germany from the Napoleonic Wars Through the Third Reich*, New York, 1975, p. 4 (German edition: *Die Nationalisierung der Massen. Politische Symbolik und Massenbewegungen in Deutschland von den Napoleonischen Kriegen bis zum Dritten Reich*, Frankfurt, 1976, p. 14).
7. *Ibidem*, p. 32.
8. See 'Albert Speer spricht über Architektur und Dramaturgie der national-sozialistischen Selbstdarstellung: Manuskript V/1528, Institut für den Wissenschaftlichen Film Göttingen', quoted in Mosse, *Nationalization of the Masses*, p. 200 (German edition p. 232). See also the chapter 'Architectural Megalomania' in A. Speer, *Inside the Third Reich*, New York, 1970.
9. Albert Speer, *Spandau: The Secret Diaries*, London, 1976, p. 262 (German edn: *Spandauer Tagebücher*, Frankfurt, 1975, p. 403).
10. *Ibidem*.

11. 'Die wesentlichen Ausführungen der Parteigenossen Ley und Schmeer in der ersten Vollsitzung der Hauptreferenten am 19. September 1937 im "Deutschen Hof", Nürnberg', Bundesarchiv Koblenz NS 1/23; quoted in Siegfried Zelnhefer, *Die Reichsparteitage der NSDAP: Geschichte, Struktur und Bedeutung der größten Propagandafeste im nationalsozialistischen Feierjahr*, Nuremberg, 1991, p. 266.

12. See Klaus Vondung, *Magie und Manipulation: Ideologischer Kult und politische Religion des Nationalsozialismus*, Göttingen, 1971, pp. 113ff.

13. See Hamilton T. Burden, *The Nuremberg Party Rallies, 1923-1939*, London, 1967. For further information see also Karl Heinz Schmeer, *Die Regie des öffentlichen Lebens im Dritten Reich*, Munich, 1956.

14. 'Erfahrungsberichte vom Reichsparteitag 1937', Staatsarchiv Bremen N I/74.

15. Quoted in Karl Heinz Schmeer, *Die Regie des öffentlichen Lebens im Dritten Reich*, Munich, 1948, p. 110.

16. Sir Nevile Henderson, *Failure of a Mission: Berlin 1937-1939*, London, 1940, p. 71.

17. 'Eröffnungsrede auf der Deutschen Architektur- und Kunsthandwerksausstellung, 22. Januar 1938', in Max Domarus (ed.), *Hitler: Speeches and Proclamations 1932-1945*, 4 vols, London, 1990, II, 1002 (German edn = *Hitler: Reden und Proklamationen 1932-1945*, 4 vols, Munich, 1965, I.2, p. 778).

18. 'Kulturrede, 7 September 1937', in *ibidem*, vol. 2, p. 927 (German edn vol. I.2, p. 719).

19. 'Hitlers "Kulturrede" auf dem Reichsparteitag 1937', in *Der Parteitag der Arbeit vom 1.-13. September 1937*, Munich, 1938, p. 53 f.

20. Quoted in Jochen Thies, *Architekt der Weltherrschaft: Die Endziele Hitlers*, Düsseldorf, 1976, p. 79.

21. Quoted in Domarus, *Hitler: Speeches*, vol. 2, p. 927 (German edn vol. I.2, p. 719).

22. Quoted in Anna Teut, *Architektur im Dritten Reich 1933-1945*, Berlin, 1967, p. 192.

23. Speech of 13 September 1936, quoted in Domarus, *Hitler: Speeches*, vol. 2, p. 836 (German edn. vol. I.2, p. 643).

24. This is confirmed by Speer's statement that he decided to stage the march of the political leaders at night under the cathedral of light in order to disguise the corpulence of the leaders, who had grown sizable paunches from the proceeds of their sinecures. See Albert Speer, *Inside the Third Reich*, p. 58 (German edn: *Erinnerungen*, Frankfurt, 1969, p. 71).

25. K. Behnken (ed.), *Deutschland-Berichte der Sozialdemokratischen Partei Deutschlands*, Salzhausen 1980, p. 903.

26. See Zelnhefer, *Reichsparteitage*, pp. 266ff.

27. 'Erfahrungsberichte vom Reichsparteitag 1937', Staatsarchiv Bremen, N 1/74.

28. *Ibidem*.

29. *Ibidem*.

30. Stadtarchiv Nürnberg, Rep. C 32/951.

11

The Theatre Aesthetics of the Falange

Sultana Wahnón
Translated by R. I. MacCandless

Introduction

In a previous study, entitled *Estética y crítica literarias en España (1940-1950)*, I postulated the existence of a fascist aesthetics in Spain which found its fullest expression in Ernesto Giménez Caballero's *Arte y Estado* (1935). In the same study, I also attempted to determine the extent to which literary criticism during the first ten years after the Civil War revealed the influence of this pre-war fascist aesthetics. It was found that the literary critics of the time adapted to the political shifts in the Franco régime and the course of events outside Spain. This evolution, often involving heated debate, led to an ever-increasing separation from the rules of fascist aesthetics that had initially inspired most Falangist writers. My conclusions on the existence of a fascist aesthetics in Spain and its decline were mainly based on general literary theory and criticism of poetry in particular. This study therefore follows on from this earlier research to deal with the Falange's aesthetics as applied to the theatre.

In February 1993, during the symposium that brought together the contributors to this volume, I was able to become more familiar with Roger Griffin's ideas on the nature of fascist ideology. As Dr Griffin's is the opening chapter in this book, it seemed natural that I should attempt to determine whether the aesthetics that I had described as fascist in 1988 fitted the characteristics of fascist ideology in general, as it is understood here. This is the aim of the first part of this chapter. The second part centres on the characterisation of fascist aesthetics as developed by Giménez Caballero, and summarises the broader study mentioned above. The third section of this chapter deals with the question of fascist theatrical aesthetics, which I analyse with reference both to Giménez Caballero and representative texts by the Falangist writer Gonzalo Torrente Ballester. The fourth and final section examines the earliest changes undergone by this approach to theatre in the post-Civil War years, again using texts by Torrente Ballester and other influential Falangist critics.

The question of Falange and Spanish fascism

Long after Stanley Payne[1] demonstrated the ideological affinity of the Falange to fascism, Spanish public opinion and, significantly, many Spanish intellectuals are still irritated by the suggestion that the Falange, which played such an important rôle in the formation of the Franco régime, had been a movement comparable to Italian or German fascism. The fierce controversy sparked off by Julio Rodríguez Puértolas' provocatively titled *Literatura fascista española*[2] should be seen in the context of this general reluctance to accept the fact that there had been Spanish writers, or politicians, or indeed simply individuals, who could be classified as fascist. For all that, Rodríguez Puértolas' decision to define a fascist as 'anyone who, in one way or another, put his pen and his thought, no matter what subtle distinctions, at the service of the political régime that arose out of the military uprising against the Second Spanish Republic on 18 July 1936'[3] was criticised even by those who, at the time, were willing to accept the existence of a fascist movement in Spain.

This abusively broad definition of the term 'fascist' has harmed rather than favoured the thesis of fascism in Spain. We should rather consider the existence of a Spanish fascist movement not by assuming an inherent correlation between Francoism and fascism, but rather between Falange and fascism. It is significant that Falange Española (FE) came close to being called *Fascismo Español* at the instigation of José Antonio Primo de Rivera himself.[4] The fact that Falange was the bearer of the fascist formula for Spain is clarified beyond doubt by an examination of the journals published by the movement in the years preceding the Civil War, such as *La Conquista del Estado, F.E., Semanario de la Falange, Haz, Jerarquía* and *Vértice*. Explicit references and admiring allusions to fascism abounded in the articles published by ideologues and collaborators of Falange, e.g., 'Fascismo es elevación' (*F.E.*, no. 3, 1934), and in original fascist documents, such as the 'Discurso de

Mussolini en la II Asamblea Quinquenal del Régimen' (*F.E.*, no. 10, 1934). While the characteristics of Spanish fascism can be detected in the texts written by Spanish Falangists themselves, the more general topics of fascist ideology were also frequently present. One of these was anti-Semitism, which is usually thought of as totally alien to a country such as Spain which had practically no Jews. Issue no. 2 of *Haz* (1935) contains the following statement: 'It saddens us to see how a few wretches still defend Marxist ideals. No Spaniard can sleep easy as long as there is another Spaniard that does not know that Marx was a disgusting Jew who trafficked in workers' flesh.'

It is in any case clear that the Falange was motivated by the ideal of national regeneration out of decadence which, according to Roger Griffin,[5] constitutes the central myth of fascist ideology. Griffin defines the fascist *minimum* as palingenetic ultranationalism, which is also the central myth upon which the ideology of the Falange was built. The Falange never saw itself as merely the restorer of an old order, but rather as the creator of a new system that took its inspiration from a glorious past. The Utopian, revolutionary aspect that distinguishes fascist from ultra-conservative discourse is constantly present in the speeches of, for example, José Antonio Primo de Rivera.

One of the arguments most commonly employed to dissociate the Falange (and to an even greater extent the Franco régime itself) from fascism is that of its adherence to the Catholic faith. However, one of the most solid convictions of the European fascist movement was that each nation had to find its own formula to attain the essential objectives pursued. The Falangists drifted towards an increasing insistence on Catholicism not only because they needed the support of the conservative forces in the country, but above all because they became convinced that the only fascist formula that could possibly succeed in Spain would have to include a Catholic component. The 'new Catholicity' for Spain was to be formulated by the major ideologue of Spanish fascism, Ernesto Giménez Caballero.

Giménez Caballero, who was first associated with the Juntas de Ofensiva Nacional Sindicalista (JONS) and later with the Falange, was a key figure in the shaping of Spanish fascism. When reconstructing its political ideology, two of his texts are of paramount importance: *Genio de España*, subtitled *Exaltaciones a una resurrección nacional. Y del mundo* (1932),[6] which ran to three editions; and *La nueva catolicidad*, subtitled *Teoría general sobre el fascismo en*

Europa: en España,[7] the two editions of which appeared in 1933. While assuming the universal character of fascist ideas, Giménez Caballero applied them in the context of what he called the Spanish nation's *genius*, and the 'new Catholicity' is presented in both of the aforementioned books as a key ingredient of Spanish fascism. It was no accident that after the publication of these works by Giménez Caballero, José Antonio decided to assert, in the first number of *F.E.*, that the 'reconstruction' of Spain had to have a 'Catholic spirit'.[8] 'Catholic' here did not just mean the restoration of traditional Catholicism, but the construction of a *new Catholicity*, by means of which the Catholic view of life would serve fascist ideals. The Catholicism of the Falange cannot be seen as an obstacle to the acceptance of the existence of a Spanish fascist movement, although we must be extremely careful to distinguish it from other, more traditional types of Catholicism present in the Franco régime.

The development of a fascist aesthetics in Spain

In *Arte y Estado*, published in 1935, Giménez Caballero expressed his desire to become 'the Spanish Goebbels': 'Fascists of Spain, I ask you to be compassionate with me when we triumph. Give me that Ministry! I would only exchange it for the Grand Inquisitor's throne.'[9] As if in reply to his request, at the very beginning of the Civil War, Giménez Caballero undertook responsibility, together with General Millán Astray, for organising the Services of Press, Propaganda and Radio. However, he was very quickly replaced, in 1937, by Antonio Tovar and Dionisio Ridruejo, who, paradoxically, was to become known as the 'Spanish Goebbels'. It may have been that the excessive zeal of Giménez Caballero's fascist militancy had something to do with his change of fortune,[10] but, nonetheless, his theories had a significant influence on the artistic policies of the new régime.

In his system of fascist aesthetics, Giménez Caballero theorised on all the arts, from architecture to theatre and music, in a half-speculative, half-political manner. *Arte y Estado* is the text containing this system and, therefore, if not quite the 'official aesthetic manual of Francoism' as Dionisio Cañas would have it,[11] it certainly must be regarded as the aesthetic manual of Spanish fascism. There is one key idea that dominates all the aesthetic choices described in the book, and that is the idea of *norm*. In

1932, Giménez Caballero confessed his disgust of Orteguian relativism and of the then topical concept of pluralism.[12] This was not because he found the idea of 'plural truths' incorrect, i.e., the idea that 'each individual has his own truth', but rather, as he said, he could not avoid 'the nostalgia of those times and those people, when all moved forward together under a single discourse, a single bell, a single, sublime comedian, under someone who disguised the dance of life so that no other truth than his was heard.'[13]

Giménez Caballero desired the appearance of 'a compassionate soul that would save us from the *horrible torment of choice*, someone who would deceive us with a supreme deceit'. Finally, he projected his desire to break free from the anguish of what we might now call the 'undecidable' in the image of a Spain converted *en masse* to Catholic fascism, – a new Spain that would not choose, but would leave decisions to a charismatic leader who, like Hitler and Mussolini, represented the Truth for all of them.[14]

Giménez Caballero, the pragmatic ideologue who saw fascist Catholicism as a way to re-establish unequivocal values in the face of the ambivalence of market-based societies, was also the only one to systematically work out a fascist aesthetics and theory of art. As one might expect, he sets himself up as representative of the aesthetic truth and as the leader who chooses values and models in order to spare the rest of the nation the horrible anguish of choice. Although I have offered an exhaustive analysis of this aesthetic system in my studies on Spanish literary criticism in the 1940s,[15] a brief review of the general principles of the system is required before the theatrical aesthetics of Spanish fascism can be characterised.

The theory of art described by Giménez Caballero in *Arte y Estado* is based on the idea of *propaganda*, which is the central idea of all fascist aesthetics. He affirms categorically that 'art is propaganda' [AyE 84] and adds: 'Win souls! Catechise hearts! Win new followers! Has art, tell me, tell me with your hands on your hearts, has Art ever had a higher aim?' [AyE 87] Having described art as the 'divine pawn in a general plan of attack', as the 'supreme combat weapon'[AyE 89], he postulates that the only difference between a crossbow and a poem is 'efficiency. Only that. A difference of distance and length of shot.'[AyE 87]

The aesthetic system proposed by Giménez Caballero, which he called *Christian classicism*, contained other commonplaces of fascist aesthetics apart from the conception of art as propaganda. Firstly, the idea that the myth of the solitary artist had to be done away with, because it exemplifies the 'arrogance' of Western art [AyE 38], and that art and the artist must be subjected, as they were in the Middle Ages, to a discipline and a hierarchy that reflect the will of the fascist State and allows for the 'humility' of the artisan. [AyE 62] This explains why Giménez Caballero, who was already complaining in 1929 of a general 'incomprehension of that magnificent phenomenon of the new social world called syndicalism',[16] displayed immense admiration towards the 'syndicalist trend in art' [AyE 212]. In his opinion, this trend showed the artists' 'desire to return to a spiritual discipline' and to destroy the romantic myth of the free artist: 'One of the lies of humanism was that the artist could live alone. The lie was confirmed by Romanticism with its bohemians: extravagance, poverty, garrets. The artist neither can, nor knows how, nor wants to live alone. Within every artist there invariably lies the comrade, in the sense of both monk and guildsman.' [AyE 214]

Secondly, all the trends in modern art since the Enlightenment and, especially, the aesthetics of contemporary and avant-garde movements, are rejected as examples of excessive individualism: 'Distrust pure artists or poets more and more. They are either retrograde or – the easier option – opportunist.' [AyE 33] Thirdly, after the rejection of aestheticism, Giménez Caballero opts for a type of art, whose content would combat 'the hypocrisy of the *purely beautiful.*' [AyE 83] Only when art once again places emphasis on content, would it be able to become a 'vehicle' for the 'points of view' of the new state, [AyE 214] i.e., become an instrument to spread the vision of the world and the values that the fascist State attempted to establish as a 'new *collective morality*' [AyE 214]:

> The artist is nothing more than a guide in life, who reveals a divine message. Art is always revelation and the work of divinity. A god communicates with his chosen one; the seer then transmits his treasure to a priestly group of initiates; and these, in turn, spread the Truth to the outer social layers of their people. [AyE 92]

Fourthly, art had to be formally and stylistically exemplary. This was required not only to propagate certain messages, but also to do so in particular ways, which, in the case of Spanish fascist art, were to be inspired by the model of the classic art of the Siglo de Oro – hence the name *Christian classicism.* In this connection, we should remember that an essential characteristic of Giménez Caballero's aesthetic system was the proposal of models for artistic creation. Since the mythical core of fascist ideology is what

Griffin calls palingenetic ultranationalism,[17] it is also a central myth of fascist aesthetics that each nation has its own perfect form of art and that this can be reborn after a period of perceived decadence. The Escorial Monastery, in which Giménez Caballero saw the 'perfect style of an entire creation' [AyE 238], is such an example of a work of art, which the nation's 'will to be' must save from decadence brought on by centuries of estrangement from the true Spanish essence:

> There is Spain with the symbol of its *supreme State* achieved once, for a few years in the sixteenth century: *El Escorial*. A State made of stone, a hieroglyphical sphinx. Today sunk in time, like an abyss, from whose depths its tower, bells, crosses and domes cry out to us in anguish, for help, like a submerged temple, for a titanic Spanish generation to return it to the light and the vertex of history. [AyE 233]

The Escorial thus becomes the *supreme model* of Spanish fascist art, as well as a political symbol of Imperial, Catholic Spain, which a titanic generation would resuscitate by its will power. The implication of its being considered an artistic model was that it offered formal and stylistic rules. What made the Escorial suitable as a model was not only its significance – its meaning as stone raised to the glory of an Imperial and Catholic Spain – but also its external appearance:

> I am certain that if all the laws emanating from that reign of the Escorial could be put in order and materialised, if they could be *reflected* in their hierarchy of values, the result would be Surprising: it would be like the monastery reflected in the garden pond: it would be the real and perfect image of the Escorial. [AyE 238]

The recovery of this symbol of the Spanish Empire, together with the resurgence of a new Imperial (imperialist) Spain was not an illusory enterprise for Giménez Caballero. The State to come would be charged with 'saving' the *old* monument from collapse precisely by seeking inspiration in that building to create a *new* architecture: 'The hour of a new architecture, of a constructive style has come. For the hour of a new State – the hierarchical, ordering genius of Rome – has come to the world.' [AyE 72]

The palingenetic myth that informs Giménez Caballero's considerations on the Escorial is also present in each of the models proposed throughout *Arte y Estado* for the different arts. The following pages are concerned with the model for drama and the performing arts under the Franco régime.

The theatrical model of Spanish fascism:
Lope de Vega and the 'return to mystery'

The ideologues of the Falange became concerned with the reor-
ganisation of the theatre at an early date. The third centenary of
the death of Lope de Vega, held in 1935, was an occasion on which
to consider the characteristics that should be present in the theatre
of the new Spain. A review of Falangist publications in 1935
shows that Lope de Vega was raised to the rank of a symbol of fascist theatre. As with the Escorial, the theatre of Lope symbolised
that 'eternal Spanish theatre' from which, by virtue of its essential
Spanishness, the new theatre should take its inspiration. The
clearest signal of the attempt to turn Lope into an aesthetic model
was an article by Eduardo Ródenas, published in *Haz*[18] and entitled 'Lope, alma de imperio'. It concluded with a call to the
reader: 'Look well on him, for Fray Félix Lope de Vega y Carpio is
a true symbol.'

Other texts appearing in the same journal between 1935 and
1936 insisted on both the eternal character of Lope's dramatic art
and on the need to create a new Spanish theatre. As regards the
former, an article called 'Lope de Vega, artesano', signed by L. B.
L. in the April 1935 issue, claimed that his theatre was 'the symbol
of the Spain of his time. It symbolises the military, Catholic, (...)
hand-crafted unity of Spain's unchanging destiny.' The July number contains a similar statement: 'Lope is the exact representation
of Spain's essence.' ('Lope de Vega en Italia'). In February 1936, G.
Sánchez-Puerta stated: 'Spanish theatre was given its definitive
shape by Lope de Vega, the Hispanic genius that arouses universal admiration', and, a little further on: 'Spanish dramatic art has
crystallised in Lope.' ('El genio del teatro español: Lope de Vega').
If these theoreticians of drama had simply intended to restore
Lope's theatre by producing his plays or inviting modern authors
to slavishly imitate him, we would be dealing with aesthetic ultra-
traditionalism. However, the fascist nature of their theorising is
indicated by the fact that, together with the insistence on the eternal character of Lope's theatre, these critics persistently refer to the
novelty of the theatre that should be written in Spain, following the
model of Lope. The most explicit propounder of this was the
author of 'Lope de Vega en Italia', who, having proclaimed that
'Lope is the exact representation of the Spanish essence', then
warned of the danger of becoming 'too enthusiastic about the

glory of the past', and proposed: 'Let us therefore seek new values that make us forget our Lope.'

However, the text that most clearly expresses the palingenetic myth in Spanish fascist theatre is an article also published in the April 1935 issue of *Haz*:

> As in all periods of profoundest national decadence, the theatre of this Second Spanish Republic is moribund, just as those of the bewitched or contemptible Monarchies of Carlos II or Fernando VII. (…) But we are not going to write an elegy for the theatre. Just the opposite. (…) We want to help it to die so that the new theatre may be born with the regeneration of Spain. Then we shall cry: 'The theatre is dead. Long live the theatre!'19

If this appeal to the old and the new, this combination of nostalgia for a lost past and revolutionary violence is one of the distinguishing features of fascist, as opposed to merely traditionalist, discourse, there is no doubt that Falangist theories of theatre in 1935 and 1936 were fascist in tone and character. As, too, was the chapter that Giménez Caballero dedicated to the theatre in his manual of aesthetics published around the same time. Under the title 'Técnicas intelectivas: el teatro vuelve al Misterio', the chapter repeats the general theory of fascism: the theatre has reached its end, its life is in danger, it is expiring with 'the dying man's last breath'. [AyE 164] Those responsible for this crisis or decadence in the theatre are the 'experimenters of a new theatre', i.e., avant-garde authors who had almost 'sunk the theatre for ever.' But the suggestion of rebirth appears beside the idea of decadence. Having said that the theatre is breathing its last, Giménez Caballero does not write it off with an elegy, but announces a miraculous recovery: 'The theatre today is safely on the way to convalescence and a healthy restoration.' The cause of this miraculous salvation lies in the theatre's return to its 'original and permanent essence', which is the *mystery*. This return is not considered in traditionalist terms, but as novelty, as a new theatre 'of our time'. [AyE 175] Here, too, the symbol was Lope de Vega, who is celebrated precisely because of his 'audacity' in 'innovating and breaking with routine.' [AyE 167]

The palingenetic myth is not the only factor contributing to fascist theorising on the theatre. Perhaps even more important is the propagandistic function attributed to theatrical production. This explains why Lope is praised above all for his capacity to 'embody innovation in the entire national mass of fervent spectators.' [AyE

167] Giménez Caballero did not hesitate to take up Mussolini's idea of an 'art of our time' in the form of a mass theatre. [AyE 172] Lope served as a model because his innovations had attracted the masses, who could then be indoctrinated in the 'new collective morality' by the 'priests' of the new régime. A new Lope de Vega had to be found to repeat this miracle, but Giménez Caballero was aware that this would not be quite so easy. He therefore proposed that 'while the poets that understand the poetic and dramatic material of our time come to the fore and achieve *our formula'*, experiments should be made with a type of theatre related to what he called *mystery*. [AyE 175]

A definition of Giménez Caballero's mysterious *mystery* will provide us with what could be thought of as the *minimum* of Spanish fascist theatre, i.e., the common denominator of all the plays with fascist pretensions, whether produced before an enthusiastic throng or not. The key to the meaning of the *mystery* of fascist theatre can be found in Giménez Caballero's description of the bullfight, which he and other ideologues of the Falange held as the only true theatrical spectacle remaining in Spain: 'In its very essence, the *Bullfight* is a religious mystery, the sacrifice of a God (totemised by the bull) by a priest (represented by the matador) before a faithful mass, who palpitate, scream, participate, become hoarse and drunk with passion, blood, enthusiasm'. [AyE 173]

The participation of God, a priest and a devoted, passionate mass of faithful followers was the *conditio sine qua non* that Giménez Caballero demanded of the new theatre until the new Lope appeared: 'The *hierarchy*, (…) the return to the *hero*, the *protagonist*, the *saint*, the *saviour*, against a background of faithful masses.' [AyE 175] This is also the distinguishing feature of fascist drama as opposed to the propaganda theatre of the Soviet Union. Although the Soviet government had fostered a theatre for the masses, this was not what Giménez Caballero aspired to as it had no place for the hero: 'No protagonists, nor dominating figures. No "individualities", nor "individualisms". A theatre for the *massman*.' [AyE 171] Unlike the Soviet theatre, fascist theatre would achieve the 'consummation of the formula of the *hero* (the West) with the *mass* (the East)'. Giménez Caballero did not hesitate to describe this as a 'profound return to the mystery.' [AyE 176] As an example of the theatre he desired for the new Spain, Giménez Caballero mentioned Copeau's production of *Savonarola* in the Piazza della Signoria in Florence before 'a mass of 4,000 spectators from all over Italy, standing in an amphitheatre constructed as if for gladiatorial combat in the time of Caesar.' [AE 172] If *Savonarola* achieved the miracle of being theatre for the masses, it was because it fitted the *mystery* formula: it is the story of 'a hero who fails in order to save a nation.' [AE 175]

The mystery of fascist theatre is thus revealed: until the arrival of the new Spain in which the new theatre would take root, fascists were to create a theatre that propagated the idea of a national community united under the yoke of a hero, who was to redeem the nation by converting it into a great imperialist power. Two other key myths were connected to the *mystery*: populist nationalism and the charismatic leader. Giménez Caballero's explicit reference to the 'myth of the State, the myth of what is national'[20] reveals the central position this myth occupies in his fascist ideology. He went on to describe it, with proverbial cynicism, as a myth which, by imposing itself 'on both the historically hostile classes', allowed fascism to preserve 'the bourgeoisie, as against the tabula rasa that Russian communism made of it.'[21]

The myth of the national community over and above social classes can be found in much Falangist discourse concerning the theatre. In the July 1935 issue of *Haz* an anonymous author[22] reflected on the difference between a 'theatre of the people' and a 'political theatre'. He believed that the theatre of Lope de Vega was theatre of the people, because its audience was 'the entire Spanish people – aristocrats, soldiers, clergy, craftsmen and rogues.' On the other hand, the 'social dramas' of Galdós, Dicenta or Benavente would be political theatre, as they had 'broken with the popular identity' and converted 'the entire Spanish people' into 'social classes in conflict'. The omnipresence of the myth of the nation in Falangist texts parallels the central place given to it by José Antonio in his speech on the occasion of the founding of the movement:

> The Motherland is a total unit made up of all individuals and all classes: the Motherland cannot be in the hands of the strongest class or the best organised party. The Motherland is a transcendental synthesis, an indivisible synthesis, with its own ends to fulfil. What we desire is that the movement of that day and the State that it creates should be an efficient, authoritarian instrument at the service of that unquestionable unit, that permanent unit, that irrevocable unit called the Motherland.[23]

The miracle of converting the antagonistic classes into an 'irrevocable unit' was to be achieved by combining the myth of the nation with that of the *hero* or charismatic leader. Suddenly, an exceptional individual would stand out from the entirety of the nation and become its saviour, leading it towards its glorious destiny. The *mystery* is, therefore, that mysterious means by which the popular and the aristocratic, or, as Giménez Caballero clearly stated, mass and hero, become united. The production of the *Savonarola* was used as a reference to exemplify the fascist concept of theatre. It showed the creation of a national community on two different levels. First, in the Piazza della Signoria, where the *'mass* of 4,000 spectators' from all over Italy had assembled to witness the spectacle; second, on the stage, where the *people* were redeemed by the *hero*. In fascist terms, this production would have been considered a work of 'popular', not 'political' theatre.

When Giménez Caballero wrote *Arte y Estado*, he found it preferable for the hero to be sacrificed, as in the most unfortunate of bullfights. The 'blood and abnegation' of the hero, who 'fails in order to save his people', was the spectacle by which he wished to achieve that 'fierce dramatic catharsis' of an intoxicated audience. The image of the hero who sacrifices himself for his people reveals the 'liturgical, hieratic, mystic, that is, *mysterious* essence' [AyE 173] that Giménez Caballero demanded of fascist theatre. Ultimately, he only manages to relate this to Catholicism by means of a daring twist in which he describes the service of mass as an equally mysterious spectacle: '*The Mass*: what other divine drama but the Mass, where the priest still acts out, still *represents* our Saviour's passion, performing the communion with bread and wine before all men?' [AyE 174]

The fascist formula for the theatre thus formed part of the broader formula of *new Catholicity*. However, a closer analysis of the *mystery* to which the theatre had to return reveals that the content and function of the proposed liturgical theatre were more fascist than Catholic. Catholicism was above all an instrument by which to accomplish the fascist aim of a totalitarian State, in which the will of the individual, converted into the mass of the people, would be subjected to the will of an aristocratic élite presided over by a charismatic leader.

We can now answer the question of whether a fascist theatrical aesthetics existed in Spain, and can state that it can be found in the chapter of *Arte y Estado* on theatre, and also in different articles published in Falangist journals. The remainder of this chapter will be concerned with the question of whether the ideas of Giménez Caballero were upheld by other Falangist ideologues and what rôle his concepts played in the post-Civil War period of the Franco régime.

Developments in fascist theatrical aesthetics in the 1940s

Giménez Caballero's theories of the new Spanish theatre found many followers. Gonzalo Torrente Ballester – at the time a Falangist – was the first to make a serious attempt to develop them further. Torrente was to dramatic theory what Luís Rosales and Luís Felipe Vivanco were to poetic theory,[24] that is, the person responsible for the assimilation of the aesthetic system elaborated by Giménez Caballero and for its adaptation to the changes in political circumstances. In 1937, in the throes of the Civil War, Torrente Ballester published his short essay 'Razón y ser de la dramática futura',[25] which he claimed dealt with 'the drama to be developed in the bright tomorrow'. [RyS 61] In this essay he confessed his allegiance to Giménez Caballero as regards the theatre, and even quoted the fragment from the chapter on theatre in *Arte y Estado*, referring to the 'original and permanent essence' of the theatre being 'no other than that of the mystery'. [AyE 73] Torrente's essay, which is little more than a replica of Giménez Caballero's chapter, provides another argument in favour of the close similarity of Falangist and fascist ideology in the years immediately preceding the establishment of the Franco régime, although it also illustrates the less aggressive, more restrained tone of the intellectuals who, like Torrente Ballester, were to centre round the review *Escorial* in the period after the Civil War.

In 'Razón y ser', which was written in a less virulent tone than the work of Giménez Caballero, the relation between the hero and the mass also constitutes the crux of dramatic theory. For Torrente, the resolution of this relation 'in perfect balance' was not only a *mystery*, but a genuine *miracle*: 'The miracle of future dramatic art must be how the relation between the hero or protagonist and the mass or chorus is resolved in perfect balance.' [RyS 66] Torrente Ballester's essay centres on an illustration of how to achieve this theatrical miracle, firstly by recommending, or demanding 'the return to the heroic'. The themes of the new drama could not continue to be the 'minor bourgeois squabbles' that were so typical of the immediately preceding theatre, because 'the multitude can only be subjugated with marvellous things, when it can follow its natural tendency for admiration of what is heroic.' However, since he was aware that a new heroic theatre could not arise out of nothing, his advice was to look back to the old national epic and 'borrow' the names of the old heroes in order to construct the new dramas that were to *subjugate* the multitude. The model invoked was, inevitably, the Spanish theatre of the sixteenth century.

On the other hand, the hero and the mass had to fulfil certain prerequisites so as to coexist on stage in perfect equilibrium. Rather surprisingly, Torrente said that the 'first and most urgent thing is that the mass ceases to be such.' His justification for such an unexpected demand was that the mass is characterised by 'multiplicity of voices' and has to become a chorus. Unlike the mass, the chorus is unanimous; its movements 'represent popular thought regarding very specific matters, and its voice is one.' [RyS 67] In short, the mass could only coexist in perfect equilibrium with the hero, when the multitude was transformed into a monolithic unit from which ideological dissent was excluded. In turn, the hero had to be 'an exceptional man' destined, as Giménez Caballero would have it, to failure and the incomprehension of his people: 'The hero or protagonist aspires to inaccessible goals, the outcome of which must always be unfortunate.' [RyS 62-63] The image of a hero sacrificed in the redemption of his people, who do not understand 'the superhuman efforts of the hero nor the solutions offered by him, as a revelation, to the deepest desires of man' [RyS 68], is the same as that of the *Savonarola* so admired by Giménez Caballero. Copeau's production provided the formula to be attempted by fascist theatre as soon as the new Spain was born, and where, one imagines, the hero would finally emerge victorious and impose his solutions on the disoriented mass. Until this fortunate situation should arise, the tragedy in which the hero fails, would contribute to making the subjugated mass feel the obligation to support the efforts of the national leader.

Once the Civil War had ended, in a Spain led by its charismatic leader Franco, the Falange had control of propaganda and the majority of cultural affairs until the end of the Second World War, especially from 1939 to 1941. Leaving aside the question of whether the Franco régime was fascist in character or not, we can say that Falange, which professed a fascist ideology, played a significant rôle in the cultural life of Spain just after the Civil War. *Escorial*, the first journal dedicated to cultural affairs in Franco's Spain, was founded and directed by Falangist poets and intellectuals, who deliberately chose an emblematic name that implied obeisance to the supreme symbol of fascist aesthetics as proposed by Giménez Caballero. Between 1940, when *Escorial* was created, and the end of 1941, no article appeared which openly challenged the aesthetic values of the Falangist élite.[26]

It was, however, the Falangist élite itself that gradually modified its positions, consequently opening the way for other aesthetic positions in the postwar years.[27] As regards the theatre, the changes can be detected quite early. Gonzalo Torrente Ballester's article of 1941, 'Cincuenta años de teatro español y algunas cosas más',[28] introduced some important modifications to the fascist model of theatre as developed in the 1930s. This essay centres on the possibility of creating a new national theatre in Spain. He defined this as a 'spectacle that displays the coinciding ideals of the Motherland, as historical subject, and its people.'[CAT 254] Torrente, who did not conceal his desire for such a theatre, explains that this could only come about when a Spanish *people* existed:

National theatres coexisted with a community of ideals between the different classes into which Spanish, or English, society is divided. Despite and above their differences, higher and lower nobility, clergy, bourgeois and villains knew themselves to be involved in something common to all and closely related to the life of the Motherland. [CAT 254]

The text did not therefore reject one of the key myths of fascist ideology: that of the national community over and above the social classes. In fact, the rest of the essay consists of a review of the history of Spanish theatre from the eighteenth century up to the avant-garde, with no aim other than to demonstrate that the *decadence* of national theatre was caused by the division between the social classes and the consequent break-up of the 'spiritual unity of Spain'. [CAT 255] Modern rationalism is presented as being closely linked with the 'death' of national theatre:

In the eighteenth century that profound communion between the Homeland and the people and also between the different classes disappeared. The Homeland adopted courses, whether good or bad, that the people neither felt nor knew; society had broken the union of its classes, who already had little in common. [CAT 255]

This situation had become worse in the last two centuries: in the nineteenth century because 'the Spanish people were much very like a family which, with no regard for anything else, had given itself up to petty squabbling'; [CAT 256] and in the twentieth century because 'Spanish society from 1898 to 1936 is divided into impenetrable strata.'[CAT 264] The conclusion is that 'the miracle of a national theatre' would be impossible as long as it is directed to 'a senseless society, inattentive to history and indifferent to the Motherland.' CAT 278] Nothing in Torrente's article suggests that since then any such miracle had taken place. The two-fold task of creating a national theatre and a national community was still entrusted to the future: 'our future as a nation is at present linked to that of our dramatic works.'[CAT 278]

Although the myth of social unity persists, the change with regard to the 1937 essay consists in the fact that there is not the slightest allusion to what the form or content of the new theatre should be. In other words, there is no explicit mention of a *formula* for the new theatre. If such a formula did exist, it would have to be culled from the positive or negative appraisals that Torrente made of the playwrights he reviewed. In this sense, Torrente's article is quite exceptional, given the context in which it was written. See, for example, what he says about Galdós: 'Galdós is an extraordinary figure of our dramatic art, worthy of being revived and studied with more love and veneration than certain scarecrows of the nineteenth century. Even though he was liberal and anti-clerical.' [CAT 258]

The generation of '98, which was officially reinstated in 1945, was also highly esteemed by Torrente who, in 1941, stood in opposition to the more inflexible sectors of culture in Franco's Spain: 'In a literary sense, the generation of '98 is the most important in Spain since the seventeenth century.' [CAT 259] He also recognises the 'very highest poetic and dramatic qualities' [CAT 277] of Valle-Inclán, Azorín, Unamuno, the Machado brothers and even García Lorca, whom he dares to mention.

Together with this abundance of positive appraisals of modern Spanish theatre, Torrente's essay also reveals contempt of all imitations of Spanish classical theatre. The theatre, he argued, could not persist in 'living off the values of a defunct social system', and historical-poetic theatre would take as 'valid a few dead things on which it attempts to base itself'.[CAT 271] Torrente's essay thus represents a modification of the fascist formula for the theatre: the heroic is not imposed here as the only formula for Spanish theatre. Just as the model for poetry based on Garcilaso began to widen its limits just after the Civil War and the technical and formal innovations of modern poetry were admitted, so the model for the theatre based on Lope gave way to a much more flexible norm, that did not demand the sacrifice of a hero for his people. Until the appearance of that new and mythical national theatre, the Falangist élite thought it appropriate to recover all that it could of the theatrical traditions, which had previously been shunned in order to give preference to what was then regarded as the only genuinely national model for a Spanish theatre.

Nonetheless, the elimination of the heroic as a component of theatrical aesthetics was slow. The most recalcitrant Falangists continued to favour a theatre with classical echoes. In 1942, Tomás Borrás, the theatre critic of *Cuadernos de Literatura Contemporánea* and one-time head of the Sindicato Nacional del Espectáculo, still made positive appraisals of works like *El estudiante endiablado* by Eduardo Marquina because of its 'classical flavour' and its 'Castilian tone, true to the spirit of Lope'.[29] However by 1942, together with the positive valuation of classical inspiration, it was common to find praise of all that revealed awareness and mastery of modern dramatic literature. The Falangist poet and playwright Eduardo Juliá Martínez, who wrote a verse drama as late as 1944, reviewed Marquina's *El esudiante endiablado*. Apart from the reminiscences of Lope and Calderón, he also emphasised the 'influence of Victor Hugo, (…) Guerra Junqueiro, Eça de Queiroz and Baudelaire', to whom he later added the names of 'Anatole France, Valle-Inclán *and other modern authors.*'[30] (My italics).

The evolution of the Falange's theatrical aesthetics did not imply that the Falange had ceased to be fascist, but rather, in response to the pragmatic nature of fascist ideology, it adapted to the changing circumstances. In general, fascism reveals its revolutionary aspect only when trying to obtain power, and when installed, it substitutes it with the fiercest conservatism.[31] If we also consider that, in the case of Spain, Falange had to share control of cultural affairs with the Ministry of Education (which Franco's eclectic régime always put in charge of traditional Catholics), it becomes clear that they could not maintain their utopian-revolutionary fervour for long. The policy of normalisation that all fascist régimes apply when they take power also affected the cultural sphere. As regards aesthetics (including theatrical aesthetics), this meant the acceptance of the most traditional forms of the preceding ages and of those trends in contemporary world theatre that were considered innocuous.

Nevertheless, revolutionary rhetoric continued to be an important component of many Falangist texts in the years immediately following the Civil War. At least until the final defeat of the Axis powers in the Second World War, it occupied pride of place along with the rhetoric of national reconciliation. To conclude, here is Tomás Borrás' 1942 interpretation of the most recent history of Spanish theatre, in which he combines the fascist myths of regeneration and populism:

> Handed over to utilitarian, profiteering impresarios, considered solely as a business, the theatre languished as a victim of the idea that only 'whatever was profitable' should be staged (…). Today, in the Spain of the Falange, the right course has been taken, and I am honoured, as head of the Union, to have been the rescuer and organiser of one of the playhouses in Spain that uphold the standard that the theatre is an art for the people.[32]

NOTES

1. Stanley G. Payne, *Falange: Historia del fascismo español*, Madrid, 1985 (1st edn 1961).
2. Julio Rodríguez Puértolas, *Literatura fascista española*, vol. 1: *Historia*, Madrid, 1986.
3. Rodríguez Puértolas, *Literatura fascista*, vol. 1, p. 9.
4. Payne, *Falange*, p. 57.
5. Roger Griffin, *The Nature of Fascism*, London, 1991. pp. 26-55.
6. Ernesto Giménez Caballero, *Genio de España: Exaltaciones a una resurrección nacional. Y del mundo*, Madrid, 1932.
7. Ernesto, Giménez Caballero, *La nueva catolicidad: Teoría general sobre el fascismo en Europa: en España*, Madrid, 1933.
8. Cited by Payne, *Falange*, p. 87.
9. Ernesto Giménez Caballero, *Arte y Estado*, Madrid, 1935, p. 88. In the following cited as AyE.
10. See Daniel Sueiro and Bernardo Díaz Nosty, *Historia del franquismo*, vol. 1, Madrid, 1986 (1st edn 1978), p. 135.
11. Dionisio Cañas, 'La posmodernidad cumple 50 años en España', *El País*, 28 April 1985, pp. 16-17.
12. See Ernesto Giménez Caballero, 'La feria de los discursos', *La Gaceta literaria. El Robinson literario de España*, no. 121, 15 January 1932, pp. 9-10.
13. Giménez Caballero, *Feria de los discursos*, p. 9.
14. *Ibidem*, p. 10.
15. See Sultana Wahnón, *Estética y crítica literarias en España 1940-1950*, Granada, 1988, pp. 22-110 and Sultana Wahnón, 'El concepto de rehumanización en el pensamiento literario del fascismo español', *Homenaje al profesor Antonio Gallego Morell*, vol. 3, Granada, 1989, pp. 477-87.

16. Cited by María Sferrazza, 'Ernesto Giménez Caballero en la literatura española desde la Dictadura a la República', in Lucy Tandy and María Sferrazza (eds), *Giménez Caballero y 'La gaceta Literaria'*, Madrid, 1977, p. 110.

17. Griffin, *Fascism*, pp. 38-44.

18. *Haz*, special edition, 1935.

19. 'Notas teatrales: Máscaras', *Haz*, April, 1935.

20. Giménez Caballero, 'El fascismo y España', *La Gaceta Literaria: El Robinson literario de España*, no. 121, 15 January 1932, pp. 7-8.

21. *Ibidem*, p. 7.

22. 'Teatro del pueblo y teatro político' in *Haz*, July 1935.

23. Cited by Payne, *Falange*, p. 60.

24. See Wahnón, *Estética y crítica*.

25. Gonzalo Torrente Ballester, 'Razón y ser de la dramática futura', *Jerarquía*, vol. 2, 1937, pp. 61-80. In the following quoted as RyS.

26. Wahnón, *Estética y crítica*, pp. 169-319.

27. For an exhaustive analysis of this process of normalisation up to 1950 see Wahnón, *Estética y crítica*.

28. Gonzalo Torrente Ballester, 'Cincuenta años de teatro español y algunas cosas más', *Escorial*, vol. 4, no. 10, 1941, pp. 253-278. In the following cited as CAT.

29. Tomás Borrás, 'Movimiento teatral', *Cuadernos de Literatura Contemporánea*, vol. 1, no. 1, 1942, p. 42.

30. Eduardo Juliá Martínez, 'Eduardo Marquina, poeta lírico y dramático', *Cuadernos de Literatura Contemporánea*, vol. 1, no. 2, 1942, pp. 109-134.

31. See Griffin, *Fascism*, pp. 26-27.

32. Tomás Borrás, 'Movimiento teatral', *Cuadernos de Literatura Contemporánea*, vol. 1, no. 2, 1942, p. 91.

12

Theatre and Falangism at the Beginning of the Franco Régime

Francisco Linares

Translated by R. I. MacCandless

With the final victory of the rebels against the Second Spanish Republic (Madrid was taken on 28 March 1939 and the last war communiqué issued on 3 April), the new State tended to intervene in all aspects of life in the country, not only because of the outcome of the war, but also because of the régime's authoritarian conception of society. Falangism provided a fascist vision of a hierarchically organised State, in which justice and culture would supposedly be achieved by overcoming petty individual interests and abolishing the class struggle. The theatre played a certain rôle in this attempt, although, as in other areas, no fully developed plan of action was ever produced. Nonetheless, the performing arts were regarded as an important instrument by which to influence public opinion and to improve the standards of Spanish cultural production, mainly by a) diffusing particular aesthetic values, and b) controlling the theatre as a socio-economic activity.

Administration and regulation of theatrical activity

When considering theatre in Spain immediately after the Civil War, we must bear in mind the question of organisation.[1] One of the most exceptional socio-economic measures taken by the new régime (on 26 January 1940) was the creation of the single trade union divided into productive branches, whose declared purpose was to make 'human relations' overcome economic interests. The Sindicato Único de Espectáculos was also meant to safeguard the artistic dimension of the theatre in the face of economic pressure. In the case of a theatre of national interest the State would cover expenses and make its patronage more effective by promoting 'advanced creativity'.[2] However, the real aim was to impose guidelines for labour relations, just as in any other area of production. Since this semi-fascist union had control over all aspects of theatrical activity, there was also the possibility of applying the as yet poorly defined aesthetics of the Falange.[3] However, in the end the entire process was reduced to little more than labour control, which effectively penalised the traditional theatre organisations and prevented the profession from achieving real improvements.[4]

During the Civil War, the Falange Epañola-JONS and its union CONS (Central Obrera Nacional Sindicalista) had promoted the formation of theatre groups with the aim of providing entertainment and propaganda. In cases such as 'La Tarumba', these companies took advantage of the aesthetic and organisational initiatives already undertaken during the Republic in order to revitalise the ailing Spanish theatre scene. It is not the aim of this essay to examine in detail the artistic and political concepts of these groups; however, it is significant that in 1938 the Falangist writer Dionisio Ridruejo[5] was named head of the press and propaganda services under control of the Minister of the Interior, Serrano Suñer. Ridruejo promoted the foundation of the Falangist theatre group that staged José de Valdivieso's *El hospital de los locos* in Segovia, later to develop into the Compañía de Teatro Nacional de FET y de las JONS, a company that was made up of non-professional actors, but supported by State subsidies. The group's organisation and objectives – in particular, their concentration on the works of classical Spanish playwrights – were frequently referred to as a model that other companies ought to emulate.

After the Civil War, many theatres were confiscated, especially in Madrid, where most theatrical activity was concentrated. The Junta de Espectáculos de Madrid, formed early in 1937 by the Republican authorities, was seized and control was handed over to the Sindicato de la Industria Cinematográfica y Espectáculos Públicos de FET y de las JONS. Nonetheless, a few days later (on 4 April 1939), the theatres, after having been purged, were returned to their owners and the pre-Civil War organisation of theatrical activity was restored on the basis of private initiative rather than State direction. Therefore, the formulae envisaged by the Falange could only be imposed in part.

The State that came into being in 1939 – which was not the State that the Falange had intended to create – concentrated on exercising rigid censorship and taking legal measures designed to maintain standards of decency and order. The only modification to the Reglamento de Espectáculos Públicos (1935) concerned article 102, dealing with the Central Consultiva e Inspectora de Espectáculos.[6] Given the power of censorship, this was not a minor intervention, but we can still say that, on the whole, the organisation of theatrical activity did not change.[7]

On the other hand, the setting up of two National Theatres in 1940 was important both in itself and in the effect it had on the commercial theatre business. In 1939, the State theatre policy as directed by the Propaganda Service under the control of the Falange could still be identified with the activity of the Falange's Compañía de Teatro Nacional.[8] The National Theatres developed out of this company, although the idea of a national theatre and of the popular nature of its activity did not originate in the Falange itself. A Junta Nacional de Teatros y Conciertos had been in existence since 1938 and was turned, in 1940, into the Consejo Nacional de Teatro.[9] Luís Escobar, who had been the first director of the Falange's Compañía de Teatro Nacional, was appointed director of the 'María Guerrero' National Theatre, but the conservatively oriented council and its president, the playwright Eduardo Marquina, acted as a counterbalance to the ideological influence of the Falange. The National Theatres stood under the control of the Ministry of National Education as distinct from the Propaganda Service. According to the law of 1940, the Comisario General de Teatros was responsible for their management and had to follow instructions from both sides.

The second National Theatre, called the 'Español', was set up a few months later by the Sindicato Nacional del Espectáculo. This project combined the constitution of a National Theatre that Felipe Lluch had favoured since the time of the Republic, with the desire for intervention of the Falangist syndicate, one of whose leaders was Lluch.

The two National Theatres, at the Teatro Español and the Teatro María Guerrero, exercised considerable influence from 1940 onwards.[10] The same can be said about the Teatro Español Universitario (TEU), which was financially supported and managed by the Sindicato Español Universitario (SEU). Apart from the TEU in Madrid under the direction of Modesto Higueras, who had been a member of Lorca's troupe 'La Barraca', the organisation comprised theatre groups in different provincial capitals, where deliberate attempts were undertaken to establish a new type of theatre. Paradoxically, despite their dependence on the Falange, these theatre groups and the publications of the SEU were vehicles for interests opposed to the Franco régime.

The first theatrical journal of the post-Civil War period[11] appeared in connection with the university theatre of Granada, where the director José Tamayo became well known, before founding the 'Lope de Vega' company towards the end of the 1940s. This was one of the few examples of rejuvenation in partial harmony with official policy, which, on the whole and certainly as regards the regulation of commercial theatre companies, merely perpetuated the most traditional forms of organisation.

Prevailing theatrical forms and attempts at creating a fascist theatre in Spain

In order to judge the impact of Falangist theatrical aesthetics on dramatic art and theatre production, we must bear in mind the development of Spanish theatre throughout the Civil War and immediately after. Researchers concerned with Spanish theatre of this period have mainly concentrated on dramatic literature[12] and have not looked in depth at the connections with Falangist ideology.[13]

The general tendency of the theatre during the Civil War did not differ greatly from the main trends of the years preceding the conflict. The taste of the audiences remained basically the same. Except for some isolated examples of formal and ideological renewal, most productions provided mere entertainment and stayed out of touch with the new social and political realities. There were some cases of a 'theatre of combat' that perceived the need for aesthetic or organisational innovation in line with the political aspirations of the Republican or National sides. These initiatives were first encouraged by intellectuals and theatre workers in the Republic,[14] and were later taken up by members of the opposing side, who attempted to demonstrate that they, too, were promoting a project of cultural regeneration (this was the case, for example, of the already mentioned Dionisio Ridruejo).[15]

This situation did not change with the end of the Civil War, except for the fact that all forms of Left-wing theatre were completely stamped out. The entertainments sections of the press in the immediate post-Civil War years show that audiences mainly preferred sentimental comedy, pseudo-folkloric plays, etc., which left little room for serious plays or scenic experimentation.[16]

Given this context of popular taste, the 'new theatre' that the Falange sought to create in post-Republican Spain was never to be more than a statement of intent.[17] Falangist collaboration with what they considered to be 'vulgar theatre' was out of the question.[18] But their initial dislike of bourgeois drama, as revealed in reviews of works by Jacinto Benavente or even Eduardo Marquina himself,[19] soon disappeared. As the Falange could not offer any valid alternatives, they were forced to accept a more or less controversial coexistence with what at the time was considered 'theatrical high culture', which consisted mainly of Spanish classical comedy transformed by the standards of bourgeois theatre praxis. Eventually, a highly eclectic attitude was adopted towards what was considered the 'best' of Spanish and world dramatic literature.

Authors such as Marquina or Benavente, who were the principal representatives of the culturally prestigious drama during the Franco years (despite the fact that Benavente was suspected of Republicanism[20]), quickly adapted to the new political situation. Some of their works show occasional signs of propaganda favourable to the new régime, but on the whole they cannot be said to fall within the category of fascist drama. The same is true of other, more deeply committed playwrights, such as José María Pemán.

Most of the embryonic renewal in the years after the Civil War was not the product of the 'new drama' proposed by the Falange, but followed dramatic trends already established in the first half of the century.[21] Falangism had, in fact, to collude with what J. Monleón has called 'Right-wing theatre' of the time. This parallels the developments in the political sphere, where Falangist authoritarianism was respected, but as a Party the Falange became isolated within a Right-wing coalition.

I shall henceforth concentrate on theatrical manifestations that fell into line with fascist ideology, although it should be borne in mind that this did not at all represent the *dominant* trend in Spanish theatre of the Franco period.

The model of Spanish classical theatre and the auto sacramental

The artistic policy of the Falange demanded that theatre, just as literature, had to follow models that predated bourgeois society.[22] Indeed, the very idea of following a model was fundamental to the Falange's aesthetics of regeneration and uniformity. In the case of the theatre this meant emulating the great Spanish drama of the Golden Age.

Before the Civil War there had been several attempts to reinstate forms of Spanish classical theatre, especially after the political crisis of 1898. Without going into detail on the theoretical aspects of this attitude, I shall, however, mention some representative ideas on the subject, held by members of the National side and taken from the review of a lecture by Eduardo Marquina:

> Since Doña Isabel made Spain the united and orderly Kingdom that was her purpose, Spain needed that magical mirror of national theatre to sense its own pulse (…) This theatre for all Spaniards was created by Lope de Vega, who placed ordinary people at the heart of his work, and came to an end with Calderón, who placed God at the heart of his work. (…) Now, at last, Spain has found a new path, even though her existence may cost life-blood and death-wail.[23]

The idea of a triumphant return of the classical theatre, especially to a theatre in the mould of Calderón, had already been heralded by Samuel Ros in his review of the production of *La Cena del Rey Baltasar* in the Retiro gardens in Madrid. Emphasis was placed more on the political aspects than the Catholic element:

> The choice of setting was the initial success of the production. To our instincts or our understanding, the sight of the cannon raised on high and bathed in intense light was like comprehending the changes brought to our time by Victory represented by a physical and audible monument. We also experienced the recovery of a style and emotion that Carlos III expelled from Spain with the Jesuits. The cries of defeat and fear of Moratín, who had attacked (…) our entire National Theatre, whirled about just offstage accompanied by the dark ages of theatre.[24]

This was the first production of the Teatro Nacional de Falange in the recently 'liberated' Madrid. Both the play and its review follow on from José de Valdivieso's *El hospital de los locos*, also staged by Teatro Nacional de Falange and reviewed in *Vértice*.[25] Here, too, the setting underlined the metaphysical conflict and subsequent victory of good over evil, to be understood as a correlative to the triumph of the National side.

However, despite several spectacular stagings of plays that belonged to the genre of the *auto sacramental*, this type of religious drama did not offer enough opportunities for the proposed renewal of the theatre. In fact, in the Golden Age, religious theatre represented the most conservative and anti-theatrical tendency, as it was more concerned with propagating religious dogmas than depicting individual characters. The problem was not that the Falange had any lack of regard for the theatre of the Middle Ages, but that the theatre-going public demanded more action-oriented drama. The Delegación de Arte of the Madrid SEU published a significant article on this question,[26] insisting that the theatre should contain a 'suggestion of humanity', a concept frequently referred to in Falangist artistic policy and, in my opinion, contrary to abstraction, but not to dogma. The Falange favoured the classical model of theatre, because apart from its allegorical or symbolic nature it also contained a heroic dimension, it possessed a propagandistic function, and was accessible to all social classes.

Falangist theatre during the Civil War

Fascist ideology in Spain was different from comparable phenomena in Italy or Germany, in as much as it was developed and took shape in the context of a civil war. Similarly, fascist theatre aesthetics were intimately linked to the prerequisites of war propaganda. But in contrast to those critics who have most recently associated all patriotic drama of the National side with fascism,[27] we must be careful not to confound the Nationalists with the Falangists. When José Antonio Primo de Rivera proposed a military-like discipline for the running of the State, he was basically referring to the functional application of discipline and not to the use of force. This means that under certain circumstances the cultural bodies would need to modify their activities in order to attend to the interests of the State. This hypothesis will be of use to us when identifying the relationship between the Falange and a type of theatre that had no clearly defined ideological orientation. First, though, let us examine some examples of productions associated with the Civil War.

On 12 December 1936, the 'dramatic comedy, in three acts, in verse' *¡España, inmortal!*, by the now fortunately forgotten Sotero Otero del Pozo, had its première in Valladolid.[28] The only aim of this play, which was also produced successfully at other theatres, was to foment the unity of the Fatherland. The drama explains the aim of the Civil War as defending the true Spain, led by the Army and the Militia, against the 'rabble and international putrefaction'. Falange Española is praised, but, in line with the call to unity, the play points out the need for it to join forces with the traditionalist Requetés.

This is, in essence, the content of the drama according to its preamble and the newspaper reviews published jointly with the text. However, the play itself follows a conventional scheme easily adapted to the theme of the Civil War, thus allowing the introduction of tirades along the ideological lines described above. The plot concerns the courtship of a seamstress and a student, rather more suited to a *zarzuela* or light comedy, if it were not for the fact that the girl's parents have been duped by the Reds and the boy is a Falangist. The dénouement is provided by the entry of the National troops into Madrid, some time before the actual event.

Although the play does the Falange no favours by suggesting that it join forces with the Requetés, the repentance of the militant pro-marxist Blas expresses a typically fascist line of thought. Blas's infliction (he has been blinded by shrapnel) makes him see the error of his ways, together with the virtues of a heroic adventure that contains 'the harmony of the violin and the perfume of a rose'. From this moment on, he belongs to the 'world of the blind', who are turned in on themselves and have been purged of their cruel instincts. This is the world of the National forces, who, although metaphorically blinded by their spiritual hierarchy, have obtained an exemplary victory – a victory that is both convincing and revealing for Blas, whom they have physically blinded. When the moment came to defend themselves, they compensated their lack of rational and empirical discernment with a daring acceptance of death:

> When the time has come
> To receive great harm
> Prepare yourself for death
> Blind, mad and violent.[29]

The idea of a regenerative catastrophe is here combined with the commonplace of the blind man who 'sees' more clearly because of his physical condition. Blas no longer has to ask forgiveness, for he has been cleansed by the war. He now perceives a more sublime reality, in which he participates by taking Holy Communion. This suggestion of spiritual enhancement arising out of a physical handicap, underlies many plays of the period and gives them a mystic dimension.

Rafael Duyos' dramatic poem, *Romance Azul*, was part of the repertoire of the Falangist combat theatre 'La Tarumba'.[30] It exalts the sacrifice of comrade Luís Platero, who, having had no regard for life, has not died, but has gone to occupy a place among the stars in Heaven. The brief plot attempts to use the emotional impact of the anecdote to draw the audience together in the same belief:

> Silence! The breeze has stopped.
> The moon as well. Silence!
> Everything seems
> Set in a dream. (...)
> A hundred thousand blueshirts
> Are singing the Credo.
> A hundred thousand blueshirts
> Mad with Peace and Empire.

On 17 December 1936, *La Nueva España*[31] by José Gómez Sánchez-Reina was performed for the first time in Granada. The theatre critic of *ABC* in Seville said of this self-proclaimed 'scenic report':

> The performance was a new work in tune with those fervently patriotic youths who, 'cara al sol', undertook the sacred task together with the Army of creating the new Spain we all desire. Was it theatre? Episodic report? A cinematographic vision of the feats and achievements of the present struggle? This new work contains a little of all this.

The novelty of the production lay in its fragmented structure, with each of the three acts being made up of three *Estampas* or 'prints', depicting different episodes of the war. The forms used ranged from farce to melodrama to the National proclamation of insurrection on Radio Seville. The aim was inflammatory rather than dramatic. In this sense, the allegorical opening and close of the play were significant, as they controlled the viewers' interpretation of the play, allegory being a classical device that became quite common in Falangist drama. The work begins with the dejection of the Motherland, represented by a woman in sixteenth-century Spanish costume, and ends with the 'vision' of the New Spain, using rather successful lighting techniques. At the première in Granada, an atmosphere of enthusiasm and excitement was created by festive garlands and the singing of anthems in the presence of high-ranking State officials.

The three examples discussed here represented different concepts of 'combat theatre' in the National zone, but they did not show any significantly new elements. Rather, they were symptomatic theatrical manifestations of fascist ideas that justified the armed uprising against the Second Republic. The same attitude persisted after the end of the Civil War, but instead of making reference to specific events in the struggle, these plays celebrated Spanish history in more general terms. Both types of drama depicted social or national conflicts as a temporary alienation from religious, historic or human values, which in the future will prevail again.

Symbolic theatre

The attempts to create modern mystery plays in the mould of the *auto sacramental* are of particular interest in the sphere of what we might call symbolic theatre, since, as we have already seen, this genre came to be associated with the events of the Civil War. However, the *auto* had already been revived at the end of the 1920s. When Rafael Alberti wrote the controversial and anti-religious *El hombre deshabitado* (published 1930, staged 1931), there was, naturally, a reaction in the form of attempts to re-establish the traditional *auto* or to reintroduce traditional religious drama in a modern format.

Gonzalo Torrente Ballester's *El casamiento engañoso* was the most significant modern *auto sacramental*,[32] since it won a competition created by Ridruejo, in which forty-seven other plays were entered.[33] This and other early plays by Torrente Ballester[34] conform to his theoretical position,[35] which in many ways was similar to the aesthetics of Ernesto Giménez Caballero and also to the Falangist concepts of order, unity and harmony that were regularly propagated on the pages of *Jerarquía*.

The link with the past can be seen in the Argumentador's initial reminder of the times when Man possessed two weapons, the sword and syllogistic reasoning, which 'fulfilled their duty by providing symbols and intelligible, accessible forms for ideas, in a world where the arts were understood in an orderly fashion.'

El casamiento engañoso presents the conflict between Man and technology. Leviathan, who is responsible for this, demands that Man relinquish his servants, Liberty, Theological Virtues and Masculine Virtues. After Man's fall into deception, the conflict is resolved with his repentance and the exaltation of the Eucharist. This intimates that there is a predetermined solution for all human conflict. Although this *auto* may seem to be only defending tradition and religion against technology, it not a religious work in the traditional sense, nor does it completely negate the values of technology. It is rather a representation of an attitude, sanctioned by the Falange, towards the troubles of Modern Man and a way to escape from them. First of all, it deals with the reinstatement of Truth, which, in the writer's craft, is expressed through poetry and symbolism. Secondly, the leaders are the incarnation of this Truth on the lower scale of ideas, which is social rather than theological. Lastly, there is an appeal to national identity, for this is the same Truth that Spain defended when it fought for Catholicism in its period of splendour.[36]

Another example of this type of drama is *En el otro cuarto*, a short play by Samuel Ros, first performed with considerable success in the Alcázar theatre in Madrid in 1940.[37] Without recourse to religious or political allegory, this play presents a poetic synthesis of a man's life while attempting to transmit the dynamics of materiality and spirituality. The man tries to escape the allure and the bounds of the female breast ('I run so that the earth will not grasp me and tie me down with roots […]. I shall only be at peace in the sea'), but after a time he feels the need to return to what he left behind. The woman understands that her fate is to be sacrificed and she stabs herself, thus preventing their reunion.

Drama on historical themes

Plays based on historical subjects had an obvious attraction for the National side, because the recollection of events or personal feats already partially legitimised by tradition offered plenty of opportunity for exalting Nationalist values. The Spanish classical theatre was not only a formal model, but also a means of making the historic period in which the plays were set intelligible to modern audiences.

Theatre in the mould of the *Siglo de Oro* (especially the so-called Spanish comedy) was employed by the Falange to unite the masses and give an epic dimension to contemporary events. However, such a 'heroic new theatre' was never brought to completion. The texts that interpreted the Civil War in these terms, such as *Y el Imperio volvía: Poema-Coral-Dramático* by Ramón Cue S.J. (staged and published in Barcelona in 1940), had no artistic value and evoked little interest in the population. One significant exception was *La mejor reina de España* by Luís Felipe Vivanco and Luís Rosales. This ambitious work was published by Ediciones Jerarquía in 1939, and was dedicated to Isabel I of Castile, who established Spain as a unified State. Mariano Tomás' *Santa Isabel de España* was staged the same year. However, apart from the vindication of the Empire, neither this play nor *Garcilaso de la Vega* by Tomás,[38] also staged in Madrid in 1939, represent any novelty in the tradition of historic verse drama.

The play by Luís Rosales and Luís Felipe Vivanco was more closely related to official literary policy, as both authors held positions of responsibility in the cultural hierarchy. It was given the subtitle 'Dramatic enactment in a prologue and three acts in verse and in prose' to distinguish it from the usual type of drama at the time. *La mejor reina de España* is a complex work that makes use of various theatrical devices from the courtly and popular traditions of the time in which it is set. It introduces different social strata in a choric fashion and uses a variety of discursive forms (courtly subtlety, troubadour verses, popular speech, etc.) in an attempt to give the impression of a multi-faceted life in the community.

The play begins with a prologue, in which a Dominican friar, representing the playwright, and a 'Voice from on High' introduce the audience to what is about to happen on stage. Since these events are well-known episodes from Spain's glorious past, the audience is able to concentrate on the ideological message, rather than having to follow the twists and turns of a complex plot. God has willed the grandeur of Isabel La Catolica, although, as the friar points out, before this can happen there will be 'ruin and desolation on the Crown of Castile'. This is the essential Truth, and the actual occurrence of what is predestined is only an 'enactment' of that Truth. The result is a work of epic character that opens up an historical (and theological) perspective on what was happening in Spain in 1939. Depicting different episodes of the Queen's life, which were crucial for the recovery of royal authority in Castile and the establishing of Spain's national unity, was part of an obvious political strategy. The Queen's painful experiences exemplify, in a poetic fashion, the desires and feelings of a whole people. Isabel's life becomes a metaphor for the fate of Spain in the Imperial age as well as the Francoist era, and affirms the necessity for an authoritarian, hierarchical order of human society.

The spectacle *España una, grande y libre* (7 April 1940) was prepared by Felipe Lluch to commemorate the first anniversary of the National victory and was also inspired by the theatrical models of the *Siglo de Oro*. The three parts 'La famosa de la unidad de España', 'Comedia heroica de la libertad' and 'Farsa alegórica de la grandeza de España' made use of classical texts and music and possessed allegorical, popular and propagandistic qualities. The production, which inaugurated the 'Español' National Theatre[39] was, in its aesthetic quality, quite original and far superior to the other premieres of the season.

Restitution of classical authors and of works of national interest

Once the new State was able to formulate a policy for the theatre, the staging of classical works that were innovative in conception and execution and appropriate to their literary status, was promoted. Both National Theatres were entrusted with the task of presenting the Spanish theatrical heritage, as well as the works of recognised contemporary playwrights such as Benavente and representative examples of classical or contemporary drama from abroad.

The productions of these plays aimed at offering a most complete realisation of the authors' conceptions. However, since the literary attributes of the works were respected above all, little room was left for creative staging techniques. It was believed that the texts contained permanent intrinsic values that made them classics in their own right. In 1942, Tomás Borrás rejected the production of *Peribañez y el comendador de Ocaña* on the following terms: 'Above all, the plays must not come second to the sets. The debate on the extent to which director and producer are to complement the author has already been concluded: the work comes first.'[40]

The critic Alfredo Marqueríe, who approved of the productions of the National Theatres, did not miss a chance to emphasise the importance of the spoken word, especially when he found that a play had been staged with 'humility' and 'simplicity': 'On stage the word is all. The scenography can be, and is, a delight to the eye and a sensual joy. But what speaks to the audience's soul is the passion of the word, the author's thoughts and what he makes his characters say.'[41]

Some years before, in 1937, the pre-eminence of the word had been proclaimed in the Falangist journal *Vértice*: 'The stage must not lose its classic tridimensional nature, which has a profound *raison d'être*, in the face of all the vain attempts to promote an open stage, where dialogue loses intimacy and subtlety. Any and all scenographic innovation is possible within these three dimensions.'[42] Although the defence of the proscenium-arch theatre was not absolute, these ideas must be kept in mind when judging the contributions made by the National Theatres. Contemporary critics who defended the work of the National Theatres, described their productions as innovatory, modern and experimental, rivalling even with the work of Bragaglia or Piscator.[43] Today, however, the prevailing opinion is that, despite the introduction of technical innovations and more meticulous procedures of stage management, the various productions of the time did not represent a significant advance in the staging of classical theatre. Indeed, this can be said of all the theatre of the period. Monleón maintains that 'year after year there was a tendency to provide ostentatious solidity and the prestige of the texts as "culture", without carrying out a genuine artistic and ideological process.'[44]

The uniform results, which were not, as Monleón suggests, the style of any school, seem therefore to have been due to the conscientious application of 'rules of the trade'. Nonetheless, the idea of production as technique and craftsmanship in the service of the grandeur of the classics was in itself an artistic and ideological position, even though it was held in the name of negating ideology. The director's 'neutrality' was not only a consequence of State patronage, but also a condition of the State's conception of the theatre.

In 1940, when the National Theatres came into being, the Falange had control over cultural policy and was to keep it at least until Serrano Suñer left the Ministry of the Interior. However, there was already a strong bias within the Falange to forego propagandistic theatre in favour of more artistic production. An increase in the number of contemporary plays in the repertoire was given official sanction and some scenographic innovations began to be imported from abroad.[45]

Even though the performative, scenic and musical aspects were not considered crucial for the understanding of a play, they were nonetheless taken seriously and carried out according to general aesthetic rules that helped to harmonise the whole production. The critics of the time used expressions such as precision, rigour or propriety when referring to a successful stage production. This would have involved, for example, the effective stage placement and choreographed movement of large numbers of characters, the use of innovative sound and lighting designs, sober, exuberant or historically accurate costumes, evocative or symbolic props and scenic objects, all in tune with an aesthetic category that we might call 'stylised realism'. From the Falangist point of view, this artistic principle was opposed to the realist-naturalist trends of late-nineteenth century theatre and sought to bring across the idealistic quality of the plays.

Mass spectacles

Finally, Falange promoted theatrical spectacles of a non-literary kind that were meant to arouse political sentiments and to foster a national community. Despite the fact that for the purposes of ideological propaganda the theatre was less effective than other media, such as radio and cinema, it had the advantage of offering room for direct participation of the audience.[46] The Falange always backed the idea that the theatre should be directed to the masses, even if this meant that these 'masses' still had to be created. Multitudinous attendance and the use of large open spaces only occurred on occasions such as the production of *autos sacramentales* at the Eucharistic Congresses.

Large gatherings of people at religious, sporting or other, not strictly political, events were exploited for propagandistic purposes. Although the leaders of the régime were aware of the possibilities that political mass meetings offered for the celebration of Nationalist values, few of these occasions were actually made use of. One reason surely was that, unlike Germany or Italy, Spain had been ravished by a civil war and the profound divisions within the population could not be disguised. However, there are examples of mass rituals held for very specific purposes, such as the transfer of José Antonio Primo de Rivera's body from Alicante for burial at the Escorial. The ceremony began on 20 November 1939 and had been devised by the Dirección General de Propaganda as a spectacular funeral cortège mainly made up of Falangist militants, who were to parade through different towns and cities along the route in order to incite people's devotion. The preparations were carried out by José Cabanas, Head of the Departamento de Ceremonial y Plástica, and Samuel Ros, who also provided a *Script for the Route and Ceremony*, according to which the participants and symbols were arranged.[47] The different elements of the spectacle were complemented by press coverage, in many cases organised by the régime's Press and Propaganda Service.

A similar mass ceremony was held in May 1940 in the spectacular setting of the Mota Castle in Medina del Campo, organised in homage to Isabel la Católica, who had died there. The objective of this type of liturgical theatre was to subject the masses to an aesthetic order, in the knowledge of the ends that could be achieved by so-called 'mass aesthetics'.[48] Federico Urrutia even went so far as to compare this to 'la liturgia nazi'.[49] He believed that this type of emotional participation would lead the individual to find an answer to his day-to-day problems and that the beauty of this liturgy would influence the participants' practical understanding of life:

> The emotion of the superfluous is experienced, and through it one senses the intensity of the necessary. It is when the Motherland is perceived in this manner that the State is conceived of as wholly totalitarian. Not because its laws are ordained by a single criterion and must be blindly and fervently obeyed, but because those who obey them are the most zealous defenders of their observance.

The ideas underlying this cultic mass theatre can be extracted from a newspaper article on a celebration organised by the Falange.[50] The incorporation of the masses was seen as being different from similar festivities in Germany or Italy. The ritual in question was a large procession of Falangists through the streets of Madrid on their way to the Escorial with a laurel wreath to lay on the tomb of José Antonio. This was the central event in the celebrations to commemorate the fifth anniversary of his death. The parade was described as a spectacle headed by the Falange, but given full significance by the emotive participation of a mass of spectators. As they marched past in silence, the individual characteristics of the participants' faces were lost in the light of the torches. The night scenery, the light effects, the rhythm of the march, the hommage to José Antonio, etc., all combined to produce an overwhelming effect: 'Beautiful were the flames and beautiful the night, as they sailed in search of the vast imperial monument! Yes, it seemed that the heart of all Spain followed after them.' The spectators followed the pageant in hushed silence and displayed an attitude that was in harmony with the 'passage of the superb theory', in other words, the abstract idea made visible. The quintessence of the spectacle that encompassed both participants and spectators was order, an order raised to the higher category of norm, but basically equivalent to discipline, harmony and coherence, which, according to Falangist aesthetics, constituted the postulates of artistic creation and, indeed, all creation. The sense of order had thus created a new Spain, Franco's Spain, as manifested in the ordered procession.

Summary

After the Spanish Civil War, conventional theatre entertainment was restored to a predominant position and functioned to offer light relief from the serious business of life. Falangism initially promoted theatrical works with propagandistic aims, but, as the movement gradually lost ideological definition, it became committed to the reinstatement of theatrical culture by the State through productions, especially of texts from the Golden Age, whose main artistic function was to provide models to be emulated by other theatres. Acts of political or religious exaltation, together with the symbols used and the emotional reactions caused by them, were considered spectacles in themselves not to be degraded by theatrical trickery. Mere aesthetic values were renounced in favour of an emphasis on content (ideology). The Falange also promoted theatrical spectacles of a non-literary, ritualistic kind, involving large numbers of participants and aiming at a representation of national unity. Mass meetings in large open spaces were organised according to liturgical principles and were used to present an image of order, discipline, cohesion and harmony under the guidance of the Nationalist leadership.

NOTES

1. This subject has not been sufficiently researched. For a first attempt see César Oliva, *El teatro español desde 1936*, Madrid, 1989.
2. This was the opinion of Felipe Lluch and Tomás Borrás, who were both syndicate leaders and promotors of the idea of a national theatre.
3. See Antonio de Obregón, 'Hacia una censura estética', *Arriba*, 12 May 1939; Tomás Borrás, 'Movimiento teatral', *Cuadernos de Literatura Contemporánea*, vol. 2, 1943, pp. 119-20.
4. The Reglamento Nacional de Trabajo para los profesionales del Teatro, Circo y Variedades regulated the composition of theatre companies and was published in the *Boletín Oficial del Estado* of 19 March 1949.
5. Dionisio Ridruejo, *Casi unas memorias*, Barcelona, 1977, p. 130.
6. *Boletín Oficial del Estado*, 3 January and 19 June 1940.
7. For a view of the situation until then, see Ricardo de la Fuente Ballesteros, *Introducción al teatro español del siglo XX (1900-1936)*, Valladolid, 1987.
8. See Antonio de Obregón, 'El teatro, en pie', *Arriba*, 4 March 1939.
9. *Boletín Oficial del Estado*, 13 March 1940.

10. See *Historia de los Teatros Nacionales I: 1939-1962*, Madrid, Centro de Documentación Teatral, 1993. This volume provides information on both the administration and productions of this institution.

11. See Antonio Sánchez Trigueros, 'Notas sobre dos revistas de teatro granadinas', *Estudios sobre literatura y arte dedicados al profesor Emilio Orozco Díaz*, vol. 3, Granada, 1979, pp. 323-37.

12. These are normally overviews of Spanish theatre in the two decades after the Civil War. An exception is César Oliva, *El teatro español* which deals with a wider period, although the immediate post-Civil War years are not examined sufficiently.

13. Among others, see José Monleón, *Treinta años de teatro de la derecha*, Barcelona, 1971; Julio Rodríguez Puértolas, *Literatura fascista española I. Historia*, Madrid, 1986; José Carlos Mainer, *Falange y literatura*, Barcelona, 1971.

14. The Republican zone is the better researched in Robert Marrast, *El teatro durante la guerra civil española*, Barcelona, 1972; the equivalent for the Franco régime in Barcelona over a longer period is E. Gallén, *El teatre a la ciutat de Barcelona durant el régim franquista (1936-1954)*, Barcelona, 1985.

15. This is the theory upheld by J. Monleón, *Treinta años*, as regards lack of innovation in Spanish theatre after the Civil War.

16. For the theatre criticism of the years 1940-1943 see Alfredo Marqueríe, *Desde la silla eléctrica*, Madrid, 1942 and the sequel *En la jaula de los leones*, Madrid, 1944, although, as Monleón, *Treinta años*, states, this can also be observed in the entertainment sections of Madrid newspapers for these years.

17. In the summer of 1941, Gonzalo Torrente Ballester was still to ponder in *Arriba* on 'What is new?' His reply for the time being was that in the arts and theatre one could only find works that were not new; see 'En torno al problema teatral', in *Siete ensayos y una farsa*, Madrid, 1942, pp. 69-86.

18. As an example of this attitude see the reviews by Antonio de Obregón in the Madrid Falangist newspaper *Arriba* throughout 1939.

19. See, for example, Antonio de Obregón's criticisms of the revivals of *En Flandes se ha puesto el sol* by Marquina, and *El nido ajeno* by Benavente, in *Arriba*, 30 April 1939 and 6 May 1939.

20. On the tribulations of Benavente's plays at this time see Monleón, *Treinta años*, in particular Chapter III.

21. Benavente was not the only detectable influence. Alejandro Casona, who was at the time silenced, can be seen to have affected the comedies of José López Rubio, Edgar Neville or Víctor Ruíz Iriarte.

22. See, in particular, Sultana Wahnón, *Estética y crítica literarias en España (1940-1950)*, Granada, 1988.

23. *ABC*, 8 November 1941, p. 6.

24. *Vértice*, August-September 1939, no page references.

25. *Vértice*, July 1938.

26. See *Arriba*, 30 June 1939.

27. This is the error of Julio Rodríguez Puértolas, *Literatura fascista española*, in his chapter on theatre.

28. Sotero Otero del Pozo, *¡España, Inmortal!*, Valladolid, 1936.

29. See Blas's speech in Act III, Scene 11 of the play, pp. 134 and 151.

30. 'Teatro. Romance azul', *Vértice*, September-October 1937.

31. José Gómez Sánchez-Reina, *La nueva España*, Granada, 1937.

32. See Hub Hermans, 'Avisos y leyendas en *El casamiento engañoso* de Gonzalo Torrente Ballester' in *Investigaciones semióticas IV. Actas del IV Simposio Internacional de la Asociación Española de Semiótica*, vol. 2, Madrid, 1992, pp. 649-661.

33. See *Arriba*, 24 June 1939.

34. Gonzalo Torrente Ballester, *El casamiento engañoso*, in *Teatro I*, Barcelona, 1982, pp. 161-212. The play was staged by the Teatro Español Universitario in 1943. More information can be found in *Historia de los Teatros Nacionales*, staging file 46.

35. See Gonzalo Torrente Ballester, 'Razón y ser de la dramaturgia futura', *Jerarquía* vol. 2, 1937, pp. 61- 80.

36. Gonzalo Torrente Ballester, *El casamiento engañoso*, in *Escorial*, Madrid, 1941. There is a reference to José Antonio in this edition, which was removed from later editions.

37. Samuel Ros, *Antología 1923-1944*, Madrid, 1948, pp. 139-155.

38. It is interesting to see how this play, doubtless inspired by the fourth centenary of the poet's death, does not follow the officially approved 'Garcilasian' aesthetics; see Sultana Wahnón, *Estética y crítica*, pp. 111 ff. and Tomás Borrás, *Garcilaso de la Vega*, Madrid, 1940.

39. See Juan Aguilera Sastre, 'Felipe Lluch Garín, artífice e iniciador del Teatro Nacional Español', in *Historia de los Teatros Nacionales*, pp. 41-65, particularly pp. 53-54. It was in November 1940 that, stimulated by the success of this production, Tomás Borrás and Felipe Lluch, as representatives of the Sindicato Nacional del Espectáculo, persuaded the City Council of Madrid to let them use the Español theatre for their project.

40. Tomás Borrás, 'Movimiento teatral', *Cuadernos de literatura contemporánea*, vol. 1, 1942, pp. 172-3.

41. Alfredo Marqueríe, *Desde la silla eléctrica*, pp. 196-197.

42. El duende azul (pseud.), 'Teatro nuevo', *Vértice*, June 1937.

43. See Alfredo Marqueríe, *Desde la silla eléctrica*, p. 184.

44. José Monleón, *Treinta años*, pp. 48-49.

45. The following figures for performance numbers give some idea of the preferences in the productions of the Español and María Guerrero theatres between 1940 and early 1945:
    Classical authors – María Guerrero 13; Español 25 (including foreign classics)
    Recognised contemporary Spanish playwrights – M.G. 12; E. 9
    New or relatively unknown Spanish playwrights – M.G. 21; E. 11
    Contemporary foreign playwrights – M.G. 14; E. 4.

46. It is curious that Radio Nacional de España contributed over the years to the propagation of theatrical culture by its broadcasts and adaptations of plays. This can be explained by the priority given to the text over the production, and also by the authorities' confidence in the useful function of radio. See, among others, Carlos Miguel Suárez Radillo, *Itinerario temático y estilístico del teatro contemporáneo español: Guiones presentados en sus emisoras para su estreno por Radio Nacional de España*, Madrid, 1975.

47. Samuel Ros, *A hombros de la Falange: Historia del traslado de los restos de José Antonio*, Barcelona, s.d. This relates the preparations for, and course of, the events and also includes, among other documents, the script of the ceremony.

48. 'Estética de muchedumbres', *Vértice*, June 1937.

49. See Urratia's article in *Vértice*, March 1939.

50. *ABC*, 20 November 1941.

13

Competing Together in Fascist Europe
Sport in Early Francoism

John London

Introduction

As a physical activity and collective ritual, sport became an integral part of the performative language of fascism. It is not difficult to explain why, since sport draws on the ritualist core of human instinct. It reinforces the sensation of belonging to a group, but encourages leaders to develop. These concepts apply equally to the team member and the spectator; the new-found strength can be literal, physical strength, as well as a strength derived from the unity of supporting the same side.

Just before the emergence of Fascism in Italy, Italian Socialists and Communists realised that sport enhanced solidarity, having previously thought that it detracted from the unity of working-class organisations.[1] Once Nazism and Fascism assumed total control over sporting activities in Germany and Italy, official statements on sports began to underline the concepts of leadership, heroism and physical strength. As far as there was a fascist ideology of sport, it posited action over intellect.[2] The spectacular culmination of this action was the Nazi Olympics of 1936 which, according to one account, constituted a success for the Germans owing to a 'supremacy in mass pageantry'.[3] Whatever one's judgement as to the identity of the real winners of the 1936 Games, the theatricality of the occasion is beyond dispute, and it was more than a secular, civic event. With the performances of the *Hallelujah Chorus* and Richard

Strauss's *Olympic Hymn*, it touched overtly on a whole tradition of religious celebrations.[4]

Such grandiose events involved a stage (the stadium), actors (athletes) and an audience – the intrinsic elements of theatrical performance. Indeed, in Fascist Italy, mass spectator sporting events triumphed over mass participatory ones.[5] One could consider this a form of political failure, but it was also a considerable achievement: the essential point was to involve citizens in the greatest possible quantities, even if the focus was spectacle rather than exertion.

However, these details give the impression merely of large-scale political control, similar to that exercised by fascist régimes on other forms of culture. In fact, the very nature of sport made the fascist organisation of it more problematic. The paradoxes lie at the heart of general attitudes towards sport itself. These attitudes range from the highly competitive to the warmly fraternal. For a game to work, rules have to be obeyed, a collaboration has to take place, even if this coming together can act as a channel for strong aggression.[6] The game can enact a kind of war or celebrate a brotherhood (even sisterhood) of friendly physical exertion in which the result is relatively unimportant and the only real enemies are fatigue and unsportsmanlike behaviour. Put in national terms, on the one hand sport can imply virulent imperialism in which physical might is symbolic of a country's military strength. On the other hand, it can suggest proselytising comradeship, in which the need to compete within one country or against another exists only to reinforce or establish links, rather than assert superiority. Mussolini's Socialist-influenced Fascism,[7] German National Socialism and Falangist National Syndicalism, with their dual emphasis on individual power and communal unity, inevitably reflect both these extremes. The extremes surface in the aesthetics as well as the politics of sporting activity.

The aim of this study is to analyse both sporting politics and aesthetics in early Francoism through an examination of Falangist ideologies and bureaucratic control of sport. Although comparisons can be made with the organisation of sport in Nazi Germany and Fascist Italy, it will also be possible to describe Spanish sporting encounters in terms of fascist spectacle in the context of international meetings with the teams of the Axis powers. While no Spanish event reached the scale of Hitler's Olympics, many sports activities in early Francoism were public ceremonies specifically designed to celebrate the national rebirth to which Roger Griffin refers.[8]

Falangist ideologies of sport

Unlike Nazi and Fascist definitions of sport, the development of Falangist ideas took place during an omnipresent armed conflict and were thus continually related to military progress. Falangists had to define their position in contrast to the conceptions of the Second Republic. Days before the outbreak of the Spanish Civil War in July 1936, activities on the Left were co-ordinated in the association called Cultura Popular. The emphasis of the Popular Front government had been on the promotion of sports which allowed mass participation and provided an element of socialisation for marginalised groups.[9] There were, in addition, several compromising links. From the perspective of those fighting against the Second Republic, one of the most incriminating of these links was the Soviet tour of the Basque football team in 1937.[10]

The Falange caricatured sport under the Second Republic as divisive and effete. As the falangist writer Jacinto Miquelarena wrote in 1937: 'Our sport has until now been a sad imitation of real sport. It served to open gulfs between the regions. (...) Winning in sport is a joy and a reason for justified pride. ¡Arriba España!' ('Long live Spain!', the Falangist motto).[11] For Miquelarena, the Second Republic was 'the period in which sportsmen were the men who did not have a daily shave; the ones who thought that sport consisted in leaving the café or the bar for two hours, perhaps every Sunday'.[12] Therefore an anonymous writer of the Falangist newspaper *Arriba* could claim in 1942, three years after the end of Civil War: 'From the former university generation of adolescents, lost in the dirty amusements of gambling dens and cafés, we have passed to the intrepid and Olympic youths born out of war and out of its heroism.'[13] Such praise did not prevent a pervasive view that sport had previously been overpoliticised. It was affirmed that money intended for popular sport was in fact channelled into the funds of 'Marxist' parties: 'Political aims almost always predominated over purely sporting objectives.'[14] Hence there was an official, ultimately hypocritical attitude that new Spanish sporting events would not be treated as political activities.[15]

However, Italian and German training systems, particularly among the young, were proposed as a basis for Spanish sport, with all the military baggage that was lumbered with them.[16] During the Civil War, Falangist theory came to view war itself as the ultimate sport: 'Those who demonstrate such a magnificent talent for that sublime and tragic sport which is war, should later find the aptitude to relax and build up their strength in the practice of ordinary sports.'[17] Following the outbreak of the Second World War, the Third Reich in particular was seen as a model for the promotion of sports among young people.[18]

Owing to this close connection between sport and war, individual sports were systematically treated as both central to the current conflict – the Spanish Civil War – and the peace which would follow it. In an article on skiing, J. Dumas praised those skiers who had responded to the 'trumpets of war'. Photographs to accompany his article show mountain battalions on the Aragon front. In a breathless sentence, Dumas goes on to say that the youths of today 'will in peace follow the advance guard which is now tracing parallel tracks, projected into infinity, longing for an Imperial Spain, the tracks which have been coloured with the blood of those skiers who fell in a posthumous tribute to sport and, for their glory, to the Fatherland which lay in danger'.[19] Similarly, an exhortation in 1938 to practise gymnastics, to be 'strong and beautiful', defined a frame of mind which was at once sporting and combative in a more general sense: 'The existence of a special sporting mentality is a fact which cannot be denied; and in these difficult times it is almost indispensable to possess this mentality, which is precisely the fighting mentality, of endurance, energy, dynamism, willpower, not forgetting loyalty and honour, inexorable rules in competitions of this kind.'[20] Although the 'competitions' refer directly to gymnastics, the competitive nature of war means that the same qualities are required for both activities.

In spite of the homages paid to foreign prototypes, the views quoted above demonstrate how Nationalism was a prominent feature of Falangist conceptions of sport. This Nationalism was exaggerated through a military view of sport and a sporting view of war. The moral worth of sport was also derived from the discipline it supposedly induced. Juan Deportista [sic] summed up what he called the 'two magnificent virtues' of sport: patriotism and discipline. According to him, the 'revolutionary transcendence' of sports reached all social classes. Moreover, spectator sport had its exemplary role to play: 'The idea of sport as spectacle is not reprehensible, because it works as a stimulus, a show of fervour and propaganda in front of hundreds of thousands of youths who are attracted and, eventually, won over.'[21] The organisation of sports events therefore needed an appropriate propagandistic reflection in press coverage.

The organisation, practice and reporting of sport in early Francoism

From the early stages of the Francoist régime, the bureaucracy of sport was dominated by the amalgamated version of the Falange created by Franco during the Civil War. General Moscardó, president of the Consejo Nacional de Deportes (National Sports Council) fixed the tone at the outset by undertaking an official visit to Nazi Germany in April 1939. He returned with a special plan for Spanish sport and explained how the Consejo would have its headquarters in the capital, Madrid, and would consist solely of military men so that Spanish sportsmen would be subject to military discipline.[22] Moscardó became head of the renamed Delegación Nacional de Deportes (National Sports Delegation) which was founded by a decree signed by Franco on 22 February 1941. Its first article read: 'The management and promotion of Spanish sport are entrusted to the Falange Española Tradicionalista y de las JONS.'[23]

The repercussions of these new measures were immediate. In 1937, an anti-Republican national soccer team had already replaced the usual red football shirts with blue ones for a match against Portugal. The blue shirts of the Falange had their rôle beyond the confines of the political Party. Once Moscardó was appointed, he made the change of colour permanent and introduced the compulsory fascist salute before the start of all football games.[24] (In 1934, the Roman Fascist salute had been prescribed for all Italian sportsmen.[25]) There was also a purge of suspect players in Spanish teams. In the realm of football, for example, although certain players were forgiven for their adherence to the side which lost the Civil War, there was a semi-official policy of cleansing among referees.[26] However, not even this can compare to the elimination of Jews and Marxists from sports organisations in the Third Reich.[27]

Spain and Fascist Italy showed a similar anti-regionalist attitude. In 1930, provincial Italian sports organisations were suppressed. The importation of non-Italian players was forbidden.[28] Likewise, as a reaction against decadent foreign influences, non-Spanish words were eliminated. (For example, the football team called Sporting de Gijón became Deportivo Gijón.[29]) The campaign against regional sport had already begun in the Francoist zone during the Civil War. In an article entitled 'Let's Make Sport National', a journalist wrote:

> Catalonia and the Basque Country, by placing the defence of their regional championships above the collective rights of the remaining federations, subjected the healthy development of the proper competitions to what was basically no more than an egotistical desire to cultivate an autonomy through sporting separatism, which was always ready to break out at any given moment. This is something which will necessarily have to end.[30]

When the stadium of Barcelona Football Club was reopened in June 1939, a 'patriotic-sporting event', presided over by General Alvarez Arenas, provided a further excuse for asserting the reincorporation of Catalonia and all its sports organisations into Spain. As the general proclaimed: 'Catalonia for Spain and Spain for Catalonia. ¡Viva España! ¡Viva el Caudillo! ¡Arriba España!'[31] The national policies dictated that regional groups in all sports were not allowed to use their own languages to describe their identity or function as teams. The restrictions against Basque and Catalan teams were particularly fierce. A centralist victory was symbolised in 1943 by Real Madrid's defeat of Barcelona by 11 to 1.

The Falangisation of sports was reinforced by the media, above all the press, which came under the control of censorship. As one article in *Arriba* proudly announced: 'With the Press Law enacted in 1938, all democratic principles sustained up until then were valiantly overthrown.'[32] Support also came from specifically Falangist publications. The sports newspaper *Marca*, founded in 1938 by the Falangist Manuel Fernández Cuesta, developed a daily circulation of up to 400,000 during Francoism.[33] As well as providing an outlet for official statements and a distinct political angle on events – above all during the Second World War – it contributed to a sporting vision of political leadership which shared common themes with Fascist Italy. The image of Mussolini as the ultimate model sportsman became a Fascist topos. In the words of one commentator: 'The Duce is a sportsman in the most elevated sense, because his physical and moral life are marvellously harmonised (...) We feel that nobody can defeat him, that nobody can bear comparison with him.'[34]

A front-page article celebrating *Marca*'s fourth year of publication fitted Franco into a similar, if less active category (Illustration 13.1). The title runs – 'A fascist salute ("brazo en alto") to all Spanish sportsmen' – and is followed by statements which confirm the anti-Republican stance of the newspaper during 'our war of salvation'. Beneath a large photograph of Franco, the Caudillo is described as the 'captain of Spain, father of our recaptured Homeland'. The military, sporting and religious metaphors continue: 'It is to him that we owe the resurrection and the noble guidance of our sport.' *Marca* joins in welcoming a new sporting era thanks to the general and shouting '¡Arriba España!'[35]

Franco's actual behaviour lagged far behind Mussolini's feats. The Caudillo never missed football matches on television, although, besides some tennis and golf, his physical efforts were concentrated above all on his long hunting and fishing trips.[36] Yet perhaps these passive and active interests were two sides of the same rough coin.

Some anthropologists believe that the origin of football is connected to the idea that the ball represents the head of a sacrificial beast which, once buried, will promote abundant crops.[37] Other theories relate how victors of a battle kicked about the heads of their enemies once the bodies were in their possession.[38] Interestingly enough, Franco displayed similar predilections during his period in Morocco. He developed a taste for brutality and hence, the exhibition of severed Moorish heads as trophies was, according to one account 'not uncommon'.[39]

Whatever the violent details of Franco's own sporting upbringing, we have observed how Falangist ideologies of sport, beyond theorising about the relationship between sport and war, locate the need for praxis in the young. During the Civil War, a training camp for young Falangists was set up and called 'Campamento José Antonio' after the founder of the movement, José Antonio Primo de Rivera. It closely resembled Italian training camps.[40] A report on the camp explained how the children played and were trained in the use of weapons 'as in a virile sport'.[41]

However, whereas membership of the Hitler Youth, with its emphasis on sporting prowess, was compulsory and the Nazi schools called Napolas involved 'war games',[42] the Falangists did not gain complete control over education owing to the important influence of the Catholic Church in the new régime.[43] Carlos Barral recounts how, in a school imbued with the rhetoric of José Antonio, patriotic songs were sung with an arm raised in the fascist salute, but gymnastics were not taken very seriously.[44] Other memoirs relate that, although football was a national obsession which began at school age, it was practised during playtime, not as part of the curriculum.[45]

The enactment of the sporting theories expounded by the Falangists was thus far from ubiquitous. Nevertheless, when important meetings of the Falange occurred, young members regularly demonstrated their regimented discipline in 'sporting festivities' (Illustrations 13.2 and 13.3). Furthermore, reports in Falangist publications could still emphasise certain ideas when events such as the first national university games took place. The connections between war, sport and patriotism remained the same:

> War was also needed so that the steps of these one thousand university sportsmen could show their strength on this dirt track.[46] It has also turned out that the fabulous and fiery world of war has even awoken the excitement of Spaniards to that beautiful adventure called sport. (...) Strong souls and muscles in the service of something as transcendent as our Fatherland. (...) The sport of the world which is emerging – our sport – is the sport which requires the training of the most immortal hours of the Fatherland. A muscle which successfully tilts the discus or javelin will be free from nerves in aiming the grenade on the necessary day.[47]

However, because of the period in which Franco came to power, sporting education remained more a product of war than a real preparation for it, as in Nazi Germany and Fascist Italy. Of course, military service for men strengthened a military education. Needless to say, when military sporting events occurred, they were given detailed press coverage.[48]

The position for women was different and is worth mentioning, not only because it involved full Falange control, but also because of the alternative rôle it assigned to female sport. In his brief discussion of sport in *Mein Kampf*, Hitler had written that the 'ideal of humanity' within the 'folkish State' was 'in the defiant embodiment of manly strength and in women who are able to bring men into the world'.[49] Falangist programmes for women's sport emphasised this secondary, servile function, while allowing for a certain personal development:

> Suitable gymnastics and sport have beneficial effects on women (...), they help women to reach the fullness of their grace and phys-

ical harmony; they develop their agility and strength; they awake in women a sense of discipline and illuminate their intelligence, thus simultaneously forming a training which is joyful, healthy and honest. They make women more suited for their maternal mission.[50]

The Sección Femenina of the Falange was under the direct control of José Antonio's sister, Pilar Primo de Rivera, who survived throughout Francoism along with her organisation. Among the most important rôles for the Sección Femenina was the running of the six-month long Servicio Social (Social Service), an obligatory female equivalent to military service, based on the Nazi *Arbeitsdienst*. Within these six months, ideological content was as important as practical maternal training in domestic tasks.[51] Sport also played its part, and the Sección Femenina organised everything from skiing competitions,[52] to more spectator-based sports exercises. At a sports display in Murcia in 1941, the submissive rôle of women according to the Falange was ideally fulfilled: they lay down in a shape, forming the national coat of arms (Illustration 13.4). Such events usually took place in the presence of military and political figures, who were capable of creating an atmosphere of bureaucratic pomp. At the closure of the Second National Gymnastics Championships of the Sección Femenina, in 1942, Franco's wife, their daughter Carmencita, Pilar Primo de Rivera, the Minister of Education and even General Moscardó were all in attendance.[53] The contest received an appropriate treatment in the Falangist press. Dr Ferreras commented in the Party paper *Arriba* that the preceding week had been a 'magnificent contribution by Spanish women to their homeland in a desire to sacrifice and excel'.[54]

The actual content of the oft-lauded 'gymnastics' shows organised by the Sección Femenina included proceedings far removed from what one might understand as sport in the usual sense (Illustration 13.5). An integral part of the Sección Femenina were the Coros y Danzas (Choruses and Dances), a group created in 1938 and dedicated to performing a debased form of folklore, which distorted regional traditions in order to exalt an imperialist, but essentially imaginary Spanish past. Movements and gestures considered coarse were excluded, as were songs judged vulgar. Dance steps and songs which were no longer taught in the villages where they originated were exclusively passed on to the Coros y Danzas so that the Falange could 'safeguard' popular tradition. Following Nationalist policy, the Coros y Danzas were meant to represent regional identities, while in fact they produced merely visual echoes of local costumes and enveloped them all in a bland uniformity free from the threatening difference of authentic historical roots.[55]

The competition in Europe: Spain in the Second World War

The extent to which Spain could engage in collective sport with fascist countries was obviously dictated by its diplomatic standing until 1945. The most significant and immediate alliance had been established with Italy and Germany through the military and financial aid granted to Franco's forces during the Spanish Civil War.[56] Nevertheless, Franco resisted full intervention in the Second World War. He claimed non-belligerency to the West and made impossible demands on Hitler, so that Germany never gained the strategic territorial advantage which would have cut off British access to the Mediterranean. Throughout the war, Franco was, according to one diplomat, a sort of 'silent ally' to the British-American forces.[57]

Yet Spain provided practical help for the Axis powers. Once Hitler turned against the Soviet Union in June 1941, Franco's anti-Communist rhetoric could be realised. During the following month, the Blue Division, consisting largely of Falangist volunteers, left for the Russian front. By the time the Division returned, at the end of 1943, about 47,000 Spaniards had fought on the Eastern front.[58] In addition, 8,000 Spanish workers were sent to Germany by a special government organisation. By May 1942, they had their own newspaper, called, symbolically, *Enlace* ('link', 'marriage').[59] Spain continued to supply Germany with wolfram throughout the war and several Spaniards took part in the final defence of Berlin.[60]

By far the most important of these pro-Axis offerings was the Blue Division, for it permitted the illusion of a genuine political, military and cultural union of fascist powers. There was a notable sporting presence in this military contribution. In November 1941, General Moscardó, already head of the Delegación Nacional de Deportes, paid the Division an official visit.[61] Back home in Spain, there were sports activities such as pelota and swimming competitions organised to raise money for Falangist comrades on the Russian front.[62] By the beginning of 1943, Barcelona football club was broadcasting local football results to members of the Blue Division every Sunday evening as a sign of patriotic solidarity.[63]

Soldiers in the Blue Division were involved in a variety of sports. They played soccer and once held a kind of mock bull-fight.[64] Skiing, that sport highlighted during the Civil War, once again had its strategic, heroic function: the patrol of Spanish skiers, headed by Captain Ordás, had to cross Lake Ilmen to support their besieged German comrades.[65] The whole nature of the deeds of the Division became clouded in an air of sporting adventure. Glorified personal accounts of the actions of the Blue Division juggle figures of casualties to set up 'scores' of dead, in which the Soviets 'lose' by disproportionately high numbers.[66]

Spanish football and the Axis powers

Sporting scores with Franco's political allies had started before the beginning of the Second World War. In 1937, an anti-Republican football team had played Portugal in Vigo. Huge portraits of Franco and Salazar were placed within the stadium. The following year, the two countries played each other again. Portugal won both games, the first by 2-1, the second by 1-0. A neo-fascist solidarity was further enhanced by the Italian referee who presided over each game.[67]

Once the Blue Division had been sent to fight against Communism, football matches could take place with German and Italian teams. The disappearance of the Nazi-Soviet Pact meant that there would no longer be any embarrassing questions about exactly where Spain stood with regard to the much feared 'Reds' who had supported the Second Republic during the Civil War. Some encounters could easily be seen within the context of an alliance of war, because they involved military teams. In November 1941, a Luftwaffe team came to play Atlético de Aviación, the new Atlético de Madrid which had been taken over in 1939 by the Spanish airforce. The Germans won by 3 to 2.[68]

By the time the Italian airforce came to play Atlético de Aviación, in December 1942, the ceremonies had been formalised well beyond the actual match. The visit was an excuse for assertions of fascist brotherhood. On the day after the arrival of the Italians, *Marca* printed the following 'greeting': 'We would not fulfil the most pleasant duty in opening this issue of *Marca*, which feels so strongly about sport and deeply about our fatherland, if we did not cordially greet our comrades with our arms raised in the fascist salute.' Italian participation in the 'crusade of liberation' (the Spanish Civil War) was remembered, and the obligatory exclamations drew the two countries together again: '¡Viva Italia! ¡Arriba España!'[69] Before the game, the Italian players, like their German colleagues in 1941, visited José Antonio Primo de Rivera's grave, accompanied by the Spanish team. Two wreaths were laid and fascist salutes were an integral part of the occasion. *Marca* displayed three photographs on its front page to illustrate the ritual (Illustration 13.6). A political homage had entered the domain of sports reporting.

When the game itself took place, the Spaniards won by 6-2, although the three pages in *Marca* devoted to reporting the match were careful to highlight the apparently balanced nature of the competition: 'The speed and fighting spirit of the Spaniards surpassed the great technical capacity of the Italians.' The match was described in terms of a friendly battle: 'A celebration of sportsmanship and comradeship, serving an elevated, beneficial aim. Brotherhoods of friendly wings, with a friendship sealed by the blood of the best. Flags, pennants, anthems. A forest of arms upraised in the fascist salute.'[70] The Italians made another visit before they returned to Italy. They went to the Alcázar at Toledo, the scene of an important siege during the early part of the Spanish Civil War.[71] It is no coincidence that General Moscardó was the main hero of that siege. When Franco started distributing aristocratic titles in 1947, Moscardó became Count of the Alcázar of Toledo.[72] In the midst of a world war, Spaniards and Italians were being reminded of another war in which they had participated.

Whereas the difficulty for those reporting the games against the Italians lay in stressing an equality of competence, the commentators of the match against the Luftwaffe had to underline a far from natural affinity between German and Spanish temperaments. This accounts for phrases such as 'that gentle game, without violence'.[73] These attempts to indicate harmony under somewhat forced circumstances were not unique. Paradoxes lay at the heart of conceptions of national football, because of forced military alliances and the problems they caused for ideas of unified identity. For the third World Football Championship in Germany in 1938, the Austrian team was absorbed into the German one.[74] During the Second World War, German teams counted Polish players amongst them.[75] Of the eight international games played by the Spanish national team in the Second World War, four were against

Portugal, and one each against neutral Switzerland, occupied France, Nazi Germany and Fascist Italy. All would bring tensions of nationhood to light, but the matches against Germany and Italy are most interesting because of the spectacle they entailed, as well as the Axis coalition they tried to consolidate.

For both events, the Spanish team travelled across war-torn Europe in April 1942. The match in Berlin brought sport closest to military activity. In the words of an anonymous article in *Arriba*: 'This friendly nation always held the talents of Spaniards in high esteem. Today, while our volunteers from the Blue Division are united with their troops to cleanse the world from Marxist impurity, Germany takes advantage of this sporting encounter to demonstrate her profound adherence to Spain.'[76] An announcer on German radio welcomed 'Spain and the soldiers of the Blue Division' and reminded listeners that representatives from the country could not be present at the inauguration of the Berlin stadium, because they were already fighting to save Europe from communism.[77]

The status of Spanish military cooperation was bolstered during the match. Beneath the presidential rostrum and alongside the pitch, accompanied by their nurses, sat wounded members of the Blue Division who were convalescing in the capital of the Third Reich. Photographs show both the 100,000 strong crowd and the players giving the fascist salute before the game. The spectators stood to sing the national anthems.[78]

Spanish reports on the game emphasise the 'church-like silence' of the stadium. The public was praised precisely for the qualities to which Falangist theorists of sport aspired, 'the sense of discipline and sporting education of such an immense mass the spectators , which incarnates the German people'. It was observed that all the German players were soldiers. There were some whistles of disapproval when Spanish players gave a slight touch of 'violence' to the encounter. But, of course, what dominated the game was a 'sportsmanship of true brothers in arms, without any incident, disturbance or violence'.[79] Efficient marking and precise tactics proved crucial for the Germans and compensated for their lack of improvisation. In any case, a 1-1 draw avoided the need for explaining the difference between two styles. In spite of this result and recent victories against Portugal, Switzerland and France, Spanish commentators were not over-jubilant, especially when they considered the forthcoming match against Italy.[80]

Events proved them right. Italy won by 4-0. In retrospect, there is plenty of irony in the comments which preceded the game and painted a picture of 'Latin' football and of two styles 'born of fraternal techniques, inspired by the same temperamental values'.[81] Even if the final score indicated different achievements resulting from these techniques, the stay of the Spanish players in Milan became a celebration of tripartite Axis bonding. There was a trade fair going on during their stay and the day before the match was declared Spanish Day. Places of honour in San Siro Stadium were given to 120 war invalids and 100 members of the German naval and air forces. The spectators, numbering over 60,000, could see the flags of Italy, Spain and Germany all around the pitch.[82] As for the Spanish players themselves, they were toured around Milan to view the places that had been so important in the early stages of the Fascist movement. They visited the Piazza San Sepolcro, the old editorial offices of *Il popolo d'Italia* (the newspaper founded by Mussolini in 1914) and placed wreaths at memorials to the dead.[83]

All were agreed, in public at least, as to the validity of the result according to performances on the day. But as if to forestall any excessive triumphalism, a bizarre reminder of greater unity interrupted the match. After twenty minutes, play was stopped and everybody was silent for a minute in memory of all those who had died fighting on land, sea and in the air.[84] It is another example of how such sports competitions were always subsumed into a political framework, in which the only losers were those not playing in the same game. In these cases, it is difficult to talk, as many have done, of Spanish football as a force for the depoliticisation of the masses.[85]

Miklos Nyiszli, a Hungarian physician and prisoner at Auschwitz, recounts how, as a member of the privileged Special Squad, he once attended a soccer game between a team representing the SS on guard at the crematorium and a group representing the Special Squad. Bets were placed, applause was voiced and players were cheered from both sides, as if the match were taking place in a village, not a concentration camp.[86] This sport, for all the superficial opposition of the game, was a confirmation of unity, and allowed only to the most special, most compromised category of prisoner. To play was to fight, indeed, to fight during a war, but on the same side as, rather than against, the opposing team.[87]

NOTES

1. See Victoria de Grazia, *The Culture of Consent: Mass Organization of Leisure in Fascist Italy*, Cambridge, 1981, p. 173.
2. See John M. Hoberman, *Sport and Political Ideology*, London, 1984, pp. 83-109 and 162-169.
3. Richard D. Mandell, *The Nazi Olympics*, London, 1972, p. x.
4. *Ibidem*, pp. 151-153.
5. See De Grazia, *The Culture*, p. 179.
6. The love/aggression aspect of sport has been taken to psychoanalytical extremes in Adrian Stokes, *A Game that Must be Lost: Collected Papers*, Cheadle Hulme, 1973, pp. 38-52.
7. For Mussolini's early Socialism, see Denis Mack Smith, *Mussolini*, London, 1983, pp. 7-32.
8. See Griffin's chapter 'Staging the Nation's Rebirth', in this volume.
9. See Christopher H. Cobb, 'The Educational and Cultural Policy of the Popular Front Government in Spain, 1936-1939', in Martin S. Alexander and Helen Graham (eds), *The French and Spanish Popular Fronts: Comparative Perspectives*, Cambridge, 1989, pp. 240-253, here p. 243.
10. See Carlos Fernández Santander, *El fútbol durante la guerra civil y el franquismo*, Madrid, 1990, pp. 27-28.
11. Quoted *ibidem*, p. 38. Unless otherwise indicated, all translations are my own.
12. *Marca*, 21 Dec. 1938, quoted *ibidem*, p. 55.
13. 'Deporte', *Arriba*, 21 April 1942, p. 1.
14. Fex, 'Deportes', *Vértice*, vol. 5, Sept.-Oct. 1937, n.p.
15. See Fernández Santander, *El fútbol*, p. 65.
16. For a recent account of Nazi sport which underlines its military emphasis, see Peter Reichel, *Der schöne Schein des Dritten Reiches: Faszination und Gewalt des Faschismus*, Munich, 1992, pp. 255-272. For the rôle of the military elements in sports education in Fascist Italy, see Felice Fabrizio, *Sport e fascismo: La politica sportiva del regime: 1924-1936*, Rimini and Florence, 1976, pp. 83-84, 91, 97, 102-105 and 126-127.
17. Fex, 'Deportes'.
18. See García-Agosti, 'Juventudes de Europa: muchachos del III Reich', *Marca: suplemento gráfico de los martes*, vol. 2, no. 24, 11 May 1943, pp. 14-15.
19. J. Dumas, 'Deportes: nieve', *Vértice*, vol. 6, Nov. 1937, n.p.
20. Lula de Lara, 'Señoras y señores: ¡Hagamos gimnasia!', *Vértice*, vol. 13, Aug. 1938, n.p.
21. Juan Deportista, 'El deporte, fuente de disciplina, escuela de patriotismo', *ABC*, 18 July 1945, p. 27.
22. See Fernández Santander, *El fútbol*, pp. 64-65.
23. Quoted in Luis María Cazorla Prieto, *Deporte y estado*, Barcelona, 1979, p. 218. For the rôle of the Falange in the francoist organisation of sports, see also Gil de la Vega, 'Sport di ieri e di oggi', *Legioni e Falangi*, vol. 2, no. 5, 1 March 1942, pp. 27-28.
24. See Duncan Shaw, *Fútbol y franquismo*, Madrid, 1987, p. 32; Fernando Vizcaíno Casas, *La España de la posguerra (1939-1953)*, Barcelona, 1981, pp. 22, 68.
25. See 'Il saluto romano prescritto agli atleti e agli sportivi', *Gazetta dello sport*, 9 Feb. 1934, quoted in Fabrizio, *Sport*, p. 48.
26. See Fernández Santander, *El fútbol*, pp. 47-48 and 57.

27. See Duff Hart-Davis, *Hitler's Games: The 1936 Olympics*, London, 1986, pp. 59-81.

28. See Fabrizio, *Sport*, pp. 42-43; Antonio Ghirelli, *Storia del calcio in Italia*, 4th edition, Turin, 1990, p. 99.

29. See Fernández Santander, *El fútbol*, p. 73.

30. Rienzi, 'Nacionalicemos el deporte', *Domingo*, 21 February 1937, p. 8, quoted in Josep Benet, *Catalunya sota el règim franquista: Informe sobre la persecució de la llengua i la cultura de Catalunya pel règim del general Franco (primera part)*, Barcelona, 1978, p. 251.

31. See Benet, *Catalunya*, pp. 252-253.

32. Santos Alcocer, 'La prensa española en el nuevo Estado Nacionalsindicalista', *Arriba*, 22 April 1942, pp. 3-4, here p. 3. For an introduction to press censorship in early Francoism, see Manuel L. Abellán, *Censura y creación literaria en España (1939-1976)*, Barcelona, 1980, pp. 45-54.

33. Shaw, *Fútbol*, p. 69.

34. A. Cotronei, 'Cesare gladiatore', *Il popolo d'Italia*, 28 November 1934, quoted in Fabrizio, *Sport*, p. 115. For Mussolini's sporting activities, see also Smith, *Mussolini*, pp. 128-131. Mussolini shared Hitler's admiration for boxing (Adolf Hitler, *Mein Kampf*, translated by Ralph Manheim, London, 1992, p. 373), a sport the Italian leader thought almost as admirable as fighting in war (Smith, *Mussolini*, p. 131). There is no equivalent statement by José Antonio Primo de Rivera or Franco, but boxing was the most popular spectator sport after football in Spain in the early 1940s. See Juan Deportista, 'Un año deportivo', *ABC*, '1943' (an undated retrospective issue on 1942), n.p.; Vizcaíno Casas, *La España*, p. 68.

35. Anon., 'Brazo en alto a los deportistas españoles' and 'Saludo a Franco', *Marca*, 25 November 1942, p. 1.

36. See Raymond Carr, *Spain: 1808-1975*, 2nd edition, Oxford, 1982, pp. 725 and 697; J. P. Fusi, *Franco: A Biography*, London, 1987, pp. 126-127; Enrique González Duro, *Franco: Una biografía psicológica*, Madrid, 1992, pp. 313-318. González Duro relates Franco's passion for hunting to his sexual frustration.

37. See Morris Marples, *A History of Football*, London, 1954, pp. 14-15.

38. See Montague Shearman and James E. Vincent, *Foot-Ball: Its History for Five Centuries*, London, 1885, pp. 4-5; Brian Jewell, *Sports and Games: History and Origins*, Tunbridge Wells, 1977, p. 70.

39. Paul Preston, 'The Discreet Charm of a Dictator', *Times Literary Supplement*, 5 March 1993, pp. 13-14, here p. 13.

40. See Tracy H. Koon, *Believe, Obey, Fight: Political Socialisation of Youth in Fascist Italy: 1922-1943*, Chapel Hill, 1985, pp. 101-102.

41. Anon., 'Flechas en España amanece', *Vértice*, vol. 5, September-October 1937, n.p.

42. See Richard Grunberger, *A Social History of the Third Reich*, Harmondsworth, 1974, pp. 350-351, 358-359 and 376-378. For an illustrated survey of the activities of the Hitler Youth, including details of the uniforms worn for different sports, see Frederick J. Stephens, *Hitler Youth: History, Organisation, Uniforms and Insignia*, London, 1973.

43. See Frances Lannon, *Privilege, Persecution, and Prophecy: The Catholic Church in Spain: 1875-1975*, Oxford, 1987, pp. 218-222.

44. *Años de penitencia: memorias I*, 4th edition, Madrid, 1982, pp. 22-23.

45. Francisco Umbral, *Memorias de un niño de derechas*, 3rd edition, Barcelona, 1986, pp. 127-128.
46. *'Pista de ceniza'*: 'ceniza' literally means 'ash', thus glorifying the tone further.
47. Anon., 'Deporte', *Arriba*, 21 April 1942, p. 1.
48. For example, 'Campeonatos nacionales militares de natación en Toledo', *Marca: suplemento gráfico de los martes*, vol. 2, no. 40, 31 August 1943, n.p.
49. *Mein Kampf*, Manheim translation, p. 373.
50. María Pilar Morales, *Mujeres*, Madrid, 1944, pp. 55-56, quoted in Carmen Martín Gaite, *Usos amorosos de la postguerra española*, 6th edition, Barcelona, 1987, p. 60.
51. See Rosario Sánchez López, *Mujer española, una sombra de destino en lo universal: Trayectoria histórica de Sección Femenina de Falange (1934-1977)*, Murcia, 1990, pp. 35-42.
52. See *Marca: suplemento gráfico de los martes*, vol. 2, no. 14, 2 March 1943, pp. 10-11.
53. See photograph in *Arriba*, 21 April 1942, p. 6.
54. Dr Ferreras, 'Divagaciones de un espectador', *Arriba*, 21 April 1942, p. 6.
55. See Sánchez López, *Mujer española*, pp. 77-79.
56. For general assessments, see Hugh Thomas, *The Spanish Civil War*, 3rd edition, Harmondsworth, 1986, pp. 939-942 and 977; Angel Viñas, 'The Financing of the Spanish Civil War', in Paul Preston (ed.), *Revolution and War in Spain: 1931-1939*, London and New York, 1984, pp. 266-283.
57. See Willard L. Beaulac, *Franco: Silent Ally in World War II*, Carbondale, 1986; Donald S. Detwiler, *Hitler, Franco und Gibraltar: Die Frage des spanischen Eintritts in den Zweiten Weltkrieg*, Wiesbaden, 1962; Paul Preston, *Franco: A Biography*, London, 1993, pp. 343-531.
58. For the most detailed historical study, see Gerald R. Kleinfeld and Lewis A. Tambs, *La división española de Hitler: La División Azul en Rusia*, Madrid, 1983.
59. See Rafael García Pérez, 'El envío de trabajadores españoles durante la segunda guerra mundial', *Hispania: Revista Española de Historia*, vol. 48, 1988, pp. 1031-1065; Iván de Madrid, 'Los trabajadores españoles en Alemania tienen ya un periódico', *Arriba*, 7 May 1942, p. 6.
60. See Kleinfeld and Tambs, *La división española*, p. 502; Felix Steiner, *Die Freiwilligen der Waffen-SS: Idee und Opfergang*, 5th edition, Preußisch Oldendorf, 1973, p. 135.
61. See Juan Ackermann Hanisch, *A las órdenes de vuecencia: Autobiografía del intérprete de los generales Muñoz Grandes y Esteban-Infantes*, Madrid, 1993, p. 41; Emilio Esteban-Infantes, *La División Azul (donde Asia empieza)*, Barcelona, 1956, p. 77; Kleinfeld and Tambs, *La división española*, pp. 194-196.
62. See *Arriba*, 20 Nov. 1941, p. 11; *Arriba*, 21 Nov. 1941, p. 7.
63. See Fernández Santander, *El fútbol*, p. 80.
64. See Arturo Espinosa Poveda, *Artillero segundo en la gloriosa División Azul (4 julio 1941 – 18 abril 1943)*, Madrid, 1992, pp. 308 and 549; José Díaz de Villegas, *La División Azul en línea*, Barcelona, 1967, pp. 92-93 and illustrations between pp. 80-81.
65. See Espinosa Poveda, *Artillero*, pp. 245-248; Kleinfeld and Tambs, *La división española*, illustrations between pp. 256-257.
66. See Espinosa Poveda, *Artillero*, pp. 661, 668; Esteban-Infantes, *La División Azul*, pp. 300-301
67. See Fernández Santander, *El fútbol*, pp. 39, 43.

68. For details, see *Arriba*, 20 November 1941, p. 8; *Arriba*, 21 November 1941, p. 7; *Arriba*, 22 November 1941, p. 5.
69. *Marca*, 18 December 1942, p. 1.
70. Barreira, Untitled article, *Marca*, 22 December 1942, p. 1.
71. See *Marca*, 23 December 1942, p. 3.
72. Thomas, *The Spanish Civil War*, pp. 409-413 and 948.
73. Flecha Dorada, 'El partido de ayer en Vallecas', *Arriba*, 22 November 1941, p. 5.
74. See Cazorla Prieto, *Deporte*, p. 294.
75. See Franz Schönhuber, *Ich war dabei*, 12th edition, Munich, 1989, pp. 45-46.
76. 'Alemania aprovecha la ocasión para mostrar su simpatía a España', *Arriba*, 12 April 1942, p. 5.
77. Anon., 'Una impresión del III Alemania-España', *Arriba*, 14 April 1942, p. 7.
78. See *Arriba*, 14 April 1942, p. 1.
79. See Anon., 'Una impresión'.
80. See *Arriba*, 15 April 1942, p. 5.
81. Flecha Dorada, 'Las dos escuelas latinas frente a frente', *Arriba*, 19 April 1942, p. 7.
82. See Luis de la Barga, 'Una vez más faltó en nuestro equipo el ataque', *Arriba*, 21 April 1942, p. 7.
83. See Luis de la Barga, 'Es probable que Martorell no pueda jugar hoy en Milán', *Arriba*, 19 April 1942, p. 7.
84. See Agencia Mercheta, 'Impresión esquemática del partido', *Arriba*, 21 April 1942, p. 7.
85. For views on football during Francoism as a form of escape and depoliticisation, see Antonio Alcoba, *El periodismo deportivo en la sociedad moderna*, Madrid, 1980, p. 252; Fernández Santander, *El fútbol*, pp. 243-246; Shaw, *Fútbol*, pp. 96, 118.
86. See Primo Levi, *I sommersi e i salvati*, Turin 1986, p. 40.
87. I would like to thank Mark Almond, Günter Berghaus, Roger Griffin and Noel Malcolm for their assistance with the writing of this article. My study was made possible by a special conference grant from the British Academy and the Queen Sofía Research Fellowship I held at Exeter College, Oxford.

14

Jacques Copeau and 'Popular Theatre' in Vichy France

Serge Added

Translated by Robin Slaughter

In 1940, Jacques Copeau was aged sixty-one. Founder of the Vieux-Colombier Theatre in 1913, great reformer of the French stage, theatre director with a long-standing, international reputation: how did he adjust his professional career to meet the profound changes France was undergoing during the Vichy years? What was the nature of his relationship with the new authorities in charge of the State?

The German offensive in May 1940 coincided with Copeau's appointment as interim Administrator of the Comédie-Française. In Spring 1941, Copeau wrote what can be considered his 'theoretic testament': *The Popular Theatre*.[1] It was also during the Vichy years that Copeau directed what he considered to be his most successful production, *Le Miracle du pain doré* (*The Miracle of the Golden Loaf*), given at the Hospice de Beaune in 1943, and wrote his last play, based on the life of St Francis, *Le Petit Pauvre* (*The Little Poor Man of Assisi*), published by Gallimard in 1946.

This period which was so decisive in the history of contemporary France was, therefore, an equally important moment in Copeau's artistic life. This raises the question of whether Copeau's theatrical thinking was at that time, when Pétain's ideas were all-pervading, contaminated by the same political ideology. The purpose of this chapter is to examine the possible links between the man, his artistic ideas and the political life of his country.

After the exodus of civilians fleeing before the occupying forces, Copeau returned to Paris and was faced with the task of organising the re-opening not only of the Comédie-Française but also of the Odéon. The latter theatre had been under the administration of Paul Abram who, being Jewish, was immediately judged undesirable by the new authorities. Copeau was asked to take over temporarily, which he did with an ill grace, asking to be replaced as soon as possible. For a while, he was exclusively pre-occupied with starting up the Comédie-Française. It is worth noting that this fitted in with the desire of the German authorities, who wanted to ensure that artistic activities were renewed as soon as possible. Driven by this professional consideration, Copeau complied with the German requirement that Jews should be excluded from the Comédie-Française, in spite of his personal feelings of compassion for those thus persecuted, as we can read in his *Journal*.[2]

Copeau was the first (and for a long time the only) stage director to be appointed as head of the Comédie-Française. Immediately on taking office, in May 1940, he organised a special programme devoted to the poetic works of Péguy, hoping to touch the heart of the public by presenting patriotic texts that echoed 'our present distress'. Copeau sought and won an emotional response from a public no longer moved by the 'classic' soirées. It seemed to him that the theatre should root itself in the historical moment and reflect the current sufferings of society.

The opening night on 7 September 1940 betrayed a worrying politicisation of the stage. It was a poetic patchwork interlaced with the watchwords of the collaborationist régime: the return to life on the land, traditional crafts, the family, the fields, in clear allusion to Pétain's *Travail, Famille, Patrie*. The evening began with a lecture by Abel Bonnard, a member of the French Academy and a panegyrist of the extreme Right. The poems had been chosen to celebrate the values then officially in vogue and were thus pressed into service under the banner of Pétain's National Revolution. Before the programme commenced, Copeau gave a speech very much in tune with the prevailing mood of self-flagellation, laying the blame for France's current misfortunes on France herself (which was the official government line):

> How is it that in the souls even of those undergoing the greatest ordeals something is already stirring, emerging from the dark and coming to life, something to which we hesitate to give a name but which, when tomorrow comes, we shall have to call Hope? Firstly, it is because we are recognising our mistakes and our sins, confessing them, condemning them and are determined to wipe out our

errors and make amends. Secondly, it is because in spite of all dis-asters we maintain a secret but unshakeable faith in the deep pow-ers of the homeland, in the soul of the race, in the lasting strength and survival of the French spirit.[3]

The same show was given another performance on 15 September, after which this type of programme was discontinued.

Next, in the autumn of 1940, arose the question of confirming Copeau's appointment as permanent. The playwright, Edouard Bourdet, had been appointed Administrator of the Comédie-Fran-çaise in 1936 by the Popular Front government. In Spring 1940, he had a car accident and was forced to take a leave. He half prom-ised Copeau that his retirement would be permanent, but once recovered, in the Autumn of 1940, he wanted his post back after all. He even took the opportunity to try to negotiate an extension of his administrative powers. The Minister of Education, Georges Ripert, apparently pronounced these proposals 'consonant with the new spirit', and his word was law in those days of unanswer-able authority. Nonetheless, he turned down Bourdet's proposals and required that he resign. Copeau, for his part, found the Administrator's chair comfortable, but the Vichy government extended his interim administration to 31 December 1940; then a decree was published that made his appointment definitive.

At that very moment, the German axe fell. The blow was dealt by Lieutenant Baumann, in charge of the theatre section at the Propaganda H.Q., even though Karl Epting, the Director of the German Institute, had tried, unsuccessfully, to make him change his mind. Baumann had been convinced that Copeau was unfa-vourably disposed towards Germany. He was right about this, as the unrelenting hostility to the German occupation, which rises constantly from the pages of Copeau's *Journal*, reveals. Baumann held a number of grudges against Copeau: firstly because the sacking of the Jewish actors had been done in a way that was designed to attract public attention (he would have preferred more discretion); secondly because Copeau rarely presented him-self at the Propaganda H.Q.; and thirdly because of the contribu-tion Copeau's son, Pascal, had made to Radio-Strasbourg during the 1939-1940 period of the war. In short, as the new year opened, the rejection of Copeau was absolute and irrevocable. The occu-pying powers threatened to close down the Comédie-Française if he stayed in his post. The Vichy government gave way to the pres-sure and Copeau was forced to resign.

Copeau thereupon returned to his Burgundian retreat. However, his contacts with Vichy were not completely severed. In fact, Copeau made several visits to the spa town in order to be able to organise lectures or set up a radio training course at Beaune in September 1942, headed by himself and Pierre Schaeffer. He also wrote an article on the theatre, which was incorporated in a propaganda brochure issued by the Ministry of Information.[4] When, in July 1943, he produced *The Miracle of the Golden Loaf*, the State was officially represented at the performances at the Beaune Hospice: Dr Ménétral, a close friend of Marshal Pétain, and Louis Hautecoeur, General Secretary of Fine Arts, turned out at the première. Georges Hilaire, who replaced Hautecoeur in April, 1944, was still considering Copeau for membership of his 'Council of Artists' which was due to advise the 'Prince', i.e., Pétain, in his project of establishing firm structures and strict supervision over cultural activities throughout the country.

As these facts indicate, Jacques Copeau was highly thought of in Vichy, the new French capital on the banks of the Allier. His conception of the rôle of the State in the domain of the theatre squared rather neatly with the idea of a dictatorial régime. A whole chapter of *The Popular Theatre* is devoted to the topic. In it, he sings the praises of strong-arm interventionist powers as sources of quality and originality: 'Strict control is a guarantee of creative power. Approval or condemnation from superiors are an insurance against disorders in public taste.' As for the reform he longed for, it could only be brought about under such leadership: 'It will only be properly guided and be fertile under the aegis of a stern authority and so long as this latter is well informed.' Perhaps, at the beginning of 1941 Copeau could see himself as adviser to the benevolent despot.

When reading *The Popular Theatre*, one is invariably struck by the extent to which it is impregnated with the Pétainist sentiments of the 'National Revolution'. From the beginning, Copeau adopted the self-flagellating tone so popular with Vichy: 'Our misfortunes have mercilessly proved how heretical our ideas were.' The reference to medieval mystery plays was intended to validate a moralistic, edifying kind of theatre, where the spectator 'feeling himself to be a sinner, would kneel and beat his breast.' Praise of the theatre festivals of Ancient Greece led naturally to a glorification of 'a human philosophy respectful of fate'. Echoing his earlier insistence on asceticism (the 'bare boards' that, in 1913, he had stipulated for a renewal of the theatre), he now demanded for the theatre a building which would be 'of simple, healthy character, a home that reflects our present poverty and, one could say, our present humiliation.' But his vision was much wider than these topical references suggest.

At the beginning of the century, the theatre-going public was, in the main, limited to one social category: the middle class. These bourgeoisie were fully satisfied with the dramatic genre that portrayed them on stage in light-hearted anecdotes: the boulevard play. The reformers of the theatre, with Copeau at their head, had to think where to look for spectators likely to follow them in their quest for a true art of the theatre. Having first addressed themselves to a cultivated, educated public, they were now seized by nostalgia for the days when the theatre had had a universally acknowledged function in the life of the people. Ancient Greece and the Middle Ages offered all the attraction of periods when dramatic art played a specific social and religious rôle, when the artist lived in close contact with his public, when the festivals had the whole population participating in them and giving the life of the City a distinct rhythm.

It is unimportant whether this vision of Athenian or medieval life was accurate or mythified. What counts here is the deeper reason for this nostalgia and its aesthetic dimension. It is not that unusual for a reformer to draw his inspiration from the past. Distance and unfamiliarity can lend long-forgotten conventions an air of novelty, indeed modernity. Greek choruses were revived in various shapes and formats, or *Commedia dell'arte* figures turned up again under various guises. However, renewal through a return to the past was not only restricted to aesthetic matters; it was also precisely what Marshal Pétain was claiming to achieve in politics! This similarity of method, which by no means indicates similarity of content, may well have led a number of these theatre reformers to put their trust in Pétain for a time.

These reformers saw their task as having to seek out those spectators, who were staying away from theatres, because ever since the French Revolution these had been dominated by the bourgeoisie. In January, 1941, Copeau's son-in-law, Jean Dasté, drew up a questionnaire which was sent to a number of theatre practitioners. Throughout it, one can detect a real hunger for a new kind of spectator. The usual Paris audiences were not considered capable of instigating a renewal of the theatre. Nor were the dramatists, who delivered the regular fare these audiences were hankering after. Copeau and his fellow reformers believed that a new organisation of the theatre would need to attract a wider and more varied public, which hence would call forth a new type of playwright. The popular masses were regarded as the fertile soil capable of giving rise to and nourishing a popular theatre, just as the *Commedia dell'arte* had been born of the people and subsequently influenced great authors right up to the twentieth century. But what constituted 'the people' in this discourse? It certainly was not the disadvantaged majority of society. Copeau's 'popular theatre' was not to follow in the steps of politically committed companies such as the October Group.[5] For him, the 'people' consisted of the City as a whole community, involving all classes of society. Ever since France had become a Republic, the theatre had been monopolised by a minority, and so now the purpose was to give it back to the entire community, thus emulating the ancient Greek drama contests or the performances in front of the porches of medieval cathedrals.

From defining theatre as a reflection of the life of society, it follows that a bourgeois society, bowing to the claims of individualism, could only produce a trivial, vulgar dramatic art:

> Once the supporting structures of society are fractured by a negative philosophy, when man's natural inclinations tend to supplant any inner discipline, when the bonds of marriage and paternal authority are loosened so far as to dismantle the family unit, when love is reduced to carnal appetite and a sense of honour is held up to derision, when social strata are mixed and beliefs discredited, (...) when man meets no opposition to his will and takes Dostoyevsky's 'Everything is permitted' for his watchword, when there are no more standards of behaviour, then there is no more comedy, nor tragedy.[6]

The decadence of the theatre was considered as being part and parcel of the decadence of an individualistic, permissive society. That being the case, only by immersing oneself in the life of the whole community could the art of drama be re-born. In this period following the French defeat, a number of dynamic personalities in the theatre (*animateurs*, as they were called by Brasillach) decided that the renewal of their art would go hand-in-hand with the National Revolution. And Jean Dasté was prophesying in January 1941:

> It seems to me that the theatre will only resume its true rôle if it is enabled to do so by a general transformation of society, like that which is already under way and for which many people are work-

ing: this National Revolution that Marshal Pétain has promised us.
I believe that when this comes about, a fresh organisation will allow
workers to flock in great numbers to the theatre as if taking part in
a public celebration.[7]

The high ideals of a theatre that is fulfilling its rôle in the life of the
City (its mission being not only to entertain but to represent ideas
and feelings), and the no less high ideals of a democratic State (to
bring together the greatest number of citizens, particularly those
that had been traditionally excluded) were welded together in 'a
theatre of the Nation. Not a "theatre of class and conflict", but a
theatre of reunion and regeneration'.[8] This dream was for a social
transformation similar to the one Pétain was preaching. Of course,
nothing of the kind was ever to take place. We have here a mis-
taken analysis of the political and cultural situation of occupied
France. The Vichy régime did not integrate the underprivileged
into society, and the social revolution never got beyond being a
theme for speeches. However, there is evidence here that the political changes that followed soon after the shock of military defeat
attracted people of the theatre to Pétain's programme of national
renewal, because they saw in it a possibility of realising their old
dreams of a reformed and democratic theatre. The government's
discourse, anti-individualistic and pro-community, could not but
touch a responsive chord in those hopeful of turning the theatre,
no longer hamstrung by mercantile considerations, into an instrument of the community.

Bearer of a global vision of their art, Copeau did not define the
theatre merely as a reflection or a mouthpiece of the public. His
concept of a 'popular theatre' carried the mark of his preoccupation with religion at this period. Theatre became like a liturgical
service. Its vocation was to gather together the whole of the City in
one place, to establish a community feeling in the public, to weld
the mass of spectators into one living body. Here, the will to
democracy (making theatrical culture accessible to all levels of
society) found its true expression. This theatre of communion was
not a promiscuous mixing of social ranks, but implied the settling
of everyone in their place in a clearly defined social hierarchy. On
closer examination, we see that the unity desired could only be
national unity. 'Popular theatre', according to Léon Chancerel, 'is
by definition a theatre which unites all the classes of a people'; it
is a powerful factor of social integration, 'which gathers together
and unites in laughter and in tears.'[9] Those who followed this line

of thinking expressed it most readily in giving great prominence to the 'classics' and above all to the celebration of feast days, both National (Joan of Arc, etc.) and religious (e.g., Christmas, Easter, St. John's Day in midsummer). For, in order to make a theatre audience feel as one, in spite of all differences and antagonisms, it was necessary to find subjects instantly understood by all and inspiring the same emotions in each and every spectator.

Copeau had called for such celebrations with a religious basis in *The Popular Theatre*, and he himself practised what he preached when he produced *The Miracle of the Golden Loaf* on the occasion of the five-hundredth anniversary of the Hôtel-Dieu of Beaune in July 1943. These performances were, as far as he was concerned, one of the high points of his theatrical career. For him, they were 'the perfect example of a sacred celebration.' The performances, in the open air, were preceded by a mass with high dignitaries of the Church and the representatives of the State. Copeau was delighted with the composition of the audience, 'this mixture of the humble people and the aristocracy', which he so much desired. 'At the end of the *Miracle*', wrote Copeau in September, 1943, 'there arose the sound of the *Te Deum* and the bells pealed out. The bishops were weeping. The whole town was caught up in the same emotion. It was like a truce in the present and an omen for the future.'[10] The 'truce in the present' nevertheless made the front page of the newspapers and magazines,[11] and the Hospice took care to hide the identity of the 'generous donor' who gave a cheque for 100,000 francs (out of a total of 511,686 francs taken). The person in question was in fact Adolf Segnitz, representative of the Reich in charge of imports and who had bought half of the grape harvest of the Hospice de Beaune in 1941.

The presence of these official representatives cannot be accepted as being without political significance. It raises at the very least one question: in spite of Copeau's conviction that he was apolitical, can we establish links between him and the ideology of the time?

Copeau's concept of 'Popular Theatre' indicated in many ways the entry of Pétainist thought into the theatre. Certainly, it is not possible to define a single Vichy ideology. From both the synchronic and the diachronic point of view it is simpler to speak in terms of plurality. But even so, the idea of the Community does constitute one of the central points in the ideological nebula surrounding the National Revolution. Being the idea that held together the triptych 'Work, Family, Fatherland', it was the object of much theorising. The salvation of France, according to a number of ideologues, lay in the restoration of the basic communities (the fatherland being the community of communities): family, province, craft guild. Pétain had declared individualism 'the source of all the ills of which we so nearly perished', and he had set an ideological trend when he proposed a French form of authoritarian régime that would put the community above the State (thus distinguishing itself from fascist theorists, who asserted the primacy of the State). Representing a 'third way', opposed equally to individualism and collectivism, it aimed at establishing a hierarchical society, a society of leaders with personal power, an authoritarian society, responsible and closely-knit. The ever-present fear of a break-up of society formed the basis of this ideological tendency. Its political expression was the theory that interpreted the defeat of 1940 as the result of class warfare and lack of solidarity in the country.

Clearly, there were political realities which explain this concern for national cohesion. The French defeat and the occupation by the German troops had been a profoundly traumatic experience with far-reaching consequences for everyone. The functioning of the economy, the whole life of society were completely disrupted. The exodus from the occupied zone led to the separation of families and above all, on a wider scale, the tearing apart of the very fabric of society. In the north, the departure of so much of the population threw everything into confusion; in the south, the influx of countless refugees posed enormous problems. The internment of nearly two million prisoners, later sent to Germany, was another painful blow. Disorganisation reigned and the spectre of massive and lasting unemployment began to haunt the country. Labour was lacking for the grape harvest, and equally in industrial enterprises.

The rifts in the fabric of society were made worse by a form of geographical dislocation: France was divided into seven 'zones'. These internal frontiers were often impenetrable, the most famous being the Line of Demarcation (dividing north from south – initially occupied and un-occupied France). Communications were cut, with serious repercussions both on the individual level (it was often difficult to obtain news of a loved one) and in the economic sphere. What is more, this break-up of the country's unity, which had already been under way for some time, became part of a process of disintegration of traditional social ties. Although the industrialisation of France had been underway for nearly a century, it is worth noting that it was only in the 1930s that the urban inhabitants of France at last outnumbered the rural population. The destruction of ancestral village communities and their loyalties had become irreversible.

The proliferation of forces that disrupted the texture of society explains why the concept of community occupied such a central position in people's minds. The question of national identity was at the heart of the prevailing ideology of the times. It also explains the powerful impact of the man who, for a while, managed to incarnate the unity of the country: Philippe Pétain. The Marshal's régime made, or tried to make, national unity the basis of its claim to legitimacy. The decision to accept the armistice, to withdraw from the metropolitan area to rural Vichy, was done in the name of this same unity. The dislocated country was supposed to reassemble around the person of the Leader of the Fatherland, still revered as the Victor of Verdun. Even collaboration with the Germans was undertaken – according to Pétain's speech of 30 October 1940 – in the name of national unity.

We can see here a convergence of Copeau's 'popular theatre' with what Henri Ghéon called 'community theatre'.[12] Copeau's ideas, discernible in all he wrote, from his *Journal* to his correspondence, are along the same lines. In an article of 1942 he asserted: 'The theatre in France, like France in her entirety, needs to be put in order', and 'in the theatre, as elsewhere, the task must be to raise a new generation filled with a new spirit.'[13] His *Journal* shows an unmistakable hostility to Nazism, a feeling of repulsion against racial discrimination, but at the same time there is also a tendency to agree with 'anti-bourgeois' authors of Right-wing persuasion, such as Bertrand de Jouvenel, whose *After the Defeat* (published in Spring 1941) led him, as he said, to re-cast *The Popular Theatre*, or Armand Petitjean (right hand of Drieu La Rochelle at the new-style *Nouvelle Revue Française* under the Occupation), whose article 'Eight Months of Defeat'[14] with its call for a 'virile socialism' gave Copeau, as he confessed, 'some solace'.

Copeau's marked religiosity (during this period he went on three retreats to the Abbey of Solesmes and one to the Abbey of Citeaux) inclined him to absorb and adopt the discourse of penitence which was in use everywhere. Again, in March, 1943, he wrote 'we have not suffered enough'! On more than one occasion he almost saw the defeat as something to be grateful for, allowing as it did a return to the simple, neglected virtues, a return to depths, to faith. And his feelings are doubtless summed up in this excerpt from an article that he wrote in the summer of 1941 for the Argentinean paper *La nacion*:

> Between those who see salvation in our immediate and total collaboration and those who would turn their backs on the conqueror and put all their hopes in an Anglo-Saxon victory, there is a middle way involving patience, dignity and firmness. This will allow us, God willing, to reach an even terrain which will make possible, together with the reorganisation of Europe (a necessity to which we have been all too blind) a renaissance of France based on the reconstruction of the genius of the French people, the punishment of our errors and the vitality of our sons.[15]

Jacques Copeau was at one and the same time hostile to Nazi Germany and its occupation of France, fairly favourable to Pétain and well-disposed towards the Resistance movement (his son Pascal lost no time in joining the Resistance and Copeau, who knew this, never condemned it[16]). Furthermore, his nephew and disciple, Michel Saint-Denis, joined the Free French in London and, under the pseudonym of Jacques Duchesne, was one of the French voices broadcasting to his occupied homeland and one who had Copeau as a regular listener. This complexity, almost incomprehensible today, seems almost typical of the confused state many French citizens found themselves in during the early 1940s. In order to understand Copeau, one should perhaps remember that among the first members of the Resistance movement there were also those who, for a time, called themselves followers of Pétain.

Putting the man and his personal political opinions aside, what we should be examining above all are his theatrical ideas. Can they be classed as Pétainist? To ask the question is already to answer it. Despite the links that I have tried to point out (and which the Vichy government, being incapable of or uninterested in formulating a theatrical policy, never itself established), the answer has to be in the negative. The conception of a community theatre, which focuses on the troupe and therefore represents a complete break with the individualistic behaviour so common in the commercial theatre, is a conception that extends well beyond its period and was voiced by men as different as Michelet, Pottecher, Rolland, Gémier and Vilar. Copeau himself did not wait for the Vichy years to put into practice this kind of theatrical idea.

It would have been possible for us to define a sort of 'Pétainist option' in the theatre. The desire to gather together the people in a spiritual communion, united, with but one soul, reveals an ambition to bring about a cultural cohesion, a sort of *unanimisme*. The purpose of this programme of unification was to exorcise the trauma of the military defeat by eliminating social antagonisms. Marshal Pétain, as symbol of renewed national unity, would have been the keystone of this edifice. However, we have to acknowledge that identical preoccupations have been expressed for more than a century, thus making it impossible for us to attach to them the political label 'Pétainist' in order to define their true nature.[17] To see them as part of Pétainism would be to credit the latter with all discourse concerning 'national unity', and that would make no sense at all. At precisely the same period, the Resistance was laying claim to the banner of national unity. Nonetheless, it is undeniable that Copeau's brand of 'popular theatre', so deeply imbued with Catholic religiosity, displayed some affinity with the Vichy mode of thinking. The Pétainist ideology did leave the imprint of its ethos on a century-old tendency in dramatic art. Thus, Copeau, inadvertently and because of his great eminence, was in a way the incarnation of that ethos.

NOTES

This article is drawn from my work, *Le Théâtre dans les années Vichy 1940 – 1944*, published by Editions Ramsay in 1992. I should like to express my thanks in particular to the ARPEGE Research Centre at the University of Rheims for all its support; also to Dr. Georges Chevaillier, who gave me the benefit of his work on the archives of the Hospice de Beaune.

1. The sixty-four page brochure was published by Presses Universitaires de France in the series Bibliothèque du Peuple. Excerpts have been translated in J. Copeau, *Texts on Theatre*, J. Rudlin & N.H. Paul (eds), London, 1990, pp. 186-195.
2. See J. Copeau, *Journal, 1901-1948*, 2 vols, Paris, 1991.
3. Copeau's introductory speech is quoted in the Comedie-Française programme of the event.
4. J. Copeau, 'Le Théâtre et son destin', in *Nouveaux destins de l'intelligence française*, issued in summer 1942 and republished in the Northern zone in 1943 under the title *La France de l'esprit*.
5. On the Groupe Octobre, Groupe Mars and similar companies see Gianfranco Pedula, 'Il sogno di mondo migliore nel teatro popolare francese', *Movimento operaio e socialista*, vol. 11, 1988, pp. 403-428.
6. Copeau, *Le Théâtre populaire*, p. 9.

7. Jean Dasté, Copeau's son-in-law, was a leader of Jeune France and an important figure in their attempt to 'rassembler le peuple et le faire communier'. This quote is taken from his own reply to the questionnaire he sent sent out to various theatre practitioners in January 1941. It is preserved in the Bibliothèque Nationale, Département des Arts et Spectacles, file Jean Vilar (Jeune France), December 1940-41.
8. Copeau, *Le Théâtre populaire*, p. 10. The same idea is expressed in 'Le théâtre et son destin'. See also Copeau, *Texts on Theatre*, p. 190.
9. Chancerel in a speech of 11 October 1941. Archives de la Société d'Histoire du Théâtre, R39, 1 to 40.
10. J. Copeau, Private archives.
11. See, for example, *L'Illustration* of 31 July 1943.
12. H. Ghéon, 'Théâtre communautaire', *Beaux Arts: Le Journal des Arts*, 30 July 1943. Already in November 1941 this Catholic playwright had declared in *Le Figaro*: 'Ne se place-t-il [i.e., the popular theatre] pas dans le fil même de cette "révolution natinale" qui tend à ressouder la France en un seul corps, un seul esprit et un seul coeur? Il devrait trouver aujourd'hui son climat rêvé; je connais tels sujets non spécifiquement catholiques qui offriraient un terrain de communion à tout un peuple unanime et ardent.'
13. J. Copeau, 'Le Théâtre et son destin'. However, in *Le théâtre populaire* he emphasises that such 'mystical' performances ought not to be modelled on the spectacular displays of the Nazis.
14. D. La Rochelle, 'Huit mois de défaite', *NRF*, May 1941.
15. J. Copeau's essay for *La nacion* is preserved in his private archive.
16. See his diary entry of 15 March 1943, where he speaks highly of Pascale's 'héroïsme' and 'liberté de l'esprit' (see his *Journal*, vol. 2, p. 663).
17. See, for example, one of Michelet's lectures of 1847, where he proclaims: 'Nourrissez le peuple du peuple. Le théâtre est le plus puissant moyen d'éducation, de rapprochement des hommes; c'est le meilleur espoir peut-être de rénovation nationale. Je parle d'un théâtre immensément populaire, d'un théâtre répondant à la pensée du peuple, qui circulerait dans les moindres villages. (…) Ah! que je voie donc avant de mourir, la fraternité nationale recommencer au théâtre!' Quoted by Romain Rolland in *Théâtre du peuple*, Paris, 1926, pp. 85-86.

15
Towards an Aesthetic of Fascist Opera

Erik Levi

Introduction

A scribing a specific political significance to such a composite art form as opera or music-theatre can pose particular problems for the cultural historian. Whilst examination of the composer's choice of subject matter and libretto may reveal a more or less clearly stated political objective, analysis of the musical setting can produce a more ambiguous interpretation of such intentions. This may simply be a question of the differing aesthetic positions occupied by drama and music – words and action appearing to present a more concrete reflection of political reality than the seeming abstractions of musical language. Yet to make a distinction between the political functions of drama and music may also seem artificial. Certainly when libretto and text are so well integrated, as in Mozart's *Le Nozze di Figaro,* Beethoven's *Fidelio* or Wagner's *Die Meistersinger,* the broad political message of each opera appears to be unequivocal and was perfectly understood by first-night audiences.

Whether such clear political messages can be discerned in the operas composed during the era of fascism in Germany or Italy is more debatable.[1] For ideologues and critics, the stylistic pluralism of music of the 1920s and 1930s proved intractable. At issue was the degree to which composers should repudiate modernism, and whether such a move necessitated a return to an older tradition of Romanticism. Few theorists offered a cogently argued solution to this problem, preferring instead to talk in the broadest terms of what was commonly termed 'a reclamation of national musical values'. How this was effected depended, of course, on the specific characteristics of each country's national traditions, and in this instance there were contrasting modes of development in Germany and Italy.

If the musical idioms employed by the most significant operatic composers working in Germany and Italy expressed a variety of aesthetic standpoints, thus compounding the difficulties of equating political ideology with artistic intent, a more useful line of enquiry may be to determine any general features which were common to the repertoire of this period. Of paramount importance is the extent to which operas of the fascist era represented a reaction against the immediate past, and whether performing traditions, reception and taste altered as a result of political influence. In the following discussion these questions will be examined alongside issues of text and musical style.

Operatic developments in Nazi Germany

Between 1933 and 1944, over a 170 new operas by German-speaking composers were premiered in the Third Reich, an impressive statistic which belies the notion that the period was bereft of creative energies in this area.[2] To a certain extent, the composition of new operas was encouraged. Under the auspices of the *Reichsdramaturg*, Rainer Schlösser, the Nazi régime evolved a co-ordinated plan in which the major opera houses were encouraged to commission and perform at least one novelty per season.[3] At a local level, numerous state prizes were awarded to composers of operas. Another important forum for performance of new opera was the music festival circuit which enjoyed an increasingly hallowed status in German musical life during this period.

Yet for all this degree of activity, opera was never deemed the ideal medium for overt political propaganda. No opera was staged in which characters wearing Nazi uniforms appeared on stage. Neither did operatic composers attempt to weave well-known political songs into the musical fabric. One possible explanation for the avoidance of such overtly political elements lies in a belief that opera represented a higher and more pure art form than drama and the spoken theatre, and as such its subject and musical matter should be divorced from contemporary realities. This argument was expounded by the Dresden critic Eugen Schmitz in 1939. Writing in the *Zeitschrift für Musik*, Schmitz claimed that whilst a spoken drama based upon the life of Horst

Wessel might have gained public acceptance, an operatic setting of the same theme, depicting the protagonist as a heroic tenor in conflict against baritone Communist agitators, would easily degenerate into the kind of nationalist kitsch that was denounced by the régime.[4]

In surveying the subject matter favoured by operatic composers during the Third Reich, the general avoidance of contemporary themes is striking. Without doubt, this represents a conscious reaction against artistic trends that evolved during the Weimar Republic. Amongst the most significant features of that period were the promotion of experimental music-theatre which flourished in state-subsidised theatres, and the growth in popularity of the *zeitoper* (topical opera) which reached wide audiences through the enormous success of Krenek's *Jonny spielt auf!* Yet during the Third Reich, composers not only avoided experimental music theatre and the *zeitoper,* but also largely refrained from setting contemporary dramas or collaborating with the playwrights that were most favoured by the régime. Censorship of chosen texts never became an important issue. Not once did the *Reichsdramaturg* withhold approval of an opera that had already been accepted for performance by a provincial opera house. Only changes in political circumstance, particularly during the Second World War, caused opera houses to withdraw certain established works after their subjects were deemed inappropriate by the Ministry of Propaganda.

Given the repressive cultural environment, it is hardly surprising that operatic texts during the Third Reich manifested the conservative cultural attitudes of the régime. Having rejected experimentation and topicality, composers turned instead to safer themes – myths drawn from either classical antiquity or Nordic legend, settings of the established classics of German literature (Goethe, Kleist, E.T.A. Hoffmann and Schiller), dramas that chronicle glorious episodes of German history, portrayals of simple village life, and perhaps most frequently of all, the fairy tale. Within these areas, it was possible to glean messages of ideological relevance – the heroism and strength of the classical warrior, the self-sacrifice for a higher ideal, intimations of racial superiority, and a strong identification with the upright values of a peasant community. It is significant, however, that the operas that gained the most public esteem eschewed even such vague political issues, and simply offered escapist entertainment to their audiences.[5]

The emphasis on escapism, or on depicting episodes from the very distant past, is indicative of a broader artistic development – that of the resurgence of the *volksoper,* a genre much cultivated during the nineteenth century, whose subject matter encompassed both light-hearted comedy and romantic legend. During the first years of the Nazi régime, the *volksoper* revival was strongly demanded by the Nazi musical press as an antidote to what was termed the 'negativism' and 'cultural bolshevism' of the operas of Kurt Weill, Paul Hindemith and Ernst Krenek. In order to educate younger composers to appreciate the values of the *volksoper,* significant changes to the repertoire were proposed for the 1933/1934 season, including the resurrection of a number of operas by minor romantic composers that had fallen into oblivion over the past twenty years. Few of these works, however, survived more than a few performances, and later attempts to salvage minor operas by Albert Lortzing, Heinrich Marschner and Otto Nicolai proved rather unsuccessful.

During the early years of the régime, the most prominent exponents of the *volksoper* were composers of an older generation, such as Paul Graener (1872-1944), Max von Schillings (1868-1933) and Georg Vollerthun (1876-1945). Largely neglected throughout the Weimar Republic, they joined the ranks of Alfred Rosenberg's *Kampfbund für deutsche Kultur* and exerted considerable influence in 1933 in persuading opera houses to stage their neo-Wagnerian works. Yet their success was shortlived. Audience reception and critical opinion remained lukewarm, with some even arguing that their creative outlooks were too redolent of a 'petit-bourgeois' past.[6]

The real turning point for this group of composers came in March 1935 after the first performance of Graener's *Der Prinz von Homburg* at the Berlin Staatsoper. Although Graener had striven to create a work of 'national artistic significance',[7] the opera failed to make a strong impression and survived for only two seasons. In the same year, however, two operas by younger composers, *Der Günstling* by Rudolf Wagner-Régeny (Dresden) and *Die Zaubergeige* by Werner Egk (Frankfurt), achieved real success and were hailed in some quarters as the first genuinely National Socialist music-theatre works. Both Wagner-Régeny and Egk had spent their formative years under the cosmopolitan influence of the 1920s. Yet they had modified their musical idioms sufficiently to make them palatable to the more traditionalist cultural climate after 1933. Besides, such a compromise between modernism and accessibility accorded perfectly with Goebbels' much-quoted demand that National Socialist art should manifest 'a romanticism of steel'.

In the case of Wagner-Régeny, the authorities' enthusiastic acceptance of *Der Günstling* seems paradoxical. The libretto, based on Victor Hugo's play, *Marie Tudor,* was written by Caspar Neher, who had a name for himself as Brecht's favourite designer and had three years earlier collaborated with Kurt Weill on *Die Bürgschaft.* Not surprisingly, such an association aroused considerable suspicion as to the political sympathies of both the composer and librettist. Yet despite post-war attempts to view the scenario as presenting some kind of resistance to totalitarianism, in reality the setting offers little opportunity either for irony or for oblique political criticism. More significantly, Wagner-Régeny's music, whilst rejecting the extravagant gestures of late Romanticism, is couched in a deliberately simple neo-baroque language modelled on Gluck and Handel.

Egk's opera, *Die Zaubergeige,* whose libretto is drawn from Franz Pocci's nineteenth-century fairy drama in which love and honesty triumph over the desire for material wealth, also presents a successful balance between traditionalism and modernism. With its judicious mixture of romantic and comic elements, it appears to be a typically escapist *volksoper,* although anti-Semitic overtones are all too apparent in the unsympathetic portrayal of the shady merchant Guldensack. In keeping with the seemingly unproblematic nature of the story, Egk's music manifests a deliberate naivety. The most pervasive elements are a strong adherence to tonality, symmetrical melodies and a frequent recourse to Bavarian folkdances. This simplicity is however punctuated by insistent *ostinati* with a percussive edge and spiced with the occasional harsh dissonance, all of which give the music a veneer of modernity.

The degree to which composers were able to employ surface features of musical modernism, without encountering official disapproval, reflects the régime's uncertainty with regard to musical aesthetics. When the Danish-born composer Paul von Klenau (1883-1946) employed Schoenberg's twelve-tone technique in his opera *Michael Kohlhaas* (Stuttgart, 1933), critics eagerly condemned the composer for utilising a culturally degenerate method of composition. Yet Klenau denied any allegiance to Schoenberg, arguing that his utilisation of twelve-tone procedures was entirely original and claiming that this technique reflected National Socialist order and discipline. Such a defence of his compositional style, coupled with the evident acceptability of Kleist's drama, ensured that

Michael Kohlhaas never fell victim to censorship. Later, the Schoenberg pupil Winfried Zillig (1905-1963) managed to camouflage his utilisation of the same technique in his one act opera, *Das Opfer* (Hamburg, 1937), based on Reinhard Goering's novel about Captain Scott's expedition to the Antarctic. Here again it was not so much the musical language that proved acceptable as the text which emphasises the heroic ideals of a man who is prepared to die for a higher cause.

Ambiguity in intention and reception

From examining the pragmatic reception accorded to the works of Klenau and Zillig, one might assume that composers of opera were allowed greater freedom of expression than playwrights and stage directors. Yet this was not always the case. In fact, some of the most significant challenges to Nazi cultural authority occurred in the opera house. In 1934, the conductor Wilhelm Furtwängler failed to secure Göring's approval for the planned first performance of Paul Hindemith's *Mathis der Maler* at the Berlin Staatsoper. Furtwängler's overt support for the composer and condemnation of artistic interference in matters of repertoire, expressed in an article published in the *Deutsche Allgemeine Zeitung* set him on a collision course with the régime. It was a conflict that Furtwängler was unable to win, and he was subsequently forced to resign his official positions in German musical life. One year later, Richard Strauss endured the same fate, relinquishing his post as President of the *Reichsmusikkammer* on account of collaboration with the Jewish writer Stefan Zweig on the opera *Die schweigsame Frau* (Dresden, 1935). The work was heard only four times before the authorities banned further performances.[8]

Both Strauss and Furtwängler were far too influential as musical figures to be consigned to oblivion. To a certain extent, the régime needed their co-operation in order to maintain cultural credibility. Yet it is still a matter of conjecture as to how far these artists actually appeased their political masters. Strauss's next opera, *Friedenstag* (Munich, 1938), to a libretto by the Viennese theatre historian Joseph Gregor, is a case in point. The scenario is drawn from an episode that took place towards the end of the Thirty Years War, a departure from Strauss's normal areas of exploration, which at this time tended to encompass escapist comedy and classical mythology. Initially, the opera met with great success, securing approval from Hitler who attended a performance in Vienna. Critics of the period drew attention to the ideologically acceptable elements of the plot – the portrayals of the heroic Commandant, who refuses to surrender when his barracks are under siege, and his submissive wife. Yet the opera's pacifist conclusion – a choral hymn rejoicing in the laying down of arms – seemed at odds with the régime's belligerent foreign policy, suggesting that the work's ultimate message was somewhat ambiguous.[9]

A similar equivocality may be gleaned from Werner Egk's *Peer Gynt* (Berlin, 1938). The opera, a free adaptation of Ibsen's drama, was commissioned by the Berlin Staatsoper, where the young composer had secured a position as *Kapellmeister*. It marked a departure from the lightheartedness of *Die Zaubergeige*, being conceived on a far more ambitious scale. Two elements of the score disturbed critics at its première – first, Egk's tendency to lavish attention upon the grotesque elements of the drama at the expense of its romantic and humanist aspects; second, the recourse to a harsher musical style, reminiscent in places of Kurt Weill and other modernists. Egk attempted to justify his use of modernist elements in the scenes depicting the Trolls, on the grounds that the dissonance of such episodes was offset elsewhere by the use of unequivocally tonal passages that were representative of positive forces.

Further examination of the Troll Scene in Act 1 of *Peer Gynt* suggests however that Egk's claim of a clear division between good (in musical terms, tonal) and evil (atonal) was somewhat misleading. When in the score Egk described the Trolls as the 'lowest form of humanity' and a 'bunch of sadists and gangsters', he appeared to be making a more than oblique reference to Nazi Storm Troopers, a point that was emphasised in the original Berlin staging. Moreover, the connection was reinforced through the parodying nature of the musical language, which at one moment recalls Weill, then lampoons a ritualistic Nazi hymn, and finally offers a grotesque distortion of the can-can from Offenbach's *Orphée aux enfers*, an operetta banned by the Nazis because of the racial origins of its composer. Egk's free adaptation of Ibsen's drama abounds in passages of Brechtian irony such as the following lines sung at the outset of the Harbour Scene (Act 2, Scene 1):

> So ist's im Leben, dem Schwachen nicht,
> dem Starken wird's gegeben!
> Und wer nicht selber tritt,
> der wird getreten,
> da hilft kein Jammern,

Winseln, Bitten, Beten! [10]
(What we doubt no longer:
the weak will die
the strong be even stronger.
It's dog eat dog
eat or be eaten!
Unless you beat your foe
you will be beaten.)

Again, one can only speculate as to how far contemporary audiences perceived the subversive undercurrent in such passages. In any case, any initial misgivings about Egk's composition were silenced after Hitler attended a performance of the opera and personally congratulated its author. Owing to this, *Peer Gynt* was nominated for performance at the 1939 *Reichsmusiktage* held in Düsseldorf, although the opera was dropped from the repertory of many theatres after the outbreak of war.

The year 1940 marked something of a watershed in terms of German operatic development. On the one hand, the Ministry of Propaganda appeared to exercise even greater control over the kind of opera that was to be performed. The banning of works by composers from enemy countries was rigidly enforced, as was the requirement to alter libretti in the light of changing political circumstances.[11] Yet at the same time, the notion of opera as entertainment that should divert the public from the realities of war was being actively promoted. This may well explain why relatively few contemporary operas exploited avowedly patriotic themes.[12] Instead, composers turned with increasing frequency to fairy tale, romance and comedy. For instance, one of the most popular escapist operas of the period was Heinrich Sutermeister's *Romeo und Julia* (Dresden, 1940), a work which attempted to reclaim a *belcanto* style reminiscent of nineteenth-century Italian opera. Another typical example was Strauss's *Capriccio*, first performed in Munich in October 1942 with financial support from the Ministry of Propaganda. Set in eighteenth-century Paris, its intimate scenario amounts to nothing more than a witty, though masterful, divertissement on the nature of opera.

This vein of 'apolitical' comedy had already been exploited with great success by Carl Orff in his opera *Der Mond* (Munich, 1939), based on a fairy tale by the brothers Grimm. Orff's musical style, which reached maturity during the 1930s, offered a striking alternative to the more conventional romanticism of many of his contemporaries. As some of its roots lay outside German music, i.e., in the work of Debussy and the neo-primitive Stravinsky (in particular, the ballet *Les Noces*), Nazi critics were initially suspicious of the composer's national credentials. At issue was Orff's fondness for percussive *ostinati* and his desire to strip his musical material to the barest essentials. Yet with the gradual acceptance of his most popular work, *Carmina Burana*, first staged at the Frankfurt Opera House in 1937, but subsequently better known in the concert hall, such objections evaporated. Besides, *Carmina Burana* revealed another more palatable aspect of Orff's style – a strong absorption of Bavarian folk music – and it was this element that profoundly influenced the idiom of *Der Mond*.

Orff returned to Grimm for his opera *Die Kluge* (Frankfurt, 1943). With its judicious mixture of closed forms and spoken dialogue, the work represents a further example of Orff's musical primitivism, although the instrumentation is much harsher here than in *Der Mond*. A number of post-war commentators have intimated that Orff was making a veiled attack against fascism in the unsympathetic portrayal of the despotic King. Yet such an intention appears to be purely speculative, for despite the fact that *Die Kluge* aroused a more mixed reception than *Der Mond*, the opera was staged at the twenty-one theatres until 1944.[13]

Continuity or change – the historical context

Analysing the nature of contemporary opera in a totalitarian society provides an obvious starting point for the definition of a fascist cultural aesthetic in the musical field. However, other considerations must also be discussed. One area which has already been mentioned is the question of performing traditions, and whether these changed as a result of political pressure. When the Nazis came to power, they were determined to sweep aside what they considered to be the cultural excesses of the Weimar Republic. To this end, they instigated a purge of German opera houses which resulted in the dismissal and emigration of numerous composers, conductors, directors, stage designers, singers and orchestral musicians. However, whilst much attention has been drawn to the effects of this exodus, it must be emphasised that the vast majority of artists remained in Germany, and that high standards of performance were maintained and even enhanced in the metropolitan opera houses. The most significant changes occurred in the composition of the repertoire which was subject to censorship by the Nazi authorities. It was no longer possible to perform works either by Jewish or 'degenerate' composers,[14] and during the war the staging of non-German works was subject to political expediency.

Yet it would be misleading to suggest that the exercise of a tighter control by Rainer Schlösser's office, the *Reichsdramaturgie*, necessarily resulted in a monolithic approach throughout Germany. Despite severe curbs on individual artistic freedom, many theatres retained some of the musical traditions that were characteristic of the 1920s. Thus whilst the Frankfurt Opera House no longer preserved its earlier reputation of promoting the avantgarde, it still proved to be one of the more adventurous of German theatres, both in the number of new operas that were staged, and in the employment of such controversial figures as Walter Felsenstein and Caspar Neher. In Berlin there were clear differences of approach and outlook with regard to the two major opera houses, since political control of the Berlin Staatsoper rested with Göring, whilst that of the Deutsche Oper (formerly Städtische Oper) was under the supervision of Goebbels. As a consequence, the artistic policy of the Berlin Staatsoper remained somewhat insulated from the strictures of the Ministry of Propaganda and appeared to be more cosmopolitan.

It is difficult to estimate the degree to which the actual performances and staging of operas were influenced by the unique political climate. In terms of singing and playing techniques, nothing really changed, since the craft of vocal and instrumental production was dependent upon solid training which had been readily available at Germany's Music Academies for many years. In any case, the major singers of the era, who included such figures as Maria Cebotari, Helge Rosvaenge, Peter Anders and Viorica Ursuleac, commanded reputations that transcended national considerations through commercial recordings and broadcasts. A more openended question is the nature of stage productions and the re-interpretation of the classical repertoire. Without doubt, producers and designers who were active during the Weimar Republic had to modify their approach. Thus the abstract and experimental interpretations of Wagner, as manifested in the controversial Jürgen Fehling productions of *Der Fliegende Holländer* (1929, Kroll Oper) and *Tannhäuser* (1933, Staatsoper) were supplanted by stagings that were more overtly naturalistic and conformed to the conservative production style that had been preserved in Bayreuth.[15] Similar tendencies can be perceived in productions of other standard nineteenth-century operas, where conventionally romantic elements were generally emphasised. Probably the most overtly politicised operatic production of the era was Benno von Arent's *Die Meistersinger*, presented in Berlin during the late 1930s.

Whilst contemporary propaganda emphasised the historical significance of Wagner for National Socialism, it is interesting to note that the number of performances of the composer's music-dramas actually declined between 1933 and 1945. How far such a statistic was a genuine reflection of public taste is open to conjecture, since economic factors certainly precluded the regular presentation of Wagner at smaller opera houses. Perhaps more significant is the rapid increase in popularity of the works of Albert Lortzing (1801-1851), whose light-hearted romantic operas both managed to fill a void left by the expurgation of the operettas of Offenbach, and to satisfy the régime's ideological allegiance to the *volksoper*. However, apart from the Lortzing revival, German opera audiences maintained a strong preference for the same handful of works, irrespective of the changed political climate.[16]

Operatic developments in Fascist Italy

Similar trends in audience taste may be perceived in Italy throughout the same period. Nonetheless, the organisation of operatic policy was far more disparate. Whereas in Germany Goebbels erected the necessary bureaucracy for the regimentation of culture within a matter of a year, the whole process was more prolonged under Mussolini. During the 1920s, the goal was the establishment of an Italian musicians' union based on the principles of Fascist corporatism, made up of composers, librettists, performers, teachers and lecturers. Yet in reality a plethora of different organisations emerged in the following years, many of them undergoing several transformations, modifications and changes of nomenclature. Only in 1935 did the régime present a more centralised approach with the founding of the Ministry of Popular Culture, which in turn created a Theatre Inspectorate for the purpose of controlling all aspects of theatrical and musical activity.[17]

One of the main functions of the Theatre Inspectorate was to promote the performance of contemporary Italian opera. To this end, a few experimental opera companies were established and a permanent committee for the examination of new opera scores was convened in 1936. Then, in 1938, the Ministry of Popular Culture commissioned ten operas by well-known Italian composers in an effort to persuade the nation's opera houses to follow suit. Statistics published in Fiamma Nicolodi's book, *Musica e musicisti nel ventennio fascista*, suggest that as a result of such propaganda a slightly larger number of productions by living Italian composers were given in comparison to those by deceased masters.[18]

Examination of the contemporary Italian repertoire most favoured by the régime in the 1930s suggests a conservative bias similar to that established in Nazi Germany. Yet prior to this, many Italian composers had embraced modernism, following a similar pattern of developments in Germany. During the 1920s, for example, composers in both countries were engaged in a reaction against nineteenth-century romanticism. In Italy, this movement was spear-headed by such figures as Alfredo Casella (1883-1947) and Gian-Francesco Malipiero (1882-1973), both of whom owed much to the 'neo-classicism' of Stravinsky.

Yet, during the following decade composers were forced to modify their creative outlooks in the face of political pressure. The first signs of a backlash came in 1932 with the simultaneous publication of a 'Manifesto of Italian Musicians for the Tradition of Nineteenth-Century Romantic Art' in three of the country's leading newspapers (*Il Popolo d'Italia, Il Corriere della Sera* and *La Stampa*). This document, signed by a number of significant composers including Ottorino Respighi, Riccardo Zandonai and Ildebrando Pizzetti, declared opposition towards 'so-called objective music, which as such can only represent sound in itself, without the living expression caused by the animating breath that creates it' and 'which does not wish to have and does not have any human content'.[19]

The impact of these statements, which manifest a clear rejection of the musical outlooks of Casella and Malipiero, was to polarise attitudes amongst Italian composers. Although the régime refrained from taking a direct stand in favour of the conservatives at this stage, the following years were to witness a growing censorship of musical activity. The first tangible repercussions were to be felt in 1934, when Mussolini banned further performances of Malipiero's opera, *La favola del figlio cambiato*, because he disapproved of the moral implications surrounding Pirandello's fantastic and bizarre libretto. As a result, Malipiero's subsequent ventures in the operatic field were confined to more traditional dramatic models, from Shakespeare (*Giulio Cesare* [1935] and *Antonio e Cleopatra* [1937]), Euripides (*Ecuba* [1940]), Calderon (*La vita e sogno* [1941]) and E.T.A. Hoffmann (*I capricci di Callot* [1942]). Moreover, Malipiero's musical style was modified to include more lyrical (and by implication, romantic) elements, and in the final C-major section of *Giulio Cesare* with its 'Hymn to Rome', a monumental glorification of Fascism.

A similar monumentalism was manifested in another contemporary opera, *Nerone*, by Pietro Mascagni, first mounted in an extravagant staging at La Scala in 1935. This work represents the final and most elaborate manifestation of the *verismo* style first cultivated by the composer in his famous *Cavalleria Rusticana*. As in Malipiero's *Giulio Cesare*, the scenario attempts to eulogise the potency of Imperial Rome, although its musical language, is, for the most part, far more conservative in outlook.

Despite the political relevance of their scenarios, neither *Nerone* nor *Giulio Cesare* attained lasting success. In the case of Malipiero, personal intrigues against the composer sabotaged further performances of *Giulio Cesare*. Likewise, Alfredo Casella's *Il deserto tentato* (1937), directly inspired by the Ethiopian campaign, aroused only a tepid response. The opera's theme concerns a symbolic encounter between pure heroes (the aviators) and barbarians (native warriors). It was first performed in Florence and bears a personal dedication to Mussolini. According to the composer, *Il deserto tentato* represented an attempt to elevate the Ethiopian war 'into a totally unreal and mythical plane... It exalts in the elevated language of poetry, the humanitarian mission of a great nation in taking possession, thanks to the exploits of her aviators, of a barren desert, carrying to it the fruits of civilisation it has been waiting for since time immemorial'.[20]

Throughout the opera, the musical material manifests both simplicity and monumentalism. As in Malipiero's *Giulio Cesare*, the final chorus is firmly anchored in the heroic key of C-major and veers dangerously close to mere bombast. Yet the earlier sections of the score seem less contrived. The quasi-Bachian polyphony of the orchestral prelude, for example, appears to be typical of Casella in affirming the principles of musical objectivity and rejecting conventional romantic bathos.

Generally speaking, the 1930s represented a decade of conservatism in which composers, who had previously explored more adventurous styles, retreated to the safety of more conventional models. To a certain extent, Mussolini's alliance with Nazi Germany strengthened such a trend, since both countries established a regular and reciprocal arrangement for the performance of each other's most representative contemporary operas.[21] The links were obvious – in both countries composers had been obliged to reject theatrical experimentation and had returned to setting literary classics. Nationalistic fervour became a central theme manifested through the glorification of historical events in an earlier epoch. Musical audacity was rejected and replaced by a more overtly diatonic idiom. One can even argue that 'neo-classicism', which in both countries was reflected through an increasing absorption of the musical idioms stemming from the Renaissance and Baroque eras, was in itself a further manifestation of staunch musical nationalism directly inspired by the prevailing political climate.

Yet for all the parallels that existed between operatic developments in Nazi Germany and Fascist Italy, there were also some striking differences. Despite the promulgation of race laws in Italy during the late 1930s, the cultural environment remained far more cosmopolitan in outlook than did the deliberately isolationist approach adopted in Nazi Germany. This explains why composers such as Bartok, Hindemith, Berg and Stravinsky were performed in Italy long after their work had been proscribed by the Nazis. In the case of opera, it is remarkable to note that Berg's expressionist opera *Wozzeck* was performed at La Scala as late as 1942 without encountering official opposition, and that after the anti-Semitic prohibitions of 1938, Lodovico Rocca's immensely successful opera *Il Dibuk* (Milan, 1934) remained in the repertoire despite its Jewish subject matter.

Checklist of the most significant contemporary operas first performed in Germany and Italy under fascism.

ITALY

1924   Boito: *Nerone* (Boito)
       Zandonai: *I cavalieri di Ekebu* (Rossato/Lagerlöf)
1925   Lualdi: *Il Diavolo nel Campanile* (after Poe)
1926   Malipiero: *Tre commedie Goldoniane* (Goldoni)
       Puccini: *Turandot* (Adami/Gozzi)
1927   Respighi: La *campana sommersa* (Guastalla/Hauptmann)
1929   Pizzetti: *Fra Gherardo* (Pizzetti)
1931   Wolf-Ferrari: *La vedova Scaltra* (Ghisalberti/Goldoni)*
1932   Casellla: *La Donna Serpente* (Lodovici/ Gozzi)*
       Respighi: *Maria Egiziaca* (Guastalla)
       Casella: *La favola d'Orfeo* (Pavolini/Poliziano)*
1933   Zandonai: *La farsa amorosa* (Rossato/de Alarcon)*
1934   Malipiero: *La favola del figlio cambiato* (Pirandello)*
       Respighi: *La fiamma* (Guastalla/Hans Wiers Jenssen)*
       Rocca: *Il Dibuk* (Simoni/ Shalom An-ski)
1935   Mascagni: *Nerone* (Tragioni-Tozzetti/ Cossa)
       Pizzetti: *Orsèolo* * (Pizzetti)
1936   Alfano: *Cyrano de Bergerac* (Cain/Rostand)*
       Malipiero: *Giulio Cesare* (Shakespeare)*
       Wolf-Ferrari: *Il campiello* (Ghisalberti/Goldoni)*
1937   Casella: *Il deserto tentato* (Pavolini)
1938   Malipiero: *Antonio e Cleopatra* (Shakespeare)*
1940   Dallapiccola: *Volo di notte* (Saint-Exupéry)
1941   Alfano: *Don Juan de Manara* (Moschino)*
       Malipiero: *Ecuba* (Euripides)
1942   Malipiero: *I capricci di Callot* (E.T.A.Hoffmann)*
1943   Malipiero: *La vita e sogno* (Calder6n)*

GERMANY

1933   Zillig: *Der Rossknecht* (Billinger)
       Strauss: *Arabella* (Hofmannsthal)*
       Klenau: *Michael Kohlhaas* (Kleist)
       Gerster: *Madame Liselotte* (von Levetzow)
1934   Kempff: *Familie Gozzi* (Kempff) *
1935   Wagner-Régeny: *Der Günstling* (Neher)
       Graener: *Prinz von Homburg* (Kleist/Graener)
       Egk: *Die Zaubergeige* (Pocci/Egk/Strecker)*

1936   Reutter: *Doktor Johannes Faust* (Andersen)
        Gertser: *Enoch Arden* (Gerster after Tennyson)*
1937   Schoeck: *Massimilla Doni* (Rüeger/Balzac)
        Orff: *Carmina burana* (13th C. Benediktbeuern MS.)*
        Zillig: *Das Opfer* (R. Goering)
        Haas: *Tobias Wunderlich* (Andersen/Ortner)
1938   Strauss: *Friedenstag* (Gregor)
         trauss: *Daphne* (Gregor)
        Egk: *Peer Gynt* (Egk/ Ibsen)*
1939   Wagner-Régeny: *Die Bürger von Calais* (Neher)
        Orff: Der *Mond* (Orff/ Grimm)*
1940   Sutermeister: *Romeo und Julia* (Sutermeister/Shakespeare)
1941   Wagner-Régeny: *Johanna Balk* (Neher)
        Zillig: *Di* e *Windsbraut* (Billinger)
        Gerster: *Die Hexe von Passau* (Billinger)
1942   Reutter: *Odysseus* (Andersen)
        Strauss: *Capriccio* (Krauss)
        Sutermeister: *Die Zauberinsel* (Sutermeister/Shakespeare)
1943   Orff: *Die Kluge* (Orff/Grimm)
        Schoeck: *Das Schloss Dürande* (Burte/Eichendorff)
        Orff: *Catulli Carmina* (Catullus)
1944   Strauss: *Der Liebe der Danae* (Gregor)

*Note: * Denotes works performed in both countries.*

NOTES

1. Examination of operatic developments in Franco's Spain is excluded from the present discussion for the reason that the régime made little effort to stimulate Spanish composers to write operas, and nor were there enough theatres in which such works could be performed. One need only cite the fact that the Teatro Real, the major forum for opera in Madrid, closed in 1925 owing to structural decay, and was not fully restored until 1966, when it was initially turned into a concert hall.
2. A complete list of these operas is published in Hans-Günter Klein, 'Viel Konformität und wenig Verweigerung: Zur Komposition neuer Opern 1933-1944' in Hanns-Werner Heister and Hans-Günter Klein (eds), *Musik und Musikpolitik im faschistischen Deutschland*, Frankfurt am Main, 1984, pp. 159-62.
3. In practice, such aspirations were only accomplished in a few centres. In Stuttgart, for example, the Württemberg State Theatre mounted only one new opera between 1935 and 1944.
4. See Eugen Schmitz, 'Oper im Aufbau', *Zeitschrift für Musik*, April 1939, pp. 380-382, quoted in Joseph Wulf, *Musik im dritten Reich*, Gütersloh, 1963/1966, pp.

308-309. Schmitz's pronouncements demonstrate considerable ignorance of developments in contemporary Nazi drama, since no major playwright contemplated basing a play around the life of Horst Wessel.

5. Richard Strauss *Arabella* (1933) and Norbert Schultze's *Schwarzer Peter* (1936) were the two contemporary operas that received the highest number of performances between 1933 and 1944. Both works bear little, if any, relationship to political themes.

6. See, for example, Hans Költzsch's damning criticism of these composers' works in 'Der neue deutsche Opernspielplan', *Zeitschrift für Musik*, October 1933, p. 997.

7. See Graener's letter to Hitler, dated 19 February 1936, inviting him to attend a performance of *Der Prinz von Homburg*; it is quoted in Wulf, *Musik im Dritten Reich*, p. 97.

8. Artistic collaboration between Aryans and Jews was officially outlawed by the Nazi régime. Yet such a policy was never implemeted with complete consistency as far as the operatic repertoire was concerned. For example, the authorities never contemplated proscribing Mozart's *Don Giovanni*, despite the fact that the librettist Lorenzo Da Ponte was a baptised Jew.

9. For a comprehensive examination of the pacifist elements in Strauss's *Friedenstag* see Pamela Potter, 'Richard Strauss's *Friedenstag*: A Pacifistic Attempt at Political Resistance', *Musical Quarterly*, vol. 69, 1983, p. 408.

10. Werner Egk, *Peer Gynt*, Mainz, 1938, p. 130.

11. Amongst the casualties of the latter policy were Klenau's *Elisabeth von England* (Kassel, 1939), whose title was changed to *Die Königin*, and Wagner-Regeny's *Johanna Balk* (Vienna, 1941), an opera whose subject matter takes place against the background of a popular uprising against the Hungarian tyrant Prince Báthory. Before this work could be staged, the authorities in Berlin demanded that the main characters and place of action were altered from seventeenth-century Transylvania so as not to offend Germany's loyal allies.

12. Exceptions such as Marc-André Souchay's *Kampfwerk 39* (Stuttgart, 1939) and Ernst Schliepe's *Marienburg* (Danzig, 1942), whose scenario is concerned with the Teutonic Knights' successful defence of a fortress in the face of attacks from Slavs and Tartars, failed to gain more than a handful of performances.

13. Hans-Günter Klein, 'Viel Konformität und wenig Verweigerung' p. 157.

14. In the light of his modernist proclivities, the 1938 German première of Stravinsky's *Persephone* in Brunswick seems extraordinary given the repressive cultural climate during that year.

15. During the Third Reich, the artistic alliance between Berlin and Bayreuth was further sealed after Heinz Tietjen, Intendant at the Berlin Staatsoper, was appointed director of the Bayreuth Festival in 1933.

16. Amongst the most frequently performed operas during the 1932/1933 season and the 1938/1939 season were Bizet's *Carmen*; Verdi's *Il trovatore*, Puccini's *La Bohème*, Wagner's *Lohengrin* and Weber's *Der Freischüt*.

17. See Doug Thompson's chapter in this volume.

18. Fiamma Nicolodi, *Musica e musicisti nel ventennio fascista*, Fiesole, 1984, pp. 23-24.

19. Harvey Sachs, *Music in Fascist Italy*, London, 1987, pp. 24-25.

20. Nicolas Slonimsky, *Music since 1900*, New York, 1971, p. 644.

21. See my checklist of contemporary operas performed in both countries.

Bibliography

Compiled by Günter Berghaus

This bibliography predominantly lists critical studies and editions of the post-war period. The sections on general history and cultural history of fascism are highly selective and contain only works of direct relevance to the subject matter of this volume.

Fascist Studies: Selected general works

Allardyce, Gilbert, 'What Fascism Is Not: Thoughts on the Deflation of a Concept', *American Historical Review*, vol. 84, no. 2, 1979

Bracher, Karl Dietrich & Valiani, Leo (eds), *Faschismus und Nationalsozialismus*, Berlin, 1991

Carsten, Francis L., *The Rise of Fascism*, London, 1967

Collotti, Enzo, *Fascismo, fascismi*, Florence, 1989

Cheles, Luciano et al. (eds), *Neo-fascism in Europe*, London, 1991

De Felice, Renzo, *Interpretations of Fascism*, Cambridge/MA, 1977

del Boca, Angelo & Giovana, Mario, *Fascism Today: A World Survey*, London, 1970

Delzell, Charles F., *Mediterranean Fascism, 1919-1945*, New York, 1970

Eichholtz, Dietrich & Gossweiler, Kurt (eds), *Faschismusforschung: Positionen, Probleme, Polemik*, Cologne, 1980

Gregor, A. James, *Theories of Fascism*, Moristown/NJ, 1974

Griffin, Roger, *The Nature of Fascism*, 2nd edn, London, 1993

Kedward, Harry Roderick, *Fascism in Western Europe: 1900-45*, Glasgow, 1969

Laqueur, Walter (ed.), *Fascism: A Reader's Guide*, Berkeley/CAL, 1976

Larsen, Stein Ugelvik et al. (eds), *Who Were the Fascists: Social Roots of Fascism*, Oslo, 1980

Ledeen, Michael, *Universal Fascism*, New York, 1972

Lubasz, Heinz (ed.), *Fascism: Three Major Regimes*, New York, 1973

Mann, Reinhard (ed.), *Die Nationalsozialisten: Analysen faschistischer Bewegungen*, Stuttgart, 1980

Mosse, George L. (ed.), *International Fascism*, London, 1979

Mühlberger, Detlef (ed.), *The Social Basis of European Fascism*, London, 1987

Nolte, Ernst, *Three Faces of Fascism: Action Française, Italian Fascism, National Socialism*, London, 1965

—— (ed.), *Theorien über den Faschismus*, Cologne, 1967

O'Sullivan, Noël, *Fascism*, London, 1983

Payne, Stanley G., *Fascism: Comparison and Definition*, Madison/WIS, 1980

Petersen, Jens, *Hitler-Mussolini: Die Entstehung der Achse Berlin-Rom, 1933-1936*, Tübingen, 1973

Plamenatz, John, *Fascism and Dictatorship*, London, 1974

Rees, Philip, *Fascism and pre-Fascism in Europe 1890-1945: A Bibliography of the Extreme Right*, 2 vols., Sussex, 1985

Revelli, Marco, 'Fascismo: teorie e interpretazioni', in N. Tranfaglia (ed.), *Il mondo contemporaneo: Storia d'Europa*, vol. 2, Florence, 1981

Robinson, Richard A.H., *Fascism in Europe, 1919-1945*, 2nd edn, London, 1989

Rogger, Hans & Weber, Eugen (eds), *The European Right: A Historical Profile*, London, 1965

Saage, Richard, *Faschismustheorien: Eine Einführung*, Munich, 1977

Schieder, Wolfgang (ed.), *Faschismus als soziale Bewegung: Deutschland und Italien im Vergleich*, Göttingen, 1983

Schulz, Gerhard, *Faschismus-Nationalsozialismus: Versionen und theoretische Kontroversen 1922-1972*, Berlin, 1974

Seidel, Bruno & Zenker, Siegfried (eds), *Wege der Totalitarismus-Forschung*, Darmstadt, 1974

Sugar, Peter F. (ed.), *Native Fascism in the Successor States 1918-1945*, Santa Barbara/CAL, 1971

Thamer, Hans-Ulrich, *Faschistische und neofaschistische Bewegungen: Probleme der Faschismusforschung*, Darmstadt, 1977

Turner Jr., Henry Ashby (ed.), *Reappraisals of Fascism*, New York, 1975

Weber, Eugen, *Varieties of Fascism: Doctrines of Revolution in the Twentieth Century*, 2nd edn, New York, 1982

Wippermann, Wolfgang, *Faschismustheorien: Zum Stand der gegenwärtigen Diskussion*, 5th edn, Darmstadt, 1989

——, *Europäischer Faschismus im Vergleich 1922-1982*, Frankfurt/M, 1983

Wiskemann, Elizabeth, *The Rome-Berlin Axis*, 2nd edn, London, 1966

Weiss, John, *Nazis and Fascists in Europe, 1918-1945*, New York, 1967

Woolf, Stuart Joseph (ed.), *The Nature of Fascism*, London, 1968

Zunino, Pier Giorgio (ed.), *Fascismo e nazionalsozialismo*, Turin, 1973

General works on Fascist culture

L'art face à la crise: L'art en occident, 1929-1939. Actes du 4e colloque d'Histoire de l'Art Contemporain, St.-Etienne, 1980

Berman, Russell A., 'Aestheticization of Politics: Walter Benjamin on Fascism and the Avant-garde', in R.A. Berman, *Modern Culture and Critical Theory*, Madison/WISC, 1989

Crispolti, Enrico (ed.), *Arte e fascismo in Italia e Germania*, Milan, 1974

Edelmann, Murray, *Politics as Symbolic Action: Mass Arousal and Quiescence*, New York, 1971

Emmerich, Wolfgang, '"Massenfaschismus" und die Rolle des Ästhetischen: Faschismustheorie bei Ernst Bloch, Walter Benjamin, Bertolt Brecht', in L. Winckler (ed.), *Antifaschistische Literatur*, Kronberg/Ts, 1977

Frank, Hartmut, *Faschistische Architekturen: Planen und Bauen in Europa 1930 bis 1945*, Hamburg, 1985

Grimm, Reinhold & Hermand, Jost (eds), *Faschismus und Avant-garde*, Königstein, 1980

Golomstock, Igor, *Totalitarian Art in the Soviet Union, the Third Reich, Fascist Italy and the People's Republic of China*, London, 1990

Golsan, Richard J. (ed.), *Fascism, Aesthetics and Culture*, Hanover/NH, 1992

Hamilton, Alastair, *The Appeal of Fascism: A Study of Intellectuals and Fascism, 1919-1945*, London, 1971

Hewitt, Andrew, *Fascist Modernism: Aesthetics, Politics, and the Avant-garde*, Stanford/CAL, 1993

Hillach, Ansgar, '"Ästhetisierung des politischen Lebens": Benjamins faschismustheoretischer Ansatz. Eine Rekonstruktion', in B. Lindner (ed.), *'Links hatte sich noch alles zu enträtseln': Walter Benjamin in Kontext*, Frankfurt/M, 1978

Hoberman, John M., *Sport and Political Ideology*, London, 1984

Jesi, Furio, *Cultura di destra: Il linguaggio delle 'idee senza parole': Neofascismo sacro e profano. Tecniche, miti e riti di una religione della morte e di una strategia politica*, Milan, 1979

Jürgens, Martin, 'Bemerkungen zur "Ästhetisierung der Politik"', in M. Jürgens et al., *Ästhetik und Gewalt*, Gütersloh, 1970

———, 'Der Staat als Kunstwerk: Bemerkungen zur "Ästhetisierung der Politik"', *Kursbuch*, no. 20, March 1970

Renzi, Renzo (ed.), *Il cinema dei dittatori: Mussolini, Stalin, Hitler*, Bologna, 1992

Sontag, Susan, 'Fascinating Fascism', in S. Sontag, *Under the Sign of the Saturn*, New York, 1980

Tabor, Jan (ed.), *Kunst und Diktatur, Architektur, Bildhauerei und Malerei in Österreich, Deutschland, Italien und der Sowjetunion 1922-1956*, 2 vols, Baden, 1994

Turits, Michael, *Mimicry and Movement: Fascism, Politics, and Culture in Italy and Germany, 1909-1945*, Ph. D. Dissertation, University of Massachusetts, 1994

Voigt, Rüdiger (ed.), *Politik der Symbole, Symbole der Politik*, Opladen, 1989

ITALY

Selected political and historical studies

Aquarone, Alberto & Vernassa, Maurizio (eds), *Il regime fascista*, Bologna, 1974

Cannistraro, Philip V. (ed.), *A Historical Dictionary of Fascism*, Westport/CON, 1982

Carocci, Giampiero, *Italian Fascism*, Harmondsworth, 1975

De Felice, Renzo, *Mussolini il rivoluzionario, 1883-1920*, Turin, 1965

———, *Mussolini il fascista, 1921-1929*, 2 vols, Turin, 1968

———, *Mussolini il Duce, 1929-1940*, 2 vols, Turin, 1981

———, *Mussolini l'alleato, 1940-1945*, 3 vols, Turin, 1990 ff.

———, (ed.), *Bibliografia orientativa del fascismo*, Rome, 1991

Gentile, Emilio, *Le origini dell'ideologia fascista*, Bari, 1975

———, *Storia del partito fascista*, Rome, 1989

Gregor, A. James, *The Ideology of Fascism: The Rationale of Totalitarianism*, New York, 1969

———, *The Young Mussolini and the Origins of Fascism*, Berkeley/CAL, 1979

Lyttleton, Adrian (ed.), *Italian Fascisms from Pareto to Gentile*, London, 1973

———, *The Seizure of Power: Fascism in Italy 1919-1929*, New York, 1973

Mack Smith, Denis, *Mussolini*, London, 1981

Mussolini, Benito, *Opera Omnia*, E. & D. Susmel (eds), Florence, 1951-1962

Quazza, Guido (ed.), *Fascismo e società italiana*, Turin, 1973

Santarelli, Enzo, *Storia del movimento e del regime fascista*, Rome, 1967
Susmel, Duilio (ed.), *Carteggio Arnaldo – Benito Mussolini*, Florence, 1954
Zunino, Pier Giorgio, *L'ideologia del fascismo: Miti, credenze e valori nella stabilizzazione del regime*, Bologna, 1985

Cultural History

Adamson, Walter L., 'Fascism and Culture: Avant-gardes and Secular Religion in the Italian Case', *Journal of Contemporary History*, vol. 24, 1989
——, *Avant-garde Florence: From Modernism to Fascism*, Cambridge/MA, 1993
Alfassio Grimaldi, Ugoberto & Addis Saba, Marina, *Cultura a passo romano: Storia e strategie dei Littoriali della Cultura e dell'Arte*, Milan, 1983
Gli anni del Premio Bergamo: Arte in Italia intorno agli anni trenta, Exh. cat. Bergamo, 1993
Anni trenta: Arte e cultura in Italia, Exh. cat., Milan, 1982
Argentieri, Mino, *L'occhio del regime: Informazione e propaganda nel cinema del fascismo*, Florence, 1979
——, *L'asse cinematografico Roma-Berlino*, Naples, 1986
Armellini, Guido, *Le immagini del fascismo nelle arti figurative*, Milan, 1980
Arte fascista: Elementi per la battaglia artistica, Sindacati Artistici Torino (eds), Turin, 1927
Benussi Frandoli, Cristina, *L'età del fascismo*, Palermo, 1978
Berghaus, Günter, *Futurism and Politics: From Anarchist Rebellion to Fascist Reaction, 1909-1944*, Oxford, 1995
Bobbio, Norberto, 'La cultura e il fascismo', in Guido Quazza (ed.), *Fascismo e società italiana*, Turin, 1973
Bordoni, Carlo, *Cultura e propaganda nell'Italia fascista*, Messina, 1974
——, *Fascismo e politica culturale: Arte, letteratura e ideologia in 'Critica Fascista'*, Bologna, 1981
Bottai, Giuseppe, *Politica fascista delle arti*, Rome, 1940
——, *Scritti*, Bologna, 1965
——, *La politica delle arti: Scritti 1918-1943*, A. Masi (ed.), Rome, 1992
Brunetta, Gian Piero, *Cinema italiano tra le due guerre: Fascismo e politica cinematografica*, Milan, 1975
Cannistraro, Philip V., 'Mussolini's Cultural Revolution: Fascist or Nationalist?', *Journal of Contemporary History*, vol. 7, nos. 3-4, 1972
——, *La fabbrica del consenso: Fascismo e mass media*, Rome, 1975
Cancogni, Manlio & Giuliano, *Libro e moschetto: Dialogo sulla cultura italiana durante il fascismo*, Turin, 1979
Carabba, Claudio, *Il cinema del ventennio nero*, Florence, 1974
Cardillo, Massimo, *Il duce in moviola: Politica e divismo nei cinegiornali e documentari 'Luce'*, Bari, 1983
——, *Tra le quinte del cinematografo: Cinema, cultura e società in Italia 1900-1937*, Bari, 1987
Carli, Carlo Fabrizio, *Architettura e fascismo*, Rome, 1980
Casucci, Costanzo, 'Fascismo e cultura', in C. Casucci, *Il fascismo: Antologia di scritti critici*, Bologna, 1961
Cavallo, Pietro & Iaccio, Pasquale, 'Appunti su cultura-propaganda-consenso nel ventennio fascista', *Prospettive settanta*, no. 1, January 1982
De Felice, Renzo (ed.), *Futurismo, cultura e politica*, Turin, 1988

De Grand, Alexander, *Bottai e la cultura fascista*, Bari, 1978

De Grazia, Victoria, *The Culture of Consent: Mass Organization of Leisure in Fascist Italy*, Cambridge, 1981

Fabrizio, Felice, *Sport e fascismo: La politica sportiva del regime, 1924-1936*, Rimini, 1976

Falkenhausen, Susanne von, *Der Zweite Futurismus und die Kunstpolitik des Faschismus in Italien von 1922-1943*, Frankfurt/M, 1979

Fioravanti, Gigliola (ed.), *Mostra della Rivoluzione Fascista: Inventario dell'Archivio Centrale dello Stato*, Rome, 1990

Forgacs, David (ed.), *Rethinking Italian Fascism: Capitalism, Populism and Culture*, London, 1986

Forges Davanzati, Roberto, *Fascismo e cultura*, Florence, 1926

Gentile, Emilio, 'Fascism as Political Religion', *Journal of Contemporary History*, vol. 25, nos. 2-3, 1990

——, *Il culto del littorio: La sacralizzazione della politica nell'Italia fascista*, Rome, 1993

Gentile, Giovanni, *Fascismo e cultura*, Milan, 1928

Gerosa, Guido, *Da Giarabub a Salò: Il cinema italiano durante la guerra*, Milan, 1963

Gili, Jean A. (ed.), *Fascisme et résistance dans le cinéma italien (1922-1968)*, Paris, 1970

——, *Stato fascista e cinematografia: Repressione e promozione*, Rome, 1981

——, *L'Italie de Mussolini et son cinéma*, Paris, 1985

Guerri, Giordano Bruno, *Giuseppe Bottai, un fascista critico*, Milan, 1976

Hay, James, *Popular Film Culture in Fascist Italy*, Bloomington/IND, 1987

Immagini di popolo e organizzazione del consenso in Italia negli anni trenta e quaranta, Exh. cat., Venice, 1979

Isnenghi, Mario, *L'educazione dell'Italiano: Il fascismo e l'organizzazione della cultura*, Bologna, 1979

——, *Intellettuali militanti e intellettuali funzionari: Appunti sulla cultura fascista*, Turin, 1979

Isola, Gianni, *Abbassa la tua radio, per favore ...: Storia dell'ascolto radiofonico nell'Italia fascista*, Florence, 1990

Italia anni trenta: Opere dalle collezioni d'arte del Comune di Milano, Exh. cat., Milan, 1989

Jürgens, Martin, 'Faschismus und Moderne: Anmerkungen zum politischen Charakter des italienischen Faschismus', in B. Hinz et al. (eds), *Die Dekoration der Gewalt: Kunst und Medien im Faschismus*, Gießen, 1979

Koon, Tracy H., *Believe, Obey, Fight: Political Socialization of Youth in Fascist Italy: 1922-1943*, Chapel Hill, 1985

Lancellotti, Arturo, *L'arte e il fascismo*, Rome, 1940

Landy, Marcia, *Fascism in Film: The Italian Commercial Cinema, 1931-1943*, Princeton/NJ, 1986

Lazzari, Giovanni, *I littoriali della cultura e dell'arte: Intellettuali e potere durante il fascismo*, Naples, 1979

Lepre, Aurelio (ed.), *La guerra immaginata: Teatro, canzone e fotografia (1940-1943)*, Naples, 1989

Malvano, Laura, *Fascismo e politica dell'immagine*, Turin, 1988

Manacorda, Giuliano (ed.), *Letteratura e cultura del periodo fascista*, Milan, 1974

Mancini, Elaine, *Struggle of the Italian Film Industry during Fascism, 1930-1935*, Ann Arbor, 1985

Mangoni, Luisa, *L'interventismo della cultura: Intellettuali e riviste del fascismo*, Rome, 1974

Marchesini, Daniele, *La scuola dei gerarchi: Mistico fascista. Storia, problemi, istituzioni*, Milan, 1976

Marino, Giuseppe Carlo, *L'autarchia della cultura: Intellettuali e fascismo negli anni trenta*, Rome, 1983

Melograni, Piero, 'The Cult of the Duce in Mussolini's Italy', *Journal of Contemporary History*, vol. 11, no. 4, 1976

Miro Gori, Gianfranco, *Patria diva: La storia d'Italia nei film del ventennio*, Florence, 1988

Mazzatosta, Teresa M., *Il regime fascista tra educazione e propaganda (1935-1943)*, Bologna, 1976

Monteleone, Franco, *La radio italiano nel periodo fascista: Studio e documenti, 1922-1945*, Venice, 1975

Monticone, Alberto, *Il fascismo al microfono: Radio e politica in Italia (1942-1945)*, Rome, 1978

Nazzaro, Gian Battista, *Futurismo e politica*, Naples, 1987

Nicolodi, Fiamma, *Musica e musicisti nel ventennio fascista*, Fiesole, 1984

Ostenc, Michel, *Intellectuels italiens et le fascisme (1915-1929)*, Paris, 1983

Papa, Antonio, *Storia della radio in Italia, 1924-1943*, 2 vols, Naples, 1978

Papa, Emilio Raffaele, *Storia di due manifesti: Il fascismo e la cultura italiana*, Milan, 1958

——, *Fascismo e cultura*, Venice, 1974

——, *Bottai e l'arte: Un fascismo diverso? La politica culturale di Giuseppe Bottai e il Premio Bergamo (1939-1942)*, Milan, 1994

Partito Nazionale Fascista (eds), *La cultura fascista*, Rome, 1936

Passerini, Luisa, *Mussolini immaginario*, Bari, 1991

Pomba, Giuseppe Luigi (ed.), *La civiltà fascista: Illustrata nella dottrina e nelle opere*, Turin, 1928

Ragghianti, Carlo Ludovico, 'Il fascismo e la cultura', in Luigi Arbizzani & Alberto Catabiano (eds), *Storia dell' antifascismo italiano*, Rome, 1964

Redi, Riccardo (ed.), *Cinema italiano sotto il fascismo*, Venice, 1979

Romano, Sergio, *Giovanni Gentile: La filosofia al potere*, Milan, 1984

Sapori, Francesco, *L'arte e il Duce*, Milan, 1932

——, *Il fascismo e l'arte*, Verona, 1934

Sachs, Harvey, *Music in Fascist Italy*, London, 1987

Salaris, Claudia, *Artecrazia: L'avanguardia futurista negli anni del fascismo*, Scandicci, 1992

Sarti, Roland, 'Fascist Modernization in Italy: Traditional or Revolutionary?', *American Historical Review*, vol. 75, no. 4, 1970

Silva, Umberto, *Ideologia e arte del fascismo*, Milan, 1973

Tannenbaum, Edward R., *The Fascist Experience: Italian Society and Culture 1922-1945*, New York, 1972

Tempesti, Fernando, *Arte dell'Italia fascista*, Milan, 1976

Thompson, Doug, *State Control in Fascist Italy: Culture and Conformity, 1925-43*, Manchester, 1991

Turi, Gabriele, *Il fascismo e il consenso degli intellettuali*, Bologna, 1980

Vittoria, Albertina, *Le riviste del duce: Politica e cultura del regime*, Turin, 1983

Zangrandi, Ruggero, *Il lungo viaggio attraverso il fascismo: Contribuito alla storia di una generazione*, Milan, 1962

Theatre Studies

Alberti, Alberto Cesare, *Il teatro nel fascismo: Pirandello e Bragaglia. Documenti inediti negli archivi italiani*, Rome, 1974

Alfieri, Dino (ed.), *La vita dello spettacolo in Italia nel decennio 1924-1933 (II-XI dell'era fascista)*, Rome, 1935

Alonge, Roberto, *Teatro e società nel novecento*, Milan, 1974

Angelini, Franca, *Teatro e spettacolo nel primo novecento*, Rome, 1988

Bragaglia, Anton Giulio, 'Lo spettacolo per masse', *La vita italiana*, July 1934

Cascetta, Annamaria, *Teatri d'arte fra le due guerre a Milano*, Milan, 1979

Cavallo, Pietro & Iaccio, Pasquale, *Vincere! Vincere! Vincere! Fascismo e società italiana nelle conzoni e nelle riviste di varietà 1935-1943*, Rome, 1981

Cavallo, Pietro, *Immaginario e rappresentazione: Il teatro fascista di propaganda*, Rome, 1990

——, *Riso amaro: Radio, teatro e propaganda nel secondo conflitto mondiale*, Rome 1994

Convegno di lettere, 8-14 ottobre 1934: Il teatro drammatico, Reale Accademia d'Italia (ed.), Fondazione Alessandro Volta, Rome, 1935

Corsi, Mario, *Il teatro all'aperto in Italia*, Milan, 1939

Curato, Baldo, *Sessant'anni di teatro in Italia*, Milan, 1947

D'Amico, Silvio, *La crisi del teatro*, Rome, 1931

——, *Invito al teatro*, Rome, 1935

——, *Il teatro italiano*, 2nd edn, Rome, 1937

——, 'Vent'anni di teatro drammatico', *Rivista italiana del teatro*, 15 November 1942

——, *Il teatro non deve morire*, Rome, 1945

De Pirro, Nicola, *Il teatro per il popolo*, Rome, 1938

Di Stefano, Carlo, *La censura teatrale in Italia (1600-1962)*, Bologna, 1964

Fontanelli, Giorgio, 'Fascismo e teatro', *Dimensioni*, no. 6, March 1978

——, 'Mussolini drammaturgo', *Dimensioni*, no. 7, June 1978

Ghislanzoni, Alberto, *Teatro e fascismo*, Mantua, 1929

Iaccio, Pasquale, 'La censura teatrale durante il fascismo', *Storia Contemporanea*, no.4, August 1986

——, *L'intellettuale intransigente: Il fascismo e Roberto Bracco*, Naples, 1992

Mussolini, Benito, *Mussolini autore drammatico, con facsimili di autografi inediti*, Florence, 1954

Pedullà, Gianfranco, 'Il "teatro di massa" nell'Italia fascista', *Ventesimo secolo*, nos. 2-3, May-Dec. 1991

Pivato, Stefano, *Il teatro di parocchia: Mondo cattolico e organizzazione del consenso durante il fascismo*, Rome, 1979

Puppa, Paolo, 'Pubblico e popolo nel teatro fascista', *Rivista di drammaturgia*, no. 18, 1980

Ridenti, Lucio, *Teatro italiano fra due guerre (1915-1940)*, Genoa, 1968

Scarpellini, Emanuela, *Organizzazione teatrale e politica del teatro nell'Italia fascista*, Florence, 1989

Simoni, Renato, *Trent'anni di cronaca drammatica*, 6 vols, Turin, 1951-1960

Trevisani, Giulio, *Il teatro italiano nell'ordinamento giuridico ed economico*, Rome, 1938

Zurlo, Leopoldo, *Memorie inutili: La censura teatrale nel ventennio*, Rome, 1952

GERMANY

Selected political and historical studies

Binion, Rudolf, '... *daß ihr mich gefunden habt.' Hitler und die Deutschen: Eine Psychohistorie*, Stuttgart, 1978

Boberach, Heinz (ed.), *Meldungen aus dem Reich: Auswahl aus den geheimen Lageberichten des Sicherheitsdienstes der SS, 1939-44*, Neuwied, 1965

Bollmus, Reinhard, *Das Amt Rosenberg und seine Gegner: Studien zum Machtkampf im nationalsozialistischen Herrschaftssystem*, Stuttgart, 1970

Bohse, Jörg, *Inszenierte Kriegsbegeisterung und ohnmächtiger Friedenswille: Meinungslenkung und Propaganda im Nationalsozialismus*, Stuttgart, 1988

Bracher, Karl Dietrich, *The German Dictatorship*, London, 1971

Bracher, K.D & Funke, M. & Jacobson, H.-A. (eds), *Nationalsozialistische Diktatur 1933-1945: Eine Bilanz*, Düsseldorf, 1983

——, *Deutschland 1933-45: Neue Studien zum nationalsozialistischen Herrschaftssystem*, Bonn, 1992

Bramstead, Ernest K., *Goebbels and National Socialist Propaganda, 1925-1945*, East Lansing/MI, 1965

Broszat, Martin, *The Hitler State: The Foundation and Development of the Internal Structure of the Third Reich*, London, 1981

Bullock, Alan, *Hitler: A Study in Tyranny*, 2nd edn, London 1964

Cecil, Rober, *The Myth of the Master Race: Alfred Rosenberg and Nazi Ideology*, London, 1972

Childers, Thomas & Caplan, Jane, (eds), *Reevaluation of the Third Reich: New Controversies, New Interpretations*, New York, 1993

Domarus, Max (ed.), *Hitler: Reden und Proklamationen 1932-1945, 4 vols.*, Munich 1965; English edn: *Hitler: Speeches and Proclamations 1932-1945*, 4 vols, London, 1990

Falter, Jürgen, *Hitlers Wähler*, Munich, 1991

Fest, Joachim C., *The Face of the Third Reich*, London, 1970

——, *Hitler: A Biography*, New York, 1974

Frei, Norbert, *Der Führerstaat: Nationalsozialistische Herrschaft 1933 bis 1945*, Munich, 1987

Goebbels, Joseph, *Die Tagebücher: Sämtliche Fragmente*, Elke Fröhlich (ed.), 4 vols, Munich, 1987

——, *Tagebücher 1924-1945*, R.G. Rauch (ed.), Munich, 1992

——, *Reden*, Helmut Heiber (ed.), 2 vols, Düsseldorf 1971-1972

Grunberger, Richard, *A Social History of the Third Reich*, Harmondsworth, 1974.

——, *Das zwölfjährige Reich: Der deutsche Alltag unter Hitler*, Vienna, 1972

Heer, Friedrich, *Der Glaube des Adolf Hitler: Anatomie einer politischen Religiosität*, Munich, 1968

Heiber, Helmut, *Joseph Goebbels*, New York, 1972

Hennig, Eike, *Bürgerliche Gesellschaft und Faschismus: Ein Forschungsbericht*, Frankfurt/M, 1977

Heuel, Eberhard, *Der umworbene Stand: Die ideologische Integration der Arbeiter in den Nationalsozialismus 1933-45*, Frankfurt/M, 1989

Hirschfeld, Gerhard & Kettenacker, Lothar (eds), *Der 'Führerstaat': Mythos und Realität. Studien zur Struktur und Politik des Dritten Reichs*, Stuttgart, 1981

Hitler, Adolf, *Mein Kampf*, translated by Ralph Manheim, London, 1992

Höhne, Heinz, *The Order of the Death's Head*, New York, 1970

Hüttenberger, Peter, *Bibliographie zum Nationalsozialismus*, Göttingen, 1980

Kehr, Helen & Langmaid, Janet (eds), *The Nazi Era 1919-1945: A Selected Bibliography of Published Works From the Early Roots to 1980*, London, 1982

Kershaw, Ian, *The Nazi Dictatorship*, London, 1985

——, *The Hitler Myth*, Oxford, 1987

——, *Der NS-Staat: Geschichtsinterpretationen und Kontroversen im Überblick*, Reinbek, 1988

——, *Hitler*, London, 1991

Koch, Hannsjoachim Wolfgang, (ed.), *Aspects of the Third Reich*, London, 1985

Koenigsberg, Richard A., *Hitler's Ideology: A Study in Psychoanalytic Sociology*, New York, 1975

Kubizek, August, *The Young Hitler I Knew*, Boston, 1955

Kühnl, Reinhard, *Faschismustheorien: Ein Leitfaden*, 2nd edn, Heilbronn, 1990

Langer, Walter C., *The Mind of Adolf Hitler*, New York, 1972

Laqueur, Walter, *Young Germany: A History of the German Youth Movement*, New Brunswick, 1962

Lewis, Wyndham, *The Hitler Cult*, London, 1939

Manvell, Roger & Fraenkel, Heinrich, *Dr. Goebbels: His Life and Death*, London, 1960

——, *Adolf Hitler: The Man and the Myth*, London, 1978

Maser, Werner, *Hitlers Briefe und Notizen*, Düsseldorf, 1973

——, *Hitler's Mein Kampf: An Analysis*, London, 1970

Mosse, George L., *The Crisis of German Ideology: Intellectual Origins of the Third Reich*, New York, 1964

——, *The Nationalization of the Masses: Political Symbolism and Mass Movement in Germany from the Napoleonic Wars Through the Third Reich*, New York, 1975

Mühlberger, Detlef, *Hitler's Followers: Studies in the Sociology of the Nazi Movement*, London, 1991

Neurohr, Jean F., *Der Mythos vom Dritten Reich: Zur Geistesgeschichte des Nationalsozialismus*, Stuttgart, 1957

Noakes, Jeremy & Pridham, Geoffrey (eds) *Documents on Nazism 1919-1945*, London, 1974

Orlow, Dietrich, *The History of the Nazi Party*, 2 vols, Pittsburgh/PENN, 1969-73

Poliakov, Leon & Wulf, Josef (eds), *Das Dritte Reich und seine Denker: Dokumente*, Berlin, 1959

Prinz, Michael & Zitelmann, Rainer (eds), *Nationalsozialismus und Modernisierung*, Darmstadt, 1991

Rhodes, James M., *The Hitler Movement: A Modern Millenarian Revolution*, Stanford/CAL, 1980

Rosenberg, Alfred, *Memoirs*, Chicago, 1949

——, *Selected Writings*, London, 1970

Ruck, Michael, *Der Nationalsozialismus: Aufstieg, Herrschaft, Folgen. Eine Bibliographie*, Cologne, 1993

Schmeer, Karl Heinz, *Die Regie des öffentlichen Lebens im Dritten Reich*, Munich, 1956.

Schnauber, Cornelius, *Wie Hitler sprach und schrieb: Zur Psychologie und Prosodik der faschistischen Rhetorik*, Frankfurt/M, 1972

Schreiber, Gerhard, *Hitler: Interpretationen 1923 – 1983: Ergebnisse, Methoden und Probleme der Forschung*, Darmstadt, 1984

Shirer, William L., *The Rise and Fall of the Third Reich: A History of Nazi Germany*, London, 1963

Snyder, Louis L., *Encyclopedia of the Third Reich*, New York, 1976

——, (ed.), *The Third Reich, 1933-1945: A Bibliographical Guide to German National Socialism*, New York, 1987

Speer, Albert, *Inside the Third Reich*, New York, 1970

Stephens, Frederick J., *Hitler Youth: History, Organisation, Uniforms and Insignia*, London, 1973

Thamer, Hans-Ulrich, *Verführung und Gewalt: Deutschland 1933-45*, Berlin, 1986

The Third Reich: A Historical Bibliography, Santa Barbara/CAL, 1984

Waite, Robert G.L., *The Psychopathic God Adolf Hitler*, New York, 1977

Wistrich, Robert, *Who's Who in Nazi Germany*, London, 1982

Zeman, Zbynek A.B., *Nazi Propaganda*, Oxford, 1964

Zitelmann, Rainer, *Hitler: Selbstverständnis eines Revolutionärs*, Hamburg, 1987

Cultural History

Adam, Peter, *The Arts in the Third Reich*, London, 1992

Albrecht, Gerd, *Nazionalsozialstische Filmpolitik: Eine soziologische Untersuchung über die Spielfilme des Dritten Reiches*, Stuttgart, 1969

——, *Der Film im Dritten Reich: Eine Dokumentation*, Karlsruhe, 1979

Atkins, Henry Gibson, *German Literature Through Nazi Eyes*, London, 1941.

Backes, Klaus, *Hitler und die bildenden Künste: Kulturverständnis und Kunstpolitik im Dritten Reich*, Cologne, 1988

Barbian, Jan-Pieter, *Literaturpolitik im 'Dritten Reich': Institutionen, Kompetenzen, Betätigungsfelder*, Frankfurt/M, 1993

Barsam, Richard M., *Filmguide to 'Triumph of the Will'*, Bloomington/IND, 1975

Bartetzko, Dieter, *Zwischen Zucht und Ekstase: Zur Theatralik von NS-Architektur*, Berlin, 1985

——, *Illusionen in Stein: Stimmungsarchitektur im deutschen Faschismus. Ihre Vorgeschichte in Theater- und Film-Bauten*, Reinbek, 1985

Becker, Wolfgang, *Film und Herrschaft: Organisationsprinzipien und Organisationsstrukturen der nationalsozialistischen Filmpropaganda*, Berlin, 1973

Berlach, Helga (ed.), *Wir tanzen um die Welt: Deutsche Revuefilme 1933-1945*, Munich 1979

Bernett, Hajo, *Nationalsozialistische Leibeserziehung: Eine Dokumentation ihrer Theorie und Organisation*, Schorndorf, 1966

——, *Sportpolitik im Dritten Reich: Aus den Akten der Reichskanzlei*, Schorndorf, 1971

Bleuel, Hans Peter, *Strength Through Joy*, London, 1973

Blunck, Hans Friedrich, *Deutsche Kulturpolitik*, Munich, 1934

Brenner, Hildegard, *Die Kunstpolitik des Nationalsozialismus*, Reinbek, 1963

Brock, Bazon & Preiß, Achim (eds), *Kunst auf Befehl? Dreiunddreißig bis Fünfundvierzig*, Munich, 1990

Buchholtz, Wolfhard, *Die nationalsozialistische Gemeinschaft 'Kraft durch Freude'*, Ph.D. Dissertation, Munich, 1976

Claussen, Horst & Oellers, Norbert (eds), *Beschädigtes Erbe: Beiträge zur Klassikerrezeption in finsterer Zeit*, Bonn, 1984.

Combes, André et al. (eds), *Nazisme et anti-nazisme dans la littérature et art allemands, 1920-1945*, Lille, 1986

Corino, Karl (ed.), *Intellektuelle im Bann des Nationalsozialismus*, Hamburg, 1980

Courtade, Francis & Cadars, Pierre, *Histoire du cinéma Nazi*, Paris 1972 (German edn: *Geschichte des Films im Dritten Reich*, Munich, 1975)

Damus, Martin, *Sozialistischer Realismus und Kunst im Nationalsozialismus*, Frankfurt/M, 1981

Davidson, Mortimer G., *Kunst in Deutschland 1933-1945*, 3 vols, Tübingen, 1988-92

Denkler, Horst & Prümm, Karl (eds), *Die deutsche Literatur im Dritten Reich: Themen, Traditionen, Wirkungen*, Stuttgart, 1976

Diller, Ansgar, *Rundfunkpolitik im Dritten Reich*, Munich, 1980

Die Dreißiger Jahre: Schauplatz Deutschland, Exh. cat., Munich, 1977

Drewniak, Boguslaw, *Der deutsche Film 1938-45*, Düsseldorf, 1987

Dreyer, Ernst Adolf (ed.), *Deutsche Kultur im Neuen Reich: Wesen, Aufgabe und Ziele der Reichskulturkammer*, Berlin, 1934

Jost Dülffer, Jochen Thies, Josef Henke (eds), *Hitlers Städte*, Cologne, 1978

Dümling, Albrecht & Girth, Peter (eds), *'Entartete Musik': Zur Düsseldorfer Ausstellung von 1938. Eine kommentierte Rekonstruktion*, Düsseldorf, 1988

Friedländer, Saul, *Kitsch und Tod: Der Widerschein des Nazismus*, Munich, 1984

Friemert, Chup, *Produktionsästhetik im Faschismus: Das Amt 'Schönheit der Arbeit' von 1933 bis 1939*, Munich, 1980

Gamm, Hans-Jochen, *Der braune Kult: Das Dritte Reich und seine Ersatzreligion*, Hamburg, 1962

Gilman, Sander L. (ed.), *NS Literaturtheorie: Eine Dokumentation*, Frankfurt/M, 1971

Grosshans, Henry, *Hitler and the Artists*, New York, 1983

Guyot, Adeline & Restellini, Patrick, *L'art Nazi 1933-1945*, Brussels, 1987

Hartung, Günter, *Literatur und Ästhetik des deutschen Faschismus*, Cologne, 1984

Heister, Hanns-Werner & Klein, Hans-Günter (eds), *Musik und Musikpolitik im faschistischen Deutschland*, Frankfurt/M, 1984

Hellack, Georg, 'Architektur und bildende Kunst als Mittel nazionalsozialistischer Propaganda', *Publizistik*, vol. 5, 1960

Herff, Jeffrey, *Reactionary Modernism: Technology, Culture and Politics in Weimar Germany and the Third Reich*, Cambridge, 1984

Hermand, Jost, *Der alte Traum vom neuen Reich: Völkische Utopien und Nationalsozialismus*, Frankfurt/M, 1988

Hinkel, Hans, *Handbuch der Reichskulturkammer*, Berlin, 1937

Hinkel, Hermann, *Zur Funktion des Bildes im deutschen Faschismus: Bildbeispiele, Analysen, didaktische Vorschläge*, Gießen, 1975

Hinz, Berthold, *Die Malerei im deutschen Faschismus: Kunst und Konterrevolution*, Munich, 1974

—— (ed.), *Die Dekoration der Gewalt: Kunst und Medien im Faschismus*, Gießen, 1979

——, *Art in the Third Reich*, Oxford, 1979

Hoffmann, Hilmar, *'Und die Fahne führt uns in die Ewigkeit': Propaganda im NS-Film*, Frankfurt/M, 1988

Hopster, Norbert, & Josting, Petra, *Literaturlenkung im Dritten Reich: Eine Bibliographie*, Hildesheim, 1993

Hull, David S., *Film in the Third Reich*, Berkeley/CAL, 1969

Infield, Glenn B., *Leni Riefenstahl: The Fallen Film-goddess*, New York, 1976

Inszenierung der Macht: Ästhetische Faszination im Faschismus, Exh. cat., Berlin, 1987 [plus suppl. vol.: *Entseelte Sinne: Nachträge zur Berliner Ausstellung 'Inszenierung der Macht'*, Berlin, 1988]

Isaksson, Folke & Furhammer, Leif, *Politik und Film*, Ravensburg, 1974

Joch, Winfried, *Politische Leibeserziehung und ihre Theorie im nationalsozialistischen Deutschland*, Berne, 1976

Ketelsen, Uwe-Karsten, *Völkisch-nationale und nationalsozialistische Literatur in Deutschland 1890-1945*, Stuttgart 1976

——, *Literatur und Drittes Reich*, Schernfeld, 1992

Kopp, Detlev (ed.), *Studien zur Literaturwissenschaft im Dritten Reich: Zur Rezeption der Dramatiker Büchner, Grabbe, Grillparzer, Hebbel und Kleist 1933-45*, Bielefeld, 1988

Kunst im Dritten Reich: Dokumente der Unterwerfung, Exh. cat., Frankfurt/M, 1974

Kunst im Dritten Reich: Special edition of *Ästhetik und Kommunikation*, vol. 6, no. 19, April 1975

Lehmann-Haupt, Hellmut, *Art under a Dictatorship*, New York, 1973

Leiser, Erwin, *Nazi Cinema*, London, 1974

——, *'Deutschland erwache!' Propaganda im Film des Dritten Reichs*, Reinbek, 1989

Lerg, Winfried & Steininger, Rolf (eds), *Rundfunk und Politik 1923 bis 1973*, Berlin, 1975

Levi, Eric, *Music in the Third Reich*, London, 1994

Loewy, Ernst, *Literatur unterm Hakenkreuz: Das Dritte Reich und seine Dichtung. Eine Dokumentation*, Frankfurt/M, 1966

Merker, Reinhard, *Die bildenden Künste im Nationalsozialismus: Kulturideologie, Kulturpolitik, Kulturproduktion*, Cologne, 1983

Meyer, Michael, *The Politics of Music in the Third Reich*, New York, 1991

Milfull, John (ed.), *The Attractions of Fascism: Social Psychology and Aesthetics of the 'Triumph of the Right'*, New York, 1990

Mosse, George L., *Nazi Culture: Intellectual, Cultural and Social Life in the Third Reich*, New York, 1968

Moyer, Laurence van Zandt, *The Kraft durch Freude Movement in Nazi Germany*, Ann Arbor/MI, 1977

Müller, Georg Wilhelm, *Das Reichministerium für Volksaufklärung und Propaganda*, Berlin, 1940

Müller-Mehlis, Reinhard, *Die Kunst im Dritten Reich*, Munich, 1976

Noèl, Bernard, *Arno Breker et l'art officiel*, Paris, 1981

Ogan, Bernd & Weiß, Wolfgang (eds), *Faszination und Gewalt: Zur politischen Ästhetik des Nationalsozialismus*, Nuremberg, 1992

Orlowski, Hubert & Hartung, Günter (eds), *Traditionen und Traditionssuche des deutschen Faschismus*, 3 vols, Halle/Saale, 1987-88

Petley, Julian, *Capital and Culture: German Cinema 1933-45*, London, 1979

Petsch, Joachim, *Baukunst und Stadtplanung im Dritten Reich*, Munich, 1976

——, *Kunst im Dritten Reich: Architektur, Plastik, Malerei, Alltagsästhetik*, Cologne, 1987

Pohle, Heinz, *Der Rundfunk als Instrument der Politik: Zur Geschichte des deutschen Rundfunks von 1923 bis 1938*, Hamburg, 1955

Pois, Robert A., *National Socialism and the Religion of Nature*, London, 1986

Prieberg, Fred K., *Musik im NS-Staat*, Frankfurt/M, 1982

——, *Kraftprobe: Wilhelm Furtwängler im Dritten Reich*, Wiesbaden, 1986

Probst, Volker G., *Der Bildhauer Arno Breker: Eine Untersuchung*, Bonn, 1978

Rabenalt, Arthur Maria, *Joseph Goebbels und der großdeutsche Film*, Munich, 1985

——, *Film im Zwielicht: Über den unpolitischen Film des Dritten Reiches und die Begrenzung des totalitären Anspruches*, Munich, 1987

Rabinbach, Anson G., 'The Aesthetics of Production in the Third Reich', *Journal of Contemporary History*, vol. 11, no. 4, 1976

Rao, Barbara L., *The Development of the German National Socialist Point of View on Art and Art Criticism as Seen in the 'Völkischer Beobachter', 1920-1937*, Ph.D. Dissertation, California State University at Long Beach, 1985

Rathkolb, Oliver, *'Führertreu und gottbegnadet': Künstlereliten im Dritten Reich*, Vienna, 1991

Rave, Paul Ortwin, *Kunstdiktatur im Dritten Reich*, Berlin, s.d. [1987]

Reichel, Peter, *Der schöne Schein des Dritten Reiches: Faszination und Gewalt des Faschismus*, Munich, 1992

Richard, Lionel, *Deutscher Faschismus und Kultur: Aus der Sicht eines Franzosen*, Munich, 1982

Ritchie, James McPherson, *German Literature under National Socialism*, London, 1983

Schäfer, Hans Dieter, *Das gespaltene Bewußtsein: Deutsche Kultur und Lebenswirklichkeit 1933-1945*, Munich, 1981

Schellack, Fritz, *Nationalfeiertage in Deutschland von 1871 bis 1945*, Frankfurt/M, 1990

Schnell, Ralf (ed.), *Kunst und Kultur im deutschen Faschismus*, Stuttgart, 1978

Schoeps, Karl-Heinz J., *Literatur im Dritten Reich*, Berne, 1992

Scholz, Robert, *Architektur und bildende Kunst 1933-1945*, Oldendorf, 1977

Schonauer, Franz, *Deutsche Literatur im Dritten Reich: Versuch einer Darstellung in polemisch-didaktischer Absicht*, Olten, 1961

Schrieber, Karl Friedrich, *Die Reichskulturkammer: Organisation und Ziele der deutschen Kulturpolitik*, Berlin, 1934

Schultz, Wolfgang, *Grundgedanken nationalsozialistischer Kulturpolitik*, Munich, 1939

Schuster, Peter-Klaus (ed.), *Nationalsozialismus und 'Entartete Kunst': Die 'Kunststadt' München 1937*, Munich, 1987

Siefken, Hinrich, 'National Socialism and German Literature', in *German Life and Letters*, no. 38, October 1985

Simon, Hans et al., *Die Körperkultur in Deutschland von 1917 bis 1945*, Berlin, 1969

Skulptur und Macht: Figurative Plastik im Deutschland der 30er und 40er Jahre, Exh. cat., Berlin, 1983

Speer, Albert, *Architektur: Arbeiten 1933-42*, Berlin, 1978

Split, Gerhard, *Richard Strauss 1933-35: Ästhetik und Musikpolitik zu Beginn der nationalsozialistischen Herrschaft*, Paffenweiler, 1987

Stollmann, Reiner, 'Fascist Politics as a Total Work of Art: Tendencies of the Aesthetization of Political Life in National Socialism', *New German Critique*, no. 14, Spring 1978

——, *Ästhetisierung der Politik: Literaturstudien zum subjektiven Faschismus*, Stuttgart, 1978

Strothmann, Dietrich, *Nationalsozialistische Literaturpolitik: Ein Beitrag zur Publizistik im Dritten Reich*, 2nd edn, Bonn, 1964

Taylor, Robert R., *The Word in Stone: The Role of Architecture in the National Socialist Ideology*, Berkeley/CAL, 1974

Taylor, Ronald, *Literature and Society in Germany 1918-1945*, Brighton, 1980

Teut, Anna, *Architektur im Dritten Reich 1933-1945*, Berlin, 1967

Theweleit, Klaus, *Männerphantasien*, 2 vols, Frankfurt/M, 1977-78 (Engl. edn: *Male Fantasies*, 2 vols, Oxford, 1987-1989)

Thoene, Albrecht W., *Das Licht der Arier: Licht-, Feuer- und Dunkelsymbolik des Nationalsozialismus*, Munich, 1979

Thomae, Otto, *Die Propaganda-Maschinerie: Bildende Kunst und Öffentlichkeitsarbeit im Dritten Reich*, Berlin, 1978

Thunecke, Jörg (ed.), *Das Leid der Worte: Panorama des literarischen Nationalsozialismus*, Bonn, 1987

Ueberhorst, Horst (ed.), *Geschichte der Leibesübungen, vol. 3.2: Leibesübungen und Sport in Deutschland vom Ersten Weltkrieg bis zur Gegenwart*, Berlin, 1981

Van der Will, Wilfried & Taylor, Brandon (eds), *The Nazification of Art*, Winchester, 1990

Vondung, Klaus, *Magie und Manipulation: Ideologischer Kult und politische Religion des Nationalsozialismus*, Göttingen, 1971

——, *Völkisch-nationale und nationalsozialistische Literaturtheorie*, Munich, 1973

Wernert, Eugène, *L'art dans le IIIe Reich: Une tentative d'estétique dirigée*, Paris, 1936

Wessels, Wolfgang, *Hörspiele im Dritten Reich*, Bonn, 1985

Wolbert, Klaus, *Die Nackten und die Toten des Dritten Reiches*, Gießen, 1982

Wulf, Joseph, *Musik im Dritten Reich*, Gütersloh, 1963

——, *Literatur und Dichtung im Dritten Reich*, Gütersloh, 1963

——, *Die bildenden Künste im Dritten Reich: Eine Dokumentation*, Gütersloh, 1963

Zeller, Bernhard, *Klassiker in finsteren Zeiten: 1933-1945: Eine Ausstellung des Deutschen Literaturarchivs im Schiller-Nationalmuseum Marbach am Neckar*, 2 vols, Marbach am Neckar, 1983

Theatre Studies

Ackermann, Volker, *Nationale Totenfeiern in Deutschland. Von Wilhelm I. bis Franz Josef Strauß: Eine Studie zur politischen Semiotik*, Stuttgart, 1990

Arndt, Karl, *Baustelle Reichsparteitagsgelände 1938/39. Edition zum Film G 142 des IWF*, Göttingen, 1973

Anderman, Walter Thomas, *Bis der Vorhang fiel: Berichtet nach Aufzeichnungen aus den Jahren 1940 bis 1945*, Dortmund, 1947

August, Wolf-Eberhard, *Die Stellung der Schauspieler im Dritten Reich: Versuch einer Darstellung der Kunst- und Gesellschaftspolitik in einem totalitären Staat am Beispiel des 'Berufsschauspielers'*, Ph.D. Dissertation, Munich, 1973

Bernett, Hajo, 'Leni Riefenstahls Dokumentarfilm von den Olympischen Spielen in Berlin 1936', in H. Bernett (ed.), *Untersuchungen zur Zeitgeschichte des Sports*, Schondorf, 1973

Bohlen, Friedrich, *Die XI. Olympischen Spiele Berlin 1936: Instrument der innen- und außenpolitischen Propaganda und Systemsicherung des faschistischen Regimes*, Cologne, 1979

Breßlein, Erwin, *Völkisch-faschistoides und nationalsozialistisches Drama: Kontinuität und Differenzen*, Frankfurt/M, 1980

Broer, Werner (ed.), *Grabbe im Dritten Reich: Zum nationalsozialistischen Grabbe-Kult*, Bielefeld, 1986

Brohm, Jean-Marie, *Jeux olympiques à Berlin, 1936*, Brussels, 1983

Bumm, Peter, *Drama und Theater der konservativen Revolution*, Munich, 1971

Burden, Hamilton T., *The Nuremberg Party Rallies, 1923-39*, New York, 1967

Dittmer, Frank, *Freilufttheater: Dramatisches ohne Dach im 20. Jahrhundert*, Ph.D. Dissertation, Berlin, 1989

Drewniak, Boguslaw, *Das Theater im NS-Staat: Szenarium deutscher Zeitgeschichte: 1933-1945*, Düsseldorf, 1983.

Düding, Dieter (ed.), *Öffentliche Festkultur: Politische Feste in Deutschland von der Aufklärung bis zum Ersten Weltkrieg*, Reinbek, 1988

Dussel, Konrad, *Ein neues, ein heroisches Theater?: Nationalsozialistische Theaterpolitik und ihre Auswirkungen in der Provinz*, Bonn, 1988.

Eichberg, Henning et al. (eds), *Massenspiele: NS-Thingspiel, Arbeiterweihespiel und olympisches Zeremoniell*, Bad Cannstadt, 1977

——, 'Das nationalsozialistische Thingspiel: Massentheater in Faschismus und Arbeiterkultur', *Ästhetik und Kommunikation*, vol. 7, no. 26, Dec. 1976

Eicher, Thomas, *Theater im 'Dritten Reich': Eine Spielplananlyse des deutschsprachigen Schauspieltheaters 1929-1944*, Ph.D. Dissertation, FU Berlin, 1992

Emmel, Felix, *Theater aus deutschem Wesen*, Berlin, 1937

Euler, Friederike, 'Theater zwischen Anpassung und Widerstand: Die Münchener Kammerspiele im Dritten Reich', in M. Broszat et al. (eds), *Bayern in der NS-Zeit*, Munich, 1979

Fischli, Bruno, *Die Deutschen-Dämmerung: Zur Genealogie des völkisch-faschistischen Dramas und Theaters 1897-1933*, Bonn, 1976

Freeden, Herbert, 'A Jewish Theatre Under the Swastika', *Year Book of the Leo Baeck Institute*, vol. 1, 1956

—— *Jüdisches Theater in Nazi Deutschland*, Tübingen, 1964

Gadberry, Glen, 'The Thingspiel and Das Frankenberger Wurfelspiel', *The Drama Review*, vol. 24, no. 1, March 1980

——*Theatre in the Third Reich. The Pre-war Years: Essays in Theatre in Nazi Germany*, Westport/CT, 1995

Gebauer, Gunter & Wulf, Christoph, 'Die Berliner Olympiade 1936: Spiele der Gewalt', in *Mythos Berlin: Zur Wahrnehmungsgeschichte einer industriellen Metropole*, Berlin, 1987

Geschlossene Vorstellung: Der Jüdische Kulturbund in Deutschland 1933-1941, Exh. cat., Berlin, 1992

Graff, Sigmund, *Von S. M. zu N. S.: Erinnerungen eines Bühnenautors (1900-1945)*, Munich, 1963

Habicht, Werner, 'Shakespeare and Theatre Politics in the Third Reich', in H. Scolnicov & P. Holland (eds), *The Play Out of Context: Transferring Plays From Culture to Culture*, Cambridge, 1989

Haider-Pregler, Hilde, 'Das Dritte Reich und das Theater', *Maske und Kothurn*, vol. 17, 1971

Hart-Davis, Duff, *Hitler's Games: The 1936 Olympics*, London, 1986

Josef Henke, 'Die Reichsparteitage der NSDAP in Nürnberg 1933-1938: Planung, Organisation, Propaganda', in H. Boberach & H. Booms (eds), *Aus der Arbeit des Bundesarchivs*, Boppard, 1977

HernØ, Leif, 'Das Thingspiel: Fragen zu seiner literarischen Untersuchung', *Text und Kontext*, vol. 8, 1980

Kemmler, Richard S., *The National Socialist Ideology in Drama*, Ph.D. Dissertation, New York University, 1973

Ketelsen, Uwe-Karsten, *Heroisches Theater: Untersuchungen zur Dramentheorie des Dritten Reichs*, Bonn, 1968

——, *Von heroischem Sein und völkischem Tod: Zur Dramatik des Dritten Reiches*, Bonn, 1970.

Koegler, Horst, 'Tanz in die Dreißiger Jahre', *Ballett 1972*, Velber, 1973

——, 'In the Shadow of the Swastika: Dance in Germany 1927-1939', *Dance Perspectives*, no. 57, Spring 1974

Krüger, Arnd, *Die Olympischen Spiele 1936 und die Weltmeinung*, Berlin, 1972

Kühn, Volker, *Deutschlands Erwachen: Kabarett unterm Hakenkreuz*, Berlin, 1989

Kulissen der Gewalt: Das Reichsparteitagsgelände in Nürnberg, Centrum Industriekultur Nürnberg (ed.), Munich, 1992.

Liebe, Ulrich, *Verehrt, verfolgt, vergessen: Schauspieler als Naziopfer*, Weinheim, 1992

Loiperdinger, Martin, *Der Parteitagsfilm 'Triumph des Willens' von Leni Riefenstahl: Rituale der Mobilmachung*, Opladen, 1987

Mandell, Richard D., *The Nazi Olympics*, London, 1972

Mellen, Peter, *The Third Reich Examined as the Dramatic Illusion of Ritual Performance*, Ph.D. Dissertation, Bowling Green State University, 1988

Mierendorf, Marta & Wicclair, Walter, *Im Rampenlicht der 'dunklen Jahre': Aufsätze über Theater im 'Dritten Reich', Exil und Nachkrieg*, Bonn, 1989

Murmann, Geerte, *Komödianten für den Krieg: Deutsches und alliiertes Fronttheater*, Düsseldorf, 1993

Nowotny, Peter, *Leni Riefenstahls 'Triumph des Willens'*, Dortmund, 1981

Panse, Barbara, *Autoren, Themen und Zensurpraxis: Zeitgenössische deutschsprachige Dramatik im Theater des Dritten Reiches*, Habilitation Thesis, FU Berlin, 1993

Pitsch, Ilse, *Das Theater als politisch-publizistisches Führungsmittel im Dritten Reich*, Ph.D. Dissertation, Münster, 1952

Reimer, Karl Friedrich, 'Die Reichsparteitage als Instrument totaler Propaganda: Appell, Feier, Kult, Magie', *Zeitschrift für Volkskunde*, vol. 75, 1979

Rühle, Günter (ed.), *Zeit und Theater, vol. 5+6: 1933-1945*, Berlin, 1974

Ruppelt, Georg, *Schiller im nationalsozialistischen Deutschland*, Stuttgart, 1979

Sauer, Klaus & Werth, German, *Lorbeer und Palme: Patriotismus in deutschen Festspielen*, Munich, 1971

Schlösser, Rainer, *Das Volk und seine Bühne: Bemerkungen zum Aufbau des deutschen Theaters*, Berlin, 1935

——, *Politik und Drama*, Berlin, 1935

Schramm, Wilhelm von, *Neubau des deutschen Theaters: Ergebnisse und Forderungen*, Berlin, 1934

Schreiner, Evelyn, *Nationalsozialistische Theaterpolitik in Wien 1938-1945 unter spezieller Berücksichtigung der Wiener Theaterszene*, Ph.D. Dissertation, Vienna, 1980

Shafer, Yvonne, 'Nazi Berlin and the Grosses Schauspielhaus', *Theatre Survey*, vol. 34, 1993

Stommer, Rainer, *Die inszenierte Volksgemeinschaft: Die 'Thing-Bewegung' im Dritten Reich*, Marburg, 1985

Sullivan, Henry W., *Calderón in the German Lands and the Low Countries: His Reception and Influence, 1654-1980*, Cambridge, 1983

Hans-Ulrich Thamer, 'Faszination und Manipulation: Die Nürnberger Reichsparteitage der NSDAP', in U. Schultz (ed.), *Das Fest: Eine Kulturgeschichte von der Antike bis zur Gegenwart*, Munich, 1988

Taylor, Jennifer Ann, *The Third Reich in German Drama, 1933-1956*, Ann Arbor/MI, 1985

Ueberhorst, Horst, 'Spiele unterm Hakenkreuz: Die Olympischen Spiele von Garmisch-Partenkirchen und Berlin 1936 und ihre politischen Implikationen', *Aus Politik und Zeitgeschichte*, vol. 31, 1986

Verspohl, Franz-Joachim, *Stadionbauten von der Antike bis zur Gegenwart: Regie und Selbsterfahrung der Massen*, Gießen, 1976

Wanderscheck, Hermann, *Deutsche Dramatik der Gegenwart*, Berlin, 1938
Wardetzky, Jutta, *Theaterpolitik im faschistischen Deutschland: Studien und Dokumente*, Berlin, 1983.
Wessling, Berndt W., *Bayreuth im Dritten Reich: Richard Wagners politische Erben. Eine Dokumentation*, Weinheim, 1983
Wulf, Joseph, *Theater und Film im Dritten Reich: Eine Dokumentation*, Gütersloh, 1964.
Wykes, Alan, *The Nuremberg Rallies*, London, 1967
Zelnhefer, Siegfried, *Die Reichsparteitage der NSDAP: Geschichte, Struktur und Bedeutung der größten Propagandafeste im nationalsozialistischen Feierjahr*, Nuremberg, 1991
Zortman, Bruce, *Hitler's Theatre: Ideological Drama in Nazi Germany*, El Paso/TX, 1984

SPAIN

Selected political and historical studies

Anderson, Charles W., *The Political Economy of Modern Spain: Policy-making in an Authoritarian System*, Madison/WISC, 1970
Brenan, Gerald, *The Face of Spain*, London, 1950
Carr, Raymond, *Modern Spain: 1875-1980*, Oxford, 1980
——, *Spain: 1808-1975*, 2nd edn, Oxford, 1982
Díaz-Plaja, Fernando, *La España franquista en sus documentos (La postguerra española en sus documentos)*, Barcelona, 1976
Ellwood, Sheelagh M., *Spanish Fascism in the Franco Era: Falange Española de las Jons, 1936-76*, Houndmills, 1987
Fusi Aizpurúa, Juan Pablo, *Franco: A Biography*, London, 1987
García Delgado, José Luis, *El primer franquismo: España durante la segunda guerra mundial*, Madrid, 1989
García Pérez, Rafael, 'El envío de trabajadores españoles a Alemania durante la segunda guerra mundial', *Hispania: Revista Española de Historia*, vol. 48, 1988
Garriga, Ramón, *La España de Franco*, 2 vols, Madrid, 1976
Graham, Helen, 'The Franco Regime', *The Historical Journal*, vol. 32, 1989
Hamilton, Thomas J., *Appeasement's Child: The Franco Régime in Spain*, London, 1943
Hayes, Carlton J. H., *The United States and Spain: An Interpretation*, New York, 1951
Linz, Juan J., 'An Authoritarian Regime: Spain', in Stanley G. Payne (ed.), *Politics and Society in Twentieth-Century Spain*, New York, 1976
Miguel, Amando De, *Sociología del franquismo: Análisis ideológico de los ministros del régimen*, 2nd edn, Barcelona, 1975
Payne, Stanley G., *Falange: A History of Spanish Fascism*, Stanford/CAL, 1961
——, 'Spanish Fascism in Comparative Perspective', *Iberian Studies*, vol. 2, 1973
Preston, Paul, *Franco: A Biography*, London, 1993
Primo de Rivera, José Antonio, *Obras completas de José Antonio Primo de Rivera*, Agustín del Río Cisneros (ed.), Madrid, 1942
——, *Selected Writings*, Hugh Thomas (ed.), London, 1972
Ridruejo, Dionisio, *Casi unas memorias*, César Armando Gómez (ed.), 2nd edn, Barcelona, 1976

Ruiz, David, *La dictadura franquista: 1939/1975*, Oviedo, 1978
Sánchez López, Rosario, *Mujer española, una sombra de destino en lo universal: trayectoria histórica de Sección Femenina de Falange (1934-1977)*, Murcia, 1990
Sueiro, Daniel & Díaz Nosty, *Historia del franquismo*, Madrid, 1986
Tamames, Ramón, *La República. La era de Franco*, 4th edn, Madrid, 1975
Umbral, Francisco, *Memorias de un niño de derechas*, 3rd edn, Barcelona, 1986
Vázquez Montalbán, Manuel, *Crónica sentimental de España*, Barcelona, 1971
Vizcaíno Casas, Fernando, *La España de la posguerra: (1939-1953)*, Barcelona, 1981
Ximénez de Sandoval, Felipe, *José Antonio: Biografía apasionada*, Barcelona, 1941

Cultural History

Abellán, Manuel L., 'Censura y práctica censoria', *Sistema*, vol. 22, 1978
——, *Censura y creación literaria en España (1939-1976)*, Barcelona, 1980
——, 'Literatura, censura y moral en el primer franquismo', *Papers*, vol. 21, 1984
——, (ed.), *Censura y literatura peninsulares*, Amsterdam, 1987
——, 'Problemas historiográficos en el estudio de la censura literaria del último medio siglo', *Revista Canadiense de Estudios Hispánicos*, vol. 13, 1989
Benet, Josep, *Catalunya sota el règim franquista: Informe sobre la persecució de la llengua i la cultura pel règim del general Franco (primera part)*, Barcelona, 1978
Beneyto, Antonio, *Censura y política en los escritores españoles*, Barcelona, 1975
Bonet Correa, Antonio (ed.), *Arte del franquismo*, Madrid, 1981
Brown, M. Gordon, 'Las actividades culturales en la España de la postguerra', *Hispania*, 25, 1942
Cirici, Alexandre, *La estética del franquismo*, Barcelona, 1977
La cultura bajo el franquismo, Barcelona, 1977
Escolar Sobrino, Hipólito, *La cultura durante la guerra civil*, Madrid, 1987
Fernández Cuenca, Carlos, *La guerra de España y el cine*, 2 vols, Madrid, 1973
Foard, Douglas W., *Giménez Caballero (o la revolución del poeta)*, Madrid, 1975; Engl. edn: *The Revolt of the Aesthetes: Ernesto Giménez Caballero and the Origins of Spanish Fascism*, New York, 1989
Gallofré i Virgili, Maria Josepa, *L'edició catalana i la censura franquista (1939-1951)*, Barcelona, 1991
García de la Concha, Víctor, *La poesía española de posguerra: teoría e historia de sus movimientos*, Madrid, 1973
Gubern, Román, *Un cine para el cadalso: 40 años de censura cinematográfica en España*, Barcelona, 1976
——, *La censura: Función política y ordenamiento jurídico bajo el franquismo (1936-1975)*, Barcelona, 1981
Hurtley, Jacqueline, *Josep Janés: El combat per la cultura*, Barcelona, 1986
Jordan, Barry, *Writing and Politics in Franco's Spain*, London, 1990
López Pina, Antonio et al., *La cultura política de la España de Franco*, Madrid, 1976
Mainer, José-Carlos (ed.), *Falange y literatura*, Barcelona, 1971
Marsal, Juan F., *Pensar bajo el franquismo: Intelectuales y política en la generación de los años cincuenta*, Barcelona, 1979
Mermall, Thomas, 'Aesthetics and Politics in Falangist Culture (1935-1945)', *Bulletin of Hispanic Studies*, vol. 50, 1973
Fifteen Years of Spanish Culture 1938-1952, Diplomatic Information Office (ed.), Madrid, 1952
Reseña, Equipo, *La cultura española durante el franquismo*, Bilbao, 1977

Rodríguez Puértolas, Julio, *Literatura fascista española*, vol. 1: *Historia*; vol. 2: *Antología*, Madrid, 1986-1987

Sanabria Martín, Francisco, *Política cultural*, Madrid, 1958

Tandy, Lucy & Sferrazza, María (eds), *Giménez Caballero y 'La gaceta literaria'*, Madrid, 1977

Vivanco, José Manuel, *Moral y pedagogia del cine*, Madrid, 1952

Wahnón, Sultana, *Estética y crítica literarias en España (1940-1950)*, Granada, 1988

Theatre Studies

Bacardit, Ramon et al., *Romea, 125 anys*, Barcelona, 1989

Berenger, Angel & Ferreras, Juan Ignacio, *El teatro en el siglo XX*, 2 vols, Madrid, 1988

Bravo, Isidre, *L'escenografia catalana*, Barcelona, 1986

Castellano, Juan R., 'El teatro español desde 1939', *Hispania*, vol. 34, 1951

Cortezo, Víctor María, 'Plástica y ornamentación escénicas', *Revista Nacional de Educación*, vol. 35, November 1943

Cramsie, Hilde F., *Teatro y censura en la España franquista*, New York, 1984

Doménech, Ricardo, 'El teatro desde 1936', in *Historia de la literatura española*, vol. 3: *Siglos XIX y XX*, José María Díez Borque (ed.), Madrid, 1974

Domínguez, Adriano, *Memorias de un actor*, Madrid, 1984

Fernández Santander, Carlos, *El fútbol durante la guerra civil y el franquismo*, Madrid, 1990

Fraile, Medardo (ed.), *Teatro español en un acto (1940-1952)*, Madrid, 1989

Fuente Ballestros, Ricardo del la, *Introducción al teatro español del siglo XX (1900-1936)*, Valladolid, 1987

Gallén, Enric, *El teatre a la ciutat de Barcelona durant el règim franquista (1939-1954)*, Barcelona, 1985

González Ruiz, Nicolás, *La cultura española en los últimos veinte años: El teatro*, Madrid, 1949

Guerrero Zamora, Juan, *Historia del teatro contemporáneo*, 4 vols, Barcelona, 1961-1967

Historia de los Teatros Nacionales, I: 1939-1962, Madrid, 1993

Hornedo, Rafael María de, '"La muralla" y el drama católico', *Razón y Fe*, no. 686, March 1955

Hoz, Enrique de la, (ed.), *Panorámica del teatro en España*, Madrid, 1973

Mallo, Jerónimo, '*La muralla* y su éxito en el teatro español contemporáneo', *Hispania*, vol. 45, 1962

Mariscal, Ana, *Cincuenta años de teatro en Madrid*, Madrid, 1984

Marqueríe, Alfredo, *Desde la silla eléctrica*, Madrid, 1942

——, *En la jaula de los leones (Memorias y crítica teatral)*, Madrid, 1944

——, *Veinte años de teatro en España*, Madrid, 1959

Marrast, Robert, *El teatre durant la guerra civil espanyola*, Barcelona, 1978

Melero, Santiago, *Teatro español contemporáneo*, Madrid, 1956

Monleón, José, *Treinta años de teatro de la derecha*, Barcelona, 1971

Mundi, Francisco, *El teatro de la guerra civil*, Barcelona, 1987

O'Connor, Patricia W., 'Government Censorship in the Contemporary Spanish Theatre', *Educational Theatre Journal*, vol. 18, 1966

——, 'Torquemada in the Theatre: A Glance at Government Censorship', *Theatre Survey*, vol. 14, no. 2, November 1973

Oliva, César, *El teatro desde 1936*, Madrid, 1989

Pasquariello, Anthony M., '*La Muralla*: The Story of a Play and a Polemic', *Kentucky Foreign Language Quarterly*, vol. 4, 1957

Ruiz-Fornells, Enrique, 'Twenty-five years of Spanish Theatre', *Drama Critique*, vol. 9, 1966

Ruiz Ramón, Francisco, *Historia del teatro español: Siglo XX*, 5th edn, Madrid, 1981

Sánchez Trigueros, Antonio, 'Notas sobre dos rivistas de teatro granadinas', in *Estudios sobre literatura y arte dedicados al professor Emilio Orozco Días*, Granada, 1979

Shaw, Duncan, *Fútbol y franquismo*, Madrid, 1987

Sirera, Josep Lluís, *Passat, present i futur del teatre valencià*, Valencia, 1981

Soldevila Durante, Ignacio, 'Sobre el teatro español en los últimos veinticinco años', *Cuadernos Americanos*, vol. 22, no. 1, Jan.-Feb. 1963

Sordo, Enrique, 'El teatro español desde 1936 hasta 1966', in Guillermo Díaz-Plaja (ed.), *Historia general de las literaturas hispánicas*, vol. 6, *Literatura contemporánea*, Barcelona, 1967

Suelto de Sáenz, Pilar G., 'El teatro universitario español en los últimos treinta años', *Thesaurus*, vol. 19, 1964

El teatro en España entre la tradicion y la vanguardia (1918-1939): Atti del seminario internazionale, Madrid, 1992

Torrente Ballester, Gonzalo, *Teatro español contemporáneo*, 2nd edn, Madrid, 1968

FRANCE

Selected political and historical studies

Aron, Robert, *Histoire de Vichy 1940-1944*, Paris, [1954]

Azéma, Jean-Pierre & Bédarida, François (eds), *Le régime de Vichy et les Français*, Paris, 1992

——, *La France des années noires*, 2 vols, Paris, 1993

Cointet-Labrousse, Michèle, *Vichy et le fascisme*, Brussels, 1987

Dunand, Elizabeth, 'La Propaganda Abteilung de France: Tâche et organisation', *Revue d'histoire de la Deuxième Guerre Mondiale*, no. 4, 1951

Durand, Yves, *Vichy, 1940-1944*, Paris, 1972

Griffiths, Richard, *Marshal Pétain*, London, 1970

Lévy, Claude, 'Organisation de la propagande allemande en France', *Revue d'histoire de la Deuxième Guerre Mondiale*, no. 64, October 1966

——, *Les nouveaux temps et l'idéologie de la collaboration*, 2nd edn, Paris, 1990

McClelland, James S., *The French Right from de Maistre to Maurras*, London, 1970

Michekl, Henri, *Les fascismes français 1923-1963*, Paris, 1963

Paxton, Robert O., *Vichy France: Old Guard and New Order, 1940-1944*, London, 1972

La propagande sous Vichy, 1940-1944, Paris, 1990

Pryce-Jones, David, *Paris in the Third Reich: A History of the German Occupation, 1940-1944*, London, 1981

Soucy, Robert J., *French Fascism: The First Wave, 1924-33*, New Haven/CON, 1986

——, *Fascism in France: The Case of Maurice Barrès*, Berkeley/CAL, 1972
Sternhell, Zeev, *Barrès et le nationalisme français*, Paris, 1972
——, *La droite révolutionnaire, 1885-1914*, Paris, 1978
——, *Ni droite, ni gauche: L'idéologie fasciste en France*, Paris, 1983; Engl. edn: *Neither Right nor Left: Fascist Ideology in France*, Berkeley/CAL, 1986
Thalmann, Rita, *La mise au pas: Idéologie et stratégie sécuritaire dans la France occupée*, Paris, 1991
Tucker, William R., *The Fascist Ego: A Political Biography of Robert Brasillach*, Berkeley/CAL, 1975
Winnock, Michel, *Edouard Drumont et Cie: Antisémitisme et fascisme en France*, Paris, 1983

Cultural Studies

Bertin-Maghit, Jean Pierre, *Le cinéma sous l'occupation: Le monde du cinéma français de 1940 à 1946*, Paris, 1989
Bertrand Dorléac, Laurence, *Histoire de l'art: Paris 1940-1944: Ordre national, traditions, et modernités*, Paris, 1986
Cervereau, Laurent & Peschanski, Denis (eds), *La propaganda sous Vichy: 1940-1944*, Naterre, 1990
Ceysson, Bernard, *Le rappel à l'ordre: L'art en France dans les années trente*, St.-Etienne, 1979
Cone, Michèle C., *Artists under Vichy: A Case of Prejudice and Persecution*, Princeton/NJ, 1992
Eck, Hélène (ed.), *Histoire des radios de langue française pendant la Deuxième Guerre Mondiale*, Paris, 1985
Ehrlich, Evelyn, *Cinema of Paradox: French Filmmaking under the German Occupation*, New York, 1985
Fauré, Christian, *Le projet culturel de Vichy: Folklore et révolution nationale (1940-1944)*, Lyon, 1989
Garçon, François, *De Blum à Pétain: Cinéma et société française, 1936-1944*, Paris, 1984
Guiraud, Jean-Michel, *La vie intellectuelle et artistique à Marseille à l'époque de Vichy et sous l'occupation*, Marseille, 1987
Jeancolas, Jean-Pierre, *Le cinéma des Français, vol. 2: Quinze ans d'années trente, 1929-1944*, Paris, 1983
Kaplan, Alice Yaeger, *Reproductions of Banality: Fascism, Literature, and French Intellectual Life*, St.Paul/MINN, 1986
Kedward, Roderick & Austin Roger (eds), *Vichy and the Resistance: Culture and Ideology*, London, 1985
Le Boterf, Hervé, *La vie parisienne sous l'occupation, 1940-1944*, 2 vols, Paris, 1974
Ménager, Yves (ed.), *La littérature française sous l'occupation: Actes du colloque de Reims (1981)*, 2 vols, Reims, 1989
Perrault, Gilles, *Paris sous l'occupation*, Paris, 1987
Ragache, Gilles & Jean-Robert, *La vie quotidienne des écrivains et des artistes sous l'occupation, 1940-1944*, Paris, 1988
Rioux, Jean-Pierre, *La vie culturelle sous Vichy*, Brussels, 1990
Serra, Maurizio, *Una cultura dell'autorità: La Francia di Vichy*, Bari, 1980
Siclier, Jacques, *La France de Pétain et son cinéma*, Paris, 1981

Theatre Studies

Added, Serge, 'L'euphorie théâtrale dans Paris occupé', in J.-P. Rioux, *La vie culturelle sous Vichy*, Brussels, 1990

———, *Le théâtre dans les années Vichy, 1940-1944*, Paris, 1992

Chamberlain, Alan, 'Theatre and the French Right in the 1920s and 1930s: Nostalgia for "un chef fort et autoritaire"', in J. Milfull (ed.), *The Attractions of Fascism*, New York, 1990

Gontard, Denise, *La décentralisation théâtrale en France 1895-1952*, Paris, 1973

Le Boterf, Hervé, *La vie parisienne sous l'occupation, 1940-1944*, Paris, 1974, vol. 1, 163-393; vol. 2, 129-150

Marsh, Patrick, *Le théâtre à Paris sous l'occupation allemande*. Special Issue of *La revue d'histoire du théâtre*, vol. 33, no. 3, 1981

Puppa, Paolo (ed.), *Eroi e massa*, Bologna, 1979

Illustrations

The editor has tried, within reasonable limits, to trace the copyright holders of the material reproduced in this volume. In some cases copyrights could not be cleared due to lack of information about the artist, the artist's estate, the successor of a publishing house or the whereabouts of their archive. Any claims arising out of this omission should be made to the editor via Berghahn Books.

Panse

8.1   *Schlageter* by Hans Johst, directed by Rudolf Schröder and designed by Adolf Mahnke at the Staatstheater Dresden in 1933.
(Source: *Künstlerbuch der Sächsischen Staatstheater*, ed. Alexander Schum, Dresden, 1934)
Schlageter was one of the fighters against French occupation of the Ruhr zone in 1923 and became a hero of the National Socialist movement. This 'cult' play by Johst, the *Chefdramaturg* of the Berlin State Theatre and from 1935 president of the *Reichsschrifttumkammer*, was one of the few popular success stories of early Nazi theatre.

8.2   *Oresteia* by Aischylos, directed by Lothar Müthel and designed by Traugott Müller at the Berlin Staatstheater am Gendarmenmarkt in 1936.
(Photo: Rosemarie Clausen; Source: Estate of Traugott Müller, University of Berlin, Institut für Theaterwissenschaft)
This production was part of a theatre festival in honour of foreign visitors to the Olympic Games. The excess of Prussian classicism in the design expressed the artistic pretensions of the Nazi régime.

8.3   *Coriolanus* by Shakespeare, directed by Erich Engel and designed by Caspar Neher at the Deutsches Theater, Berlin, in 1937.
(Source: Karl Blanck & Heinz Haufe, *Unbekanntes Theater: Ein Buch von der Regie*, Stuttgart, 1941)
Engel and Neher were both collaborators of Brecht, but decided to stay in Germany right through the Nazi period. Their artistic survival tactics were relatively successful, for example by restaging this masterful production stemming from the Weimar period (1925).

8.4   *Der Untergang Karthagos* by E.W. Möller, directed by Franz Evert and designed by Caspar Neher at the Hessisches Landestheater in Darmstadt in 1938.
(Source: Karl Blanck & Heinz Haufe, *Unbekanntes Theater: Ein Buch von der Regie*, Stuttgart, 1941)
Möller worked in the theatre section of the Reich's Ministry of Propaganda and was a major figure in the *Thingspiel* movement. After the enforced demise of this genre, he pursued his quest for a 'nordic' form of tragedy with this rather classicist parable of the fall of Carthage. Rosenberg understood the play to be a warning of a Nazi *Götterdämmerung* and ordered its withdrawal from the repertoire.

8.5   Gustaf Gründgens in *Richard II* by Shakespeare, directed by Jürgen Fehling and designed by Traugott Müller, Preußisches Staatstheater Berlin, 1939.
(Source: University of Hamburg, Theatre Collection)
A good example of how classical drama could be used by oppositional theatre artists to elucidate contemporary issues. Fehling underlined the topical relevance of Shakespeare's analysis of the abuse of power in his directorial concept. Whereas Goebbels 'only' voiced his objection to Müller's abstract stage design, Schlösser denounced the whole production as 'cultural Bolshevism'.

8.6   Josef Fenneker, Scenic design for *Prinz Friedrich von Homburg* by H. von Kleist (1777-1811), directed by Jürgen Fehling at the Schiller Theater Berlin, 1940.
(Source: University of Cologne, Institut für Theaterwissenschaft)
Schlösser declared this play to be a `cornerstone of our repertoire of steely romanticism' and obliged every German theatre to perform it. Fehling's Expressionist production focussed on Homburg's internal turmoil and eschewed all nationalist undertones. Fenneker's subdued designs in delicate, impressionist colours eliminated all references to the usual Prussian pomp and baroque excesses.

Schültke

9.1   *Oresteia* by Aischylos, directed by Hans Meissner and designed by Helmut Jürgens at the Schauspielhaus Frankfurt/M in 1941. The scenic design of this production was inspired by fascist classicism *à la* Breker or Thorak.
(Source: Estate of H. Meissner, University Library Frankfurt/M, Department of Music, Theatre, Film, Fine Art and Media)

9.2   *Rebellion in Preußen* by Bethge, directed by Hans Meissner and designed by Helmut Jürgens at the Schauspielhaus Frankfurt/M in 1939.

(Source: Estate of H. Meissner, University Library Frankfurt/ M, Department of Music, Theatre, Film, Fine Art and Media)

Thamer

10.1 March of the *Reichsarbeitsdienst* columns past the main tribune of the Zeppelinfeld. More than 50,000 of these 'soldiers of labour' participated in the subsequent call-up.
(Source: Centrum Industriekultur Nürnberg)

10.2 'Community Day' on the Zeppelin Field in 1938. The fascist notion of community was symbolised in the ornament of the masses, the costumes of the participants and the choreographic patterns harking back to old folk customs.
(Source: Centrum Industriekultur Nürnberg)

10.3 Hitler greets the marching Hitler Youths from the balcony of the Deutscher Hof. The annually repeated event became part of the Nuremberg festive calendar.
(Source: Centrum Industriekultur Nürnberg)

Linares

12.1 *El hospital de los locos* by José de Valdivieso (1560? - 1638), directed by Luis Escobar for the Teatro Nacional de la Falange at the Teatro Capitol de Madrid in 1939.
(Source: Revista Nacional de Educación, November 1943)
This *auto sacramental*, previously performed in the atrium of the cathedral of Segovia and in this photograph in the cathedral of Càdiz, amalgamated the aesthetic, political and religious ideals of the Falange and inaugurated their national theatre enterprise.

12.2 *Don Duardos* by Gil Vicente (1465?–1537?), directed by Huberto Pérez de la Ossa for the National Theatre at the Teatro María Guerrero in 1942.
(Source: Revista Nacional de Educación, November 1943)
The double nationality of the author was used in 1940 in Lisbon to celebrate the political brotherhood of Spain and Portugal and his popular status to revindicate the virtues of classical hispanic culture. The scenic and costume design of the production aimed at a 'realistic' reconstruction of the late-medieval world.

12.3 *Fuente Ovejuna* by Lope de Vega, in a version by Ernesto Giménez Caballero, directed by Cayetano Luca de Tena and designed by Sigfrido Burgman for the Teatro Español in 1944. (Source: Cuadernos de Teatro, no. 1/1944)
The classic text about a popular uprising against a repressive régime of noblemen was re-interpreted to denounce the partial

interests of the nobility and to show the need for binding the 'people' to a strong central State. The superior political and judiciary position of the State is symbolized in the Tower of La Mota shown in this photograph.

London

13.1   General Franco on the front page of *Marca* to celebrate the sport newspaper's fourth anniversary.
(Source: *Marca*, 25 November 1942)

13.2 + 13.3 Two examples of 'sporting festivities' which took place at a meeting of the Falange in Malaga in 1942.
(Source: *Legiones y Falanges*, vol. 2, no. 20, July 1942)

13.4   The Spanish coat of arms arranged by the Sección Feminina at a sporting demonstration in Murcia.
(Source: *Legioni e Falangi*, vol. 1, no. 8, 1 June 1941)

13.5   Regional folk dance as a form of gymnastics, performed at the closing ceremony of the Third Women's National Gymnastics Championships in 1943.
(Source: *Marca: Suplemento gráfico de los martes*, vol. 2, no. 20, 13 April 1943)

13.6   A fascist homage as 'sports news' on the front page of *Marca*. The three photographs show a wreath-laying ceremony at El Escorial, where the Italian airforce team and the Atlético de Aviacion honoured José Antonio Primo de Rivera with a pilgrimage to his grave.
(Source: *Marca*, 19 December 1942)

Levi

15.1   *Die Bürger von Calais*, by Rudolf Wagner-Régeny, directed by Werner Jacob at the Duisburg Opera House in the season 1939/1940.
(Source: Carl Niessen, *Die deutsche Oper der Gegenwart*, Regensburg 1944)
The heroic citizens of Calais withstand the siege of the King of England. Fritz Mahnke's designs symbolize the oppressive forces of the enemy in a set that offers more than a fleeting reference to Nazi monumentalist architecture.

15.2   *L'Orfeo* by Carl Orff based on Monteverdi's score, directed by Heinz Arnold at the Opera House in Dresden in 1940.
(Source: Carl Niessen, *Die deutsche Oper der Gegenwart*, Regensburg 1944)
The designs by Emil Preetorius turned the Arcadian landscape which has traditionally been associated with the Orpheus myth into a German scenery reminiscent of Caspar David Friedrich's Romantic paintings.

15.3   *Doktor Johannes Faust* by Hermann Reutter, directed by Walter
Felsenstein at the Städtische Bühnen Frankfurt/M in the season
1935/1936.
(Source: Carl Niessen, *Die deutsche Oper der Gegenwart*, Regensburg
1944)
Ludwig Sievert's designs were based on paintings of the German
Reformation, celebrated during the Nazi period as masterpieces of
true German art.

15.4   *Der Günstling* by Rudolf Wagner-Régeny, directed by Josef Gielen at
the Sächsisches Staatstheater in Dresden in the season 1934/1935.
(Source: Carl Niessen, *Die deutsche Oper der Gegenwart*, Regensburg
1944)
Based on Hugo's *Maria Tudor* in the translation by Georg Büchner,
the libretto by Brecht's erstwhile designer Caspar Neher deals with
the machinations of a corrupt and power-hungry aristocracy at the
court of Westminster. Neher, who also designed this production,
avoided all local colour and gave the sets a universal quality which
veered between monumental classicism and Piranesi's prison
nightmares.

Notes on Contributors

Serge Added is a theatre practitioner and a Research Fellow at the Institut d'Histoire du Temps at the Centre National de la Recherche Scientifique. He holds a doctorate in Historical Studies and has published *Le théâtre dans les années Vichy, 1940-1944*.

Günter Berghaus took his Ph.D. in Theatre Studies at the Free University of Berlin in 1977, taught at the University of London from 1978 to 1983, and is now a Reader in Theatre History at the University of Bristol. He specialises in Renaissance and Baroque theatre, dance history, twentieth century avant-garde performance, and theatre anthropology. He has written and edited eight books, amongst others on J.N. Nestroy, Andreas Gryphius, the English Civil War, Theatre and Film in Exile, F.T. Marinetti, Futurism and Politics.

Pietro Cavallo is an Assistant Professor of Contemporary History at the University of Salerno, where he teaches history of political parties. His research and publications have been concerned with Fascism, the Second World War, the Communist movement and the American Myth. His latest books are *Immaginario e rappresentazione: Il teatro fascista di propaganda* and *Riso amaro: Radio, teatro e propaganda nel secondo conflitto mondiale*. He is currently engaged in writing a book on the Italian national identity during the Second World War.

Emilio Gentile was Professor of Contemporary History at the University of Camerino and is now teaching at the Department of Political Sciences at 'La Sapienza' in Rome. He sits on the editorial board of the Journal of Contemporary History and specialises in the political and cultural history of Italy during the period 1860-1945. His many books include *"La Voce" e l'età giolittiana*, *Mussolini e "La Voce"*, *Le origini dell'idelologia fascista*, *L'Italia giolittiana*, *Il mito dello Stato nuovo*, *Storia del partito fascista*, *Il culto del littorio* (soon to be published in an English edition), *La via italiana al totalitarismo*.

Roger Griffin is Principal Lecturer in History at Oxford Brookes University. His research has mainly been concerned with the ideological dynamics of generic fascism and nationalism. He is author of *The Nature of*

Fascism and of the documentary sourcebook *Fascism* in the Oxford Readers series. He has also contributed chapters to Eatwell & Wright, *Contemporary Political Ideologies*, Larsen, *Was There Fascism Outside Europe?*, Eatwell, *European Political Culture*, Cronin, *The Failure of British Fascism* and has published many articles on aspects of generic fascism.

Reinhard Kühnl has held the position of Professor of Political Sciences at the University of Marburg since 1971. He has been guest professor at the University of Tel-Aviv and has published 16 books, dealing with German and international fascism, theories of fascism, German social and political history. His works have been translated into fourteen languages.

Erik Levi is a Senior Lecturer in Music at Royal Holloway, University of London, a critic for *BBC Music Magazine* and *Classic CD*, and a musician who has made many recordings for the BBC. His latest publication is *Music in the Third Reich*.

Francisco Linares is a Titular Professor of Literary Theory at the University of Granada. His main areas of research are semiotics of literature, the novel and drama. Some of his publications have focused on post-war Spanish writers such as Francisco Ayala, Luis Rosales and Camilo José Cela.

John London has been lecturer at Exeter College, Oxford University, Alexander von Humboldt Research Fellow at the Institute of Theatre Studies at the Free University Berlin, and is now Leverhulme Research Fellow at University College of Swansea. His publications include *Claves de 'La verdad sospechosa'*, *El teatre de la página*, *The Unknown Lorca* (an edition of performance texts), and translations of Spanish and Catalan plays. He has co-edited *An Introduction to Contemporary Catalan Theatre* and is currently writing a study of the reception of Spanish drama during the Third Reich.

Barbara Panse is currently a Professor at the Institute of Theatre, Film, Television at the Ruhruniversität Bochum and has previously been a member of the research project 'Structural History of German Theatre, 1933-45', based at the Free University Berlin. She took her Ph.D. in 1981 with a thesis on Peruvian theatre and has been lecturing at various Latin American universities. Several of her publications have been concerned with theatre in Peru, Colombia and Mexico. She has recently completed her Habilitation thesis on censorship practices and German drama during the Third Reich.

Bettina Schültke wrote her Ph.D. thesis on the municipal theatre in Frankfurt/Main during the Third Reich. She lectured at the Institute of Theatre Studies at the Free University Berlin, worked as *dramaturg* at the State Theatre Hanover, Volksbühne Berlin, and is now employed by the Bavarian State Theatre in Munich.

Hans-Ulrich Thamer is Professor of Modern History at the University of Münster and member of an inter-disciplinary research team 'Conflicts in the Context of Social and Cultural Diversity'. He has published on French social and intellectual history of the eighteenth and nineteenth centuries, European fascism and German National Socialism. Other research interests include the resistance movements in Westphalia during the Third Reich and the cultural history of collecting and museology.

Doug Thompson is Professor of Modern Italian Literature and History at the University of Hull. Latterly, he has moved into the area of computer-assisted learning and plays a directorial role in a national academic consortium producing language-learning software for the higher education sector. He has written and edited several books, amongst which *Cesare Pavese: A Study of the Major Novels and Poems; An Introduction to Pirandello's 'Sei personaggi in cerca d'autore'; Transfiguration and Reconciliation in Eliot's 'Four Quartets'; State Control in Fascist Italy: Culture and Conformity, 1925-43*.

Mario Verdone is Emeritus Professor of History and Criticism of Film at the University of Rome. He has widely published in his main research areas: contemporary theatre, Futurist literature and theatre, avant-garde cinema, *Commedia dell'arte*, masques, circus and popular theatre. He has also written on a variety of Italian authors, such as Vasari, Ginna, Corra, Chiti, Settimelli, Pirandello, Govoni.

Sultana Wahnón is Titular Professor of Literary Theory at the University of Granada. Her main research areas are contemporary Spanish poetry, fascist aesthetic theories, and the history of literary theory. Her books include *El irracionalismo en la poesia de Miguel Fernández, Estética y crítica literarias en España (1940-1950), Introducción a la historia de las teorías literarias, Saber literario y hermenéutica, Lenguaje y literatura*. She is currently preparing a new edition of her book on fascist aesthetics in Spain.

Index

This index lists Mussolini, Hitler and Franco only when quoted or referred to as active persons. Excluded are passing references, such as 'Mussolini's régime, Hitler's Party, Franco-Spain'. Equally omitted are the names in the opera checklist (pp. 274-275) and in the bibliography, but authors quoted in the notes to each essay have been incorporated.